𝑚𝑳 Binding

This textbook has an ML-BINDING designed for exceptional durability and long lasting use. The ML-BINDING is distinguished by:

Extensive Testing for Durability

The ML-Binding has endured highly sophisticated testing that approximates the wear and tear of heavy classroom use.

Reinforced Stress Points

A specially designed reinforced endsheet assembly strengthens the joint area and relieves stress on the first and last signatures. This also enables the book to stay open easily.

Maximum Cover Adhesion

Latex-impregnated kraft liners are the strongest available providing superb adhesion to the backbone and cover of the book.

Flexible Spine for Ease of Use

Tubular liners add strength and also enhance flexibility at normal stress points on the spine of the book.

The ML-BINDING exceeds the Manufacturing Standards and Specifications set forth by the National Association of State Textbook Administrators.

McDougal, Littell
ENGLISH

Dear Student,

You are entering a challenging and exciting period of your life. Your view of the world is becoming more mature and more complex. The textbooks you use should reflect this growth. They should encourage you to think new thoughts and explore new ideas. Most of all, your textbooks should help you discover and develop your own special talents and skills.

McDougal, Littell English was created to help you achieve these goals. The photos, fine art, and literature selections were chosen to fire your imagination and expand your knowledge of the world. The text was designed to appeal to your interests and abilities while at the same time challenging you to improve your writing and speaking skills.

We hope you will enjoy working with the images and ideas in this book. More important, we hope that using the book will give you confidence in your abilities and an eagerness to try out new ideas. In the process, you will even discover that language can be lively, exciting, and even fun.

The Editors

*"Each moment . . .
has its own beauty."*
Ralph Waldo Emerson

McDougal, Littell
English

Green Level

ML

McDougal, Littell & Company

Evanston, Illinois
New York   Dallas   Sacramento   Raleigh

Allan A. Glatthorn
Brenda C. Rosen

Consultants

Naomi Arabian, District Curriculum Coordinator of Middle School Reading, Fresno Unified School District, Fresno, California

David R. Collins, English/Creative Writing Instructor, Moline Senior High School, Moline, Illinois

Sr. Mary Dawson, IHM, Director of Curriculum and Instruction, Diocese of Rockville Centre, Education Department, Rockville Centre, New York

Dr. Joy C. Fowles, Coordinator for Secondary Education, Clear Creek Independent School District, League City, Texas

Richard Fluck, Superintendent, Cary School District 26, Cary, Illinois

Dr. Donald Gray, Professor of English, Indiana University, Bloomington, Indiana

Elizabeth W. McDonald, Secondary Language Arts Consultant, Pontiac, Michigan

Judy Powers Money, English Teacher, Fort Recovery High School, Fort Recovery, Ohio

Janet Morrow, Teacher Specialist, Staff Development, Mesa Public Schools, Maricopa, Arizona

Debra Olsen, Teacher, Garside Junior High School, Las Vegas, Nevada

Jerome Smiley, English Coordinator, Elmont Memorial Junior and Senior High Schools, Elmont, New York

Sr. Mary Theiss, SSSF, Coordinator of Curriculum, Archdiocese of Milwaukee, Milwaukee, Wisconsin

Gay D. Wells, Supervisor of Language Arts, Neshaminy School District, Langhorne, Pennsylvania

Cover Photograph: © 1989 The Image Bank/Benn Mitchell
Cover Quote: From "Nature" by Ralph Waldo Emerson

Acknowledgments: see page 697

90 / 15 14 13 12 11 10 9 8 7 6 5 4 3

ISBN: 0-8123-5760-4

Composition

Beginning with You

Choosing a Process for Writing

For a list of literature selections and other featured writers, see the last section of this table of contents.

Writing for Different Purposes

Resources and Skills

Grammar, Usage, and Mechanics

Featured Writers

David Attenborough

Mary Austin

Ray Bradbury

Dr. Kenneth H. Cooper

Tui De Roy

Joan Didion

T. S. Eliot

Victoria Furman

Joseph Krumgold

Barry Lopez

Harvey Manning

Alfred Meyer

Mary Britton Miller

W. O. Mitchell

Samuel Eliot Morison

Steve Osborn

Katherine Anne Porter

Marjorie Kinnan Rawlings

James Reaves

Kate Seredy

B. J. Walker

Jonathan Weiner

E. B. White

Virginia Woolf

Longer Literature Selections

Composition

Writers, like painters, develop their compositions through experimentation and exploration. Both make exciting discoveries during this process. Then, both share what they have worked to discover. The painter shares through colors, shapes, and images; the writer shares through words.

1
The Senses and Journal Writing

If you experienced the seasons only with your sense of sight, think what you would miss: the cold, wet feel of snow, the crisp crackle of leaves, the sweet smell of grass, and much more.

Careful observation using all of your senses is the basis of all good writing. One way to train your senses is to keep a journal.

A journal is a personal record of your thoughts and experiences. This chapter explains how a journal helps you practice using your senses and how it can serve as a sourcebook for discovering writing ideas.

1
Using the Senses

There were some days compounded completely of odor, nothing but the world blowing in one nostril and out the other. Some days were days of hearing every trump and trill of the universe. Some days were good for tasting and some for touching. And some days were good for all the senses at once. From *Dandelion Wine* by Ray Bradbury

Have you ever awakened in the morning to discover that a storm had occurred while you slept? While you are asleep, your senses of sight, hearing, touch, smell, and taste are less active. You are not very aware of the world. Now imagine that same storm occurring during the afternoon. You are aware of the sharp cracks of lightning and the drumbeat of the thunder. When you are awake, you are open to the information provided by your senses.

The more in touch you are with your senses, the more effectively you will be able to write. That is because all good writing and speaking depend on the ability to observe your world and communicate what you learn to others.

Training the Senses

Training the senses involves taking the time to really know and feel what you see, hear, taste, smell, or touch. For example, it is possible for you to develop the ability to observe in greater detail and to listen with extra care. Doing so will make it easier to communicate and share your experiences with others.

Using a Journal   You can develop your judgment and ability to observe by "exercising" your senses. There are many ways to do this. For example, you could sit in a room and describe all the sounds you hear. You could go for a walk and then you might describe all the aromas in the air.

Another way to exercise your senses is by recording in a journal what you see and experience. A **journal** is a written record of your thoughts and experiences. Concentrate on all five senses when you write. Use specific words, such as the following, to describe what your senses experience:

Sight	Hearing	Touch	Smell	Taste
azure	screech	satiny	buttery	sour
oval	grate	rough	fishy	tangy
wavy	rustle	slippery	musty	bitter
sparkling	hum	wet	smoky	burnt

For your first journal entry, look carefully at the picture of a festival. Observe the colors and shapes in the picture. Imagine the noises that might be heard. How would different objects feel? What tastes and smells would you experience? What kind of mood, or overall feeling, do the details create?

Writing Activity *Using Your Senses*

For one week, concentrate on a different one of the five senses each day. Describe in your journal everything you experience through the sense you have chosen. Compare and contrast different sensations and be as specific as possible.

2
The Journal as a Sourcebook

Literary Model
I have never written a story in my life that didn't have a very firm foundation in actual human experience—somebody else's experience quite often, but an experience that became my own by hearing the story, by witnessing the thing, by hearing just a word perhaps. It doesn't matter; it takes just a little—a tiny seed. Then it takes root, and it grows.

Katherine Anne Porter quoted in *Writers at Work*

One of the most difficult aspects of writing is getting started. Before you can write, you need something to write about. One way to come up with creative, interesting writing ideas is to use your journal as a sourcebook.

To keep a sourcebook, just set aside a portion of your journal or use a small notebook or spiral-bound pad you can carry around. Then, record in your notebook anything that catches your attention or makes you think. Gather writing ideas from as many different sources as possible: books, magazines, newspapers, radio, television, and movies; and conversations with friends, relatives, and teachers. You can even record events you observe firsthand. Paste in favorite photographs and clippings from magazines. Then, when you want to find a topic for writing, look through your journal for ideas. Here's how one student, Cheryl, came up with a writing idea. She had written the following entry in her journal.

> At the mall today, I saw a little boy at the "lost and found" station. He was tearful, but he was trying very hard to be brave. It made me think about all the different models for bravery children follow. Was this boy trying to be like Superman? Was he thinking of some personal hero?

Later, when Cheryl needed a writing topic, she looked through her journal and saw the entry about the lost boy. She then decided to describe some children's heroes and write about the qualities they represent. Cheryl came up with a writing idea based on experience. Now see how another student came up with an idea based on something that he clipped from a daily newspaper.

O'Hare cougar lets a probe of transport out of the bag

By Jack Houston

Federal authorities Wednesday continued to investigate the attempted export from O'Hare International Airport of two cougars, named Ron and Nancy, to a man with a traveling circus in the Persian Gulf state of Qatar.

The shipment, which may have been illegal, was discovered Tuesday after one of the 35-pound cats escaped from its crate and ran loose at the airport for three hours before its capture. . . .

After its capture near a runway, the cougar and its companion were confiscated by Fish and Wildlife Service agents and taken to Lincoln Park Zoo to be held as evidence. . . .

The cougars, from a wildlife farm in Plymouth, Minn., were being shipped to Muhammed el

The cougar escaped from a shipping cage Tuesday at O'Hare Airport

Heleu, a trainer with the Central National Circus, said Jeff Howard, owner of the farm. . . .

Howard, 34, said he has about 100 animals on his 70-acre farm, including llamas, bobcats, wolves and cougars.

From the Chicago Tribune, January 8, 1987

This article and photograph present some very interesting news. I wonder how animals are shipped to different zoos? I wonder who checks to see that animals are transported carefully? There could be several good writing ideas in this article.

Notice that Rick clipped this material from the newspaper and pasted it into his journal. Then he recorded the source of the passage so that he could find the entire article again if he needed it. Finally, Rick jotted down some writing ideas that the passage suggested to him.

Remember, you can copy or cut out items that attract your attention and include them in your journal. You might see a thought-provoking headline, a funny sign, or an interesting photograph. Advertisements, bulletin board notices, and store windows are also full of interesting material. If an item doesn't fit in your journal, write a description to help you remember it.

Writing Activity *Keeping a Sourcebook*

A Find five articles in magazines or newspapers that interest you. Paste these in your journal. Beneath each one, jot down two or three possible writing topics based on that article.

B At the end of each week, read over the entries in your sourcebook. Put the three best ideas in a special list of writing ideas at the back of the notebook.

3
The Journal as a Diary

Literary Model
So the point of keeping a notebook has never been, nor is it now, to have an accurate factual record of what I have been doing or thinking . . . *how it felt to me:* that is getting closer to the truth about a notebook.
From "On Keeping a Notebook" by Joan Didion

In addition to being a sourcebook, your journal can also serve as a diary—a daily record of events. A diary can help you explore how you feel about your experiences.

Set aside time each day to write about what was important to you and why. Examine your feelings, desires, and goals. Also think about the feelings of others. Consider the following diary entry from Kim's journal.

I was late for my flute lesson and running like crazy, when I heard Chopin's "Minute Waltz" coming from Ms. Jenner's studio. I thought, will I *ever* be able to play that well? I ran upstairs and burst into the studio, gasping, "I wish I could play like that!" Ms. Jenner smiled. "Practice," she said. And I will.

Notice that Kim not only told what happened but also how she felt about it. Then she thought about her experience and drew a conclusion. She decided to practice more.

When keeping a diary for class, be sure to include only the thoughts and feelings that you want to share. You may wish to keep another, more private, diary for yourself. A private diary can help you sort out thoughts that you might want to write about later.

Writing Activity *Keeping a Diary*

Begin keeping a diary in your journal. Describe events that seem important or outstanding to you. At the end of a week, look through your diary entries for writing ideas. Add these ideas to the list of writing ideas at the back of your journal.

Starting from Literature

from *One Writer's Beginnings*

Eudora Welty

The following literature selection is from a writer's autobiography. It is a glimpse into the writer's past, a memory—not unlike a journal or diary entry—about her sensory education.

*L*earning stamps you with its moments. Childhood's learning is made up of moments. It isn't steady. It's a pulse.

Senses of sight and smell introduced

In a children's art class, we sat in a ring on kindergarten chairs and drew three daffodils that had just been picked out of the yard; and while I was drawing, my sharpened yellow pencil and the cup of the yellow daffodils gave off whiffs just alike. That the pencil doing the drawing should give off the same smell as the flower it drew seemed part of the art lesson—as shouldn't it be? Children, like animals, use all their senses to discover the world. Then artists come along and discover it the same way, all over again. Here and there, it's the same world. Or now and then we'll hear from an artist who's never lost it.

In my sensory education I include my physical awareness of the *word*. Of a certain word that is; the connection it has with what it stands for. At around age six, perhaps, I was standing by myself in our front yard waiting for supper, just at that hour in a late summer day when the sun is already below the horizon and the risen full moon in the visible sky stops being chalky and begins to take on light. There comes the moment, and I saw it then, when the moon goes from flat to round. For the first time it met my eyes as a globe. The word "moon" came into my mouth as though fed to me out of a silver spoon. Held in my mouth the moon became a word. It had the roundness of a Concord grape Grandpa took off his vine and gave me to suck out of its skin and swallow whole, in Ohio.

Sense of taste introduced

This love did not prevent me from living for years in foolish error about the moon. The new moon just appearing in the west was the rising moon to me. The new should be rising. And in early childhood the sun and moon, those opposite reigning powers, I just as easily assumed rose in east and west respectively in their opposite sides of the sky, and like partners in a reel they advanced, sun from the east, moon from the west, crossed over (when I wasn't looking) and went down on the other side. . . .

Sense of sound introduced

Sense of touch introduced

The night sky over my childhood Jackson was velvety black. I could see the full constellations in it and call their names; when I could read, I knew their myths. Though I was always waked for eclipses, and indeed carried to the window as an infant in arms and shown Halley's comet in my sleep, and though I'd been taught at our diningroom table about the solar system and knew the earth revolved around the sun, and our moon around us, I never found out the moon didn't come up in the west until I was a writer and Herschel Brickell, the literary critic, told me after I misplaced it in a story. He said valuable words to me about my new profession: "Always be sure you get your moon in the right part of the sky."

Trying Out Sensory Writing Eudora Welty wrote, "Learning stamps you with its moments." Use your journal to record a special moment. Choose your words carefully to express what you experienced with your senses during that moment.

Creative Writing

A Have you ever ordered something from a restaurant menu simply because the description made your tastebuds tingle or your nose perk up? Restaurant owners know that people eat for reasons other than hunger. That is, diners respond to the way that food looks, smells, feels and even sounds. For example, what do you think about when you read these items: crunchy granola, piping-hot pizza smothered with melted white cheese, warm rolls flavored with fresh cinnamon? With your diner's senses in mind, create the ideal menu for a restaurant of your own. Describe your favorite foods in a way that makes them mouth-watering and absolutely irresistible.

B Think of a familiar story or myth, such as *The Wizard of Oz*, and retell it by concentrating on making it come alive through the senses. Add "sense" words and phrases to recreate the characters, settings, and events for your readers. Be as creative as you can.

C Write a letter to a friend or relative telling about an event or vacation you've experienced. Use strong adjectives and other "sense" words so that your reader can almost see, hear, smell, taste, and feel the scene at home. Describe the sights and sounds, the foods, and all other sensations. Make your letter the next best thing to being there.

Trouville. Raul Dufy.

Application and Review

A **Training the Senses** Identify the sense (sight, hearing, smell, touch, or taste) that is associated with each of the following words. Then list another sense word that is closely related to each word below. For example, *hot* and *feverish* (sense of touch).

1. stench
2. dash
3. sugary
4. jangle
5. sparkling
6. bitter
7. squawk
8. fuzzy
9. ivory
10. lukewarm
11. gaseous
12. clang

B **Using the Journal as a Sourcebook** Read the following excerpt from an article in the October, 1986 issue of *National Geographic World*. Then think of four topics you might write about based on ideas from the article. Write those ideas in your journal.

> Black rhinos are in danger of becoming extinct.
> . . . In March 1984, a jumbo jet streaked over the Atlantic Ocean from Africa to the United States. Aboard were several huge crates, each of which held an adult black rhinoceros. The rhinos would be roaming the range in Texas. Two of them would find themselves on a large spread near McAllen. There, rancher Calvin Bentsen had set aside 80 acres where the animals would live. . . .
> Black rhinos live in parts of Africa south of the desert called the Sahara. In 1970 more than 60,000 black rhinos roamed the plains. By 1985, only 7,000 remained. African countries have passed laws forbidding the hunting of these animals. But poachers, or illegal hunters, continue to kill the rhinos for their horns.

C **Using the Journal as a Diary** In your journal, write a one- or two-paragraph entry about today. Then identify one writing idea in that diary entry. Write the idea in your journal.

2
Writing and Thinking

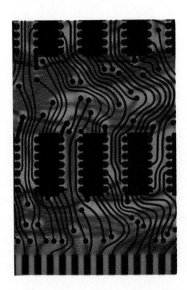

The most complex computer is simple when compared to the human mind. By itself, your mind keeps your body functioning while dealing with thousands of other tasks. It can plan strategies in sports, compose new music, create artwork, explore the frontiers of science, and much more.

You can learn to use your "personal computer" more effectively and creatively. In this chapter you will learn strategies to find and explore ideas. You will experience the exciting process of combining imagination with clear thinking to produce writing that is uniquely your own.

1
Discovering Ideas

In the fifteenth century, Johann Gutenberg invented the printing press. Books could then be printed quickly and in large quantities. The printing press created an information explosion that gave birth to the modern age.

The secret of Gutenberg's success was his ability to use familiar materials in a new way. He created his printing press from ink, paper, carved wooden blocks, and a cheese press. You too can learn how to tap what you already know to discover new ideas for your writing. You can use several techniques for finding ideas: brainstorming, freewriting, clustering, imaging, and charting.

Brainstorming and Freewriting

Brainstorming is a simple technique for coming up with ideas. First, you choose a topic, or starting point. Then, you list all your ideas as quickly as possible. Keep adding to your list until you run out of ideas.

Freewriting is a variation of brainstorming. After you have chosen a focus, you write whatever comes to your mind as you think about your focus. Write nonstop, for about three to five minutes, without lifting your pen or pencil from the paper. Do not worry about using complete sentences or appropriate grammar, spelling, or punctuation.

The following journal entry shows how Wally used freewriting to find a topic for a paper.

> Baseball. I love everything about it. The park. Statistics. Who's leading the league in home runs. Best earned-run average. Highlights on the news. Tomorrow they're going to announce who will get into the Hall of Fame. What a fantastic tribute— *the* Hall of Fame! Think of all the great players in it—and what about all the fine players that never made it! Who's going to make it this year? I wonder how they decide . . . I could find out and write my paper on that . . . .

Clustering

Clustering is another method for exploring and developing ideas. When you use this technique, you make a visual map of your thoughts. Here is one way to cluster:

1. Write your focus in the center of your paper. Circle it.
2. Think about your focus. Write outside the circle any related ideas that occur to you. Circle these and draw lines connecting them with the main circle.
3. Think about the related ideas. Write down other ideas that occur to you. Circle these and draw connecting lines.

Janet wanted to convince her parents to buy a home computer. Here is how she used clustering to come up with reasons to buy the computer.

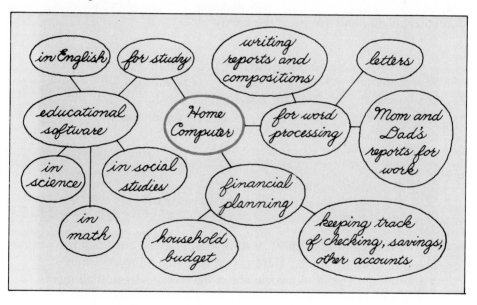

An idea related to clustering is tree diagraming. For an example of a tree diagram, see page 27.

Imaging

Much of what you know is stored in your mind as whole pictures or images. To recall these pictures in detail, use the technique known as **imaging**. First, free your mind of distractions by repeating your subject, or focus, silently to yourself. Then picture in your mind the subject that you want to recall. Imagine looking at the subject from a distance. Then imagine moving closer to observe the details.

Suppose, for example, that you want to recall a train trip that you made last summer on the *Super Chief*. Repeat the name of the train several times. Picture yourself at the station. Was the platform crowded? Was it noisy? Who took your ticket? What did the train look and sound like when it arrived?

Charting

Charting is one way to recall and organize ideas. A simple chart may consist of columns of items set under headings naming the main parts of a subject. Other types of charts you might use are a time line or a list of pros and cons. Here is a simple chart that Adele made when she was planning to write about animals, entertainers, and events at the circus.

What I Saw at the Circus

Animals	Entertainers	Appearance
lions	trapeze artists	three rings
bears	jugglers	ropes arcing
tigers	clowns	from tall poles to
monkeys	strongmen	the ground
horses	bareback riders	blue and pink
elephants	the human	lights
	cannonball	sawdust

The second kind of chart, a **time line,** is useful for thinking about a series of events. Here is one that Miguel made when working on a yearbook article about his school's basketball team.

This Year's Basketball Season

October 16	October 21	November– January	February 6
preseason loss to Roosevelt Jr. High	coach recruits two exceptional players	team undefeated in regular season games	team loses play-offs

The third type of chart lists pros and cons. **Pros** are the advantages of something. **Cons** are the disadvantages. Mary made a pros-and-cons chart to help her decide whether to take an after-school job.

An After-School Job

Pros	Cons
1. I could use the money for a new guitar.	1. I won't be able to play the guitar as much.
2. I might meet some new people.	2. I won't see my old friends.
3. I will be able to take care of my own expenses.	3. I'll lose study time.
	4. I won't be able to play softball after school.

When you come up with an idea by using one of these techniques, jot the idea down in a special section of your journal called an "Idea Notebook." Doing so will help you keep track of new writing ideas that occur to you.

Applying Thinking Skills

Use *brainstorming, freewriting, clustering, imaging,* and *charting*:

- to come up with ideas for speeches and writing
- to gather information about a topic
- to recall what you have learned when studying
- to come up with ideas for creative projects
- to think about choices when solving a problem or making a decision

Writing Activities *Finding Ideas*

A Choose one of the following subjects. Use freewriting to record your thoughts about the subject in your journal.

concerts	the Olympics
space	horses
home	peer pressures
rain	board games
jobs	favorite books

The Beach at Trouville, 1870. Claude Monet. The National Gallery, London.

B Choose one of the following subjects. Use clustering to record your thoughts about the subject in your journal.

beaches	bells	color
friends	high school	anger
music	ghosts	Saturdays
parks	animals	holidays

C In your journal, make a time line listing the five most important events in your life. Begin the time line with your birth. Save this chart to use as a source of writing ideas in the future.

D Think of something you are trying to make a decision about. Make a pros-and-cons chart in your journal. Write down all your reasons in the appropriate columns. Do the reasons in one column outweigh the reasons in the other? Can you make a decision based on your chart?

E Use the thoughts you recorded in Activity A, B, C, or D as the basis for a short composition or poem.

2
Exploring Ideas

An idea cannot go anywhere unless you take it there. Once you come up with an idea, you must then explore and develop it fully. Here are several techniques for exploring ideas: observing features, inquiring, noting connections, analyzing, classifying, and comparing and contrasting.

Observing Features

Most ideas involve people, places, or things. Therefore, one way to explore an idea is to **observe** the people, places, or things involved and to note specific features. When you observe the features of something, you note its parts and characteristics. Features to look for include the following:

size	height	feel
shape	depth	duration
color	width	function
weight	taste	condition
age	sound	importance
quantity	smell	value

Here is an example of how Ellie used the skill of observing features to identify someone.

> One day when Ellie was home alone, a man came to the door asking for her mother. He left without leaving his name. When Ellie later told her about the visitor, her mother was puzzled and asked what the man looked like. Ellie said, "I remember that he was short, and he had dark eyes and black curly hair . . . He was wearing a faded straw hat and carrying a blue notebook in his hand. Also, he spoke very slowly in an accent."
>
> Her mother's face brightened. "Oh, that must have been Mr. Fizazzi, who has just moved here from Atlanta! He asked to see our garden and learn about the Garden Club."

Inquiring

One of the simplest and most successful methods for exploring an idea is **inquiring,** or asking questions. Reporters use this method when they cover a news story. First they prepare questions beginning with *who, what, where, when, why,* and *how.* Then they attempt to find answers to each question, one by one, as in the following example.

What happened?	The food drive
Who led the drive?	Allen King
Where did he do it?	In the Lakeview neighborhood
When was the drive?	In November and December
Why did Allen do this?	He heard that many local families might go hungry during the holidays.
How did he do it?	He organized the students at Lakeview High to ask their neighbors and local merchants for food.

Of course, some answers may lead to further questions, such as, "How many local families were helped?"

Making Connections

When you study the relationships between things, you look for the ways in which things are connected, or related. By observing relationships, you can often find out why something is the way it is or how it affects other things. This chart shows some of the most important relationships.

Types of Relationships	
In Time	Ask yourself, "When did each event or action happen?"
In Space	Ask yourself, "Where is each thing in relation to the others?"
Of Degree	"Is one more or less familiar, important, or specific?" "Is one greater or lesser than another in some way?"
Of Cause and Effect	Ask yourself, "Does one cause the other? Is one an effect of the other?"

Here is a situation in which Naomi used the skill of making connections.

> For her science class, Naomi prepared a presentation on natural disasters. She gathered information from encyclopedias, yearbooks, and almanacs. Then she had to decide whether to present her material—how many disasters occurred, where they took place, what damages they caused—in order of time, or cause and effect.
>
> Naomi noted the connection between earthquakes and tsunami, or tidal waves. She decided to present these disasters as a cause and effect. She drew a diagram showing how a tsunami hit Hawaii after an earthquake in Alaska.

Grammar in Action

In writing and speech, adverbs are often used to signal relationships. (See pages 509–510.)

> Adverbs that show relationships in time: *first, then, finally, later,* and *meanwhile*
>
> Adverbs that show relationships in space: *up, down, above, below, near,* and *far*
>
> Adverbs that show relationships of degree: *less, more, least,* and *most*
>
> Adverbs that show relationships of cause and effect: *because, since, consequently,* and *therefore*

Use these adverbs in your speech and writing to make the relationships between your ideas clear.

Analyzing

Another useful method for exploring ideas is analyzing. When you analyze something, divide the subject or idea into its parts and then examine each part. Here is how Frank used this thinking skill:

> Frank's social studies class is studying his hometown, Atlanta. Frank decided to write a paper explaining why Atlanta had grown so much in the last few years. Frank divided his subject, Atlanta, into several parts: location and climate, transportation, job opportunities, colleges, and cultural attractions. Then he listed the following observations about each.
>
> *Location and climate:* northwestern Georgia, mild winters and summers
>
> *Transportation:* Atlanta is the railway center of the region. Many of the country's largest transportation companies have offices here.
>
> *Job opportunities:* good in wholesale and retail trade, tourism
>
> *Colleges:* over twenty-five, including Emory University and Georgia Institute of Technology
>
> *Cultural attractions:* Atlanta Symphony Orchestra and Alliance Theater Company

One simple way to analyze something is to draw a chart or a tree diagram representing its parts. You have already seen how to set up a chart. To draw a tree diagram, follow these steps:

1. Write your subject at the top center of a piece of paper.
2. Below the subject, list its major parts. Draw lines to the subject.
3. Then, either break each part down further or describe each part in detail.

At the top of the next page is a tree diagram that María created when working on a plan for her school's yearbook. Note how her diagram has three basic sections: a subject head, major parts, and details related to each part.

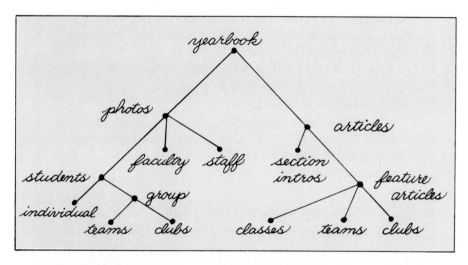

Classifying

One way to organize information is by **classifying** it, arranging it according to class or category. Suppose, for example, that you wish to classify physical activities. Follow these steps.

1. List the things you want to classify.
   Physical activities: baseball, bowling, football, hiking, skating, soccer, swimming
2. Look for a feature that some of the things have that the others do not have.
   Some can be done alone. Others require a team.
3. Divide your list into groups or classes under the headings from Step 2.

Activities that require a team	Activities that can be done alone

Comparing and Contrasting

A way to organize information about two subjects that have something in common is by **comparing and contrasting** them. Here is how you would go about comparing and contrasting a weaver and a spider.

1. List the things that you want to compare and contrast.
   weaver   spider
2. Observe the characteristics of things.
   Weaver: uses threads, yarns, makes patterns, designs, works

on a loom, provides basic necessities (clothes, blankets)
Spider: spins, makes patterns, silk, designs, web, provides
basic necessities (home, trap for food)
3. Look for similarities between the things (comparison).
Both use a type of fiber in their work.
Both make intricate patterns.
Both provide basic necessities.
4. Look for differences between the things (contrast).
Weaver must gather his or her materials.
Spider makes silk from materials in its body.

Applying Thinking Skills

Use *observing features, inquiring, making connections, analyzing, classifying,* and *comparing* and *contrasting* when:

- thinking about ideas that you hear or read
- limiting or developing a topic for a paragraph, composition, speech, or report
- solving problems and determining how to achieve goals

Writing Activities **Exploring Ideas**

A Choose some plant, a type of tree, houseplant, or flower. Make a list of its features—its parts and characteristics. Then use this list to write a paragraph describing the plant.

B Make a family tree for your natural or adopted family. Your teacher can demonstrate how one is supposed to look. Start by writing the name of the earliest member of your family that you know about. Then list others according to their relationships to each other.

C Read the items in the following groups. What is the relationship among the items in each group? Then write the items in a logical order. Be ready to explain why you organized the items as you did. Use encyclopedias, atlases, or other reference works as necessary.

1. Vietnam War, Civil War, World War I, Korean War, World War II, Revolutionary War

2. develop film, focus the lens, buy film, load the camera, take some pictures
3. half dollar, penny, quarter, dime, nickel, dollar
4. Pacific Ocean, Antarctic Ocean, Arctic Ocean, Indian Ocean, Atlantic Ocean

D Imagine that you are a newspaper reporter in Texas. Some fishermen in the Gulf of Mexico have captured an enormous sea creature that looks something like a dinosaur. Your editor has asked you to go to Corpus Christi, Texas, where the creature is being held in a marine aquarium. Make a list of questions that you will try to answer when you arrive there.

E Analysis is useful for thinking about processes—things that happen in stages over a period of time. Think about one of the following processes. First, divide the process into stages or steps. Next, organize the steps according to their relationships in time (first, second, third, and so on). Then write a paragraph describing the process.

1. Preparing and delivering a speech
2. Doing a job around the house
3. Operating a machine of some kind

F Compare and contrast the following:

1. ideas and viruses
2. football and baseball
3. people and robots
4. newspapers and television news programs

G Classify the following: *monkeys, elephants, horses, zebras, cows, giraffes, dogs, pigs, lions, chickens,* and *bears.*

3
Using Other Sources of Information

In the last two lessons you learned several techniques for finding and exploring ideas. When using these techniques, you gather information through recall or through direct observation.

Suppose, however, that you are doing a report on the planet Saturn. To gather information about Saturn directly, you would have to use a powerful telescope. If you do not have such a telescope, you must rely on information gathered by professional astronomers.

As this example shows, you will often have to depend on information gathered by other people. Ways to gather information from other people include interviewing, reading, and using nonprint media, such as filmstrips, films, and videocassettes.

Interviewing

To **interview** someone, first prepare a list of questions about your subject. Perhaps your subject is the person you are interviewing. Then try to learn something about him or her that will make the interview interesting. A question such as "What would you like written on your tombstone?" will reveal more about a person than, say, "What are your plans now?"

Prepare ahead of time for the interview. Have your list of questions ready, and bring materials to make notes. For more information on interviewing, see pages 296–297.

Reading

Another way of gathering information is reading books, magazines, newspapers, and other printed materials. Before reading about a topic, prepare as you would for an interview. Make a list of questions to be answered as you read.

Make sure that your written sources are up to date and reliable. An up-to-date source is current. It has the latest information available. You should use an up-to-date source even when studying a historical event, since new facts about the past are always being discovered. A reliable source is one you can depend on. It should have been written by an expert. For information on finding written materials in a library, see pages 310–327.

Using Other Media

Your school or local library has probably acquired many new reference resources recently. You may find filmstrips, films, videocassettes, or audiotapes on your subject.

Applying Thinking Skills
To gather information when direct observation is impossible, try *interviewing, reading,* and *using nonprint media* such as filmstrips and videocassettes.

Writing Activities Using Other Sources

A Imagine that you can travel through time to conduct research. Choose a historical figure who interests you. Do some reading about this figure. Then write a list of questions that you would ask this person in an interview.

B Explain why each of the following would not be a reliable source of information.

1. Advice on dieting in a magazine interview with a soap opera star
2. A map of Africa from a 1959 atlas
3. A report about UFO sightings in a newspaper devoted to gossip about celebrities and sensational stories about lost civilizations, miracle cures, and fantastic creatures

Queen Elizabeth I,
England, 1558–1603.

C Choose one of the topics below. Go to the library and find five sources of information about the topic. Three should be print sources, and two should be nonprint sources.

Mexico   automobiles   sports
careers   computers   health

4
Inferences and Drawing Conclusions

After exploring an idea and gathering information about it, the next step is to draw conclusions. The thought process you use when you draw a conclusion is called **inference**. When you infer, you analyze information, looking for ideas that are implied but not actually stated. A **conclusion** is a statement that seems logical based on both the information you have gathered and the inferences you have made about it. Drawing conclusions is the most exciting step in any thinking process. By doing so, you go beyond what is already known to come up with ideas that are uniquely yours.

The first step in drawing conclusions is to put the information that you have gathered into statement form. You can draw conclusions from a single statement or several statements.

Drawing Conclusions from a Single Idea

To infer a conclusion from a single idea, study the statement carefully. Try to see what is there besides the obvious. Ask yourself, "What other statements are probably true if this statement is true?" Consider the following statement:

Sue placed tenth in the Boston Marathon.

Based on this one statement, you can conclude that the following statements are probably true:

1. Sue is in good shape.
2. Nine people ran the marathon faster than Sue did.
3. Sue has been to Boston.
4. Sue enjoys running.

Notice how Lee used the skill of drawing conclusions from a single observation:

Mr. Akins announced to his class that he would be retiring at the end of the year. He planned to move to a cabin in the country to work on a book about teaching. Lee and several other students wanted to get Mr. Akins a going-away present. Based on the information that Mr. Akins would be living in the country, Lee drew these conclusions: In the country there are many birds. People who live in the country can watch birds. Bird watchers use binoculars. We could get Mr. Akins a pair of binoculars that he could use to watch the birds around his cabin.

Drawing Conclusions from Several Statements

When you draw a conclusion from several statements, you look for some relationship or connection between them. Suppose that you are doing a science report about establishing colonies on other planets. You have the following information about temperatures on other planets.

Mercury: −315° to 648° Fahrenheit
Venus: 850° Fahrenheit
Mars: −191° to −24° Fahrenheit
Jupiter: −236° Fahrenheit
Saturn: −285° Fahrenheit
Uranus: −357° Fahrenheit
Neptune: −360° Fahrenheit
Pluto: −342° to −369° Fahrenheit

You notice that the temperatures on the other planets are all extremely high or extremely low. Based on this observation, you can draw a conclusion. You might conclude that people living elsewhere in the solar system would have to be protected from extreme temperatures.

Applying Thinking Skills

Use the skill of *drawing conclusions:*
- when you study material presented in textbooks or in class
- when you think about information gathered for a speech, composition, report, or project
- when you have a problem to solve or a decision to make

Writing Activities *Drawing Conclusions*

A Read each of the following observations. Then, for each, make a list of three statements that would have to be true if this observation were true.

1. Ms. Lupico voted in the last presidential election.
2. A swift can fly faster than any other bird.
3. John Elway is a quarterback for the Denver Broncos.
4. Elizabeth I was Queen of England from 1558 to 1603.
5. The largest library in the world is the Library of Congress, in Washington, D.C.
6. In 1979 Michael Cairney set up and toppled a row of 169,713 dominoes.
7. The printing press, which is used to make printed books, was not invented until the early 1400's.

Writing Inside Out

Meet Mrs. Linda Hurst. Mrs. Hurst is not a famous writer or poet. She doesn't write television commercials or scripts for movies. Yet, Mrs. Hurst is a writer. She writes journals. Journals are like diaries. People use them to record memorable events during their lifetimes or to sort out their feelings and emotions. Over the years, Mrs. Hurst has raised three daughters, run a household, and managed a family-owned business.

Yet, she has still managed to find time to write.

Q. Why did you start writing journals?

A. I've always been a letter writer. I do so much better in writing a letter than I do in talking. So writing is another aspect of my personality for me.

Q. Do you keep journals for more than one purpose?

B Read the following groups of observations. Then, for each group, write a single conclusion that you can draw based on these observations.

1. Mount McKinley is 20,320 feet high.
   Mount Everest is the highest mountain in the world.
2. Bactrian camels have two humps.
   Arabian camels have one hump.
   The dromedary is a special kind of Arabian camel.
3. Rick plays the violin.
   Rick plays the flute.
   Rick sings in the choir.
4. Kim bought tickets for the ice-dancing show.
   Kim owns an expensive pair of ice skates.
   Kim has a picture of a famous ice-skater on her wall.

A. Yes, this has been mainly about trips. I like to have a reminder of the good times. Every day is special on a trip for me. Then, I started doing it at work, and I've done some personal things. When I was confused, I would sort out my thinking.

Q. What do you write in your travel journals?

A. I would say mainly chronological things—a short paragraph about each day. Then, if I wanted to remember what I did, it would be there and when I did it. One time a big wind came up and our tent blew down. That went into the journal—silly things like washing and what we had to eat, that's always in there.

Q. Why did you start a journal for your business?

A. I never thought I'd be in business—managing it, doing the buying! I just wanted to keep records.

Q. Was your personal journal like a diary?

A. Yes! Whatever I was feeling came tumbling out. Usually it was negative feelings, trying to sort them out, trying to see what was bothering me. Writing it down helped me to see what I was thinking.

Q. When do you write?

A. I like to write in the morning. That's my quiet time.

5
Thinking Creatively

The word *creativity* may make you think of artists, writers, actors, musicians, and inventors. However, creativity is important to everyone. Creative thinking helps people find original solutions to problems and approach everyday tasks in new ways. It is also valuable for its own sake. Here is how Brian used creative thinking to solve a practical problem.

> Last summer Brian's family adopted a small dog. They named the dog "Murphy." Brian and his mother built a doghouse for Murphy in the back yard. When it began to get cold, Brian became worried. How would Murphy keep warm? His mother would not let Murphy sleep in the house, and the garage was not heated. He asked, "What if we connect our house with Murphy's house some-how, so that the heat from our house can warm his house, too?" Brian and his mother added a door to the doghouse and connected the two dwellings by a length of large, insulated tube. Heat flowed in a steady stream from house to doghouse. Murphy stayed warm and happy all winter.

Creative Approaches to Thinking

Brian solved his problem by connecting two things that were not usually connected. Making new connections between things is one of many approaches to creativity. To begin to think creatively yourself, follow this plan:

1. Turn off the part of your mind that evaluates and criticizes. Play with ideas without worrying whether they seem foolish or silly. Consider new, unusual, original alternatives.
2. Use your imagination. Ask yourself "What if?" questions, such as the following:
   a. What if I combined or connected two objects that are normally separate? (The hard metal bronze was created by combining two softer metals, copper and tin.)

b. What if I used this object in a new or unusual way? (The American artist Louise Nevelson created beautiful sculptures from "found" objects—pieces of woodwork, chairs, and old utensils.)

c. What if this person, place, object, event, or idea had never existed or happened? (Imagine the world without electricity.)

d. What if I changed just one part of this thing or situation? (What would happen if the world's oil supplies were used up?)

e. What if I changed what this object is made of? What if I changed its shape in some way? (Several designers have created clothes made of paper.)

f. What if the connections between certain people, places, objects, or events were different? (What if New Year's Day fell on July 1?)

g. What if I put these opposing ideas together? (What if I crossed an onion with a rose?)

h. What if I changed the location of something? (What if classes were held not in schools but in museums, libraries, parks, zoos, factories, and businesses?)

i. What if people changed their roles or actions in some way? (What if the members of our family took turns doing the household chores?)

Applying Thinking Skills

Use *creative thinking:*

- to come up with ideas for writing, speeches, projects, inventions, and works of art
- to solve problems and make decisions
- to see yourself and the world in new ways

Writing Activities *Thinking Creatively*

A Use "What if?" questions to come up with three creative ways to use or change television.

B List problems that face your school or community. Brainstorm with friends about them, asking "What if?" questions. Come up with ways to begin solving each of the problems in your list.

English and Math

"Alice rode in a bike-a-thon. Her sister pledged $ .05. per mile. Alice rode 30 miles. How much money did her sister owe?"

$$30 \times .05$$

What is the difference between these two problems? They are the same problem, but one is expressed primarily in words, the other in numerals only. Unfortunately, many people become confused when they read "word problems" or when they are asked to solve math problems in everyday life. This confusion makes the problems seem harder than they really are.

The thinking skills you learned in this chapter can help you solve word problems in math. You've learned how to analyze a problem and break it up into smaller, more manageable parts. You've also learned to brainstorm for new solutions. These skills, and the system below, lead to successful problem solving.

1. Analyze all of the information carefully, looking for numbers and facts.
2. Compare this problem to a similar problem that you've solved.
3. Think about how the numbers and facts are related and use a sketch, formula, diagram, or mental map to outline the problem.
4. Make a guess or do the computations.
5. Check your answers.

Activity

Two trains are traveling on parallel tracks from Chicago to New York. Train **A** stops for fifteen minutes in Gary, Indiana, and for thirty minutes in Cleveland, Ohio. Train **B** stops for twenty-five minutes in South Bend, Indiana, for fifteen minutes in Youngstown, Ohio, and for fifteen minutes in Allentown, Pennsylvania. Train **A** arrived in New York ten minutes before Train **B**. Which train was traveling at the fastest rate of speed?

Creative Writing

A Have you ever tried to invent something that's both brand new and fabulous? Succeeding on either count takes a bit of brain power, but accomplishing both at the same time is like hitting a grand slam homerun in the World Series. A feat like this can bring you fame, fortune, and fun. Using your developing skills of brainstorming and freewriting, work alone or with a partner to invent the greatest new game you'll ever play. The invention can be a board game, a sport, or any other creation of your imagination. It might help if you brainstorm about what you like most about existing games. Make up the invented game's objectives, rules, size and makeup of teams (if any), scoring, and design of the playing board or field. Write up a description and include diagrams of anything that requires additional explanation.

B Select any two items that do not at first seem to be similar or related in any way, such as a photograph and a pencil. They can be objects, people, or activities. Take at least five minutes and use your freewriting techniques and your imagination to put down on paper everything that you can think of to describe the items. Rely on your observations, opinions, feelings, associations, and memories. Try to find at least two or three characteristics that are shared by these two items. Write a short paragraph explaining the connection. Be as creative as you can. Stretch your mind as you write.

Application and Review

A Recognizing Connections Read the items in each of the following lists. Note the relationship among the items in each group. Then write the items in a logical order.

1. Horse, fox, mouse, elephant, rabbit
2. May, December, April, February, October
3. Teaspoon, cup, gallon, quart, tablespoon
4. Noon, dusk, morning, midnight, dawn

B Classifying Information The items listed below each describe the game of football. Form three columns on your paper under the headings: *Scoring, Team Players,* and *Bowl Games.* Place each listing under the proper classification.

- A touchdown is worth six points.
- Eleven team members are allowed on the field at once.
- Three points are earned for each field goal.
- On New Year's Day, highly-ranked college teams play in bowl games across the country.
- The quarterback leads the offense.
- Passes are thrown to wide receivers and running backs.
- Hawaii is the home of the last professional football game of the season—the Pro Bowl.
- The defense earns two points for a safety.
- The Super Bowl decides the NFL championship.

C Drawing Inferences Read the statements below. For each one, write two other statements that are probably true.

1. Jeremy likes carrots more than he likes apples.
2. Aubrey skis in the Rocky Mountains every weekend.
3. Jane won a trophy for being the most valuable player on her softball team.
4. Felix starts on both the basketball and football teams, and he is an "A" student.
5. Carol plays four musical instruments, and she has also formed a highly-praised band.

Starting Points

Ideas for Writing

Your world is brimming with ideas for writing. The pictures and quotes on the following pages can help you discover them. Use these pages, and the questions below, to free your creativity.

Pictures

1. How could I describe or explain this picture?
2. Does this picture remind me of something that I know about or have experienced?
3. Can I find out more about the subject through research?
4. What might have happened *before* the scene in the picture or just *after* it?
5. Would the people in the picture make interesting characters in a story?
6. Does the picture bring to mind other experiences or topics that are worth exploring?

Quotations

1. What is the main idea? Do I agree or disagree with it?
2. How does the quotation apply to my own life?
3. Does the quotation remind me of someone I know or admire?
4. Can I think of an example that illustrates this quotation?

You may go beyond *Starting Points* with these questions. Apply them to any of the photos, art, or ideas that appear throughout the text.

Starting Points

Flight

Albrecht Durer's 1493 woodcut was the first picture of flight ever printed. The detail above shows the mythical Daedalus in flight.

I have a small-town soul.
It makes me want to know
Wee unimportant things
About the folks that go
Past on swift journeys.

Violet Alleyn Storey

Dorothy's ruby slippers, from
The Wizard of Oz, *1939.*

Travelers are always discoverers,
especially those who travel air.

Anne Morrow Lindbergh

In 1927, Charles A. Lindbergh made the first solo
nonstop flight across the Atlantic Ocean.

Duo seeks aviation's 'last plum'

Author once
directed Air
& Space
Museum, is
22-year Air
Force veteran

By Walter Boyne
Special for USA TODAY

Dick Rutan and Jeana
Yeager are attempting something never done before — a
flight around the world nonstop and non-refueled. They
lifted off Sunday morning
from the 15,000-foot runway of
California's Edwards Air
Force Base in the Voyager, a
strange white aircraft that
looks like an airborne catamaran.

Much is at stake besides the lives of two brave people and
establishing a record Rutan calls "the last big plum" in avia-
tion history.

As the numbing effects of the Challenger tragedy begin to
wear off, a successful flight by the Voyager — with its innovative design and revolutionary new materials, and with
Rutan and Yeager as role models — could spark a vitally
needed revolution of the American air and space spirit.

The modern equi_____ f Charles Lindb___ ___d Ame-

More Ideas to Explore

Space Flight
Flying Machines
Outer Limits
Pioneers of Flight
Flights of the Imagination

Americans

We must learn to
live together as
brothers, or
perish together as
fools.
Dr. Martin Luther King, Jr.

*Detail from mural
by Thomas Hart Benton*

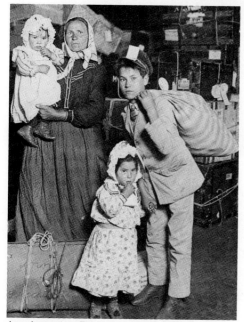

Immigrants at Ellis Island, circa 1910.

I realize that patriotism is not enough.

Edith Cavell

Public opinion in this country is everything.

Abraham Lincoln

Vietnam War Memorial.

More Ideas to Explore

Rights and Responsibilities
American Heroes
The First Americans
Growth and Change
Different People, Different Cultures

Friendship

It is only with the heart
that one can see
rightly; what is essential
is invisible to the eye.

Antoine de Saint-Exupéry

No person is your friend
who demands your silence
or denies your right to grow.

Alice Walker

We love the things we
love for what they are.

Robert Frost

More Ideas to Explore

Teamwork
Love and Hate
Getting Respect
Conformity
Independence
Trust

Discovery

> Everything has its
> beauty but not
> everyone sees it.
>
> Confucius

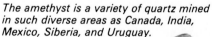

The amethyst is a variety of quartz mined
in such diverse areas as Canada, India,
Mexico, Siberia, and Uruguay.

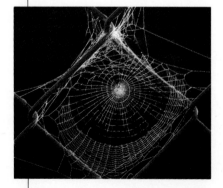

That's always the way
when you discover
something new:
everybody thinks
you're crazy.

Evelyn Smith

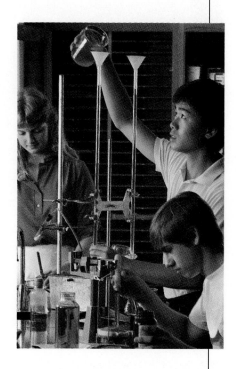

Discovery consists of looking
at the same thing as everyone
else and thinking something
different.

Albert Szent-Gyorgyi

More Ideas to Explore

A Surprise Ending
Discoveries for the Future
Failure and Success
A Discovery that
  Changed the World
A Great Experiment

Starting Points

Nature

Moonlight is sculpture.
Nathaniel Hawthorne

Slot Canyon, near Page, Arizona

Wild animals and
people have something
in common; they love
to look at each other.
Maxine A. Rock

It is not possible to step in the same river twice.

Heraclitus

In every outthrust
headland, in every
curving beach, in every
grain of sand there is a
story of the earth.

Rachel Carson

More Ideas to Explore

Natural Disasters
Conservation
Wilderness
Survival
The Stars and Planets
Frontiers

Free Time

The days are all
too short when one
goes fishing.

Theodore Gordon

It is better to have
loafed and lost than
never to have loafed at all.
James Thurber

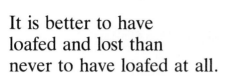

In dreams begin responsibility.
Kenneth Grahame

More Ideas to Explore

Hobbies, Games, and Crafts
An Incredible Challenge
Arts and Books
Sports
Daydreams

3
Prewriting Strategies

Every writing experience is like an adventure. Often the outcome is unknown. You are not quite sure of your focus, and you may explore different paths, make false starts, and come up with new ideas before the adventure ends.

Many of the most successful undertakings—in real life or on paper—are those that are thought out beforehand. That's why prewriting, or planning your writing, is so important.

Good planning is essential to good writing. In this chapter you will ask basic questions, make choices, and identify an individual writing approach that works best for you.

1
The Writing Process

Every writer has a unique way of writing, just as every person has a unique way of thinking. Most writers, however, go through the following basic stages while writing.

Prewriting During the prewriting stage, you plan your writing. At this time, you determine your topic, audience, purpose, and form. You research or think about your topic, make notes you can refer to later, and organize your ideas.

Drafting The goal of drafting is to get your ideas down on paper, without worrying about spelling or punctuation. You may find that you revise as you draft, or discover that you need to gather more information or reorganize.

Revising In this stage, you read through what you have written and make changes to improve it. You may enlist the help of a peer editor, or read your writing aloud to an audience. As a separate step, you proofread the final draft to correct errors in spelling, grammar, usage, and mechanics.

Publishing and Presenting This stage gives you a chance to share your writing in a meaningful way. There are many ways to find an audience for your writing, from class magazines to oral readings.

A Flexible Series of Stages

The writing process is flexible. You can move back and forth among the stages until you are satisfied with your writing. For example, after Frank finished drafting his story, he read it aloud to a friend (presenting). Then he used his friend's suggestions to plan a new ending for the story (prewriting). Frank drafted a new ending, then asked his friend to evaluate it and suggest improvements (revising). Frank's process of writing is illustrated on the next page.

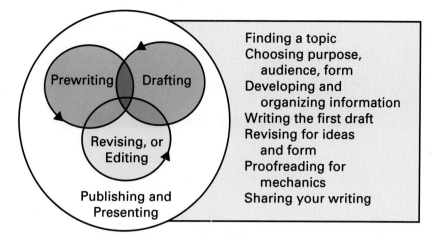

Finding a topic
Choosing purpose, audience, form
Developing and organizing information
Writing the first draft
Revising for ideas and form
Proofreading for mechanics
Sharing your writing

A Problem-Solving Process

To understand the writing process, you may find it helpful to think of it as a way of solving problems in writing. Each stage of the process may be viewed as a problem-solving step.

In prewriting, you first **identify the task or problem**. Then you **examine alternatives,** considering different ways of gathering information or presenting material. Finally, **you choose an approach**.

The drafting stage allows you to **try out the approach**. You may experiment with different ways of expressing your ideas, or share your draft with a friend, asking for comments.

In the revising stage, you **evaluate results** by judging the effectiveness of your paper. Then you make any needed revisions.

Writing Activity *The Writing Process*

Answer the following questions to help you understand the writing process you use now.

1. How do you usually get ideas for writing?
2. What kind of planning or prewriting do you usually do?
3. Do you draft with a pencil, pen, typewriter, or word processor? Where do you usually do your writing?
4. Do you generally revise as you draft? Have you ever shared an unfinished draft?
5. Do you ever read your work aloud while revising? What other revising techniques do you use?
6. How carefully do you proofread your writing?
7. Who have been your audiences?

2
Prewriting: The Planning Stage

Professional writers often spend more time preparing to write than they do actually writing. They know that finding a topic, determining their purpose, analyzing their audience, and choosing a form are essential preliminary steps for many kinds of writing.

Finding a Topic

To find something to write about, you could use some of the thinking skills you learned in Chapter 2. For example, you might keep a journal of your thoughts, ideas, observations, and feelings. Your journal could contain an account of a movie or concert you attended. Or it could contain a description of a place you visited or a funny experience you had. Entries like these can provide material for a review, story, or other piece of writing. You might also use your journal to practice freewriting or clustering, as described on pages 18–19.

You should also be alert to potential writing ideas while you are reading, watching television, visiting a public place like a museum or zoo, or just talking to friends. This method of gathering ideas, called gleaning, is described on pages 64–65. Finally, when you want to write a story or poem or think of a new approach to a familiar subject, you might try creative thinking, as described on pages 36–37.

Let's see how one student writer found a topic for writing. Cathy's science class was studying oceans. Her teacher asked each student to choose an ocean animal and report on it to the class.

> Cathy began by brainstorming. She made a list of ocean animals that she was interested in or that she wanted to learn more about: *lobster, shark, eel, octopus, whale, horseshoe crab, porpoise.* She read over her list several times, and thought about the animals. She remembered an exhibit she had seen at an oceanarium about whales. She decided to write something about whales.

Setting the Limits

Once you have found a subject, it is usually necessary to set the limits. This means you narrow your focus to a topic you can cover thoroughly. One way to do this is by inquiring, as described on page 24. Listing questions about your subject may help you choose which questions to answer. Another way to narrow your focus is by analyzing—breaking the subject into parts and studying those parts. This was described on pages 26–27. Here is how Cathy analyzed her subject:

> First Cathy divided the subject of whales into parts: *kinds of whales, habitat, physical characteristics, myths about whales, behavior, life cycle,* and *whales in captivity.* As she read over her list, she remembered an interesting kind of whale behavior she had learned about at the oceanarium—whale songs. She decided to find out what kind of whale produces songs. An encyclopedia entry on whales provided the answer—humpback whales sing. She would report on humpbacks, the singing whales.

Determining Your Purpose

There are four main purposes for writing: **to express yourself**, **to entertain**, **to inform**, and **to persuade**. Sometimes the topic itself determines the purpose. For instance, if Cathy had decided to focus on how the whaling industry has endangered the survival of humpback whales as a species, her main purpose would probably be to persuade the reader that hunting whales is cruel and should be stopped.

Other times you decide on the purpose of your writing by reflecting on your thoughts and feelings about your subject. You ask yourself questions such as the following: why does this subject appeal to me? Why do I want others to know about it? What effect do I want my writing to have on my audience? Here is how Cathy answered these questions.

> The exhibit I saw on whales was really interesting. They are gentle and intelligent animals. Their songs are haunting and beautiful. I want my classmates to understand what makes humpback whales unique. The main purpose of my report is to inform my

classmates about humpback whales and to convince them that whales should be protected from hunters.

Analyzing Your Audience

Sometimes you can choose your audience. When you write an article for a science fiction fan magazine, you have chosen readers who share a common interest in science fiction. Other times your audience is chosen for you. Cathy's audience, the members of her science class, had been chosen for her by her teacher. However, there are other audiences with whom Cathy could have shared her writing. She could have written an article on humpbacks for the readers of a nature magazine.

Once you know your audience, you analyze them so that you can suit your writing to them. You decide what part of your subject might interest them, what information they need, and what level of language would be best. If Cathy was writing a

Writing Inside Out

Since the early 1970's Leon Forrest has emerged as one of America's most highly praised novelists. Born and raised in Chicago, he writes with imagination and zeal about black American life. Mr. Forrest was a journalist before he turned his attention to writing fiction. Today he is a full-time writer and professor in the Afro-American Studies department at Northwestern University.

On becoming a writer:

"You don't start off knowing that you're going to be a writer. What leads you to writing is a lot of reading."

"It starts off with your love for some book, story, tale, or folklore—so much that you'd like to imitate it."

children's story about a whale; for example, she might have focused on a young whale and told how it learns to avoid dangers. She would have used short sentences and simple words.

Choosing a Form

The **form** is the type of writing in which your message is expressed. Common forms are stories, plays, poems, articles and essays, and school reports. You choose a form by thinking about your topic, purpose, and audience.

Sometimes the topic determines the form. If Cathy's topic had been about saving the whales from extinction, she might have written a persuasive piece, perhaps a letter to a newspaper.

Other times the purpose determines the form. If Cathy's purpose had been to entertain, she might have written a journal account of an all-day whale watching trip she went on. Since Cathy's purpose was to inform, she decided to give a slide talk to

"Most early writing is imitative, but that's all right."

"A writer comes out of a library; that's the most important thing. A library feeds the imagination and then out of that something new is made."

On writing:

"Writing doesn't come easily to me; I have to work for it. I write a section and put it away and work on several other things. When I come back to it, I can look at it with a more critical eye, and see if the patterns of events are flowing well and associating clearly with my overall vision for the whole novel."

"This idea of doing something in process is very important. I was raised by a seamstress and I have a sense of that from her. She was always working on something."

"The writer develops something like a memory bank of impressions. Everything you've read and all the stories you've heard work together in a strange kind of chemistry."

her science class. She planned to read her report to the class and to illustrate her talk by showing slides of whales and by playing a recording of whale songs.

Using the Prewriting Process

Often one or more of the prewriting decisions is made for you. For instance, Cathy knew that the audience for her report would be her science class. She also knew the general subject area of her report (ocean animals). However, she had to decide on the specific topic, set the limits of that topic, determine her purpose, and choose what form her report would take.

If you do not have decisions made for you, reflect about the prewriting issues in any order. For example, you might decide first that you want to write about sanctuaries to protect hump-back whales (topic). You decide next that the best form for your writing is a letter and that the letter should be sent to your senator (audience). You decide that your purpose is to persuade your senator to support legislation to create whale sanctuaries off the northwest coast of the United States.

Writing Activities Planning

A Below are several statements. Tell whether each is about topic, purpose, audience, form, or a combination of these.

1. I want to write something to express how surprised I was.
2. I have to write an article for my class magazine.
3. I feel like writing a poem.
4. I want to write something about computer games.
5. I want to convince students to attend volleyball games.

B **Writing in Process** Use a thinking technique like free-writing, clustering, or gleaning to come up with an idea for a short composition. As one possible source of ideas, look through Starting Points on pages 41-53. You may also want to refer to Ideas for Writing in the Writer's Handbook on pages 655-656. Set the limits of your topic by analyzing or inquiring. Determine your purpose, audience, and form. Make a special writing folder and save your notes in it. You will also use this folder in other chapters to store notes, drafts, and revisions of your writing.

3
Gathering Information

Once you have planned your writing, you should gather information about your topic. There are a number of ways to gather information.

Analyzing and Inquiring

Analyzing, or dividing your topic into parts, can help you discover what issues you need to find information about. Since Cathy had analyzed her topic of humpback whales during prewriting, she used another thinking technique called **inquiring** to gather information. Inquiring means that you make a list of questions you need to answer about each part of your topic. Here are the questions Cathy asked herself about the topic of humpback whales.

Topic: What are the most important characteristics of the humpback whale?

Parts and Questions:
Part 1: Physical characteristics of humpback whales
1. How big are humpbacks?
2. Why are they called "humpback" whales?
3. How are humpbacks different from other whales?

Part 2: Behavior of humpback whales
1. What unique behavior do humpbacks have?
2. What are whale songs?

Watercolor by Ken Lisbourne

Part 3: Life cycle of humpback whales
1. Where are humpbacks found?
2. How do humpback whales care for their young?
3. What enemies do humpbacks have?

Using Reflecting to Gather Information

Another useful way to gather information about your topic is by **reflecting** about what you already know. When you do imaginative writing, such as stories, plays, and poems, you will have to create characters, settings, or images in your mind. You can do this by reflecting about people, places, and events in your daily life. You might find it helpful to use your journal to record impressions. Reading your entries later can help you recall your thoughts and feelings. These impressions can be used in a story. You will learn more about developing stories in Chapter 10.

Reflecting is also a good way to gather material for informative writing projects, like reports and articles. For example, you might try freewriting or clustering to help you discover what details you know and what details you will have to find by some other method. (See pages 19–22.) Here is some freewriting Cathy did to discover what she remembered about whale songs:

> The whale songs I heard at the oceanarium were
> beautiful but eerie. They sounded something like
> birds chirping, but the notes were longer and deeper.
> They sounded like a combination of crying and whis-
> tling. There were also groans and clicking noises.
> Sometimes patterns of sounds were repeated over
> and over. I should use this description of whale
> songs in my report. I'll also try to find out why
> whales sing and what the songs mean.

Using Gleaning to Gather Information

Probably the most useful technique for gathering information for an article or report is **gleaning**. Notice that Cathy had started gleaning information from the exhibit she saw at the oceanarium and from the encyclopedia entry she read. She also used the card catalog in her school library to find a book about humpback whales. The book gave her a lot of useful information and also had pictures that Cathy could show her class on the opaque projector to illustrate her talk.

Cathy also decided to interview a marine biologist who worked at the oceanarium. She prepared a list of questions about whale behavior and took notes on the biologist's answers. Following are Cathy's questions and the notes she took during her interview.

Question: Why do humpback whales sing?
Answer: No one knows for sure. Males usually sing before or during yearly migration.
Question: What do the songs mean?
Answer: Songs seem to be a kind of communication. Whale separated from herd will sing or call for hours. Whales in the Atlantic and Pacific sing different songs. Songs change from year to year.
Question: What other behaviors are unique?
Answer: Humpbacks are very playful. They "breach," or jump out of the water. They also slap the water with their flippers and tail fins ("flukes"). Often, humpbacks stroke each other with their tail fins. They have even been seen following ships.

After her interview, Cathy compared the notes she had taken to the information she had gleaned from the book on humpbacks. She found that by combining the two sources of information, she gained a better understanding of the answers to her questions than she could get from one source alone.

Writing Activities *Asking Questions*

A Choose one of the topics listed below. Write five questions you might want answered in a short composition about the topic. Review the technique of inquiring on page 63 to help you think of questions. Then tell how you might find the answers if you were gathering information to write the composition.

1. Planning a backpack trip
2. The first railroad across America
3. Summer jobs and how to find them
4. Observing stars and comets
5. Wild horses in the United States

B Writing in Process Take out your notes from Activity B on page 62. If you decided to write a story or other imaginative composition, use freewriting or another reflecting technique to gather information. If you decided to write an article or report, use analyzing or inquiring to decide what information you need. Then use gleaning to gather notes about your topic. Keep your notes in your writing folder.

4
Organizing Your Ideas

After you have gathered information, you have to organize it. A good plan of organization makes your ideas clear to your reader. There are two main tasks to complete when you organize. First, you arrange your information in a logical order. Second, you decide what information should be deleted and what information you still need.

Choosing a Logical Order

Ideas can be organized in many ways. To choose a method of organization, look for relationships among the gathered ideas.

Relationship in Time   Sometimes your ideas are events that occur at different times. If so, you can use **chronological order**. Here are some notes Cathy made about the migration of North Atlantic humpbacks. The numbers next to the notes show how Cathy arranged them in chronological order.

③ The journey of up to 4,000 miles takes one to two months.

② The first to leave are the females with year-old calves. The last to leave are pregnant females.

① North Atlantic humpbacks begin to move south in October.

④ By December, the first whales have reached the warm waters of the West Indies.

Relationships by Position   Sometimes the details you have gathered are related to one another by position. If so, you can use **spatial order**. For example, when Cathy writes about the physical characteristics of humpbacks, she could move from the front of the whale to the back. First, she could describe its mouth. Next, she could tell about its blowhole and ears. Then she could describe its long pectoral fins. Next, she could give information about its body size and shape. Finally, she could tell about its flukes or tail fins.

Relationships of Amount or Degree At other times, your details differ from one another in degree. You can arrange them in **order of familiarity**, or **order of importance**, by starting with the least important or familiar idea and ending with the most important or familiar. For example, read Cathy's notes about how people are an enemy of the humpback. The numbers show how she arranged her ideas in order of familiarity, starting with least familiar example and ending with the most familiar.

③ Water pollution threatens whale feeding grounds.

① Noise from ship traffic disrupts migration patterns.

② Though whaling is illegal, some hunting still takes place.

Adding and Deleting Information

After organizing your material, make sure that each detail fits your topic and purpose. For example, look again at the notes on page 65 that Cathy made during her interview. The fact that whales in the Atlantic and Pacific sing different songs and that whale songs vary from year to year are interesting, but these details do not really answer the question "What do the songs mean?" These facts should probably be deleted.

You should also make sure that you have enough details to fulfill your statement of purpose. You have to look at your material from your reader's point of view and ask yourself whether all their questions have been answered. In looking over her notes about people as an enemy of the humpback, Cathy decided her readers would wonder whether whale watching expeditions bother humpbacks. Here is the note she added.

> Whale watching is big business in some humpback feeding grounds. No one knows for certain what damage this might do.

Writing Activity *Organizing Notes*

Writing in Process Take out your notes from Activity B on page 65. Decide which method of organization is best suited for each part of your composition. Arrange your information in the order you have chosen. Add additional information, and delete information that does not fit your topic or purpose. You will continue this writing project in Chapter 4.

English and Science

You've learned about the writing process, but did you know that you've been involved with other types of processes all your life? For example, your experience with and study of science is all about processes. Science asks questions about how things work and how events happen, progress, and end.

The actual process of any science experiment can be broken down just as the process of writing was outlined in this chapter. An experiment involves the following steps: (1) *Preparation and Prediction.* You assemble all the necessary equipment and decide what hypotheses (or predictions) you are going to test. (2) *Testing.* You check your predictions by performing certain tasks under controlled conditions. (3) *Results.* You examine and analyze the results to see if your predictions were true.

Activity

Select a simple scientific experiment, such as testing the reaction of combining baking soda and vinegar. You may make up an experiment or use one from a science book. (Check with your science teacher to make sure the experiment is safe.)

Write a laboratory report describing the experiment and the results, using the following form.

Experiment: (What are you testing?)
Preparation: (How did you set up the experiment?)
Prediction: (What do you think will happen?)
Observations: (What happens as the experiment progresses?)
Results: (What actually happened? Was your prediction correct?)

Application and Review

A Identifying the Stages of the Writing Process Read the following list of writing activities. Write whether each activity is most likely to be prewriting, drafting, revising, or sharing.

1. Reading your composition to the class
2. Looking through your journal for writing ideas
3. Writing a conclusion
4. Correcting spelling errors
5. Reorganizing paragraphs into a more logical order
6. Constructing an outline
7. Proofreading your writing
8. Writing the body paragraphs
9. Defining your audience
10. Printing an article in the yearbook

B Using Inquiry to Gather Information Read the writing topics listed below. Choose two of them. For each one, write four questions that could be answered in a short composition on the topic.

1. Famous racecars and their drivers
2. Auditioning for a school play
3. The earth's active volcanoes
4. Growing a Venus flytrap plant
5. Maintaining an aquarium at home

C Organizing Ideas Look through the writing topics below. Tell which method of organization (chronological order, spatial order, order of familiarity, order of importance) is best for each topic.

1. A description of a video arcade
2. A trip down the Mississippi River
3. The different vitamins your body needs to survive
4. The renovation of the Statue of Liberty
5. A comparison of grits, oatmeal, and mush
6. A history of the National Football League

4
Drafting

The artist has decided what she wants to paint, and now she is putting her vision on canvas. She will try different colors and patterns as she goes along. Chances are, her vision will change as the painting takes shape.

Writers, too, try out ideas, rearrange them, and change them as they write. Drafting is the process of putting ideas down on paper and revising them. Different writers use different methods; this chapter will help you find a method that works for you.

1
Preparing to Write

There are many ways of drafting a piece of writing. The method you choose will be determined by your purpose and by the style of writing that is most comfortable for you. Think for a moment about two piano players. Each is practicing an unfamiliar piece of music. The first works through the music slowly, measure by measure. He plays the same phrase again and again, correcting his errors, until he is satisfied he has it right. The second pianist plays through the whole piece quickly, without worrying about mistakes. Then she goes back to work out difficult passages.

Like the first pianist, you might prefer a slow and methodical drafting method. On the other hand, your style might be more like the second pianist. You might prefer to get everything down quickly. Experiment with the drafting methods described in this chapter. Then choose a method that is right for you.

Take Stock As you prepare to begin drafting, you should first use reflecting to take stock of the prewriting choices you have made. Ask yourself questions to make sure your writing is planned as you want. Here are some questions you might consider:

> Have I limited my topic?
> Do I know my purpose?
> Have I analyzed my audience?
> Have I chosen an appropriate form?
> Have I organized my information logically?
> Do I have enough information to fulfill my purpose?
> Have I deleted information that is not relevant?

Cathy thought about these questions as she prepared to draft her report on humpback whales. She was satisfied with how she had narrowed her topic, analyzed her audience, and determined her purpose and form. As she read over her notes, such as those on page 65, she realized that she still needed a plan of organization. She decided to start with the least important whale behavior, tail slapping, and end with the most important, whale songs.

Find a Time and Place The second step in preparing to draft is choosing a good time and a good place. Writing takes concentration. You will probably do your best work when you have a block of uninterrupted time. A good place to write might be the desk in your room, a library carrel, or even a quiet place outside.

Choose and Gather Materials The last step is choosing and gathering the materials that you need. Some writers prefer to draft in pencil. They revise by erasing to keep their rough drafts as neat as possible. Other writers like the free flow of writing with a pen. They revise by crossing out or drawing arrows. Today many writers use typewriters or word processors. Typewriters produce readable drafts that can be revised later with pen or pencil. Word processors allow writers to revise as they work. With a few keystrokes the writer can eliminate mistakes and move words and sentences around on the screen before printing the final copy.

Self Portrait, Winnie Ng, Student Artist.

Other materials might include your prewriting notes, any pictures or photographs you want to describe, a dictionary, and a thesaurus to help you choose the right word. For some drafting projects, you might also need a library book or a reference book, such as an encyclopedia or atlas, to check details. Cathy, for example, decided to have the book on humpback whales on hand so that she could refer to the illustrations and to quickly check facts and details as she drafted.

Writing Activities *Drafting*

Writing in Process Take out your writing folder and look over the notes you made for your composition. Answer the questions listed under *Take Stock* on the previous page to check whether your planning is complete. Add additional information to your notes if needed and go over your plan of organization. If you are satisfied with your planning notes, save them in the folder for the next activity. Decide what materials you need to begin drafting, and gather them together.

2
Drafting Techniques

Drafting means putting your ideas down in sentences and paragraphs. You are free to experiment, cross out ideas, add details, or reorganize information. If you wish, you can wait until the revising stage to correct mistakes in spelling, grammar, usage, and mechanics. If you get stalled, you can start all over again. The most common methods of drafting are the loosely structured draft, the highly structured draft, and the bridge-building type of draft. Each of these can be either a quick or a slow draft.

The Loosely Structured Draft For a loosely structured draft, you work from rough prewriting notes. You experiment with ideas and organization as you draft. This method works well when you are not sure what you want to say or how you want to say it.

Here is a loosely structured draft Cathy wrote from the notes on page 65. Notice that Cathy changed the order of details as she drafted. She also added examples and transitions.

Humpbacks are very playful. *Humpbacks also* ~~They sometimes~~

stand on their heads in the water and slap the water

with their *flukes* ~~tail fins~~. This makes a huge splash and a

lot of noise. Other times humpbacks use their long

flippers to stroke other whales or to splash water.

they
~~Humpbacks~~ sometimes follow ships. Scientists are

not sure if the whales think the ship is another whale

or if they are just curious. *Their most spectacular behavior* ~~In breaching,~~ the whale
is called breeching.
jumps out of the water, arches over, and lands on its

side or back.

> **I should describe this behavior first.**

> **I should add a transition.**

The Highly Structured Draft When writing a highly structured draft, you work from very complete prewriting notes. You follow your writing plan carefully, changing very little in the content or organization. You can, of course, add further details if they occur to you. This method works well for those who already have a clear idea about what they wish to write or who have a lot of details to include. Here is an example of how Cathy might have written a highly structured draft from her notes on page 66 about the migration of humpbacks.

In October, humpbacks begin to move south from

their summer feeding grounds in the North Atlantic

I should tell why. to their tropical breeding grounds. The first to leave I'll add another detail here.

are females with their year-old calves. Pregnant

who swim more slowly ∧ *The herd follows the same route*
females bring up the rear. ∧ Their journey of up to *every year.*

4,000 miles takes one to two months. By December,

the first whales have reached the warm waters of the

West Indies.

Bridge Building When using the bridge-building method of drafting, you begin with three or four main ideas. Then you build "bridges," or logical connections, between them. This method is useful for more personal writing, in which research is not important or when you discover ideas as you go along. Here, for example, is a paragraph that Cathy might have written by the bridge-building method on people as the enemies of the humpbacks. Notice that the main ideas are connected by the bridge *in ways we may not even realize.*

People are enemies of the humpbacks in ways we may not even realize. We seldom think about the ocean as being noisy, but noise from ship traffic may make it difficult for humpbacks to communicate. This might disrupt their migration and breeding. Even whale-watching expeditions might disturb the whales in some way. Everyone knows about pollution in our lakes and rivers, but few people realize that the oceans are polluted too. Ocean pollution may threaten humpback feeding grounds. Whale hunting, which people think is the greatest human threat to humpbacks, is actually the least serious problem today.

The Quick or the Slow Draft? You can complete whichever drafting method you choose by writing a quick draft or a slow draft. When you write a **quick draft**, you can use prewriting notes if you have them. However, your goal is to get your ideas down on paper quickly. When you have completed your paper, you can go back over it to reorganize your material, refine ideas, add or delete information, and correct errors. You may wish to write a quick draft if you find that frequent stops interrupt your flow of ideas or make you lose track of your ideas.

When you write a **slow draft**, you work slowly and carefully. You draft one sentence or one paragraph at a time, revising as you go along. You may wish to use this method if you are uncomfortable with leaving an idea unfinished.

Writing Activities *Drafting*

A Jim made the following prewriting notes for a paragraph he is writing about the advantages of canoes. Choose one of the drafting methods discussed in this section and write a draft of a paragraph using Jim's notes.

- inexpensive and long-lasting
- light, portable, and easily maneuverable in the water
- can carry two people and camping gear for several weeks
- can be used in marshes, streams, shallow rivers
- easily carried around dams, sand bars, and other obstructions
- can be stored in basement or garage in winter

B Writing in Process Look over your notes from Activity B on page 67. Use one of the drafting methods described in this section to write a first draft about your topic. Keep the draft in your writing folder.

3
Reflecting After Drafting

When you have finished drafting, it is a good idea to wait a day or two before you start revising the draft. Postponing your revision will allow you time to reflect on what you have written. Here are several techniques to help you think creatively about your draft before you revise it.

Read Your Draft Silently When you read your draft silently, imagine that you are the reader, not the writer. Try to identify places where the reader might be confused or need more information. Ask yourself questions the reader might ask, such as "What does this sentence mean?" or "Why do you think that?"

Read Your Draft Aloud When you read your draft aloud, your ear often detects problems that you miss when you read silently. For example, you might become aware of missing words or ideas, awkward phrases or sentences, or problems with logical organization. Don't worry about correcting these problems. Concentrate, instead, on identifying the parts that you will want to revise.

Share Your Draft Asking a family member, a friend, or a classmate to read your draft is another good way of identifying problems before revision. Tell your reader to point out any part that does not make sense or that lacks details.

As you use these reflecting techniques, look for answers to the following questions.

Checklist for Reflecting after Drafting
1. Can I identify places where I need more information or where I can delete some information?
2. Are there places where the reader might be confused?
3. Can I identify places where words or ideas are missing?
4. Are there any awkward phrases or sentences?
5. Can I identify any problems in the logical order?

Speaking and Listening

Do you shy away from positions of responsibility because you may be asked to talk before a crowd? Relax. There are ways to make public speaking a comfortable experience.

The best way is to think carefully about what you want to say. This is where your prewriting and drafting skills can help you, because a good speech needs to be as well-planned as a report. List and outline what you want to say, arranging the main points in a logical order. You now have a clear plan to follow.

Let your plan guide you through your speech, but don't be afraid to change what you want to say. As you speak, you can explore new ideas that were not part of your original plan. In addition, your audience's reaction can influence your speech. You may decide to change what you want to say or how you want to say it because your audience is not responding as you expected.

Activity

Select a topic for a five-minute speech. You might tell about a personal experience, a favorite person or pet, or a place or thing you find interesting. Or, you might try to persuade your audience about a strong opinion you hold. Write out a plan as suggested above. Deliver the speech to your class. If possible, have your teacher or one of your classmates record the speech. Listen to the tape and note how you changed the plan as you were speaking. If a tape recorder is not available, pass out a copy of your plan to your classmates before you speak. Then let them evaluate the changes you made.

Application and Review

A **Preparing to Write** Pretend that you are about to draft a report on electricity. Use reflecting to take stock of the prewriting choices you have made. Make a list of the questions you might ask yourself to be sure you have a good writing plan.

B **Identifying Types of Drafts** Answer the following questions.

1. What is drafting?
2. What are the most common methods of drafting?
3. In what method do you experiment with ideas and organization as you draft?
4. In what method do you follow very complete prewriting notes?
5. In what method do you begin with three or four main ideas?
6. What is the goal when you write a quick draft?
7. When would it be a good idea to write a quick draft?
8. How do you write a slow draft?
9. When would it be a good idea to write a slow draft?

5
Revising and Presenting

The lights dim, the audience grows silent, and music fills the auditorium. The ballerinas dance onto the stage. The difficult preparation is all behind them now—the perfecting of the arabesque, the long practices, the changes in routine. Only the beauty of the dance matters now, only the sharing and enjoyment of talent.

Like dancing, writing should be shared. In this chapter you will learn how to revise and proofread your work. Then, like the performing artists in these pictures, you will be ready to enjoy sharing your work with others.

1
Revising, or Editing

When you have finished drafting, you make the final revisions in your writing. You correct errors in spelling, grammar, usage, and mechanics and change anything that does not work well or that you think you can improve. Your main tasks, however, are to make sure that you have expressed your ideas clearly, organized your information logically, and used the right words to express your meaning.

Choosing a Method   Choose a revising method that suits your personal style and the kind of writing you are doing. Here are some common methods.

> ### Methods of Revising
> 1. **Self-editing**   Set your draft aside for a day or two. Then read it carefully, silently or aloud. Correct any problems you find.
> 2. **Peer Editing**   Share your draft with another student or a group of students. Use the questions and comments of your readers to guide your revisions.
> 3. **Teacher Conferences**   Share your draft with your teacher. Ask questions, such as "How can I improve the organization of this paragraph?" or "How can I make this idea clearer?"
> 4. **Performance**   Ask a friend or a classmate to follow directions that you have written explaining how to do something. Look for directions that are unclear, incomplete, or confusing.

Cathy began with self-editing when she revised her report on humpback whales. Then she read her report aloud to a small group of students in her class. She used their questions, such as "Whales don't really talk, do they?" and "What do whale songs sound like?" to guide her revision. On the next page is a paragraph that shows her revisions.

fascinating

The most ~~interesting~~ thing about humpback whales

haunting and

is there ^ beautiful songs. Male humpbacks sing just

before or during their migration to the Tropics. ~~Each~~

It

→ ~~fall whales migrate to warmer water.~~ ,A song is a

cries, whistles, moans and clicks ←

complex sequance of ~~sounds~~ that is repeated exactly.

communication

The songs seem to be a method of ~~talking~~. Male

humbpacks may sing to atract females or to tell

their location

other whales ~~where they are.~~ a typical song lasts

from fifteen minutes to one hour.

I don't need this sentence.

This makes my description clearer.

This sentence is out of place.

Revision Checklist When revising, ask yourself the following questions. A peer editor may also use these questions.

Revision and Peer-Editing Checklist

1. Is all essential information included? Are there any unnecessary or unrelated details?
2. Is each main idea clearly expressed and thoroughly developed?
3. Does the organization clearly show how ideas are related? Are transitions used to link ideas and paragraphs? Does anything seem out of place?
4. Are there any confusing sentences or paragraphs?
5. Are vivid and precise words used?
6. Do the tone, mood, and level of language suit the audience?

Writing Activity *Revising*

Writing in Process Share the draft you wrote in Activity B on page 76 with a classmate to get suggestions for revision. Then use the revision checklist to self-edit your draft. Save your draft in your writing folder.

2
Proofreading

Proofreading is the last step in revision, when you pay close attention to finding and correcting errors in spelling, grammar, usage, and mechanics. Try proofreading your work several times, each time looking for a different kind of error. To correct mistakes in spelling and hyphenation, use a dictionary. Refer to your textbook for corrections of grammar, capitalization, punctuation, and usage.

Proofreading Checklist As you proofread your draft, look for the answers to the following questions. (Additional information on these concepts can be found on the indicated pages in your textbook.)

Proofreading Checklist
1. Do all verbs agree with their subjects? (Pages 570–581)
2. Are there any run-on sentences or sentence fragments? (Pages 392–393, 415)
3. Have I used the correct form of each pronoun? (Pages 438–457)
4. Are all the adjectives and adverbs used correctly? (Pages 504–525)
5. Are all the first words capitalized? Are proper nouns and proper adjectives capitalized? (Pages 600–601, 609–610)
6. Does each sentence have the proper end mark? (Pages 618–620)
7. Are commas, semicolons, apostrophes, hyphens, and quotation marks used correctly? (Pages 634–645)
8. Have I checked the spelling of all unfamiliar words in the dictionary? (Page 337)
9. Are all plural and possessive forms spelled correctly? (Pages 427–431)

Proofreading Symbols Use the proofreading symbols at the top of the next page to change and correct your draft.

Proofreading Symbols

∧	Add letters or words	⌒	Close up
⊙	Add a period	¶	Begin a new paragraph
≡	Capitalize a letter	⋏	Add a comma
/	Make a capital letter lowercase	∿	Trade the position of letters or words

— or ⌒ Take out letters or words

Here is how Cathy proofread the revised paragraph from her report on humpback whales.

¶ The most fascinating thing about humpback whales is their haunting and beautiful songs. Male humpbacks sing just before or during their migration to the Tropics. a typical song lasts from fifteen minutes to one hour. It is a complex sequence of cries, whistles, moans and clicks that is repeated exactly. The songs seem to be a method of communication. Male humpbacks may sing to atract females or to tell other whales their location ⊙

Writing Activities **Proofreading**

A Proofread and rewrite this paragraph.

It was the most important game of the season against our archrivel, hillside. During the first three Quarters, I warmed the bench. On the first play of the forth Quarter our reciever Jay watson hurt his knee. the coach sent me in to play. On the next play, the Quarterback calls my number. I went deep and caught touchdown pass to take the lead.

Jelly bean art, Peter Rocha.

B **Writing in Process** Take out the draft you revised in the activity on page 83. Use the proofreading checklist and the proofreading symbols to correct your revised draft. Make a neat final copy.

3
Publishing and Presenting

This stage of the writing process involves sharing your work, which can be accomplished through a form of publication or presentation, such as the ones listed below.

Bulletin Boards Your class, club, or library might use a bulletin board to post writing about a specific topic.

Booklets Your class, club, or friends could put together a booklet. The booklet might contain writing about one subject, such as backpacking, or of one type, such as short plays or movie

Writing Inside Out

In the late 1970's a group of young musicians grew disenchanted and bored with the way rock and roll was being played. As a result, they formed their own bands and began to play their own brand of rock and roll music. Lisa Wertman, a songwriter and member of the band *Get Smart!*, is a part of this movement.

Q. Lisa, what is your movement trying to do?

A. It's a DIY approach—do it yourself. Hey, anybody can form a band, and you don't have to wear fancy costumes, or have a big light show, or play stadiums. The original idea was to bring rock and roll back to the people, bring it back to where the fathers of rock and roll started, like Chuck Berry and Little Richard.

Q. You're a songwriter, but so are Frank and Marc. How do the three of you work together to write songs?

reviews. You could illustrate the booklet with art.

Newspapers and Magazines You could submit your writing to your school newspaper or to a local newspaper that prints student writing. Many fan magazines also accept articles about favorite movie or television characters.

Letters You can write letters to relatives or friends. You can write a letter to the editor of a magazine or newspaper about an issue that concerns you. You could also write a letter to a pen pal.

Performances You and your friends could adapt a story or poem and act it out for your class or club. You could also read a report to your class and illustrate it with projected pictures and background music. This is how Cathy will share her report on humpback whales.

A. There's never a set formula because you have three individuals who write differently. Some of us will come to practice with a sheet of lyrics. We'll just jam for a while to see if we can come up with some music for it. Other times, in our rehearsal space, we'll be jamming and all of a sudden words will come to one of us, and we'll start singing and eventually that may turn into a song.

Often, I have this idea for a song and as a result of the two other people in the band inputting what they think, the song might go from one point all the way to another point. For example, I had this song, basically a rock song, and I started playing it. There was something wrong with the chorus, and we kept going back to it. This isn't working. What's wrong? And then as a joke, we started playing it as a country song, and then we looked at each other and it sounded good. That was the best thing that happened to that song. But I never would have brought a song to practice and said that I think this is probably going to be a country song.

This is an example of how an opinion from someone else is really important sometimes, because here it really changed the song, made it better. Also, it opened me up to something I would have never done.

Here is the final copy of part of Cathy's report. She shared it with her science class while giving a slide presentation.

Student Model

The most unusual thing about the humpback is the way it behaves. One of its playful behaviors is called tail-slapping. A humpback stands on its head in the water and slaps the water with its flukes. This makes a huge splash and a lot of noise. Other times, a humpback uses its long flippers to stroke other whales or to splash water. The most spectacular humpback behavior is called breaching. A whale jumps out of the water, arches over, and lands on its side or back.

Of all the unusual behaviors of humpback whales, however, the most fascinating is its haunting and beautiful songs. Recordings of humpback songs have been used to accompany orchestras and singers. Marine biologists have discovered that male humpbacks sing just before or during their migration to the tropics. A typical song lasts from fifteen minutes to one hour. It is a complex sequence of cries, whistles, moans, and clicks that is repeated exactly. The song seems to be a method of communication. Male humpbacks may sing to attract females or to tell other males their location.

Choosing a Process for Writing

You have learned that writing is a process made up of four stages—prewriting, drafting, revising, and sharing. However, you will rarely complete these stages in one step-by-step process. Some writers, for example, like to start by writing a first draft. Others like to carefully follow a prewriting plan. Still others move back and forth between stages, jotting down a few ideas, beginning a draft, jotting down more ideas, revising, and then completing the draft. You will not need to use every stage of the writing process for every writing task. A science report might require much prewriting, but a letter may involve none.

Writing Activity *Presenting*

Writing in Process Share the writing you completed in Activity B on page 85 in one of the ways described.

Speaking and Listening

Have you ever been in a play in which you and your fellow actors revised the way you said some of the lines or changed some of the stage movements during rehearsals? For example, consider these lines from Lorraine Hansberry's play, *A Raisin in the Sun*. A young woman named Beneatha is asked by her mother if she will ever get married.

> Oh, I probably will . . . but first I'm going to be a doctor, and George, for one, still thinks that's pretty funny. I couldn't be bothered with that. I am going to be a doctor and everybody around here better understand that!

In the first performance, perhaps the actress faced the mother and pointed her finger. When that did not seem effective, she may have decided on a change for the next show—facing the audience and putting more emphasis on the last sentence.

Activity

Divide your classmates into small groups. Choose either a scene from a popular play or a story that everyone knows well. Have each group work out its own interpretation of the same scene or story. Work closely with the members of your group to rehearse your version. Then perform the scene or story for your class. Discuss the differences in each performance. Then have each group tell how they would revise their scene for the next performance.

Creative Writing

A Each of the stories and books you read and the movies you watch usually has a distinctive setting. Change a story's setting and you change the story. For example, suppose the "Wizard of Oz" had taken place anywhere but Oz. What would have happened if Dorothy's house had landed in present-day New York City instead? She might have hopped in a cab to the airport, taken the next airplane back to Kansas, charged it all on Auntie Em's credit card, and effectively ended the story right there. Think about what would happen to a familiar book or movie if the time or place were changed. Rewrite the story using the new information.

B Can a dishwasher become a new type of oven? Can a wristwatch record and play music? These ideas may sound wild, but inventors find new uses for old things all the time. One day, someone might realize that the hot water and steam in a dishwasher could be used to cook food. Today, the computer chip already allows wristwatches to sing "Happy Birthday" to us. Tomorrow, they may even record what we have to say.

Changing an everyday item can make it more useful or interesting and, sometimes, make the inventor very wealthy. The famous "pet rock" is a great example; a man sold millions of plain old rocks (and not for pennies) just because he advertised them as quiet, easy-to-care-for pets. To become the next star inventor, select a common, everyday item and think of a new and exciting use for it. Write out an advertisement, telling the world about your great invention.

Application and Review

A Recognizing Proofreading Symbols Rewrite the paragraph below by correcting the errors marked. If necessary, use the symbol chart in this chapter.

I was amazed to learn that Popeye is based on a real person. ~~popeye is~~ that loveable spinach-chomping cartoon sailor, Elzie Segar had created a cartoon strip *named* *Trimble Theatre* in 1920. In 1928 he needed a sailor for the strip and thought of a character from his hometown named Rocky Feigle. Rocky worked at the local saloon *and* ~~Rocky~~ had a reputation as a skillful fighter *He* ~~Rocky~~ always had a pipe clenched between his teeth. ~~Rocky is a lot like a man named Joe who lives on my street.~~ Rocky became the model for Popeye. Even today, popeye, inspired long ago by Rocky Feigle, lives on in his own comic strip, ~~And~~ on television. The current comic strip is written by Bud Sagendorf.

B Using Proofreading Symbols Read the sentences below. Copy them on your paper. Then insert proofreading symbols wherever corrections are needed. There are at least three errors in each sentence.

1. During the Homecoming dance the casette player broke down and the school had to rely on an amatuer band of students.
2. They didn't know many good songs and thier instrument out of tune and they were just plain bad so some of the kids wanted to leave the dance.
3. The principle, mrs Kearns, asked everyone to stay at the Dance and she brought out the radio from the office for our music.

6
Writing Effective Paragraphs

"In autumn down the beechwood path
The leaves lie thick upon the ground . . ."

From "Beech Leaves" by *James Reaves*

A single leaf shows us a small part of the beauty of autumn. A multi-colored collection of leaves shows us much more.

Similarly, a single sentence tells us something about a topic, but it usually takes a paragraph to express a thought fully. This chapter explains how paragraphs are organized. You will learn to use the writing skills presented in the preceding chapters to create coherent and unified paragraphs.

1
Analyzing Paragraphs

A **paragraph** is a group of related sentences that explain or develop a single idea. In a well-developed paragraph, the main idea is expressed clearly and all the sentences work together logically to support that idea.

Read the following paragraph and look for the main idea. Note how the sentences work together to develop that idea.

*Student
Model*

> My cousin and I learned most of our family's history by playing in Grandmother's attic. In one corner stood a brass-bound trunk, filled with forgotten dolls once treasured by aunts and mothers. Beside the trunk was a plain metal rack. Grandfather's World War II uniform hung proudly on the rack, next to once-stylish dresses and suits. When we dressed up in the old-fashioned clothes, we felt that the past was truly part of our lives.

The writer stated the main idea in the first sentence. The related sentences tell you how the writer learned about family history by exploring the corner of an attic.

The paragraph about the attic corner is a **descriptive paragraph**. By using specific details, it creates a picture of the attic. This is one of four basic types of paragraphs that you are likely to read or write. Another is the **narrative paragraph,** which tells a story or describes an incident by using details about the setting, the characters, the actions, or the conflict. A third is the **expository paragraph,** which explains a subject, using factors or examples. A fourth is the **persuasive paragraph,** which uses reasons, facts, and examples to persuade the reader to adopt the writer's opinion. Sometimes these four types of paragraphs also appear in combination with one another.

Writing Activities **Main Ideas**

Read each paragraph and identify the main idea. Some of the paragraphs have a sentence that strays from the main idea. Identify each, and tell why it does not belong in the paragraph.

1. Wise shoppers follow four steps before they make an important purchase. First, they think about what they need and the features it should have. Second, they compare brands and read about the item in consumer magazines. The school library does not carry these magazines. Third, wise shoppers compare prices in different stores. Finally, they find out if the item is covered by a warranty, in case it needs to be returned or repaired later.

2. I thought professional baseball was dull until I discovered the secret language that is spoken throughout a game. Look at the catcher who is giving the pitcher codes that tell him how to pitch. One finger means fast ball; two fingers mean curve. Now, when I watch a baseball game, I no longer look at the pitcher and batter. I watch "the signs."

3. Our yard looked magically different after the heavy winter snow. The bare branches of the maple trees were outlined in shimmering white. The bird bath near the house had become a frosty snow cone. In front of the garage, the bushes drooped, heavy with snow blossoms. The old garage wore a fresh white coat of snow-paint. Our snow blower will certainly be busy this year.

4. Computers are taking over our lives. We use computers to add two and two. Most of our dishwashers, telephones, televisions, alarm clocks, and cars have computers in them. We use computer software to write reports, check our spelling, and even draw pictures and graphs. If we are not careful, we will become a generation of computer addicts who may be too lazy to do anything for ourselves.

2
Writing Topic Sentences

The main idea of a paragraph is usually expressed in the **topic sentence**. This sentence helps the writer focus on the most important idea, and it helps the reader understand what the paragraph is about.

Limiting the Main Idea

Do not try to cover too much in one paragraph. If your main idea is too broad, your paragraph will become too large and difficult to manage. One way to prevent this is to study your topic sentence. Can it be more specific? Look at the following chart for examples of how general subjects can be made into specific subjects.

General	Specific
American music	Gospel music
Rivers of Germany	The Danube River
Where I live	My bedroom

You could not begin to write all there is to know about music, German rivers, or where you live in just one paragraph. You could, however, explain what gospel music is, trace the path of the Danube, or describe your bedroom in a paragraph.

Positioning the Topic Sentence

Usually the topic sentence comes at the beginning of the paragraph, as in the following example:

Writing Model

Jeff Daniels is deaf, yet he knows when his telephone rings or his alarm clock goes off. His "hearing ear" dog, Rags, tells him. Trained by the American Humane Association, Rags alerts his master whenever someone knocks on the door or the telephone rings, and he leads Jeff to the source of the sound.

The topic sentence at the beginning tells you immediately that the paragraph will discuss how Jeff Daniels, a deaf person, knows when there is a sound in his apartment.

Sometimes the topic sentence sums up the ideas in a paragraph. Notice how the sentences in the following example build up to the topic sentences at the end.

Writing Model
    It is dawn. Ten people huddle together on the rocky hillside, armed with binoculars and telephoto lenses. As the light breaks slowly, an expectant hush falls over the group. Suddenly, a fountain of spray shoots up from the watery horizon and the people cheer. Once more, as hundreds do every year along the California coast, the people gathered here have witnessed the annual migration of the mighty gray whales.

Some paragraphs do not need a topic sentence. Instead, the main idea is implied throughout the paragraph. This kind of paragraph is most common in stories, where the purpose is to move the action along or establish a setting. The following paragraph, for example, establishes a setting.

Professional Model
    The sun poured brightly through his window; sparrows were shrill and pigeons hiccoughed on the small projection of roof that separated the second and third floors. For a moment Brian lay watching the small boys on his wallpaper. They were all fishing with bent rods.

    —W. O. Mitchell

Writing Interesting Topic Sentences

A well-written topic sentence not only states the main idea but also catches the reader's interest. If a topic sentence is dull, the reader may skip over the paragraph. If the topic sentence is interesting, the reader is eager to know more. Study the following topic sentences and decide which ones would make you want to continue reading.

1. I would like to write about one of the world's most graceful animals—the vicuña.
2. The lithe vicuña leaps about the Andes Mountains with the grace of a ballet dancer.

3. I think everyone should learn about how to give first aid to choking victims.
4. What would you do if the person next to you in the cafeteria began to choke?
5. One of the strangest of all the mythical creatures is the basilisk.
6. Stay away from the fearsome basilisk—looks from this beast can kill!

All of these sentences are topic sentences because they state a main idea. However, the writers of sentences two, four, and six used techniques to make their topic sentences more interesting: stating an unusual fact, asking a question, or giving a command.

Stating an Unusual Fact One way to catch a reader's eye is to use an unusual or interesting fact in the topic sentence. In sentence two, the writer chose an interesting characteristic of the vicuña and compared the animal to a ballet dancer. The related sentences in the paragraph might continue the comparison or develop ideas about the gracefulness of the vicuña.

Asking a Question Another technique for making a topic sentence interesting is to change it into a thought-provoking question. Sentence four poses a question about something that could happen to anyone.

A related technique is to turn the topic sentence into two sentences—a question and an answer. For example, the sentence following topic sentence four might answer the question about how to aid a person who is choking:

> If you knew first aid, you would use the heel of your hand to give the choking person four sharp blows between the shoulder blades.

Giving a Command A third way to make a topic sentence interesting is to turn it into a command. Topic sentence six is a command telling the reader to beware of the basilisk. Chances are good that the reader will want to know more about a creature whose "looks can kill." The related sentences might then describe the dangerous-looking characteristics of this mythical creature or beast.

Grammar in Action

Writing interesting topic sentences requires a solid knowledge of the four kinds of sentences: declarative, interrogative, imperative, and exclamatory. (See pages 618–619.) Each kind has its own way of getting a reader's attention. Read the following examples of topic sentences from four magazine articles. Do they make you want to continue reading?

Declarative sentences make statements or express opinions: Last year, for the first time, soft drinks displaced coffee as the nation's favorite drink.—*Discover*

Imperative sentences state commands or make requests: Sit back and think of all of the all-girl groups or bands of today.—*Black Teen*

Interrogative sentences ask questions: Suppose they gave a hockey game and nobody watched? —*Sports Illustrated*

Exclamatory sentences express strong feelings: Boston is booming!—*Newsweek*

Writing Activity You are assigned to write four short articles for your favorite magazine. Select four topics and then write a different kind of topic sentence for the beginning of each article.

Writing Activities Topic Sentences

A Read the following topic sentences. Some are too general; others are not interesting. Decide what is wrong with each one. Then rewrite the sentence to make it an effective topic sentence.

1. I would like to explain why astronomy is fascinating to me.
2. The history of America is filled with heroes.
3. In this paragraph, you will learn about the American pioneers in the nineteenth century.
4. Watching television can be educational.
5. Here is how I earned enough money to buy ice skates.

B In the following paragraphs, the topic sentence has been removed. Read each paragraph and then write a topic sentence. You may want to refer to the techniques for writing interesting topic sentences on pages 97-98.

1. *(Topic Sentence)* The skill of embalming was perfected in Egypt about 3500 years ago. In the small town of Arica, Chile, near the Atacama Desert, diggers unearthed a 7,810-year-old mummy. That ancient mummy, whose age was determined by carbon-14 dating, is only one of the hundreds that have been discovered in the area.

2. *(Topic Sentence)* Abraham Lincoln, for example, learned to live with many nicknames such as the Rail Splitter, Honest Abe, and Old Abe. However, he probably did not like the name Ape, which was a pun on his name and reference to his physical appearance.

3. *(Topic Sentence)* Daisy is a snob, but Oscar is very friendly. On the other hand, Juno will only be friendly when he's hungry. Then he purrs softly and rubs against my legs. I like them all.

4. *(Topic Sentence)* They took him into a room where there were only some boxes and three bananas hanging from the ceiling. They wanted to see how long it would take the chimp to pile up the boxes and climb on them. The chimp did not touch the boxes. He pushed one of the men under the bananas, crawled up on his back, and brought the bananas down.

3
Developing Paragraphs

The topic sentence catches the reader's interest and states the main idea, but the sentences that support it are equally important. If you want to keep the reader's interest, you must choose details that will develop and support your main idea. For instance, you may choose facts, examples, or anecdotes to develop your paragraph fully.

Facts Facts are provable statements. That means they can be looked up in a reliable reference source or observed firsthand. How many facts can you find in the following paragraph?

Professional Model   Promptly every night at the National Archives Building in Washington, D.C., the Charters of Freedom are put to bed. Hermetically sealed in individual helium-filled bronze-and-glass containers, the Declaration of Independence, pages of the Constitution, and the Bill of Rights are lowered by mechanical scissorjacks from their bulletproof display case into a vault twenty-two feet directly below. Built of steel and reinforced concrete, the fifty-five ton vault was thought to be atom-bomb proof when it was installed in the early 1950's.

—Alfred Meyer

Examples Examples give the reader concrete instances of the main idea. In the following paragraph, notice how the general topic statement is made more specific by the example.

Writing Model   Speed has become an obsession with some Americans. Designers and engineers are even experimenting with ways to make the simple bicycle move faster. One designer, Gardner Martin, has made a bicycle that looks like the nose cone of a rocket. Martin's machine has been ridden at a speed of over sixty-five miles an hour. This breakthrough in speed may change bicycle racing forever.

Anecdotes Anecdotes are short narratives or stories that can be entertaining or dramatic, depending on the main idea and purpose of the paragraph. The following paragraph contains an anecdote.

Writing Model

Sometimes children can be cute and endearing, but other times they can be embarrassing. When my family traveled to Florida, we stopped for lunch at a restaurant in South Carolina. My little sister wanted to know about the "white stuff" on her plate. Mom asked the waitress, who replied, "Why, those are grits." My sister's eyes grew big with horror. Pushing the plate away, she shouted, "I'm *not* going to eat guts!"

Definitions In developing a paragraph you may wish to use a word or term that may be unfamiliar to the reader. To make certain that the term is not misunderstood, provide a definition. Include in your definition the term, the general class to which the term belongs, and the characteristic that sets the term apart.

term   general class   characteristic
A **quarterback** is a **football player** who **directs the team.**

As your writing skills grow, you will probably use more than one kind of detail to develop a paragraph. For example, you might use facts and an example or a definition and an anecdote to support the main idea in your topic sentence.

Writing Activities *Developing Paragraphs*

A Read the following topic sentences and the list of details listed below each one. Tell whether each detail is a *fact, example, anecdote,* or *definition.*

1. If you want to know how Southwest Indians really live, visit a pueblo.
   a. A *pueblo* is a type of village built by the Indians of the Southwest.
   b. The eighteen major pueblos are located along the Rio Grande, between Taos and Albuquerque.
   c. The Taos pueblo resembles a group of apartment buildings that are connected to one another.

2. Many people think puppets are only for children, but Gary Jones runs a puppet theater for all ages.
   a. The Blackstreet, U.S.A. Puppet Theatre started fifteen years ago.
   b. Many adults like the life-size puppets, which are five feet tall.
   c. The tap-dancing puppet, Mr. Stomp, once performed at City Hall.
3. The first year I played softball was a disaster for me as well as my team.
   a. I came to my first practice wearing football cleats instead of baseball shoes!
   b. With me on the team, we ended with a season record of one win and fourteen losses.
   c. It was the bottom of the ninth inning, bases loaded, two outs, and I was up to bat.

B Each of the following topic sentences may be developed into a paragraph by adding details. Choose three sentences and make a list of details that might support the main idea. Label each detail *fact, example, anecdote,* or *definition.* If necessary, you may use books and other sources to find details. Write the details in related sentences that support the topic sentence.

1. Have you ever tried to discuss popular music with your grandparents?
2. Try to live one week without watching television.
3. Many people say that Columbus discovered America, but other people came to America before Columbus.
4. Teen-agers should be given more freedom.
5. If you want to operate a computer, you must learn an entirely new language!
6. Some people, like my uncle, are natural storytellers.
7. When you're learning a new sport, it's hard to try and try again.
8. I was baby-sitting my little brother when the storm hit.

4
Achieving Paragraph Unity

Like pieces of a jigsaw puzzle, all the parts of a paragraph must fit together. In other words, the paragraph must be **unified,** with all the sentences relating to the main idea.

Just as you limit the topic of a paragraph, you must also limit the related details. If you try to squeeze in unrelated details, no matter how interesting they are, you only confuse the readers and lose their interest.

The following paragraph comes from a description of life in the Arctic among the Inuits (what the Eskimos call themselves). Here, the author describes the features of a typical sled.

Professional Model   The sled itself was a remarkable piece of equipment. The sled runners were cross-braced with lengths of caribou antler, lashed to the runners with sealskin thongs. The bottoms of the runners were shod with a mixture of pulverized moss and water, built up in layers. On top of the peat shoeing came an ice glaze, carefully smoothed and shaved. The result was a flexible sled that could be sent over the surface of the snow with a flick of the wrist. . . .

From *Arctic Dreams* by Barry Lopez

Notice how all of the sentences following the topic sentence describe how the sled was made and why it was remarkable. Thus, the paragraph is unified because there are no extra details that might distract a reader.

Writing Activities *Achieving Unity*

A Read the following groups of sentences. Each group has several sentences that work together to support a main idea. Find the sentence in each group that strays from the main idea. Then eliminate the sentence as you rewrite the unified paragraph.

1. Hurricanes are born over warm oceans and grow as the winds in the atmosphere push them along. Whirlwinds of air spin counterclockwise around an eye, or low pressure center.

Winds have been measured at 200 miles per hour . .
eye. In the Pacific Ocean, hurricanes are called typhoons. .
hurricane continues to grow in energy until it reaches land
or cold water. Then it loses its force and gradually dies out.

2. Many Native American legends relate the mischievous antics of pranksters. Usually in these legends, the prankster plays
tricks on people or animals that are proud, powerful, or rich.
Coyote, a favorite character, appears in legends told by the
Sioux and the Apache. In European legends, the prankster is
usually a fox.

3. Like fashions, first names have come and gone in popularity
over the years. For most of our country's history, the most
common names for men were John, William, and James. The
name John has many variations in other languages—Johann,
Juan, Giovanni, and Ivan. However, in recent times, the most
common names changed. The top five names for boys became
Michael, David, John, Mark, and Christopher.

B Look at the following topic sentence and the list of possible
details. Write the numbers of the details you would choose to
keep the paragraph unified.

> Venus may be a fascinating planet to visit,
> but you wouldn't want to live there.

1. The 1978 *Pioneer* satellite probes discovered
   winds of up to 200 miles per hour on
   the planet's surface.
2. Temperatures on the surface can reach
   600 degrees Fahrenheit.
3. Venus is the name of a Roman goddess.
4. The planet's atmosphere is made up
   mostly of carbon dioxide.

C Select one of the following topics or use one of your own.
Make a list of details that support the topic and write a unified
paragraph. Remember to state the main idea interestingly in the
topic sentence.

1. Popular songs of 19____   3. Practice makes perfect
2. Why keep a diary?   4. If I had a million dollars

...ving Paragraph Coherence

A paragraph has **coherence** when there is a clear and logical link, or relationship, between the sentences. You learned that all the sentences must relate to the main idea to make the paragraph unified. However, the sentences must also connect logically to one another to make the paragraph coherent.

Read the following paragraph. Notice how the writer uses transitions to carefully connect one event to another.

Professional Model

When you watch the evening news, do you ever think about how stories from all over the country are gathered and then presented on the screen to you? Follow me on a journey through TV news. *First,* a story happens. *Second,* the network dispatches a reporter and a camera crew from that region to cover the story. *At the scene,* they ask questions and film the event. *When they return,* the story is fed by satellite into the network's headquarters in New York. *There,* editors examine the film, deciding what parts to keep and what to throw away. *Once these decisions are made,* producers outline all of the news stories for that day, figuring out in exact minutes and seconds just how much time each story will get on the air. *Finally,* it is time: the announcers are ready. The anchorpersons are seated in front of the cameras. The videotape machines are cued. Lights, cameras, action, "Good evening, America. This is the six o'clock news."

—B. J. Walker

Organizing Your Paragraph

One of the best ways to achieve coherence is to use an appropriate order, or organization, for your paragraph. Often the kind of paragraph you are writing, the purpose of the paragraph, or the kinds of details you include may suggest a logical organization.

For example, in the paragraph about TV news, the writer uses chronological or time order to give the reader a step-by-step picture of how a story gets on the evening news. Four of the most commonly used orders are chronological, spatial, order of importance, and general to specific. Sometimes one paragraph may combine two kinds of orders.

Chronological Order If you are writing about an incident, event, or process, you may organize your sentences in chronological order. Chronological order is time order. That means you tell about the experience in the order that it happened, from the beginning to the end.

Writing Model

Even I became crabby when I tried to catch a glimpse of the speedy ghost crab. First, I selected a place on the beach in view of two or three of the telltale crab holes in the sand. Then, as the sun began to set, I made myself as still as a marble statue, because the slightest movement sends the little crabs skittering into their holes. Soon, the light faded to dusk. I spotted a claw, followed by a round eye on a stalk. I held my breath, but it vanished. Finally, the crab gained enough courage to come three-fourths of the way out of its hole. I had seen a ghost crab! Unfortunately, the sight was quick because I shivered in the cool evening breeze and the crab darted away.

Notice how the writer uses transition words to make the order clear: *first, then, soon,* and *finally.* These words connect the sentences logically and show the order in which things happen.

Spatial Order Organizing a paragraph in spatial order means describing something in relation to its position or direction. Using this order, you can describe an object or scene from bottom to top, inside to outside, right to left, or near to far. Which spatial order did the writer use in the following paragraph?

Writing Model

The new building looked as though a giant child had been playing with translucent building blocks. Three glassy stories perched on top of the building like a rectangular knob. The shiny gray stories below the knob were straight in back with arms that stuck out at acute angles from either side, as if the giant had tried to keep his building from toppling over. Halfway down the structure, extensions of the lower stories jutted out. There, the steel gray glass shrank, each square pane surrounded by beige concrete slabs. Across the bottom floor, the giant child had strung a drooping banner: "Metro South Office Building—Now Renting."

Notice how the writer used transition phrases such as *on the top, halfway down,* and *across the bottom* to link sentences and to move the reader through the paragraph's spatial order.

Order of Importance When you organize a paragraph by order of importance, you can begin with the most important detail and move to the least important, or you can start with the least important and move to the most important. What did the writer do in the following paragraph?

The Hmong people from Southeast Asia have preserved their culture in *pandau*, which means "cloth made beautiful like a flower." Without using patterns or machines, Hmong women have been embroidering and appliquéing figures and designs on cloth for centuries. They turn the finished *pandau* into clothing, home decorations, and wraps for babies. The most important *pandau,* however, are large tapestries that tell the history of the people in tiny stitches and colorful cloth and threads.

In this paragraph, the writer began with the least important details and moved to the most important. Notice how the writer clearly signals the most important detail.

General to Specific Order You can begin a paragraph with a general picture and gradually focus on one specific detail. Imagine you are seeing the subject through a zoom lens. First you take in the general surroundings, or information, and then zoom in on the specific subject, as in the following paragraph.

Professional Model When a hurricane batters a tropical seacoast, all life seems in peril. Savage winds that can uproot trees and reshape entire dune lines often pound grounded pelicans and other seabirds to death. Yet soaring high above, in the very teeth of the storm, one denizen of the seashore is oblivious to it all: the frigate bird.　　　　　　　　　　—Tui De Roy

In this paragraph, the writer gives clues to the order she has used. Notice how she begins with the general words *all life,* zooms in a little closer with *pelicans and other seabirds,* and then focuses sharply with *frigate bird.*

For some paragraphs none of the four most common orders seems to work. Then use another order that is logical. Be sure, however, to use the transitions that make the order clear to the reader.

Writing Activities *Achieving Coherence*

A Select one of the following topics. Write a list of supporting details that you could use to write a paragraph. Look carefully at your list. Decide which order is the most suitable for your paragraph: chronological order, spatial order, order of importance, or general to specific order. Remember to use transition words in your paragraph. After drafting your paragraph, revise it. Finally, share the paragraph with your classmates.

1. Thomas Edison's inventions
2. A beautiful sunset
3. A memorable birthday
4. An endangered animal
5. An exciting sports event
6. How a _____ works

B **Writing in Process** Look through Starting Points (pages 41–53) or Ideas for Writing (pages 655–656). Think of a topic for a paragraph, and then limit the topic to one that would be interesting to your classmates. List the details you might include and then select the ones that are related to your main idea. Decide on an appropriate order for your details, and then write a rough draft of your paragraph. When you revise the paragraph, check its unity and coherence.

Speaking and Listening

When you're playing a song on the radio or stereo, do you ever really listen to the words? Try tuning in to the words of different songs. You'll see that most songs tell a story.

To tell a story, a songwriter organizes his or her ideas in a particular way. That is, each song has a main idea and related sentences that support the main idea. In this way, songs are much like the paragraphs you might write for any story or essay.

In many songs, the main idea is spelled out in a chorus. The chorus usually consists of four or five lines that are repeated throughout the song. This is often the section of the song that you recognize and remember.

The main storyline of a song is developed in the verses. The verses of a song come before and after the chorus, and give details that help support the main idea presented in the chorus.

Like a good paragraph, a good song is unified. That is, all of the verses relate to a chorus, much like supporting sentences relate to a paragraph's topic sentence.

Activity

Choose a song from a record or cassette and copy down the words. Read the words over while you are listening to the music. Do the verses fit with the chorus? What is the song trying to say? Summarize the song by writing its main idea and listing details from the verses that support the main idea.

Application and Review

A Writing Topic Sentences Read the following three writing topics. First, limit each topic so that it can be covered in one paragraph. Then, write a topic sentence that captures the reader's interest and attention by either stating an unusual fact, asking a question, or giving a command.

1. Water sports   2. Pets   3. Museums

B Achieving Unity and Coherence Read the paragraph below. Write a topic sentence for it that both preserves the paragraph's unity and sparks the reader's interest. Identify the sentence that doesn't fit properly.

> (topic sentence). The ones with open mouths that spit out rainwater are called gargoyles. Gargoyles are statues carved out of stone to look like animals or people. Usually the carvers exaggerate the features so that the creatures can be seen easily from the street. The word *gargoyle* is an Old French word meaning *throat*. While gargoyles add interest to a building, they also have an important function. They are attached to gutters, and they throw rainwater away from the stone buildings. In that way, they protect the walls from erosion. A gargoyle is more than just an ugly face!

C Organizing a Paragraph Read the paragraph below, and write which type of order best fits the topic. Rewrite the paragraph by adding appropriate transition words or phrases.

> A pizza has a special design all its own. Roll and shape thin, thick, or chewy crust. Spread a thick tomato sauce filled with spices over the crust. Add whatever toppings the eaters desire: sausage, mushrooms, green peppers, or pepperoni. Sprinkle on a mixture of mozzarella and parmesan cheeses. On to the oven for this work of art!

7
Developing Compositions

"... And now they have grown
So gigantically high
They nudge the new moon
And scrape the blue sky ..."

From "Houses" by Mary Britton Miller

Building a skyscraper involves developing a structure and then organizing the materials so they will form a unified whole. The process requires thoughtful planning and careful execution.

Writing a composition also involves structure and organization. This chapter explains how the paragraphs of a composition work together to express a complete idea.

1
Analyzing the Parts of a Composition

A **composition** is a group of closely related paragraphs that develop a single idea. Like a paragraph, a composition may be narrative, descriptive, explanatory, or persuasive. In the chapters that follow you will learn in more detail how to write specific types of compositions.

The paragraphs in a composition serve specialized functions. Usually, a composition begins with an **introductory paragraph.** It tells the reader what the composition will be about. This opening paragraph introduces the main idea of the composition, just as the topic sentence of a paragraph introduces that paragraph's main idea.

The **body paragraphs** of a composition develop the idea introduced in the first paragraph. For example, if a student wrote a composition about why he or she loves Phoenix, Arizona, the first paragraph might tell about the climate, the second about the scenery, and the third about the life style.

The final paragraph, or **conclusion,** of a composition signals "The End" to the reader. The conclusion might restate the main idea of the composition, summarize the supporting ideas, or present one last thought on the subject.

Read the following example of a well-developed narrative composition.

Student Model

The Perfect Day

Introductory Paragraph
July 27th was no ordinary summer Saturday. After a week of cloudy, rainy weather, the day was absolutely perfect. After considering options such as swimming and baseball, I decided that the day was made for bike riding on the beautiful trails a few miles away. I called my friend Ron and asked him to join me.

Body Paragraphs
Ron said he'd like to go, but explained that he had to deliver some cookies to his uncle first. He suggested that I come with him so we could start

our ride immediately afterwards. We were half-way there when Ron told me that we were on our way to a nursing home. That was the last place I wanted to be on such a glorious day.

Ron steered me up the steps, through a hallway, and into an old-fashioned living room. Ron's uncle was sitting in a wheelchair by the window. A half dozen other people sat around the room that smelled like cough medicine. I could feel my precious day slipping away. As I edged toward the door, I tripped over someone's feet. A quiet old man murmured an apology. I noticed then an unusual set of wooden chess figures on the table beside him. He invited me to look at a piece. He explained that he had carved the complete set by hand but that he had never played with it because he had no visitors and no one at the home played chess.

When I saw that Ron was still talking to his uncle, I offered to play a quick game before setting off for the bike trails. Three hours later I was still playing chess! Mr. Watson was the best player I had ever met. He beat me seven straight times.

Conclusion It was almost supper time when Ron and I finally left. Ron apologized for causing me to miss my afternoon of biking and asked if we could go the next Saturday. I suggested that since we couldn't really depend on the weather to be fine enough for biking, we should plan to visit his uncle again. After all, the weather is always perfect for a game of chess!

This composition, like the other sample compositions you will study in this chapter, is made up of several paragraphs. Notice how they work together to tell the story.

- The introductory paragraph of this composition introduces the main topic of the composition.
- The body paragraphs develop the main topic. The second paragraph discusses Ron's errand and the writer's reaction to it. The third paragraph relates what happened inside the nursing home. The fourth paragraph describes the experience of playing chess.

- The conclusion shows the results of that summer afternoon. It suggests that the writer discovered a new enthusiasm and a new friend.

Writing Activities *Prewriting*

A Write the main idea of the composition entitled "The Perfect Day."

B Writing in Process Turn to *Starting Points: Ideas for Writing* on page 41. Look at the pictures and read through some of the ideas on those pages. Then brainstorm about an experience you have had, a place where you've been, something you would like to explain, or an opinion you would like to persuade someone to adopt. Read over your notes and choose one idea that could be developed into a composition. Then write the main idea of your composition. Save your notes in your writing folder.

Writing Inside Out

People who work for the federal government have their own internal court system. If they get fired, suspended, or demoted at work, federal employees can appeal through the United States Merit Systems Protection Board. Judges like Jennifer Gee in San Francisco hear these cases and decide whether or not the charges filed against an employee are true or not. After hearing a case, Ms. Gee writes out her decision, explaining why and how she made her ruling.

Q   Ms. Gee, how do you write a decision?
A   It varies, because sometimes I can make up my mind very easily. I just sit down and put down the facts that support

2
Planning a Composition

First you must find a subject. Use some of the thinking skills you learned in Chapter 2 (pages 16–40). Select a subject that you know something about and that interests you. The next step is to write down all the ideas you have about your subject. For example, if you chose to write about summer jobs, your notes might look like these.

Lawn care, gardening, painting
Baby-sitting, cleaning
Community service organizations
Jobs that spring from interests or hobbies

the decision I am going to make. Sometimes, it's harder to come to a decision for one way or another. Then, what I will actually do is sit down and start writing. I'll start developing the case. I'll describe what has happened in the case, what the allegations are, what the dispute covers, and then I will start summarizing the facts and the law on both sides of the case. And then I'll pull back and look at it very carefully to see which side really has the stronger case.

Q   What information do you include in a decision?
A   In my decisions, I give a background so the reader will understand why this person was charged and what the basis was for the charge. After I do the background, I summarize exactly what the charges were. Then, after I finish the summary, I go into an analysis of the facts that were presented. Sometimes I just say right off the bat that I find the charge is sustained, which means that it's true. And then I'll discuss why I reached the decision I did, bringing in the evidence that was made available to me and the testimony that I heard.

The next step is to identify your main points. When you read over your list of details, you will find that most of them fit under a few key ideas. Write down those main points.

1. The usual ones
2. Volunteer work
3. Starting up a new business

Once you have your main points, you will see that they relate to one another in some way. This will determine how to organize the ideas in a logical way. The topics in a composition can be arranged in chronological order, spatial order, order of familiarity, or order of importance. When Nathan wrote a composition about jobs, he arranged the main points in order of familiarity, from most familiar to least familiar.

First Main Idea: The usual ones
                        Child care
                        Lawn care and gardening
                        Painting
                        Cleaning

Second Main Idea: Starting up a new business
                        Businesses that use special talents
                            (growing plants, etc.)
                        Businesses that fill a need (pet sitting)
                        Examples of friends who have succeeded
                            (bike repairs, magic shows, garage sales)

Third Main Idea: Volunteer work
                        For a hospital
                        For a church
                        For a service organization
                        For a campaign

Notice that Nathan has expanded the original list of ideas. Nathan will now use this list as a guide for writing a first draft.

Writing Activity *Prewriting*

Writing in Process List details for the subject you chose in Activity B on page 116. Then identify and write down your main points. Organize them in a logical order, and add additional details if you need them. Save your notes for the next activity.

3
Writing the Introduction

You have chosen your topic, listed details, grouped your points, and arranged the groups in a logical order. Now you are ready to write your introduction. (Keep in mind that some writers like to write their introductions last, after they have developed all their ideas.) The introduction tells what the composition is going to be about. However, the introduction must do more than that. It also must catch the reader's attention so that he or she will want to finish reading what you have written.

When you write your introduction, you should keep your audience in mind. Who will read your composition? Write your introduction so that it will be interesting to your particular audience.

The following introduction is for Nathan's composition entitled "Summer Jobs in Your Neighborhood." Although it tells the reader what the composition is going to be about, it probably would not be very interesting to your audience or to any other writer's audience.

> I am going to write about summer jobs. I think you will be interested in these ideas.

Following are some ways you could make this introduction more interesting.

Show a Benefit Gained from Reading the Composition	One way to fill the long, lazy hours of summer is with a neighborhood job. With a little creative thinking, you can find a job that will help to make your summer super—and maybe increase the size of your bank account at the same time.
Repeat an Interesting Quotation	Mark Twain once said, "Work and play are words used to describe the same thing under different conditions." With a little creativity, you might be able to find a summer job that is interesting and so much fun that it won't seem like work.

Ask a Question	What did you do last summer? If you cannot remember, it must not have been very great. This year you should find a neighborhood job that will make this summer memorable and maybe even profitable.
State an Interesting Fact	Last summer eight students in our class earned enough money to buy new ten-speed bicycles. You could join this group if you got one of the many neighborhood jobs available this summer.

All of these introductions tell what the composition will be about. They also catch the reader's attention and make the reader want to read more about the topic.

Writing Activities *Writing the Introduction*

A Rewrite the following introductions by adding more information or by making them more interesting.

1. The first time I worked on a computer, I didn't like it. I was still a bit nervous the second time too. By the third time, though, I realized that computers might be useful after all.

2. There's something about Halloween night that always frightens me, even though I'm too old to believe in that stuff. I think it's the darkness and the shadows. Even the sound of a neighbor's cat sounds different, somehow.

3. I think every citizen ought to vote. If I could, I would make it a law that every citizen had to cast a ballot in every election.

4. There are many different kinds of pollution. Among them are noise pollution, water pollution, and air pollution. Pollution is a problem that requires our immediate attention and a problem that we should all try to solve.

B **Writing in Process** Look over your prewriting notes from Activity B on page 118. Think about your audience. Who will read your composition? Then write a good introduction for your composition, one that will appeal to your audience. Save your introduction in your writing folder.

4
Writing the Body

The body is the most important part of a composition. It is in these paragraphs that the main idea presented in the introduction is supported or explained with descriptive details, events, facts and figures, examples, incidents, or definitions.

The body of your composition must also have coherence. To develop coherence, use transitions to connect the main idea in one paragraph with the main idea in the next paragraph. Following are examples of some transitions you can use.

Transitions

Transitions to Show Time	always, before, finally, first, immediately, last, later, meanwhile, now, sometimes, soon, then
Transitions to Show Place	above, around, beneath, down, here, there, inside, outside, over, under, near, within
Transitions to Show Order of Importance	at first, first, second, last, former, latter, primarily, secondarily
Transitions to Show Cause and Effect	as a result, because, therefore, so, for that reason

Following is the body of Nathan's composition on summer jobs. The three paragraphs follow his organizational plan.

Student Model

The first kind of summer job that comes to mind is the familiar kind—such as baby-sitting, mowing lawns, and other odd jobs. These jobs should not be overlooked just because they are so ordinary. The reason they are plentiful is that so many people need these services. No matter how many of your friends are doing these chores, dozens of your neighbors will still be eager to hire someone to wash windows, prune plants, or paint porches. Just

knock on a few doors, and you'll soon have several customers.

The second kind of job is a little different. Try starting a business of your own. Many teen-agers have been quite successful with this approach. Consider your skills and interests and try to make them profitable. For example, two twelve-year-olds I know do bike repairs. Another girl does magic shows at children's parties. Three eighth-graders raise and sell plants. Another way to get an idea for starting a business is to consider what the people in your neighborhood need. If many have pets, for example, you might start a pet-sitting service for people on vacation. You might even organize a day camp for neighborhood children.

The last kind of summer job may be more satisfying than any of the others. This is volunteer work. Such work really helps other people and also gives you a worthwhile experience. One good place to do volunteer work is at a hospital, where many aides are needed. Another place to volunteer is at a church or temple, which usually has service projects. A third possibility is to work for a community service organization, such as an ecology group. Finally, you might like to campaign for a cause you believe in. The rewards that come from helping in any of these volunteer jobs can far outnumber the dollars you might earn at a paying job.

The first sentence in each paragraph of the body expresses the main idea of that paragraph. Each one tells what kind of job will be explained in that paragraph. Since this composition is told in order of most familiar to least familiar, the transitions *first*, *second*, and *last* were used to connect the three body paragraphs.

Grammar in Action

Transitions are verbal links in a chain. A writer uses them to move from one related idea to another related idea. Time and place transitions are words called **adverbs** or **prepositional phrases** used as adverbs. (See pages 509 and 536.)

> The detective hid behind the heavy gold-colored drapes in the living room. **Within ten minutes,** he saw the doorknob slowly begin to turn. **Then** the door opened, and a woman in a black cape quietly slid into the room, dragging something behind her.

Writing Activity Finish this story or write a brief mystery of your own. Be sure to use transitions to connect your ideas.

Writing Activities *Writing the Body*

A Write the main idea in each paragraph of the body of the following composition, "Harness Training My Cat Muffin." Then write the transitions that were used to develop coherence.

> The first time I tried to take Muffin for a walk, we never even got out the door. I couldn't get Muffin to wear a harness and leash. When I first put the harness on her, she immediately became paralyzed, or at least it seemed that way. I couldn't get her to stand because her legs turned to mush. It was a silly sight. Every time I held her up, her legs would collapse under her. After twenty minutes of trying, I finally gave up and took the harness off her. Without hesitating for a minute, Muffin jumped up and ran to her food bowl. Her "paralysis" was miraculously cured.
>
> About two weeks later, the momentous day came when I took Muffin outside for the first time. Eventually, after about fifty more tries with the harness, Muffin had given in. She had finally shown me that she could walk with a harness on—if she wanted to. At first Muffin seemed scared of the open space

outside. After all, the backyard is much bigger than any room in our house. However, within just a few minutes any fearfulness on Muffin's part was soon forgotten and replaced with the excitement of the new, delicious smells on the ground. That day Muffin's nose touched every square inch of soil within a fifteen-foot radius of the door.

Now Muffin and I go outside every afternoon. She eagerly stands and waits while I put on her harness, and she's always the first one out the door. We enjoy our walks together, but I have learned that there's a big difference between walking a cat and walking a dog. When I walk my friend's dog, I can go where I want to go, but when I walk Muffin, I have to go where she wants to go!

B Writing in Process Write the body of the composition you started in Activity B on page 120. Include at least three paragraphs. Be sure that each paragraph has a main idea and that you use transitions to connect the paragraphs.

5
Writing the Conclusion

After you have written the body paragraphs of your composition, you are almost finished with the first draft. One step remains—writing the conclusion.

The conclusion presents the last idea the reader will take away from your composition. Therefore, it should be as clear and interesting as the introductory paragraph. The final paragraph should also tie everything together. You can do this in one of three ways.

1. Describe a result.
2. Write a short, interesting statement that signals "The End" to the reader.
3. Summarize the ideas in the composition. The concluding paragraph of Nathan's composition on summer jobs is a good example of a summary paragraph.

> Whatever kind of summer job you choose, you will be sure to benefit from it if you do it well. A job well done not only pleases the people you work for, but it also introduces you to the pride of accomplishment. That's a very special way to make sure that your summer doesn't just slip away.

Once you have written your conclusion, revise and proofread your entire composition. Turn back to the revision and proofreading checklists in Chapter 5 (pages 83–84). You can also use the following short checklists to help you.

Checklist: Revising Compositions
_____ precise language
_____ coherent order
_____ use of transitions
_____ unity of ideas
_____ informative or interesting introduction
_____ effective conclusion

In summary, you have now seen that a composition begins with an introduction that is followed by body paragraphs and ends with a conclusion. Each paragraph, including the introduction and conclusion, is built around a main idea. Each sentence in a paragraph supplies supporting details about the main idea, just as each paragraph in the body relates to the main idea in the introduction.

Your composition will have unity when all the ideas in the body paragraphs support the main idea in the introduction and when all the related paragraphs are connected with transitions.

Writing Activities *Writing the Conclusion*

A Read the following conclusions. Decide which ones would make good conclusions. Tell why the others are weak.

1. We stood at the edge of the marsh long after the last of the geese had disappeared from view. Now the water was still, and the sky showed nothing more than an ordinary fall sunset. Yet we knew that the picture that would remain in our minds would be that of a cyclone of Canadian geese whirling across the marsh, trumpeting their eerie cries to the wind, clouds, and water.

2. My coach told me to keep on practicing. She said that was the only way to get better. I'll take her advice.

3. Some of Ted's friends are still kidding him about trying to change the world. After all, they say, being a Big Brother to Jimmy is not going to have too much of an impact on anything. Somehow, though, Ted doesn't believe them. I don't think Jimmy does, either.

Marco Polo embarking from Venice, painted circa 1340.

4. Painting miniatures can be a fascinating and extremely satisfying hobby. Once you have mastered the basic techniques, there will be no limit to what you and your paintbrush can do.

5. These were my reasons for feeling that movie producers should come out with more family films. Perhaps not everyone agrees with me, but I think they should. Everyone would benefit, so why not?

B **Writing in Process** Write the conclusion of the composition you started in Activity B on page 120. Then revise and proofread your entire composition. Use the checklists on pages 83–84 to help you. For example, when revising you might have to rearrange some ideas or eliminate some sentences to create unity. You also might need to add words and phrases to develop coherence in your composition. When proofreading, check for errors in grammar, usage, capitalization, punctuation, and spelling. When you have finished, write the final copy of your composition.

English and Reading

When you read any of your textbooks, you are trying to understand the message of the author. You should keep one goal in mind: *To understand what I am reading, I must reconstruct the author's message.* You can use thinking strategies to help you reconstruct what the author is saying.

One such strategy is called **surveying**. In this chapter you learned that a well-developed composition has an introduction, a series of body paragraphs, and a conclusion. You also learned how to identify and organize main ideas when you write a composition. When you survey a text, you look for these composition elements and use them to reconstruct the author's message.

First you look at the titles and subtitles, the pictures, graphs, and charts. Then you skim the text before you actually begin to read. Try to figure out how the text is organized, what questions the author is trying to answer, and what you already know about the subject.

Activity

Select a chapter from this book that you have not studied yet. Survey the chapter, using the strategy outlined above, and write your answers to the following questions.

1. What is the chapter about?
2. What main ideas are covered?
3. How is the chapter organized?
4. How are pictures and charts used?
5. What do you already know about the subject?

Application and Review

A **Organizing Details** Arrange these ideas in logical order.

1. First, we blended wet ingredients, eggs and buttermilk.
2. They baked in the oven for fifteen minutes.
3. We read over the recipe for bran muffins.
4. We poured the batter into the greased muffin tins.
5. Our afternoon snack was quite a treat!
6. We added in the bran flakes, flour, and other dry things.
7. We set out the necessary ingredients on the counter.

B **Writing a Strong Introduction** Rewrite the following introduction. Use an interesting question, fact, quotation, or anecdote in your new introduction.

> If you keep your eyes and ears open, you can find some interesting people in your own neighborhood. Mr. Madison, our mail carrier, is a good example. For as long as I can remember, he has been delivering mail to our house. Through the summer heat and winter snow, he always appears.

C **Using Transitions** In each section below, the first sentence concludes one paragraph and the second sentence begins the next one. Add a transition word or phrase that best joins the two paragraphs.

1. Sam continued opening his birthday presents with his friends, and found a new baseball mitt from Steven.
   _____, in the kitchen, his father was lighting the last of the candles on Sam's cake.
2. As we stopped on the bridge, we looked around before travelling onward.
   _____, we could see tiny fish and water insects floating by.
3. I walked on to the next house and rang the doorbell, no longer expecting anyone to sponsor me for the walk-a-thon.
   _____, before I could even rehearse my opening line, an older woman came to the door and showed me inside.

8
Revising Sentences

What is craftsmanship? Look at an intricate woven rug, or a hand-turned piece of pottery, or a beautifully finished piece of sculpture. What you admire is not just the design, but also the care the craftsperson devoted to making it.

Crafting sentences involves more than just putting words together. You must work and rework your sentences, smoothing the rough edges and eliminating unnecessary words and phrases. In this chapter you will learn how to become a craftsperson when you create sentences.

1
Combining Sentences and Sentence Parts

A sentence is a group of words that states a single main idea. Suppose you want to add one or more smaller, related ideas to your main idea. You may begin by expressing the related ideas in separate sentences. The result may be writing that is choppy and dull. Worse, your reader may not understand how the separate ideas are related to one another. When you revise, look for ways of combining related sentences and sentence parts.

Combining Sentences

Two sentences may contain ideas that are equally important. The sentences may express similar ideas, contrasting ideas, or a choice between two ideas. Often these sentences can be combined into one sentence.

If the ideas are similar, use a comma and the word *and*.

> Alaskan brown bears are the largest species of bears.
> Malayan bears are the smallest species of bears.

> Alaskan brown bears are the largest species of bears, **and** Malayan bears are the smallest.

If the ideas contrast, use a comma and the word *but*.

> Alaskan brown bears can grow up to nine feet long.
> Malayan bears grow only to about three feet long.

> Alaskan brown bears can grow up to nine feet long, **but** Malayan bears grow only to about three feet long.

If there is a choice between two ideas, use a comma and *or*.

> We could see bears in the zoo.
> Instead, we could go to see bears in the national park.

> We could see bears in the zoo, **or** we could go to see bears in the national park.

Combining Sentence Parts

The ideas in two sentences may be so closely related that words are repeated in the sentences. Often you can combine the sentences by keeping the important parts and leaving out the repeated words.

For similar ideas, use *and* (repeated words or ideas are shown in italics):

> Bears eat meat. *They also eat* berries.
> Bears eat meat **and** berries.

For contrasting ideas, use *but*.

> Bears are usually peaceful. *Bears* get angry quickly.
> Bears are usually peaceful **but** get angry quickly.

For a choice between ideas, use *or*.

> Sloth bears sleep under shrubs. They also sleep in shallow caves.
> Sloth bears sleep under shrubs **or** in shallow caves.

Writing Activities *Combining Ideas*

A Rewrite each pair of sentences as one sentence. Use the word given in parentheses. Eliminate the words in italics.

1. A brown bear might weigh over 1,500 pounds. *A brown bear* can move quickly when it is angry. **(but)**
2. Bears have small eyes. *They* cannot see well. **(and)**
3. Bears will rip apart beehives to get honey. *Bears will rip apart* the nests of wild bees *to get honey*. **(or)**
4. Bears are intelligent. *Bears* can learn tricks. **(and)**

B Combine each pair of sentences. Decide on your own what combining word to use and what words, if any, to leave out.

1. Bears usually live alone. They never gather in packs.
2. One blow from the front foot of an adult grizzly bear can kill a person. One blow from the front foot of an adult polar bear can kill a person, too.
3. A female bear may have one to four cubs at a time. A female bear usually has two cubs at a time.
4. Bears try to avoid a fight. They run from danger.

2
Adding Words to Sentences

You may sometimes write two sentences whose ideas are not equally important. When you revise, you find that the second sentence has only one important word to contribute to the main idea. Add that one word to the first sentence, and get rid of the rest. The result will be a tighter, clearer sentence.

> We saw a kind of bicycle on a small side street. *It was strange.*
> We saw a **strange** kind of bicycle on a small side street.

> A man was pedaling it. *He was pedaling* furiously.
> A man was pedaling it **furiously**.

> *He was in a* reclining *position*. His position was amazing.
> His **reclining** position was amazing.

You can combine more than two sentences when one sentence carries the main idea and each of the others adds only one important detail. Sometimes when you add more than one word, you will have to add a comma or the word *and*.

> *The bike was* unusual. The bike had one front wheel and two rear ones. *The front wheel was* small.
> The **unusual** bike had one **small** front wheel and two rear ones.

> Handlebars were under the seat. *The handlebars were* short. *The seat was* low.
> **Short** handlebars were under the **low** seat.

> Finally, the cyclist pulled up to the curb. *He pulled up* slowly and carefully.
> Finally, the cyclist pulled up to the curb **slowly and carefully.**

Sometimes an important word must be changed before you can add it to another sentence. The most common change is the addition of an ending such as *-y, -ed, -ing,* or *-ly*. Often, words ending in *-ly* can appear in various positions in sentences.

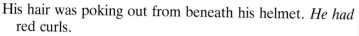

His hair was poking out from beneath his helmet. *He had red curls.*

His **red curly** hair was poking out from beneath his helmet.

He stepped back from his bike to look at it. *The bike had three wheels. He looked* proud.

He stepped back to look **proudly** at his **three-wheeled** bike.

The bike had been painted yellow. *The color* gleamed.

The bike had been painted a **gleaming** yellow.

He locked his bike with a heavy chain. *He was* cautious.

He **cautiously** locked his bike with a heavy chain.

Writing Activities *Adding Words*

A Combine each group of sentences. Eliminate the words in italics, and follow any other direction that is given in parentheses.

1. The spokes sparkled in the sun. *The spokes* shone. (Use **-ing**.)
2. The seat looked strange. *It was* large. *It was made of* cloth.
3. "It's the most comfortable bike in the world," the cyclist said, grinning. *His grin was* broad. (Use **-ly**.)
4. We were standing on a busy corner. *The* wind *was blowing around the corner.* (Use a comma and **-y**.)
5. "I can ride this bike in any kind of wind. *The ride is* safe. *It is also* smooth." (Use **-ly** and the word **and**.)
6. A police officer helped us. *She had a* uniform *on*. (Use **-ed**.)

B Combine the following sentences by eliminating unimportant words. Decide whether you need to change any words.

1. The officer looked at him. She looked impatient.
2. "Do you understand the traffic rules? Are they clear to you?"
3. The officer wrote out a ticket. The ticket was for speeding.
4. The cyclist looked up. The expression on his face was proud. It was also unhappy.
5. "I can't help showing off this bike. It's terrific!"

C Rewrite the passage on the next page, eliminating the words in italics. Sentences that can be combined are enclosed in parentheses. Look for single words that can be used in other sentences. Use connecting words, or add an ending: *-y*, *-ed*, *-ing*, or *-ly*.

(Rowboats are human-powered machines. Tread-mills *are also human-powered machines*.) (Both kinds have been important in history. The most wide-spread human-powered machine is the bicycle, *how-ever*.) (The history of the bicycle is fun to read. *The history* fascinates *the reader*.)

(One drawing by Leonardo da Vinci shows a bi-cycle. *The drawing shows many* details *of the bicy-cle*.) (This early design was clever. The first modern bicycle was actually built 400 years later.)

(The Draisienne was invented by Karl von Drais. *The invention was a* success.) (It looked like the popular hobbyhorses of the day. *It* could be steered, *however*.)

D Using combining techniques, revise the following passage.

Kirkpatrick Macmillan added pedal drive in 1839. James Starley invented the wire-spoked wheel around 1870. A bicycle called the *high-wheeler* was de-veloped. It was light and fast.

A bicycle craze started in the 1870's. Clubs with riders would crowd the roads on Sundays. The riders wore uniforms. The roads were covered with dust. A bugler would give signals. He would keep the group together. Few women rode in those days. Clothing made cycling hard. Customs made cycling hard, too. The clothing was restrictive. The customs were restrictive, too.

By the 1890's, a new kind of bicycle had been developed. It had two wheels. The wheels were of equal size. It had pedals. It was chain driven. This new design caused a revolution in women's clothing. It also caused a revolution in their behavior. Now women were sud-denly mobile. They became more inde-pendent.

3
Adding Groups of Words

Sometimes when making revisions you may wish to add a group of words from one sentence to another. There are several ways to combine such sentences.

Adding Without Changing Word Forms

You may be able to add a group of words to another sentence without changing the form of any of the words. Place these words close to the person, thing, or action they describe.

> The Egyptians buried their kings' bodies beneath pyramids. *They buried them* in secret chambers that were filled with treasures.
> The Egyptians buried their kings' bodies beneath pyramids **in secret chambers that were filled with treasures**.

Adding Groups of Words with Commas

You can add a group of words that merely renames, or defines, one or more words in another sentence. Set off these added words with a single comma or a set of commas.

> The tombs and temples of many ancient peoples were pyramids. *Pyramids are* large structures with triangular sides.
> The tombs and temples of many ancient peoples were pyramids, **large structures with triangular sides**.

Adding Groups of Words with -ing or -ed

You may be able to add a group of words by adding *-ing* or *-ed* to a word in the group. Sometimes, there is already a word in the group that ends in *-ing* or *-ed*.

> The sides of a pyramid reminded the Egyptians of the slanting rays of the sun. *The pyramid's sides* slope.
> The **sloping** sides of a pyramid reminded the Egyptians of the slanting rays of the sun.

Indians of Central America built pyramids. *Their pyramids had* flat tops.

Indians of Central America built **flat-topped** pyramids.

In Egypt thirty-five pyramids remain. *They are* standing near the Nile River.

In Egypt thirty-five pyramids remain **standing near the Nile River.**

Writing Activities *Adding Word Groups*

A Combine each pair of sentences. Eliminate the words in italics. Use any other clues provided in parentheses.

1. King Tutankhamon ruled Egypt from 1347 to 1339 B.C. *King Tutankhamon is* often called King Tut. (Use commas.)
2. King Tut's tomb had four rooms. *They were* filled with treasures.
3. In the tomb were three coffins. *The coffins* rested one inside the other. (Use **-ing**.)
4. Tutankhamon's mummy lay in the innermost coffin. *This coffin was* made of solid gold.

B Combine each pair of sentences, using what you have learned.

1. Carter discovered King Tut's tomb in Luxor. Luxor is in the Valley of the Kings.
2. A hidden entry led to a sealed door with a special mark. The mark identified the tomb as a royal burial place.
3. By candlelight Carter saw strangely shaped animal figures and statues. They glinted of gold.
4. The press reported Carter's every move from tents. The press had pitched their tents hastily.
5. The treasures that Carter discovered were placed in the National Museum. That museum is in Cairo, Egypt.

4
Combining with who, that, *or* which

Sometimes you may find that you have repeated ideas unnecessarily. You may have introduced an idea in one sentence, then gone on to give further information about that person, place, or thing in the next sentence. You can avoid needless repetition by combining such sentences when you revise.

Adding Groups of Words with who

You can use the word *who* to introduce a word group giving information about a person.

> Certain women were once thought to be odd. These women liked science.
> Women **who** liked science were once thought to be odd.

> Grace Hopper never thought that she was odd. She invented a computer language.
> Grace Hopper, **who** invented a computer language, never thought that she was odd.

In the first example, the added words help to identify a particular group of women. The added words are essential to the meaning of the sentence. Therefore, no comma is used before *who*. In the second example, Grace Hopper is identified as a particular person, and the added words merely provide additional information about her. You could delete the added words without changing the meaning of the sentence. Therefore, the added words are set off with commas.

Adding Groups of Words with that *or* which

You can use the word *that* or *which* to introduce a word group giving details about a thing or a place.

> Here is an invention that helps many people.
> Many students use computers, which are in classrooms.

In the first example, the words following *that* give an important detail about what kind of invention is meant. They cannot be omitted. The words probably appeared in the first draft. The writer is not likely to have placed the words in a sentence by themselves.

In the second example, the words following *which* merely give additional information about some particular computers. Therefore, the word *which* is used to introduce the words, and a comma is used to set them off. The writer possibly wrote them as a second sentence in the first draft: *Computers are in classrooms.* In combining sentences, use *which* preceded by a comma if the information from the second sentence is merely an extra detail.

Writing Activities who, that, *or* which

A Combine each pair of sentences. Eliminate the italicized words, and follow the clues given in parentheses.

1. Ada Lovelace was another important woman. *She* was a pioneer in computers. (Use **who**.)
2. Weaving looms gave her the idea for computer programming. *The looms* used punch cards. (Use commas and **which**.)
3. Charles Babbage invented the automatic computer. *Babbage* was a mathematical genius of the 1800's. (Use commas and **who**.)
4. His computer used Lovelace's punched cards. *It* was not electronic. (Use commas and **which**.)
5. A new computer language was introduced around 1980. *The language* bears Ada's name. (Use **that**.)

B Combine each pair of sentences. Decide whether to use *who, that,* or *which* and whether to use commas.

1. BASIC is a simple computer language. Many people learn that language first.
2. COBOL is a complex business-oriented language. Grace Hopper developed it.
3. Charles Babbage never got to build the "analytical engine." He designed the engine.
4. Ada Lovelace was Babbage's colleague. She thought of using punched data cards.

C Revise the following passage. Groups of sentences that can be combined are enclosed in parentheses. Use what you know about sentence combining to eliminate the words in italics. Use *who, that, which,* or *-ing,* with or without commas.

(Some dieters use technology to lose weight. *These dieters* are computer buffs.) (Several dieting and nutrition programs are available. *They can be bought* in stores. *These programs* give the calories and nutritional content of many foods.) (Other computer programs include exercise guides. *These programs* pop up on many screens.) (A tiny figure guides viewers through the exercises. *The figure* dances on the screen.) (You can enter your progress on the computer. *The computer* will track it for you.) (Another technology used by dieters is the VCR. *These dieters* need help.) (Videocassettes guide dieters through aerobics. *Aerobics is* a special kind of exercise.)

D Revise the following passage, using what you know about combining sentences. Some sentences can remain the same.

Many people are concerned about their weight. These people weigh too much. Many prejudices still exist. These prejudices are in favor of thin people. These prejudices keep people from appreciating one another. The prejudices are promoted in magazine articles and on television programs.

Television schedules exercise programs. These programs are designed to help people lose weight. Jane Fonda has made exercise videotapes. She is enthusiastic. She is a movie star. Her exercises are quite difficult. At least they are difficult at first. You could start out by trying to do all of her exercises. Doing them gradually is a better idea, though. Some computer programs and videotapes tell people how to lose weight. These resources are part of the information revolution. This revolution has changed our lives. The changes in our lives have taken place in the last ten years or so. Information alone will not make you thinner. Eating less and exercising more will make you thinner.

5
Correcting Empty Sentences

Some groups of words have the form of a sentence but say very little. These sentences simply repeat an earlier idea. Other sentences make a statement that is not supported by a fact, reason, or example. Such sentences are **empty sentences**. Watch for empty sentences and revise them in your writing.

Sentences That Repeat an Idea

When you revise your work, eliminate repeated ideas by condensing or combining sentences. Look at these examples:

Faulty   The horse frisked, tossed her head, and ran to greet me. She seemed glad to see me.
(Omit the second sentence. It merely repeats the idea.)
Revised The horse frisked, tossed her head, and ran to greet me.

Faulty   I was once afraid of this magnificent horse. My fear of this horse was such that I couldn't even look at her.
(*Afraid* and *fear* are similar. *This horse* is repeated. The two sentences can be combined.)
Revised I was once so afraid of this magnificent horse that I couldn't even look at her.

Writing Activity *Repeated Ideas*

Revise the following sentences. Leave out repeated ideas or combine them in new sentences. There is no one "correct" way to revise the sentences.

1. At first, the rest of the crew laughed at my fears. They laughed because the idea of anyone being afraid of a horse was funny to them.
2. Then Richards, the boss, let me in on a secret. He told me something that he had never told anyone. The secret was that he had been afraid of horses, too.

3. I was curious to know what he had done about his problem. I asked him what he had done to get rid of his fear.
4. He said that a horse like Maya could sense a person's fear. Maya could tell if a person was afraid.

Unsupported Statements

Empty sentences can result if statements are not supported by reasons, facts, or examples. What unsupported statement can you find in this paragraph?

> There are over 250 breeds of horses. Some are lightweight ponies, some are middleweights, and some are huge heavyweights. The heavyweights are the most fascinating.

There is certainly a lot to know about horses, but you might not share the writer's admiration of the heavyweights. The writer never really justifies his opinion.

As you revise your work, look for unsupported statements that can be strengthened by adding reasons, facts, or examples. Adding the following detail, for instance, might help justify the writer's opinion:

> The heaviest weight on record is held by a horse that weighed 3,200 pounds. That's heavier than some cars!

Writing Activity *Unsupported Statements*

Revise the following statements by adding necessary reasons, facts, or examples. You may have to do research.

1. The Shetland pony is small and a great favorite of children. It deserves to be as popular as it is.
2. The original Shetland ponies came from the Shetland Islands of Great Britain. People used them to pull cars in the mines. They were cheap to keep.
3. Shetlands were imported to the United States as children's pets. Children preferred them to other horses.
4. Shetlands are no longer used for work or transportation. People can still admire them for recreation and entertainment.

6
Correcting Stringy Sentences

Can you take combining too far? Yes, if the result is a stringy sentence. A **stringy sentence** is one in which the word *and* links a series of main ideas. The reader has no clue about how the ideas are related. Look for stringy sentences when you revise. For clearer, more powerful writing, break up the complete thoughts into separate sentences. Use transition words or other combining techniques to show relationships between the ideas.

Stringy The house stood on a hill overlooking the ocean, and it was outlined against the sky, and the sky was growing dark.

Revised The house stood on a hill overlooking the ocean. It was outlined against a darkening sky.

Stringy I looked up and saw a dim light in an upper window, and I thought that the light was strange, and then I remembered that the house was supposed to be abandoned, and my heart stopped.

Revised I looked up and saw a dim light in an upper window. I thought that the light was strange. Then I remembered that the house was supposed to be abandoned, and my heart stopped.

Stringy I approached the door, and my heart was in my mouth, and I started to knock, and then the door opened.

Revised My heart was in my mouth as I approached the door. When I started to knock, the door opened.

Writing Activities **Stringy Sentences**

A Revise the sentences that follow on the next two pages. Remember these points:

- Separate each sentence into two or more shorter sentences.
- Reduce the number of *and*'s.
- Try to show a logical connection between ideas. Use words like *as, when, then, but, with,* and *because.*
- Use sentence combining techniques when you can.

1. There was no one behind the door, and so I began to feel brave, and so I went on into the old house.
2. Dust lay thick on the floor, and the floor creaked, and I left tracks in the dust.
3. It was very gloomy, and the outline of the stairs was barely visible, and so I crept forward, and I didn't know what to expect.
4. In a dimly lighted room I saw nothing but a coffin, and there was no other furniture in the room, and so I went in.
5. I approached the coffin and it began to move toward me and I was so scared that I froze to the spot.
6. I began to back away, and for every step I took, the coffin moved a few inches toward me.
7. The house was too dark to run in, and so I began to walk as fast as I dared, and the coffin followed me out of the room.
8. I was not very familiar with the house, and I took a wrong turn, and soon I came to a stairway going up, and it led to the attic.
9. Still the coffin came on, and it moved when I did, and it stopped when I did, and with each move it came a little closer.
10. The attic stairs were covered with dust, and I was afraid I would slip and fall against the coffin, and I felt my way along as best I could.

11. At the top of the attic stairs was a tiny room, and there was hardly any room to turn around, and I could hear the coffin.
12. I heard a loud creak, and I turned to face the coffin, and I could see that the lid was lifting up, and there was an eerie light inside it.
13. Just then I reached into my pocket and discovered an old cough drop, and I desperately threw the cough drop into the coffin, and that was just what I needed to stop the coffin.

B Revise the following passage. Combine or condense any empty sentences. Eliminate unsupported statements or give facts or reasons for them. Separate stringy sentences and try to show a logical connection between ideas.

High on a ridge she stood, outlined by the silver light of the moon. The moon shone its silver light on her. No one had ever caught this wild horse. This wild horse was a mare and wild horses are the most beautiful horses.

This horse was huge; no one in the countryside knew of any larger. No one had ever seen her by day. She showed up only at night. Usually at the time of the full moon, people would hear a loud neigh followed by sound like a clap of thunder. They would rush out of their houses, and they would run to any open space, and then they would look around for the horse.

This female mare would be seen rearing up on her hind legs in back, pawing at the air. It often seemed that she was pawing at the moon, and many legends grew up around this.

One girl, for example, has said that the mare was really a princess looking for her prince. In the girl's imagination, she pretended that the prince was a golden palomino that appeared only in daytime. The two horses could meet only when the moon was low in the sky before the sun went down. Then the horses would gallop from one end of the sky to the other, and they would make a lot of noise, and she was the rain, and he was the lightning.

7
Correcting Padded Sentences

Padding is sometimes useful. It protects football and hockey players from injuries, keeps things from breaking in the mail, and makes some clothing fit better in the shoulders. In sentences, however, padding serves no purpose.

A **padded sentence** is one containing unnecessary words or phrases. A padded sentence may be grammatically correct, but its wordiness keeps the reader from following the ideas. There are two common types of sentence padding. One type consists of extra words that merely repeat an idea. The other type consists of whole groups of words that could be reduced to shorter phrases without affecting the ideas behind them. When you revise your work, take out the padding or cut it down to size.

Taking Out Extra Words

Here are some examples of wordiness that can get in the way of your ideas. Following each example is a more direct method of saying the same thing.

"Fact" Expressions	Reduced
because of the fact that	because, since
on account of the fact that	because, since
in spite of the fact that	although
call your attention to the fact that	remind you

"What" Expressions	Reduced
what I want is	I want
what I mean is	(Just say it!)
what I want to say is	(Just say it!)

Other Expressions to Avoid

the point is	the thing is	it happens that
the reason is	being that	

Sentences are clearer and less wordy when you avoid the kinds of padding shown in the examples on the next page.

Padded *It just so happens that* Oliver hasn't spoken to Lydia for a week.

Revised Oliver hasn't spoken to Lydia for a week.

Padded Terry was confused by *the fact that* the cat refused to come out from under the porch.

Revised Terry was confused by the cat's refusal to come out from under the porch.

Padded *The thing that happened was that* Edison kept trying until he succeeded.

Revised Edison kept trying until he succeeded.

Reducing Groups of Words to Phrases

Often groups of words beginning with *who is, that is,* or *which is* can be simplified. Study the following examples.

Lengthy Algebra, which is often taught in junior high, is like a whole new language.

Revised Algebra, often taught in junior high, is like a whole new language.

Lengthy The cave that was in France has prehistoric wall paintings.

Revised The cave in France has prehistoric wall paintings.

Lengthy The lead actors, who were in *Romeo and Juliet*, have taken difficult roles before.

Revised The lead actors in *Romeo and Juliet* have taken difficult roles before.

Writing Activities *Padded Sentences*

A Revise each sentence. Get rid of extra words that do not contribute to the meaning. Look for *who, that,* and *which* word groups that can be simplified.

1. What I want to say is that I think the play I saw at the Theater for the Deaf was similar to the story of Helen Keller's life.
2. Helen Keller had difficulties on account of the fact that she could neither see nor hear.

3. Being that Annie Sullivan, who was Keller's teacher, was so persistent, Keller eventually learned to communicate.
4. The reason that I admire Sullivan is that she combined love and determination.
5. The fact of the matter is that many people who have no handicaps do not communicate well.
6. What I mean is that few plays or films about handicapped people are as inspiring as the one about Helen Keller, which is called the *Miracle Worker*.

B Revise each of the following passages. You should see opportunities to use the following techniques:

- combine sentences and parts of sentences
- add words and groups of words to sentences
- use *who* and *which* to combine sentences
- combine or condense "empty" sentences
- separate stringy sentences
- take the stuffing out of padded sentences

1. Putting in a home garden is one of the best summer pastimes to do at home in the summer. You can have vegetables. The vegetables will be fresh. They will also be inexpensive. Even the smallest plot can give good results. You just need to prepare the soil. You also need to tend the garden. You should tend it carefully.
2. In the city, a container garden works well. Tubs of soil on the roof can be used to grow tomatoes. The tubs can also be used to grow summer squash. You just turn over the soil, and then you spread on fertilizer, and plant the seeds, and cover the seeds with a layer of hay or black plastic. The hay is better to look at than the plastic.
3. An interesting family lived in our neighborhood. Their name was Anderson. The Andersons grew all their vegetables in containers. The containers were on the roof. They used a special method. The method is French intensive gardening. Seeds are planted in the spring. They are planted close together. The garden is covered with hay. Because of the fact that the garden is covered, there are very few weeds. The point is that French intensive gardening gives very good results in small places.

Creative Writing

A Have you ever wondered what it would be like to wander around the halls of Count Dracula's legendary castle, or visit the unusual settings for such movies as *The Wizard of Oz* or *Raiders of the Lost Ark*? Choose a famous mythical location from a book or movie that you've heard about or seen. Pretend that you are writing instructions on how to design the set for a movie using that location. Describe the way you imagine the set should look, and where each item of scenery should be placed. The crew doesn't have much time to read, so write one or two concise paragraphs that give as much information as possible. Write the directions out quickly from your thoughts first. Then go back, revising and combining sentences where necessary.

B Imagine that you have suddenly figured out the technology needed to make a computer or robot do anything you want it to do. What would you ask it to do first? In one or two paragraphs, tell what would happen on the computer or robot's first day on the job. What would it accomplish, and how? Read over your first draft carefully to make sure all of the sentences are clear and well-written. Rewrite any padded, stringy, or empty sentences.

Application and Review

A **Combining Sentences** Read the paragraphs below and combine sentences where needed to keep the writing clear, concise, and flowing.

Tide pools are natural aquariums. They are found along coastlines of seas and oceans. The pools of water are protected from heavy waves by walls. These barriers are made of rock. Animals such as starfish, crabs, sea urchins, and herons live in the tide pools. Sea plants like algae and sponges live there also.

The lifeforms in these pools can usually survive all sorts of natural assaults in the form of storms. They often are defenseless against human contact. Some visitors collect things from the pools to display at home. Other people take things just to possess the objects. Either way, the pool life suffers. California was among the first states to protect tide pools by law. California has many valuable tide pools. It is located on the Pacific coast.

B **Improving Sentences** Revise the sentences below that are empty, stringy, or padded.

1. People shouldn't be allowed to visit tide pools.
2. Because of the fact that the wentletrap snail can extend its snout three times the length of its shell, which is one centimeter long, I would like to say that it can stand up to its larger neighbors quite well.
3. The Monterey Aquarium, which is what you'd call a well-respected institution, has displays of artificial tide pools.
4. Waves bring in food for the inhabitants of the tide pool and much of this is plankton and sand-castle worms pull the plankton toward their mouths with their tentacles.
5. Tide pools are openings to the sea and they are sometimes called windows between land and sea. They are openings that allow you to see from the land into the life of the water.

9
Descriptive Writing

Pretend you are a diver. You want to show your friend how beautiful it is underwater, but he is afraid to dive. What can you do?

You can take an underwater picture, or you can "show" him the beauty of the sea through description. Good descriptive writing allows your reader to know exactly what people, places and things are like. It can make a reader imagine the exotic colors of ocean fish or hear the screeching halt of a powerful engine.

Description plays an important role in many types of writing. In this chapter you will improve your writing by creating specific images with words that appeal to the senses.

1
Analyzing Descriptive Writing

A good writer can use words to paint pictures, play music, and create smells, tastes, and feelings. This is not magic—it's just a matter of knowing how to use descriptive writing.

Almost any writing can benefit from good description. In stories and poems, description can create powerful images and unforgettable moods. In articles and essays, description can clarify ideas by projecting people, places, and things into the reader's mind. Sometimes writers devote an entire paragraph to description. More often, however, they weave descriptive words and phrases throughout a piece of writing.

Read and Think Effective description can create strong feelings or **moods** by appealing to our senses of sight, sound, smell, taste, and touch. Following is a poem entitled "Prelude 1." As you read the poem, identify words and phrases that appeal to your senses? Which senses do they appeal to?

Literary Model

The winter evening settles down
With smell of steaks in passageways.
Six o'clock.
The burnt-out ends of smoky days.
And now a gusty shower wraps
The grimy scraps
Of withered leaves about your feet
And newspapers from vacant lots;
The showers beat
On broken blinds and chimney-pots,
And at the corner of the street
A lonely cab-horse steams and stamps
And then the lighting of the lamps.

From "Prelude I" by T.S. Eliot

The poem appeals to our senses of feeling, sight, and smell. The day is burnt-out; the leaves are withered; the steaks are cooking; the blinds are broken; the lamps are lit.

In expository texts, writers also use description to explain a process, show cause and effect, or make a comparison. For example, in the following selection, the author describes how some frogs use their toes to fly.

Birds are not the only creatures that may sail past you through the air. . . . A few frogs have also taken to gliding. They use the membranes between their toes that are part of a standard frog's swimming equipment. The flying frog has greatly elongated toes and when they are extended, each foot becomes in effect a tiny parachute, so that when the frog leaps it can glide considerable distances from one tree to another.

From *The Zoo Quest Expeditions* by David Attenborough

Mood is not important in this passage. Instead, the author is more concerned with explaining how frogs fly. Making an idea clear to the reader is the primary goal in a text like this.

Think and Discuss Discuss the following questions with your classmates.

1. What mood does the first selection create? Which details help to create that mood?
2. What details does the second selection use to explain its main idea? Could you now tell someone else how frogs fly?

Follow Up Description appeals to our senses. Writers can use description to create images or moods or to clarify ideas. Keep these features of descriptive writing in mind as you read the literature selection on the next four pages.

Description in Literature

from *A Bevy of Beasts*

Gerald Durrell

Figurative language

Winter came upon us like the sudden opening of a tomb. Almost overnight it seemed that the last multi-colored banners of autumn leaves had been wrenched from the trees by the wind and built up in great moldering piles that smelled like plum cake when you kicked them. Then

Sensory language

came the early-morning frost that turned the long grass white and crisp as biscuit, made your breath hang in pale cobwebs in front of you and nipped at your fingertips with the viciousness of a slamming door. Then came the snow, in great flakes like Madeira lace, settling in a smooth milk-white coating over the countryside, a layer up to your knees and drifts seven feet deep, a covering that muffled all sound except its own squeaking and rustling voice as you walked on it. Now the wind whipped unrestricted across at you like a saber-cut, squeezing the tears from your eyes, freezing the melting snow on the trees and guttering into fluted icicles like a million melting candles.

I had been moved from my love affair with the giraffe and was now working in the section of the zoo known as "The Camels." On this section the main animals were the herd of Bactrian camels, a herd of yaks, a pair of tapirs, and sundry antelopes and deer. . . .

The main herd of camels, consisting of six females, was led and ruled by Big Bill, a huge animal with overstuffed humps like a French armchair, great plus-fours of curls on his

Vivid details

legs, and an expression of such sneering superiority that you longed for him to trip over something and fall down. He would stand towering over you, his belly rumbling, squeaking his long, greeny-yellow teeth together and staring at you with a disbelieving disgust as though you were a child mur-

derer or something similarly obscene. Apart from this posi-
tively Victorian belief in his superiority he was an untrust-
worthy beast and would not hesitate to lash out at you with
one of his great pincushionlike feet if he felt that you were
not giving him the respect that was his due. As you were
never quite sure what Big Bill considered to be an affront to
his dignity, life with him was hazardous.

Once, on my way to feed the tapirs, I decided to take a shortcut by climbing the fence and crossing the camel paddock. Big Bill was standing in the middle of the paddock ruminating, and as I got near him I greeted him.

"What ho, Bill old boy!" I said jovially.

Vivid details

It was obvious that my familiar attitude did not appeal to such a superior animal. Big Bill's jaws stopped moving, and his pale yellow eyes fastened on me. Then he suddenly stepped forward very swiftly, his head lunged down with open mouth, and he sank his long, discolored teeth into the clothing on my chest, lifted me off my feet, shook me and dropped me. Mercifully, I was wearing a thick tweed coat and a very thick rolltop pullover, so that his teeth sank into this instead of the wall of my chest. As I lay on the ground he wheeled round and lashed out with his hind leg. Desperately I rolled to one side, and his great hoof missed my head by inches. I got to my feet and fled. It was the last time I took a shortcut across Big Bill's paddock.

The most elderly of Bill's wives was a sedate matron known as Old Gran, and while I was on the section she gave birth. The baby must have been born early one morning, for when we arrived at eight o'clock we found him lying in the straw under his mother's bulging stomach, looking utterly bewildered and dejected, his fur plastered down and wet from Old Gran's greeting wash . . .

Transition

After twenty-four hours the baby could walk, or, to be more accurate, he could, after considerable effort, hoist himself onto his legs. After this preliminary effort the whole performance began to lack reality. He had not as yet obtained full control of his lanky legs with their great, bulbous joints. In fact, at times it seemed as though some other power were in control of these necessary adjuncts and that he was trying manfully to get possession of them. He would stagger a few steps, his knees buckling under him, and the more they bent the more worried became his expression. Then he would come to a stop, swaying violently, and consider the problem. But the longer he stood still the less inclined his legs became to support him. His knees would fold up, his body would lunge wildly from side to side, and then, quite suddenly, the whole scaffolding of his limbs would cave in and he would fall heavily to the ground, his legs sticking out at such weird angles that it was only their elasticity that prevented them from being snapped. Grimly determined, he would climb upright again by painful stages and then set off at a brisk run, but even this method was no use. His legs would shoot out in the most unpredictable directions and he would stagger wildly. The faster he went, the more involved became the antics of his legs. He would leap in the air in an effort to disentangle them from each other, but the knot would be too intricate and once again he would fall in a heap on the ground. But he persisted in these exercises every morning, while nearby his mother would stand chewing the cud and watching him proudly.

Details
support
comic
mood

After two days he had at last succeeded in controlling his legs to a certain degree, which was really quite an achievement. He was so proud of his accomplishment that he took daring risks such as gamboling like a lamb, which sometimes ended disastrously. This gamboling was as laughable as his first attempts to walk. He would frisk around his mother, bucking and bouncing, his hump flaps waving like pocket handkerchiefs out of a train window. Sometimes his legs would let him down and he would fall heavily to the ground. This would have a sobering effect, and when he got to his feet he would walk behind his mother very sedately. Then his feelings would get the better of him and he would be off again. The rest of the herd considered him a nuisance, for he was not a very good judge of distance and would frequently bump into one of them, tripping them up and causing a hiatus in their orderly progression. Quite frequently he would receive a kick from an outraged matron whose rear he had assaulted by tripping over his own feet while executing a particularly complicated and beautiful gambol.

.

Trying Out Descriptive Writing Big Bill made a lasting impression on Gerald Durrell. In your journal, vividly describe a person, place, or animal that made a lasting impression on you.

2
Prewriting: Description

To begin writing a description, first identify the people, places, or things you want to describe. Then determine the mood or feeling you want to create and collect sensory details that support the mood.

Identifying What to Describe

Description is not just icing on the cake. It is one of the essential ingredients of good writing. If you don't include description, your writing may be flat and unappealing. For example, in an article on mountain climbing, you might want to describe the terrible dangers that mountain climbers face. Imagine how much more effective it would be to describe the tension of walking on the narrow ledge of a cliff than it would be to just list the dangers of mountain climbing.

To identify the things you should describe, ask yourself what purpose your writing has and if description can help you accomplish that purpose. For example, in an expository article, descriptions can be used to give readers a clear picture of the article's subject. In an editorial, descriptions can be used to present specific people, places, or things that support your arguments. And in fiction writing, descriptions can be used to create vivid characters, settings, and moods.

Identifying a Mood

The simplest way to identify a mood is to ask yourself: what feelings do I want my readers to have? Select sensory words and details that help create those feelings. For instance, if you intend to write a description of a subway platform, spend some time on the platform, or imagine yourself there, and notice your feelings. Is the platform a frightening place, or a friendly one? Look around and notice the details that influence your feelings. Does the tunnel make you feel afraid? Do the crowds make you feel helpless? Or do you feel secure in the midst of so many people? When you write, use those feelings in your descriptions.

The Port of Collioure, Andre Derain, 1905.

Sometimes you do not want to create a specific mood in your description. For instance, in writing a science report, you might be explaining a process or an idea. Then, your descriptions need to be more objective because you are writing to clarify something, not to create a mood.

Collecting Sensory Details

To write effective description, you must collect sensory details that show how something looks, sounds, smells, tastes, and feels. For example, even a blank piece of paper has color, size, shape, weight, texture, and smell. It makes a sound when you wave it in the air, and it has its own way of falling to the ground.

Remember, you can't create a good descriptive mood just by writing, "The house was scary." You have to show the details that make the house scary. Describe the cobwebs in the corners, the creaking floorboards, the muffled thuds from the cellar. Sensory details like these can be collected in a number of ways.

Observation If you are writing about something that you can observe, you can collect details simply by studying the subject closely. In collecting details about a car, for example, study what the car looks like, what the motor sounds like, what it feels like to sit in the seats, what the interior smells like, and so forth.

Memory If you want to collect details about something that occurred in the past, try to get a clear picture of the event in your mind. This technique is called **imaging**. For example, if you want to describe a trip you took to the mountains, try to remember images from your trip and focus on the details in each image. What did the mountains look like? What sounds could you hear? What smell was in the air? What did the wind feel like?

Imagination If you want to describe something that you have made up, all you have to do is use your imagination. You can invent any details you want. Try using the imaging technique as you add details to your creation. That way, you will get a clear picture of whatever you are imagining.

You can use several methods for writing down details that support a specific mood. The simplest is just to list the details that you think support the mood. Another method is to write different categories and fill them in with details. If you are describing a certain door, your categories might include: color, shape, size, type of doorknob, type of material, closing sound, and so on. Yet another method is to group your details by senses, separately listing details for each sense.

Writing Activities *Prewriting*

A Use the imaging technique to collect details about a place you visited in the past. Pick a place that you remember fairly well, such as an amusement park, the seashore, or a tall building. Determine the mood that you want to create and list the details that support that mood. Next, imagine what the place might look like fifty years from now and list details that support the mood. Finally, compare the two lists.

B Writing in Process Find a person, place, or thing that you would like to describe. You might want to look through *Starting Points: Ideas for Writing* (pages 41–53) for a subject that interests you, or you might want to find something on your own. Once you have decided on a subject, determine the mood you want to create and make a list of sensory details that support the mood. Save your list in your writer's folder for a later activity.

3
Drafting: Organizing a Description

Your list of sensory details will form the basis of your description. Before drafting the description, however, you will need to organize your details. There are two basic ways of organizing descriptive details: spatial order and order of impression.

Spatial Order

Spatial order shows the position of details in relationship to other details, giving your readers a logical and well-organized picture. For example, you might describe details as they appear from the top to the bottom of an object, from left to right, from front to back, or from outside to inside. The location of each detail is given as you develop the description. You might start a spatial-order description of a diesel truck by describing the outside of the truck first, moving to the interior, and ending with the engine under the hood.

Notice which type of spatial order is used in the following selection.

Professional Model   The view from the upper deck at Wrigley Field is simply magnificent. Straight in front of you, of course, is the famed baseball diamond, with its dirt infield and emerald-green grass, encircled by an ivy-covered brick wall. The sun-bleached wooden bleachers, filled with screaming fans, sit behind the wall, and are crowned with a magnificent hand-operated scoreboard, the last of its kind. Beyond the bleachers lie the brick houses and apartment buildings of northern Chicago, and beyond those Lake Michigan gleams in the sunlight, its surface crowded with sailboats.

—Steve Osborn

The description starts in the front of the scene and moves slowly toward the back. First you see the baseball diamond, then the outfield wall, then the bleachers and scoreboard, then the houses, and finally the lake.

Spatial-order descriptions are mostly used to describe places. They can give readers a good general idea of what a place looks like. Because spatial-order descriptions are logical and objective, they are often found in factual articles and other expository types of writing. Of course, fiction writers also use spatial order to describe story settings and sometimes to establish a mood.

In the description of the baseball park, the words *in front, behind,* and *beyond* help you see the spatial order. These words, and others like them, are called **transitions**. Which transitions might a left-right spatial order use? Which transitions might a top-bottom spatial order use?

Writing Inside Out

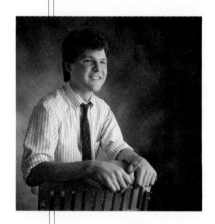

Spanish is the native language of over 17 million Americans. Many television and radio stations, magazines, and newspapers serve the nation's Spanish-speaking communities. When companies want to advertise their products on these stations, they hire advertising agencies like Conill in New York.

Lucio Arce is a young copywriter, working for Conill. As a copywriter, Lucio generates ideas for commercials. That is, he tries to come up with ideas that will help sell a client's products.

Lucio was raised in Argentina, where he studied advertising and started his career as a copywriter. In high school, he remembers that he loved to write about almost any topic and that he always did very well. Apparently, that love and talent for writing are what pushed him toward his present occupation. Today, Lucio believes passionately in what he does. He says,

Order of Impression

Sometimes, when you observe a person, place, or thing, you notice one detail at a time, in no particular order, starting with whatever makes the greatest impression on you. You can write an **order-of-impression** description to show these changing impressions.

Unlike a spatial-order description, the details are not arranged in a logical spatial order, such as front to back. Instead, a presentation or arrangement of the details depends on the personal view of the observer.

In the description that follows on the next page, notice the girl's changing impressions of the scene.

"I believe in what I do. I will defend it. I will stand behind it."

At Conill, Lucio writes copy for all kinds of products—from America's most popular hamburgers to the "plop-plop, fizz-fizz" tablets people take for stomach distress. Products may differ, but copywriters often use the same approach to tackle them all.

They sit around a table, discuss the product, its features, its uses, and the client's image. Then they brainstorm—sometimes for hours. They talk about crazy ideas as well as down-to-earth ones. Finally, they settle on two or three ideas to develop, and the copywriters go to work. Each develops copy to present the product in an attractive, memorable image. Copy is not just words. It may be dialogue for a television or radio announcer. It may be jingles or songs. It also may be pictures, illustrations, or other graphic images—anything that helps to describe the product for the potential customer.

Ideas are the heart of a copywriter's work. Without them products may not sell. Yet, there are times when even the most creative copywriter runs out of ideas. When this happens, Lucio and his co-workers look to each other for help. Lucio says that people "are always willing to help because they have gone through the same thing." It is an unwritten understanding: "I'm helping you now; someday you'll help me."

She looked around. She saw the great Hungarian plain unfold before her eyes. Something in her was touched by the solemn beauty of it. Its immense grassy expanses unbroken by mountains or trees, shimmering under the spring sun. The dark blue sky, cloudless, like an inverted blue bowl. Herds of grazing sheep, like patches of snow. No sound, save the soft thud of the horses' hoofs on the white dusty road, and now and then the distant tinkle of sheep's bells, or the eerie sound of a shepherd's flute, the tilinkó.

From *The Good Master* by Kate Seredy

As she looks around, the girl sees the grassy expanses. Then she looks up at the sky and back down at the sheep, which make her think of snow. Next, she hears the different sounds and sees the dusty road. Through her, we get a strong impression of the scene—*her* impression. If the writer had used a spatial order, our understanding of the scene would be entirely different.

Writing Activities *Organizing a Description*

A Tell whether you would use spatial order or order of impression for each of the following descriptions. Explain your answers.

1. An apartment building on your block was gutted, and the shell was completely renovated inside. As the real estate agent, you must describe the new apartments.
2. Raccoons are invading your neighborhood. Help people figure out the difference between a squirrel and a raccoon.
3. To teach a class on playing chess, you need to write directions describing how to set up a chessboard.
4. Someone has asked you to describe for a food magazine what a roasted, uncarved turkey looks like.
5. Helen tried to dye her hair red, but it turned out purple. Tell what she looks like now.

B **Writing in Process** Draft two descriptions of the same subject, using the sensory details that you listed in Activity B on page 162. Use spatial order for the first description. Use order of impression for the second. When you finish, compare the drafts. Which order seems better suited to the subject? Why?

4
Drafting and Revising: Descriptive Language

Descriptions should not only be well organized, they should also make effective use of words. Good descriptions usually contain sensory images, specific words, and figurative language.

Sensory Images

Sensory images are composed of words that describe sights, sounds, smells, tastes, or feelings. The following selection creates a number of sensory images through a careful choice of words.

Literary Model

He rolled up the hems of his blue denim breeches and stepped with bare dirty feet into the shallow spring. His toes sank into the sand. It oozed softly between them and over his bony ankles. The water was so cold that for a moment it burned his skin. Then it made a rippling sound, flowing past his pipe-stem legs, and was entirely delicious. He walked up and down, digging his big toe experimentally under smooth rocks he encountered.
From *The Yearling* by Marjorie Kinnan Rawlings

The sensory images allow us to use our senses in a number of ways. We see the character's clothes and feet, as well as the spring that he steps into. We feel the sand oozing between his toes and the cold water burning his skin. We hear the water rippling past his legs. All of these images combine to create a rich and pleasurable mood.

Specific Words

In order to create strong sensory images, you need to use specific words. A sentence such as "The driver shouted loudly" can be vastly improved by adding a few specific words. "The enraged taxi driver let loose with an ear-splitting yell." Because it uses specific words, the second sentence creates a stronger sensory image.

Specific words include specific nouns, adjectives, verbs, and adverbs. You should use specific nouns and adjectives to give objects their precise names and describe what they look like. Use specific verbs and adverbs to show individual actions and how they are performed. In the following selection, notice how the specific words bring the scene into sharp focus.

Literary Model

There was a far off rumble. And over the hill came a glare that spread through the sky until suddenly it narrowed down to a long beam of headlights. Right after, came another pair of headlights shooting high in the air. They leveled off as the top of the hill was reached. They were the first trucks from Burke's Lumber Yard, a couple of big two-ton trailers.

—Joseph Krumgold

What begins as a far off rumble becomes two sets of headlights and finally ends up as specific trucks coming from a specific place. The headlights don't just shine. They glare, narrow down suddenly, shoot high in the air, and level off. The trucks aren't just trucks. They're a couple of big two-ton trailers from Burke's Lumber Yard.

Figurative Language

Language can be literal or figurative. In **literal language,** the words mean exactly what they say. In **figurative language,** the words mean more than their usual meaning. For example, "She runs fast" is literal. The words mean exactly what they say. "He runs like a snail" is figurative. The words say that he runs like a snail, but they mean that he runs slowly.

Figurative language makes you think. When you read a description that uses figurative language, you have to think about what the writer means.

Two of the most common types of figurative language are similes and metaphors. **Similes** compare two different things, such as a person and a snail, and use the words *like* or *as.* Here are some similes:

Her skin was as clear as porcelain.
The cat's eyes were like emeralds.
The man glided through the crowd like a snake.

Metaphors also compare two different things, but they don't use the words *like* or *as*. Metaphors take different forms. In one form, they are very much like similes. The first two similes on the previous page, for example, can be changed into metaphors simply by dropping a few words:

> Her skin was porcelain.
> The cat's eyes were emeralds.

In another kind of metaphor, specific verbs can be used to imply comparisons. For example, the noun *snake* can be changed into a verb:

> The man snaked through the crowd.

The metaphor is still comparing two things—the man and a snake—but it doesn't make the comparison directly.

Metaphors are often not as obvious as similes. The comparison is only implied, not stated directly with *like* or *as*. Which comparisons are implied in the following metaphors?

> The swimmer's arms sliced through the water.
> The man's eyes smoldered with anger.

Using figurative language can give your readers a much deeper understanding of your subject than literal language can. For example, you might write, "The boxer had a thick neck." Your readers will see the boxer and his thick neck, but that's all. However, you might also use figurative language by writing, "The boxer had the neck of a bull." Your readers will still see the boxer and his thick neck, but they might also think of other ways in which the boxer is like a bull: strong, wild, easily angered. These details would strengthen your descriptive picture.

In the following selection, notice how the figurative language helps you see and think about the exploding sun.

Professional Model Then the Sun will collapse upon itself, and the energy released by this infalling will heat it rapidly to 100 million degrees centigrade. It will expand violently—becoming a red giant. As it grows, it will swallow first Mercury, then Venus, and then, perhaps—if it keeps expanding—it will engulf our Earth and Moon.

From *Planet Earth* by Jonathan Weiner

Grammar in Action

You can use present and past participles and participial phrases as adjectives to add life to your writing.

> *Bewildered,* the dog scratched at the secret panel *hiding* its owner.

> *Laughing* with glee, the magician pulled a rabbit from a hat *suspended* in mid-air.

For more information on participles and participial phrases, see page 587.

Writing Activities **Using Descriptive Language**

A Rewrite the paragraph below so that it contains sensory images, specific words, and figurative language.

> The pond is a nice place. It has fish, ducks, and frogs. There's some grass around the edge and a boat you can use. The water is kind of strange, but we swim in it anyway. We're there almost every day in the summer.

B Write a simile and a metaphor to describe each of the following items:

falling snow	the movement of a shark
sunrise	a car's sputtering engine
silence	the cry of a wild animal

C Writing in Process Revise one of the descriptions you wrote for Activity B on page 166. Include sensory images, specific words, and figurative language in your revision.

5
Revising Descriptive Writing

The last step in writing a description is to make a careful revision of your draft. The revision checklist below can help you or a peer editor decide which parts of your draft need revision. As you make your revisions, keep reading your description to see if it gives a good image of whatever you are describing. Once you are satisfied, go back and correct any awkward sentences or phrases. Complete the revision by proofreading the description and correcting any spelling or mechanical errors.

Revision and Peer-Editing Checklist
1. Does the description use specific nouns, verbs, adjectives, and adverbs? Are the words precise and accurate?
2. Does the description create sensory images? Do the words appeal to the senses?
3. Does the description use figurative language? Do similes and metaphors help readers understand the subject?
4. Does the description create a specific mood? Do the sensory details support the mood? Could any other details be included?
5. Is the description organized? If spatial order is used, is the order clear and logical? If order of impression is used, does it show the impressions that an observer might have?

Once your description is completed, you should share it with an audience. Find out if they can picture the things you have described and ask them to identify the mood of your description. You may make further revisions based on their comments.

Using the revision checklist, Hector revised the following description. Notice his thoughts as he worked.

took a strong pair of legs and a set of earplugs

It ~~was hard~~ to stand near Coach Caldwell during

explosive   drive

basketball practice. His ~~loud~~ voice could ~~force~~ you

with a single blast   turn

back, and his piercing green eyes could ~~make~~ your

to jelly

knees ~~shake.~~ When he did allow you to speak, you

choked   collapsed in a fit of coughing.

~~stumbled~~ on your words and ~~started to cough.~~

rifled

Then there were times when he ~~tossed~~ the ball to

someone and asked him to demonstrate a shot. If

ranted and raved   condemned to

the player missed, Coach ~~shouted~~ and ~~gave~~ him ten

grueling

laps.

> This helps the sensory image.

> Figurative language and specific words might help throughout here.

Writing Activities *Revising a Description*

A Revise the following description to give it a more frightening mood. Add sensory images, specific words, and figurative language. Also rewrite the awkward sentences.

> Joan crept along the dark hallway. She heard strange noises. The walls felt bad. She could see a little bit of light in front of her. Somebody was saying something. She felt cold without her jacket. Suddenly, the floor under her feet gave way and she fell into a pit.

B Writing in Process Make a final revision of the description you completed in Activity B on page 170. Use the questions in the checklist on page 171. Then share your description with an audience and find out how well they can "see" the images.

English and Art

Have you ever watched an artist at a fair or carnival draw funny, quick sketches of the people who pass? The artist picks out one or two of the person's most notable traits (size, hair color, dimples) and then exaggerates those traits in the sketch. This type of drawing is called a *caricature.* Famous actors and politicians are often the subjects of these unique drawings. Check your newspaper's political cartoons for some examples.

Sam Spade   Tina Turner   Margaret Thatcher

While some artists use pencils to create caricatures, others use words. Exaggeration in description can be funny and can give us a quick snapshot-like picture of a character at the same time. In writing, the artist's greatest tools are strong adjectives, descriptive verbs, and vivid, specific details. As an example, read the following caricature, and try to form a picture in your mind of this character from the novel *The Maltese Falcon.*

> Samuel Spade's jaw was long and bony, his chin a jutting *v* under the more flexible *v* of his mouth. His nostrils curved back to make another, smaller *v*. His yellow-gray eyes were horizontal.

Activity

As a caricature artist, you want your subject to be instantly recognized from a few quick strokes of your pencil. Therefore, choose a famous person to sketch. Draw a caricature sketch, concentrating on one or two main traits. Create a word sketch for your artwork. Have a classmate guess who your subject is.

Creative Writing

A Have you watched a movie recently where the star was a person or creature from a different planet, culture, or time? You might have laughed to see this alien try to identify and use such common American items as an escalator, can opener, or television set. For now, imagine that an alien of your choice and design has just appeared in your neighborhood. Describe what it would find in your home, using its eyes as your own. Try to see things as if you had never seen them before and didn't know what they were. You might have to make up new and creative uses for them.

B Coming up with creative new twists on everyday clothes and accessories has become very popular and profitable in recent years. Watches have become colorful play-fashion items and basic white gym shoes are now made in a rainbow of colors and styles. Select an item of clothing that seems common and ordinary, and imagine a way to jazz it up. Add sparkles or bangles or stripes, anything that gives the item new life. Describe your fashion invention in detail for the waiting public.

C Imagine that you're writing the year's next blockbuster movie. Create a character (person or creature) that you think will be both interesting and appealing to an audience. How would this character look, sound, act, speak, dress, and move? Make it come alive in a written description.

Application and Review

A Analyzing a Description Read the following paragraph. Answer the questions below.

> He stood by the window again. It was raining, but the whiteness had gone. Save for a wet leaf shining here and there, the garden was all dark now—the yellow mound of flowering tree had vanished. The college buildings lay round the garden in a low couched mass, here red-stained, here yellow-stained, where lights burnt behind curtains; and there lay the chapel, huddling its bulk against the sky which, because of the rain, seemed to tremble slightly. But it was no longer silent. He listened; there was no sound in particular; but, as he stood looking out, the building hummed with life. There was a sudden roar of laughter; then the tinkle of a piano; then a nondescript clatter and chatter—of china partly; then again the sound of rain falling, and the gutters chuckling and burbling as they sucked up the water. He turned back into the room.
>
> From *The Years* by Virginia Woolf

1. To which senses does the selection appeal? For each of those senses, list five details from the selection.
2. Does the man at the window share in the cheer of the party sounds? How do you know?
3. What sort of mood or feeling does the selection create? Which words help to create the mood?
4. In what order does the author describe this scene?

B Using Specific Description Replace each word or phrase with a more specific term. Write a sentence using each specific term.

dog	touch	pretty
little	water	said
plant	good	fight
a little bit	over there	a white building

10
Narrative Writing

"When I hear the old men
Telling of heroes,
Telling of great deeds
Of ancient days . . ."

From "A Song of Greatness" by Mary Austin

We hear stories all the time. Some are about the old days, some are about recent events. Some stories are true; some are imagined.

Narrative writing is writing that tells a story. In this chapter you will learn to develop characters, create settings, and construct plots in your narrative writing.

1
Analyzing Narrative

A **narrative** is a story. Often, the story is about something that actually happened. When you tell a friend how you learned to love fishing, you're relating a narrative. An anecdote telling how your parents met is a narrative. So is a diary entry about your family's yearly reunion.

A narrative also can tell a story that the writer created in his or her imagination. This sort of narrative is called **fiction**. Novels and short stories are fictional narratives. So are most movies and television programs.

Read and Think Read this entry from Sara's writing journal. Think about the way she presents the information in her story about an airplane ride.

Student Model

I was already nervous about being in a plane on such a cloudy day. So when the pilot asked us to fasten our seat belts, my heart skipped a beat. I glanced around to see whether anyone else looked as scared as I felt. The other passengers seemed bored. Some were reading. The woman next to me was asleep. There's nothing to panic about, I told myself. Everyone else seemed at ease.

The pilot began to talk again. In a falsely jolly voice, he warned that the ride was going to get rough. I peeked outside, and saw raindrops zipping past the window. Lightning flashed below me right next to the plane! I clutched the armrests, closed my eyes, clenched my teeth, and tried to wish myself to the ground.

Think and Discuss Think about the following questions. Then discuss your answers with your classmates.

1. Who are the characters in this story? Where are they?
2. What is the problem facing the characters?
3. Do you think this is a story about something that really happened to Sara? Why or why not?

Read and Think Here is the first paragraph of a published short story. As you read it, think about how the author introduced the characters and the story situation.

Literary Model

The morning of the dog-sled race, Debbie and her brother Mark were up before the sun had lightened the cold New England sky to finish the chores around the family kennels. They packed their racing equipment in the farm truck—the harnesses made of white bands with each dog's name stitched in red, the hitching lines, water pans, and the medicine kit. Mark tied the light ashwood racing sled on top, where it sat like a strange wild bird. The team of five strong husky dogs was lifted into individual boxes built into the truck. When everything was ready, Mark took the wheel, and Debbie hoisted herself into the seat beside him.

From "The Race" by Victoria Furman

Think and Discuss Think about the following questions. Talk about your ideas with your classmates.

1. What do you know about the characters in this story?
2. In what part of the country does the story take place? During what time of year? How can you tell?
3. What are Debbie and Mark going to do in this story?

Follow Up All narratives have a few elements in common. They all have **characters**—the who or what of the story. Also, every narrative tells about a series of events that occurs at a particular place and time. In fictional narratives, the series of events is called a **plot**, and the place and time of the story is called the **setting**.

In this chapter you will learn how to create characters, imagine settings, and construct plots for narratives. Keep these features of a narrative in mind as you read the literature selection on the next four pages.

Narration in Literature

"The Death of a Whale"

Ada and Frank Graham

Main character and setting introduced

*F*or some years a writer and naturalist named Farley Mowat lived with his wife, Claire, in the fishing village of Burgeo on the south coast of Newfoundland. There he had the kind of experience that very few people have had with a whale. It ended in the death of a single whale at a time when many thousands were being killed all over the world. But Farley Mowat had a special regard for whales. The book he wrote about the experience, *A Whale for the Killing*, helped a great many other people to start thinking about whales in a new way. . . .

Sometimes small family groups of fin whales were seen near Burgeo in winter when they came to feed on herring. The Mowats got great pleasure from watching the whales feeding in a lonely cove near their home. Once they flew in a small plane over a family of whales swimming just below the

surface. They marveled at the graceful movement of the whales through the water. "It's like watching a fantastic ballet," Claire Mowat said. "They aren't swimming through the water—they're dancing through it!"

One day after a big storm in January an astonishing thing happened. Near Burgeo there was a little saltwater pond, partly cut off from the sea by rocks. Somehow a large female fin whale got over the rocks and into the pond. The storm had been fierce, the tide high, and the whale had probably been chasing a school of herring. When the whale finished feeding in the pond, the storm was over and she was trapped.

Word that a giant whale was trapped in the pond quickly spread through the town. For some reason several men in the town decided that it would be great fun to go to the pond and shoot at the whale.

"The five men wasted no time," Mowat wrote in his book. "Some dropped to their knees levering shells into their rifles as they did so. Others stood where they were and hurriedly took aim. The crash of rifle fire began to echo from the cliffs enclosing the pond and, as an undertone, there came the flat satisfying *thunk* of bullets striking home in living flesh. After an hour the men had exhausted their supply of shells."

But the men returned with more ammunition the next day. They fired hundreds of bullets into the thick blubber of the frightened whale. Her skin was scarred with bullet holes but she did not seem to be seriously hurt. A curious part of the incident was that another large whale, surely her mate, was often seen in the ocean near the entrance to the little cove, keeping the trapped whale company. Sometimes it seemed as if the big whale outside was trying to drive schools of herring into the cove for his mate to eat.

Farley Mowat was wild with anger when he learned that men were shooting at the trapped whale. He made up his mind to help her. He arranged to have a Royal Canadian Police officer patrol the cove to keep people from shooting at her or chasing her around the shallow little pond in their motorboats. Many of the townspeople, even some of his old

friends, were angry with Mowat for trying to help the whale.
They believed they had a right to shoot at it if they wanted to.

Mowat knew that time was short. Even if the whale was
not killed by the high-powered rifles, she might soon die of
hunger. He hired some local fishermen to help him drive
schools of herring into the cove. He made long-distance telephone calls all over the United States and Canada to try to
get help for the whale.

The Newfoundland government promised to send a big
fishing boat to help, but it did not arrive in time. Newspapers all over the world carried stories about the trapped
whale and Mowat's attempt to help it. People who had never
given a second thought to the slaughter of two million
whales now were in sympathy with this one fin whale as she
fought for her life.

Mowat hoped to keep her alive until another high tide
might help to float her over the rocks and back into the sea.
Every day he and a fisherman friend went into the cove to
stay with her. Her mate was always waiting just outside the
cove.

One day when Mowat rowed across the cove the great
whale swam slowly under his boat. For the first time he

heard her voice. "It was a long, low, sonorous moan with unearthly overtones in a higher pitch," he wrote later. "It was unbelievably weird and bore no affinity with any sound I have heard from any other living thing. It was a voice not of the world we know."

Mowat wrote that he will always believe that his trapped creature had tried to communicate with him—to reach out across the space that separates two species.

He failed, yet it was not a total failure. "So long as I live I shall hear the echoes of that haunting cry," he went on. "And they will remind me that life itself—not human life—is the ultimate miracle upon this earth. I will hear those echoes even if the day should come when none of her nation is left alive in the desecrated seas, and the voices of the great whales have been silenced forever." . . .

Toward the end the whale could no longer keep herself afloat. Several times she dragged her huge body up on the beach. Each time she rested her head on the rocks, then pushed off again. Mowat heard her cry only once more.

End of action

"It was the most desolate cry I have ever heard," he wrote in his book. He knew that this was her leavetaking. The next day she drowned, sinking to the bottom of the little cove, too weak to push herself back to the surface to breathe. "It was dark, and there was none to know that I was weeping," Mowat wrote, "weeping not just for the whale that died but because the fragile link between her race and mine was severed."

Trying Out Narrative Writing Think of an interesting topic for a story. It can be based on your own experience or an imaginary event. Choose your characters, plot, and setting; then write your narrative. After you have finished, reflect about the act of writing. What part of your story was the most difficult to write? Why? What part was the easiest? What are the strongest and weakest parts of your story? Why? The following pages will help you to learn more about writing an effective narrative.

2
Prewriting: Finding Ideas

Getting started can be hard for any writer, but you can call on your thinking skills to help you. Glean ideas from books, newspapers, and magazines. Reflect about the people you meet or see. Generate ideas by asking yourself questions about the things you see and hear. See Chapter 2, pages 16–40, for a review of these thinking techniques.

Use a method like freewriting or clustering to get ideas down on paper. Later you can expand the ideas for a story. You might begin by focusing on one aspect of the narrative—character, plot, or setting.

Start with a Character

The world is full of characters, from the passengers on a bus to your neighbors down the street. Look for the traits that make people interesting. You might notice a style of dress, a certain walk, or a special way with words. Jotting down these colorful features or traits when you notice them can help you create an interesting character later.

Another way to create a character is to do brainstorming. Make a list for yourself of names, appearances, hometowns, hobbies, and personality traits. Write down whatever comes to mind. Then choose several details and combine them to create an interesting character. Below is an example of this kind of character portrait.

Terri Stevens 14 years old 5'4" 103 lbs.
- wears casual clothes, no matter what the occasion
- lives in Milwaukee in a second-floor apartment with her mother and two older brothers
- goes to a pottery studio after class every day
- likes art and all kinds of music
- is friendly but has no close friends at school
- helps support the family with the pottery she sells

Start with a Plot

When most people recall a story, they remember the problem or conflict in the story, the events that happen because of the problem, and how the problem is resolved. This organized series of events is the plot.

A second way to begin planning your story is to think of a plot idea. You might draw on your imagination or personal experience. If you once wanted to join a circus, for example, you could write a story about someone who actually does join a circus. Real events you've read about also could be turned into plot ideas.

You can also try asking yourself some *what-if* questions: what if two friends had to compete for the same job on the high school radio station? What if your best friend were moving away? What if someone suddenly turned blue? The questions you ask yourself might suggest a problem and a plot idea for your narrative.

Start with a Setting

A third way to begin planning your story is to start with an interesting setting. Think about where and when a story might take place. Don't worry about the plot. Just try to see the details of the setting in your mind. One way to think of a setting is to use books and pictures. Read about different places, or look at pictures, magazines, or artwork to get ideas. Combine or exaggerate elements of famous settings you have seen. You can use freewriting to get the details down. Focus on a setting and write about what your imagination sees and hears.

This method of planning your story will work best if you choose a setting that is special for you. If you're fascinated by the Old West, you could try to imagine a dusty cattle-trail town in the 1870's. If you yearn for faraway places, you could freewrite

Pony Tracks in the Buffalo Trails, 1904. Frederic Remington.

about an island somewhere in the Pacific. You can write about imaginary characters or incidents in your favorite place or a place you don't like at all. Send your imagination on a trip.

Following is an entry from Glenn's journal. Read it to see how he found an idea for a narrative.

> My little brother asked me to fix a toy for him the other day, and I almost destroyed it before I got it fixed because I didn't know what I was doing. It got me thinking: what if someone pretended he was an expert at something, and then put people in danger by not knowing what he was doing? What might happen?

Now answer these questions about the journal entry.

1. Did Glenn focus on a character, plot, or setting?
2. What problem or conflict is emerging as a story idea?

Writing Activities *Finding Narrative Ideas*

A Use listing or freewriting to expand on one story starter from each category below. Write at least five details about each character, plot, and setting that you choose.

Character
1. A man named Wolf
2. A teen-ager from Los Angeles who loves swimming and surfing but has moved to Alaska

Plot
1. A basketball team loses its lead in the big game.
2. A girl who works at the neighborhood grocery store catches a neighbor's child shoplifting.

Setting
1. A resort on another planet
2. A tropical island after a hurricane that has destroyed all the homes

B **Writing in Process** Find two or three story ideas. You may begin with a character, with a plot, or with a setting. If you wish, use one of the ideas in Activity A, or look through *Starting Points: Ideas for Writing* (pages 41–53) for story ideas. Use the suggestions in this lesson to help you get your ideas down on paper. Save your work in your writing folder for a later activity.

3
Prewriting: Planning Your Narrative

You have come up with an idea for a story. Now you can develop that idea into a plan for the characters, plot, and setting. Some writers might develop their idea by writing about all three elements at once, but you will probably find it easier to think about one element at a time.

Know Your Characters

Your story will probably have two or three main characters. You should try to describe each of them briefly. Close your eyes and imagine each character in action. Listen to the characters talking. You might try looking at pictures of people to trigger your imagination. List features that not only tell how the character looks on the outside but also how the character feels on the inside.

The selection below shows how author Gerald Durrell pictures a character called the Rose-Beetle Man.

> He had a sharp, foxlike face with large, slanting eyes of such a dark brown that they appeared black. They had a weird vacant look about them.

Sharp, detailed descriptions not only make your writing more interesting, they also help you focus your ideas about a character or setting.

Focus the Setting

As you develop your story idea, you may need to think further about the setting. If you were writing about a marathon, for example, you might need to describe how the weather affected the race. If you were planning to write a mystery, you might want to add details about a dark old mansion, foggy streets, or a dog howling in the woods. Try to include details that will give your setting the mood, or feeling, you want.

Explore Plot Events

A plot idea can be simply a situation. To plan a complete plot, you develop the situation so that it has a beginning, middle, and end.

The beginning of the story should introduce a problem or conflict. The middle should expand on the problem. The end of the story should resolve it. You link the beginning, middle, and end with a chain of events.

One way to construct a plot is to try to imagine a number of scenes. Each important event is a different scene. By coming up with just a beginning scene, a middle scene, and an ending scene, you have a plot outline from which to begin writing.

Organize with a Scenario

You will need to organize the different notes you made for your narrative. A good way to organize your notes is to develop a scenario. A **scenario** summarizes the characters, setting, and plot of a narrative. Following, on the next page, is Glenn's scenario, which is based on his journal entry from page 186.

Writing Inside Out

Phyllis Whitney is well over eighty years old. She has been writing novels for over forty-five years.

How does a novelist like Ms. Whitney get started on a story? She says, "There are many, many times when the writer has no ideas at all, when we start from scratch. We then do need a springboard to launch us into that first idea, to which other ideas will keep attaching themselves until hundreds of pages have been filled."

When Phyllis Whitney begins work on a new novel, her own springboard is the setting. She says, "A real setting furnishes

Scenario for a Narrative

1. Who are the characters?

- Kyle, a pioneer boy in Missouri. He is new in the settlement and wants to make a name for himself. Sometimes he brags to get attention.
- Julia, an older girl in the settlement. She's friendly to Kyle, but kind of distant.

2. What is the setting?

- a nearby forest. It has clearings, paths, and large wilderness areas.
- the one-room town hall, where meetings take place

3. What are the events of the plot?

- On an overnight trip to a neighboring settlement, Kyle brags that he is an expert at surviving in the wilderness, but he accidentally starts a fire that gets out of control.
- With help from the others, Kyle manages to put out the fire. He does not confess to anyone that he started it.
- The other travelers treat Kyle like a hero and brag about him when they reach the settlement.
- Kyle has to decide whether to tell the truth.

endless ideas for story scenes." In addition, she feels that a setting may introduce her to people who can help her develop her own characters. However, Ms. Whitney doesn't like to use these real people in her stories because "they would never behave as I want them to." Instead, she uses real people to help her create more realistic fictional characters.

As soon as she selects a setting, Ms. Whitney takes a trip there or to somewhere much like it. For example, she once had a dream about a stone bull standing on a mountain. That dream eventually became a novel called *The Stone Bull*. To begin writing the novel, Ms. Whitney went to the Catskill Mountains in New York for a week—hiking, driving around, taking pictures, collecting maps, postcards, brochures, and books from the region. She says, "Once I am in the place of my choice, I work very hard every minute. I fill a notebook with random description and set down any plot ideas that may come to me, inspired by the place."

Writing Activities *Developing a Narrative*

A List the details of plot, setting, and character that you might use to focus on one of the following situations.

1. School gym on the night of a rock concert after the band cancels
2. A mysterious woman who never goes out during the day
3. Hospital room where one child is seriously ill and another is slowly recovering

B Writing in Process

1. Choose one of the story ideas you thought of for Activity B on page 186. Write a scenario for the idea. Save the scenario in your writing folder for a later activity.
2. Write a story idea based on the picture below. Then write a scenario for the idea. Save the scenario in your writing folder for a later activity.

4
Drafting Narrative Writing

Your scenario can guide you as you write the first draft of your narrative. But you don't have to follow the scenario blindly. In fact, many writers feel that they don't really find out what they want to say until they begin to draft.

Create a Strong Beginning

As a reader, you know how important a good beginning is. If the beginning of a story is uninteresting or confusing, you might not read any further.

If you want people to read your story, get immediately into the action or events of the story. The passage below shows how Glenn drafted the beginning of his narrative.

I want to show the setting right away.

Loneliness was the worst part of ~~moving to~~ *settling in* a new *territory* ~~place,~~ *as he dangled his feet out of the wagon.* Kyle thought ∧ He missed his friends, he

missed the shopkeepers he had known, and he even

missed Jeremiah, who had thrown mud at him dur-

I should show a little about her character.

ing every rainstorm since they were kids. Now he glanced shyly at Julia ∧ *, who was laughing with her father* More than he had ever want- *in the next wagon.*

ed anything, Kyle wanted Julia for a friend. But she *older than he was,* was ∧ well-liked, clever, and confident. Why should

Reader should know that this is just friendship, not a love story.

she even look at him?

1. What information does Glenn give about his characters, setting, and plot?
2. How does this beginning catch your interest?

Develop the Setting

To make your narrative effective, you need to provide details that appeal to your readers' senses. Let your readers see, hear, smell, taste, and feel whatever you are describing. If you want to show bad weather at a lake, for example, describe the rolling black clouds, the whitecaps crashing against the dock, the cold spray stinging your character's face.

Below is a part of Glenn's first draft using sensory details.

heavily

Kyle dropped his pack to the ground and began

> I want to describe how the pack felt.

walking. Three steps into the woods, he tripped on

an exposed root. His hands landed in cold, wet mud.

> Use the sense of smell.

moldy, rotten-smelling

His pants were covered with ~~dirty~~ leaves. He sighed,

and wondered why he'd ever said he was an experi-

enced fire builder. Bits of pine cones and damp

> Put the most important detail at the end.

limped along the path   *ing*

wood chips littered the path. Kyle ~~got up and~~ looked

> I want to describe Kyle's actions.

~~around~~ for wood. Ten yards in front of him lay a

long, heavy branch. He wondered how to get the

branch through the narrow path back to the clearing.

1. Which of the five senses do Glenn's details appeal to?
2. What do the details tell you about Kyle's state of mind?

Show the Characters

To keep your readers interested in your story, you need to get them involved in your characters. Whenever possible, show your characters in action rather than telling about them. Instead of telling your audience that a character is happy, show your character jumping into the air and shouting. Instead of telling them that a character is shy, show how the character avoids being seen.

You can also use dialogue to show what kinds of people your characters are. Doctors talk differently than students, for example. Most people speak differently when they're happy than they do when they're angry. You can communicate the ages, personalities, and life styles of your characters through their speech. You might read your dialogue aloud to friends, in order to find out whether the characters sound the way you want them to sound.

Notice how Glenn used action and dialogue to show the characters in his first draft.

"What's the matter, Kyle?" Julia asked, looking at

him with concern.

Kyle considered confessing the truth, but just thinking
about it made him turn
pale.

I want to show how Kyle felt.

^"Nothing," mumbled Kyle.

"Maybe you're ill from being out in the cold,"

She felt Kyle's forehead and frowned.

Julia suggested. "Do you want me to ask my mother

I want to show Julia's concern.

for a remedy?"

"No. But thank you," Kyle sighed. Julia was

being so friendly, and all Kyle wanted was to get

Use more dialogue.

"I've got to go now, Julia," Kyle stuttered.
away. ^ *"I'll see you later."*

1. In which sentences did Glenn show rather than tell about Kyle's feelings? In which sentences did he show Julia's feelings?
2. When did dialogue help you understand Kyle better? When did dialogue help you picture Julia better?
3. What else could Glenn show about his characters?

Grammar in Action

Using a series of adjectives and adverbs is not the secret to good descriptive writing. In fact, adding too many adjectives and adverbs can sometimes bog down writing. Descriptive writing usually works best when it depends on clear, specific nouns and verbs.

Compare the descriptive effect of the two sentences in each pair below.

A 1. A **well-dressed** man **walked slowly** into the room.
    2. The man in the **tuxedo shuffled** into the room.

B 1. The **classic** car **moved slowly** in the parade.
    2. The **Model T Ford crawled** in the parade.

C 1. The **shy** boy **walked timidly** to the podium.
    2. The boy who **was always blushing crept** to the podium.

See pages 424 and 468 for additional information on nouns and verbs.

Writing Activities **Drafting**

A Write a strong beginning for one of the following situations. Make sure you introduce the setting, plot, and at least one character. Remember to *show* rather than tell.

1. A girl who must decide whether to have her old dog put to sleep
2. A popular boy who finds he must take sides between two groups of friends
3. A lonely woods that is suddenly invaded by the roar of a bulldozer

B Writing in Process Using one of the scenarios you developed in Activity B, page 190 and the suggestions in this lesson, draft your narrative. Then save your draft in your writing folder. You will work on it in a later activity.

5
Revising Narrative Writing

Revision is more than correcting misspellings and putting in commas. To revise, you have to take out things that don't work, rewrite other parts, put in some new ideas—perhaps even change the way the story ends. Revision turns your rough draft into an enjoyable story.

Here is the end of Glenn's revised draft.

Kyle was grateful that Julia was next to him as he

walked toward the campfire to explain to the others

"Thank you for coming with me", he said. "I know I have been an idiot."

why he shouldn't be called a hero anymore. ∧

> **I want to show Kyle's gratitude.**

"Don't worry," said Julia. "You'll be fine". ~~At least~~

"Julia, I don't want to go", he whispered.

~~it will be over with soon."~~ ¶ Kyle caught his breath, ∧

Julia replied.

> **Dialogue here would better show their feelings.**

is   *you are*

¶ This ~~was~~ no time to be timid. ∧ If ~~he was~~ going to tell

you must

the truth, ~~he wanted to~~ do it calmly and bravely."

¶ *Kyle gulped.*   *frowning and gravely*

~~Yet,~~ he kept imagining his father, being ~~very angry~~

reminding him of the danger he had caused.

~~with him.~~

> **I want to describe Kyle's feelings.**

1. What kinds of revisions has Glenn made?
2. How has Glenn changed the ending? Do you think the revised ending is better? Why or why not?

However good the draft of your narrative looks and sounds, chances are you can make it better. If you have the time, let the draft sit for a day or two. Then reread it. The time away from your narrative will help you see the draft less as a writer and more as a reader.

As a final step, you may want to read your narrative aloud to friends or give your story to someone to read. A person who reads or hears the story for the first time will have a fresh viewpoint. In the chart below are some questions you should ask yourself and others about your narrative as you work at revising and completing it.

Revision and Peer-Editing Checklist
1. Will the beginning catch the readers' interest and make them want to read on?
2. Are enough sensory details used so that readers have a vivid picture of the setting, characters, and events? Does the description use specific nouns and verbs?
3. Does the narrative *show* the characters in action rather than just *tell* about them?
4. Is dialogue used as effectively as it could be to carry the action and to reveal what types of people the characters are?
5. Are the events of the story complete? That is, will readers understand what the characters are doing and why they are doing it? Are the events believable? Is the ending satisfying?

Writing Activities *Revising a Narrative*

A Revise each of the following. Use the suggestions in parentheses as a guide.

1. This is a story about three friends on a treasure hunt in the Florida Keys. One of them finds a strangely shaped coin on the beach. (Begin the story by showing the characters in action.)
2. One of the friends wants to tell his parents about the coin. The other two want to hunt for more treasure first. (Use dialogue.)
3. The search involves danger, and the friends are frightened, but they do not give up. (Use an incident to show what

B **Writing in Process** Refer to the checklist above as you reread the first draft of your narrative. Then revise the draft, and save it in your writing folder.

6
Proofreading and Presenting

Proofreading

When you send your narrative out into the world, you want it to represent you at your best. So before your narrative is really finished, you need to find and correct any errors in spelling, punctuation, and grammar. Look especially closely at the dialogue. The words that each character speaks should be set off with quotation marks. You should also start a new paragraph for each change in speaker. See pages 639–641 for more about punctuating dialogue.

Here is how Glenn corrected a few mistakes in part of his narrative.

"Julia, I'm in trouble," murmured Kyle. He turned away, and looked out the cabin window. "What's troubling you? asked Julia.

"Julia, I didn't save your life," sighed Kyle. He paused for a moment to calm himself.

"Well, not ~~direckly~~ *directly*," Julia relied. "But if you hadn't known so much about fires and camping, everyone of us might have been caught up in that fire." A knot of frustration ~~cought~~ *caught* in Kyle's throat, "Julia, I *started* that fire! ~~he finally blurted out.~~

Publishing and Presenting

Once you have proofread your story, you can share it with an audience. You might want to read it to someone. You could give a copy to a classmate or a friend, or mail a copy to a relative who lives far away. Maybe your teacher would like to post several stories on the class bulletin board.

You and your classmates might even collect all your stories in a booklet and make copies to be shared.

Writing Activities *Proofreading and Presenting*

A Below is a passage of dialogue that needs to be proofread. Rewrite the passage, adding your own corrections of the spelling, punctuation, and grammar. Circle each correction.

> Vicki opened the book and pointed to a pitcher of an old coin.
>
> Wow! said Jerrod. That looks exactly like the coin we found on the beach!
>
> The book says its a sixteenth-century Spanish coin said Vicki. A gold coin, she added in a whisper.
>
> I bet more, said Carrie excitedly. A treasure ship probably sank during a storm or something like that.
>
> But it could have happened miles away said Jerrod. The current would of carried it to shore.
>
> I guess well just have to go on a treasure hunt, said Vicki.

B Writing in Process Carefully proofread your story. Make a neat, final copy. Then, with three or four classmates, brainstorm ideas for sharing your stories. Share your group's ideas with the ideas of other groups. Use the ideas to help you decide how you want to share your narrative.

Speaking and Listening

Did you ever get half a block from your home only to have your sister yell out the door to you? You can't hear her, but you can see her waving and putting her hand to her ear. The message comes through that you have a phone call, but how did you know? If you think about it, you'll find that you often communicate with your hands and face instead of words.

Artists who communicate without words are called *mimes*, and they perform *pantomimes*. Pantomimes can be performed alone or with a group. Mimes often paint their faces white, dress in black, and act out dramas on city sidewalks. They use expressions on their faces and gestures of their bodies to tell a story. These performers move very slowly and exaggerate every movement. Everything they do and every expression they make relate directly to the story being told—its setting, characters, and plot.

Activity

Congratulations! You've been hired by the city to perform pantomines for a special festival. Begin by practicing simple acts, such as eating different pieces of fruit, using the telephone, or crossing the street. Then, form a small group and create a short wordless story to perform together. Some examples are: auditioning for a part in a circus or band, helping friends move from an apartment on the third floor, or taking a group of five-year-olds to the zoo. Let the characters interact with one another to tell an active story. Make it interesting. Share it with the class.

Creative Writing

A Have you ever gone to a movie simply because you liked the ad poster displayed at the movie theater or the advertisements printed in the newspaper? The saying, "a picture is worth a thousand words," is very important to movie advertising. An ad picture can give you a quick feeling for the actors, style, action, and setting of a movie. Then, you are left to use your imagination to figure out what the movie might be about. If you like what your imagination comes up with, you might choose to see the movie. For now, select a picture ad for a movie that you have not seen. Using the picture as a starting point, imagine how the story might develop. Write out your version.

B Sometimes, a dream can be so vivid and startling that it wakes you up right away. Most of us have had dreams like this. They are so real they jolt us from sleep. Usually, we awaken at some dramatic or critical moment, and when we return to sleep the moment has passed. Most of the time, these dreams are never whole stories. Instead, they are bits and pieces of a story we sometimes remember and most often forget. Try to remember parts of a dream you recently had. Use what you remember to construct the entire story. Write the story.

Application and Review

A Analyzing Narration Read the story excerpt below. Answer the questions that follow.

> When I was thirteen, I took on the job of breaking a pony for the Hagens up the road. They had sent to Colorado for this pony for their ten-year-old daughter; and after it came, nobody could do a thing with it. The pony cost a hundred and fifty dollars, and Mr. Hagen offered me a hundred to break it. That made a pretty expensive pony, it seemed to me, but I was glad of the chance to earn the money. There was a beautiful Mexican saddle at the Merc that I had my heart set on.

1. Who is the main character in this scene?
2. What do you know about the main character?
3. What problem does the author introduce?

B Using Time Order Put these events of the story in chronological order.

- Maggie, the young girl, saw the pony for the first time.
- Soon, she was able to ride the pony.
- Maggie took Grandma's advice and rewarded the pony when it was good.
- "Use love with your pony," Grandma advised.
- Maggie stayed at Grandma's until her arm healed.
- The pony ran toward Maggie and bit her arm.

C Using Dialogue Rewrite the paragraph below as dialogue.

> Maggie noticed that Mr. Hagen's daughter carried a whip. She advised the younger girl not to use the whip, not even to carry it. The girl ignored the advice. The whip had been a birthday present, and she insisted that she would use it if she felt like it. She mounted the pony and raised the whip. The pony bucked and threw her to the ground.

11
Expository Writing

HAWAII—The latest eruptions of the Kilauea volcano have provided scientists with new information on the causes and effects of volcanic action.

If you wanted to know more about volcanos, you could consult with a volcanologist or look for information in a book or a magazine. In each case, you would be learning from someone's explanation. That is why explanatory writing is so important—it is the means by which we share knowledge.

Chapter 11 will help you understand the process of explanatory writing. Then you will be able to clearly explain the things you know.

1
Three Kinds of Exposition

Exposition is writing that informs or explains. One kind of expository writing explains a **process,** such as how to cook spaghetti or how a video camera works. Another kind of expository writing explains **causes and effects.** A cause-and-effect explanation might tell what causes earthquakes, for example, or what effect the new coach has on your football team. A third kind of expository writing explains through **comparison and contrast.** For example, you might want to explain how a violin and a cello are alike and different.

Read and Think The coaches of the boys' and girls' basketball teams at your school have decided that both teams should start an aerobic exercise program. Here is their explanation of the process of doing a safe aerobic workout.

Writing Model   The first part of a safe exercise session is a five-minute warm-up. The warm-up increases the pulse rate and stretches the muscles. You begin with simple exercises like head rolls, shoulder lifts, and toe touches. Once you have begun to limber up, increase the pace of your warm-up by jogging in place or doing jumping jacks. The second part of a safe exercise session is a well-balanced workout that strengthens each part of your body. Beginners should do a three- or four-minute series of exercises for the arms, waist, abdominals, legs, and hips. The last part of a safe workout is a three-minute cool-down. The cool-down helps circulate blood to your heart while your muscles relax slowly. Breathe slowly and deeply while doing cool-down exercises.

Next the coaches explain the effects of exercise on a person's outlook on life. They found the following cause-and-effect explanation in a workout book.

Professional Model   Take self-image. . . . It's the discipline itself, the fact that one has set a challenge and has over-

come it by sticking regularly to the exercise program, that seems also to affect the self-image in
a positive way. People get a sense that they *can*
do what they set out to do, . . . and this gives a
sense of accomplishment and independence
many haven't felt so strongly in a long time.
—Dr. Kenneth H. Cooper

Finally, the coaches compare and contrast aerobic and anaerobic exercise.

Aerobic means "with oxygen." Aerobic exercise
is done at a pace that is easy enough for the
heart and lungs to supply all the oxygen your
body needs to continue the exercise. Any rhyth-
mic, repetitive activity that can be continued for
several minutes without huffing and puffing is
probably aerobic. For most people, jogging,
swimming, and bicycling are aerobic. In *anaerobic* exercise, on the other hand, your body uses
oxygen faster than your heart and lungs can supply it. Usually all-out anaerobic exercise can be
performed for one minute or less. For example,
running as fast as possible is anaerobic.

Think and Discuss Think about these questions. Discuss your
answers with your classmates.

1. What specific examples of warm-up exercises are given in the
   process paragraph? Why is it important that these examples
   are given in the correct order?
2. According to the cause-and-effect paragraph, how does
   exercise affect a person's mood?
3. How are the aerobic and anaerobic details arranged in the
   comparison paragraph?

Follow Up When you write to explain, you write to tell the
reader how something is done, what something is, or why something is so. In this chapter, you will learn how to describe a
process clearly, explain causes and effects, and explain through
comparison and contrast. Keep these features of explanatory
writing in mind as you read the literature selection on the next
two pages.

Exposition in Literature

"The Bloomer Outfit"
Jean McLeod

*I*n 1851, as Elizabeth Smith Miller traveled to visit her cousin, Elizabeth Cady Stanton, in Seneca Falls, New York, it is unlikely that she knew her trip would be making clothing history. Miller brought with her a new style of outfit she had bought in Europe. The costume so impressed Stanton, an advocate for women's rights, with its practicality and comfort, that she promptly made one for herself.

The outfit contrasted sharply with the fashion of the day. Instead of the waist-tight dress with long, heavy petticoats dragging along the ground collecting dust and mud, this new outfit consisted of a loose-fitting tunic and a skirt that ended just below the knees. And under the skirt, long, puffy pantaloons (trousers) gathered at the ankles.

"What incredible freedom I enjoyed!" Stanton wrote. "Like a captive set free from his ball and chain. . . ."

While in Seneca Falls, the cousins, wearing their new outfits, visited Amelia Bloomer, an advocate of dress reform. In the next issue of her feminist paper, *The Lily*, Bloomer mentioned briefly that she was trying out the new outfit. Within days, hundreds of women wrote letters to her asking for more information and patterns. Bloomer gladly supplied sewing instructions for what quickly became known as the "bloomer outfit." Although she gave full credit to Elizabeth Smith Miller for introducing the outfit, the name "bloomer" stuck.

Not everyone was enthusiastic about the new costume. Many men and women, boys and girls, heckled the "bloomer girls" wherever they went. . . . Newspaper editors ridiculed the outfit in much the same way they made fun of other ideas developing in the women's movement.

As opposition grew, many women felt that the outfit was drawing attention away from more important issues, especially those giving women the right to vote. Susan B. Anthony

Main idea introduced

Comparison

Chronological order

Transition

wrote, "The attention of the audience was fixed upon my clothes instead of my words."

Elizabeth Cady Stanton was one of the first to discard the outfit. Within three years of trying it on, she put it aside, and others soon followed. In a letter to Anthony, she said, "We put the dress on for greater freedom, but what is physical freedom compared to mental bondage? . . . It is not wise, Susan, to use up so much energy and feeling that way. You can put them to better use. I speak from my experience."

1850

1850

1872

1897

1916

Conclusion   While the bloomer outfit caused controversy, it helped bring about significant changes in women's clothing. Although the outfit may not have been accepted, women discovered that they had a right to decide what they wanted to wear.

Trying Out Expository Writing Search through Starting Points (pages 41–53) or Ideas for Writing (655–656) to find an interesting expository topic. You can explain how something is done, what something is, or why something is so. After writing, think about the problems you encountered while writing. The rest of the chapter will help you to solve those problems.

2
Explaining a Process

When you explain a process, you will have one of two purposes in mind. Your purpose may be to help your reader make or do something by following your step-by-step instructions. On the other hand, it may be to help your reader understand how something works or how something is done. For instance, you might explain to a new member of your Bike Club how the gears on a ten-speed bicycle work.

Read and Think Here are some instructions that explain what to do if hikers become lost.

Professional Model If lost, what then? . . . First, as soon as you are confused, *stop;* don't plunge onward, getting more thoroughly lost. Sit down, rest, and have a bite to eat. Think calmly. Do not let fear lead to panic. If two or more persons are lost together, discuss the situation—and do not henceforth get separated. The annals abound in incidents where every member of a party was found except the one who went for help.

Second, mark the location. Chances are the trail is not far away. Conduct short sorties in all directions, returning to the marked spot if unsuccessful. Third, shout—and listen for answering shouts . . . . Friends or strangers may answer, their shouts guiding the way back to the trail. Fourth, prepare for the night well in advance. Conserve strength for the dark, cold hours. . . . Build a fire if possible, not only for warmth but because searchers may see the flames or smoke.

The hiker lacking considerable experience in cross-country navigation should, if first efforts fail, concentrate not on finding the way but on letting rescuers *find him or her.* Above all, this means staying in one place.

From *Backpacking: One Step at a Time* by Harvey Manning

Think and Discuss Think about these questions. Discuss your answers with your classmates.

1. List in order the five major instructions the writer gives to a lost hiker. Why are the instructions in that order?
2. What transitions are used to introduce each new instruction?

Read and Think Here is a science report that Tyrone wrote explaining how a bat uses sound waves to "see" in the dark. Notice the steps in the process he describes.

Student Model

A bat does not have good eyesight. Instead, it uses sound to find its way in the dark and to hunt for food. The process is similar to sonar that is used on ships to find the depth of anything beneath them. The bat produces a series of high-pitched squeaks from its mouth or nose. These squeaks cannot be heard by people. The squeaks bounce off objects such as trees, buildings, or flying insects. Then the bat's sensitive ears pick up the returning echoes. From the direction, loudness, and pitch of the echoes, the bat can determine where things are. It can even determine the direction, distance, and speed of a flying insect. This helps the bat catch its dinner.

Think and Discuss Carefully reread the paragraph. Then discuss the following questions with your classmates.

1. Can you list the three steps in the process the writer explains?
2. How are the details in the explanation arranged?

Follow Up These two examples of explaining a process had different goals. In the first, the writer wanted lost hikers to follow step-by-step instructions. In the second, the writer wanted the reader to understand an interesting natural process. However, each writer used specific details and a logical order to describe the process being explained. In the section that follows, you will learn to plan, write, and revise an explanation of a process.

Prewriting: Explaining a Process

Like the writers in the two previous selections, you will often find yourself in a situation where you have to explain a process. You may need to explain something you have done many times. For example, you might write directions for your younger sister who has borrowed your bicycle on what to do in case of a flat tire. She might also be curious about how the gears work. Either would be a good topic for a process explanation.

Gather Information When you are explaining a process, begin by writing down what you already know about the process. Next, read books or articles to build on what you know. Then analyze the process by looking at its various stages or steps (see Chapter 2, page 26).

For example, Janet is writing an article for her Craft Club magazine on how to make a miniature cactus garden. Since she has already made a cactus garden, she begins by listing the steps she used. She adds information from a book on house plants, which she found in the library.

Organize the Information Once Janet has her information together, she must organize her explanation logically. Following are some useful steps that can help Janet organize her explanation:

1. Tell why the process is important, useful, or worth understanding.
2. Tell what supplies or equipment are needed, or what parts are involved.
3. Explain the steps of the process in chronological order—the order in which they should or did happen.
4. Tell what the results of the process are.

Drafting: Explaining a Process

There are a number of ways to draft your process explanation. The following steps provide one method you might try.

Introduce the Subject After Janet organizes her information, she needs to think of a good way to introduce her explanation.

Remember that a good introduction identifies the subject and catches (and holds) the reader's interest. Here is the opening paragraph of Janet's explanation of how to make a miniature cactus garden.

Student Model

A miniature cactus garden is just the thing to bring the beauty of the desert into your house. A shallow container, a few stones for rocks and outcrops, and a selection of cacti and succulents can cheer up any windowsill.

Notice that the first thing Janet does is introduce her subject in an interesting way. She also tells what equipment or parts are needed for the process and explains why the process is useful.

Help the Reader As you explain the steps of the process, use carefully selected details. Try to anticipate questions people might ask, and then answer them. Since Janet thinks her readers might not know about plant types and names, she describes each plant she mentions, defines the word *succulents,* and gives useful background information.

Student Model

To make your garden interesting, use cacti and succulents with different shapes. For instance, include a round cactus such as a rose pincushion and a column-shaped cactus such as an apple cactus. Succulents, water storing plants not of the cactus family, add more interest. You might choose the spiky aloe or the trailing sedum. The same plant is often sold under different names, so buy plants by shape rather than by name.

Use Transitions Transitions such as *first, next, as soon as, then, later, after,* and *finally* are especially useful in a process explanation since they indicate chronological order. Notice the transitions Janet uses in this paragraph.

Student Model

To prepare the container, put in some gravel. *Then* cover the gravel with potting soil. *Next,* position some shapely stones. Use a stick to tamp down the mix *as* you plant. *Finally,* create paths with small gravel chips.

Write a Conclusion An effective conclusion for a process explanation tells what has been produced or what value the process has. Here is how Janet ends her composition.

Student Model

Your cactus garden makes a lovely centerpiece or room decoration. Since cacti and succulents thrive in shallow containers, your garden will stay beautiful for years.

Revising: Explaining a Process

Answering these questions can help guide your revision.

Revision and Peer-Editing Checklist

1. Is the subject introduced in an interesting way? Is the usefulness of the process explained?
2. Are the steps explained in chronological order? Are transitions used to organize the writing?
3. Is there an explanation of necessary preparations, equipment, or parts?
4. Do the details help the reader understand the process?
5. Are all special terms clearly defined?
6. Are the results explained?
7. Is there an effective conclusion?

Grammar in Action

This, that, and *which* are often vague when they refer to a whole idea rather than to a specific noun. To make the reference clear, add a specific noun. Look at the following example from a process explanation.

Vague: Smoke breaks a beam of light in your smoke detector.
   That triggers an alarm.
Clear: Smoke breaks a beam of light in your smoke detector.
   That broken beam triggers an alarm.

For additional information see pages 444 and 445.

Writing Activities Explaining a Process

A Mike is planning to write a paper explaining how to train a dog to heel on command. Which questions from the following list do you think Mike should answer? Add three questions of your own to the list.

   Why should a dog heel?
   What kind of dog is easiest to train?
   What does the word *heel* mean?
   How long should it take before a dog
      learns to heel?

B Writing in Process Think of a process you can explain. If you need help in choosing a topic, you might look through *Starting Points: Ideas for Writing* (pages 41–53). Begin by developing a subject that you might need to explain to someone. Write down what you already know about the process. Do some reading to gather additional information. Organize your information. You may want to use one of the graphic organizers described on pages 657-658. Then write the explanation. Begin with an effective introduction. Use important details and smooth transitions to help the reader follow your explanation. Be sure your conclusion explains the significance of the explanation. Finally, reread your explanation and revise it according to the checklist on page 212.

3
Explaining Causes and Effects

When you explain causes and effects, your purpose is to help your reader understand the connection between an event and its causes or between an event and its effects. For instance, you might write a report for history class explaining the causes of the American Revolution. A question on a home economics test might ask you to explain how wearing a red sweater affects a person's mood.

Read and Think   This selection by a professional writer explains some of the effects of a new invention, the automobile, during the early years of the 1900's.

Professional Model   Model T was the car that revolutionized American life. The farmer now had a vehicle that he could use for pleasure, with a pickup truck attachment to carry crops to market or, with rear wheel jacked up and a homemade attachment, he could saw wood, fill the silo, and do everything (it was said) but wash the dishes. The skilled worker in town or city could live miles from his job and drive his family into the country after supper or on Sundays. The automobile, in connection with gasoline-driven agricultural machinery, emancipated the western wheat farmer from his land. Without animals to feed, he could shut up house as soon as the crop was harvested and roll to California or Florida for the winter.

From *American Heritage* by Samuel Eliot Morison

Think and Discuss   Read the following questions. Think about how to answer them. Discuss the ideas with your classmates.

1. According to Morison's topic sentence, what is the cause in his explanation? What is the major effect?
2. What other effects of the automobile are explained?
3. What are some modern-day effects of the automobile that the writer does not mention?

Read and Think   Matt was giving a speech at a meeting of his Science Fiction Fan Club. His subject was the causes or reasons for the continuing popularity of *Star Trek* movies and TV reruns. Here is part of his talk.

Student Model

What has caused *Star Trek*'s continuing popularity? For one thing, it shows a world of limitless technological achievement. Thanks to faster-than-light travel, men and women can literally reach the stars, while starships equipped with food synthesizers and sonic showers make them feel comfortably at home. For another thing, *Star Trek* gives us a cast of characters we have come to know and love. Courageous Captain Kirk, logical Mr. Spock, and emotional Dr. McCoy are both heroes and familiar friends. The most important cause of *Star Trek*'s popularity, however, is that it shows us that we do have a future. *Star Trek* says that we can solve our problems, even end the threat of nuclear destruction.

Think and Discuss   After reading the following questions, discuss your answers with your classmates.

1. What three reasons does Matt give for the continuing popularity of *Star Trek?*
2. What specific examples of technological achievement does Matt mention? Why are these examples important?
3. What transitions does Matt use in this paragraph?

Follow Up   The first example you read explained effects; it told you what happened next. The second explained causes; it told you why something happened. In the following section, you will learn to plan, organize, and write cause-and-effect explanations.

Prewriting: Explaining Causes and Effects

A subject is suitable for a cause-and-effect explanation if you find yourself thinking about one of these questions:

> What caused _____?
> What effect has _____ had?

For example, Gary is writing a report on personal computers. His first prewriting step is to state his subject as a question: What effect have personal computers had on our daily lives?

Gather and Organize Information Your next step is gathering information about your subject by thinking about what you know, by reading books and magazine articles, and by interviewing people who know about the topic. (Review Chapter 2, page 30, for additional hints on how to gather information.) Keeping your main idea in mind will help you decide what information is important. Also, you need to set up your notes in a manner that will help you show causes and effects. For example, you might write *C* in the corner of each note card that lists a cause and *E* on each card with an effect.

Here are some facts and examples that Gary gathered for his report about the effects of personal computers. The numbers show the order in which Gary has decided to present his ideas.

(4) Computers help people pay bills, figure their taxes, plan their budgets, and balance their checkbooks.

(1) Computer games for adults and children turn computers into home entertainment centers.

(3) At work, personal computers help people write letters and reports and keep track of appointments and messages.

(2) At school, computers help students practice reading and math, find books in the library, and study for tests.

Here are three methods for organizing the details in a cause-and-effect explanation.

1. Use **chronological order.** Start from the beginning.
2. Use **order of importance.** Start with the most important or least important cause or effect.

3. Use **familiar to unfamiliar order.** Start with the cause or effect that is most well known. Look again at the order of Gary's ideas. Notice that he has chosen this method of organization.

Drafting: Explaining Causes and Effects

Like a process explanation, a cause-and-effect explanation needs an interesting introduction, a body of informative details, and a conclusion that ties the argument together.

Write an Introduction The opening sentences of a cause-and-effect composition should state the cause-and-effect relationship to be explained. The introduction can also indicate what kind of examples you plan to present.

Student Model

Personal computers are changing the way people live. Someday, they will be as commonplace and as essential to our daily lives as the car and the telephone. Already computers affect the way people play, learn, work, and manage money.

Develop Examples Fully As you write the main part of a cause-and-effect composition, use well-chosen, specific examples to develop each cause or effect fully. For example, Gary will mention several computer games to show the entertainment value of personal computers.

Write a Conclusion An effective conclusion for a cause-and-effect composition restates the main idea and summarizes the information you have presented. It may also draw a conclusion or make a prediction, as in Gary's conclusion.

Student Model

Personal computers have had wide-ranging effects on our society. We have seen examples of these effects and can now understand how personal computers have made many everyday tasks easier and more enjoyable. Someday, every home, every office, and every classroom may have its own computer.

Revising: Explaining Causes and Effects

Answering these questions can guide your revision.

Revision and Peer-Editing Checklist
1. Is the topic suitable for cause-and-effect explanation?
2. Is the introduction interesting and informative?
3. Are specific examples and details used to explain each cause and effect?
4. Is the organization logical and easy to follow?
5. Are transitions used to show cause-effect connections?
6. Does the conclusion restate the main idea and summarize the information presented in the paper?

Writing Activities Causes and Effects

A Beth is writing a paper that answers this question: What can we learn from traveling? Which examples from the following list do you think Beth should develop? Add three examples of your own to the list.

> A trip to Washington will teach you how government works.
>
> Last summer our family visited Niagara Falls.
>
> A canoe trip will show you how early explorers saw America.

B **Writing in Process** Write a cause-and-effect explanation on a subject that interests you. If you need help thinking of subject ideas, see Starting Points (pages 41–53) or Ideas for Writing in the Writer's Handbook (pages 655-656). Decide upon an idea that is appropriate for a cause-and-effect explanation. Gather information by reading and interviewing. Decide on the best way to organize your facts. Then begin to write. State your main ideas in the introduction, and develop them in the paragraphs that follow. Then write a conclusion that restates your main idea and summarizes the explanation. If possible, come to a decision about your topic and make some predictions. Finally, revise your explanation, using the checklist at the top of this page.

4
Explaining With Comparison and Contrast

We are always making comparisons. We compare television programs, athletic teams, and political candidates, for instance. When you make a comparison, you tell the important similarities and differences between two related things in order to make an important point about them.

Read and Think Holly wrote the following comparison of the redwood and giant Sequoia trees of California.

Student Model

The redwood and giant Sequoia trees are close relatives. Both are ancient kinds of trees. Most were swept away by the glaciers that also wiped out the dinosaurs. The few giant trees that remain grow in small clusters. The giant Sequoia grows only on the western slopes of the Sierra Nevada in central California. The coast redwood grows near the Pacific Ocean between Monterey and southern Oregon.

The redwood is the tallest living thing on earth, many growing to more than 300 feet. The Sequoia is the world's most massive tree; the largest are thirty to forty feet in diameter at the base and weigh more than 1,000 tons. The Sequoia's limbs are heavier and more angular than the redwood's. Though their appearance is different, both trees are majestic and beautiful.

Think and Discuss Think about your answers to these questions. Then discuss your answers in class.

1. What is the main idea of Holly's comparison?

2. Can you list the similarities between redwood and Sequoia trees? Can you list the differences?
3. How would you describe the difference between the first and second paragraphs of Holly's comparison?
4. Why do you think Holly's comparison includes many facts and statistics?

Read and Think Some comparisons make their point through humor. For example, here is a comparison of a hen and a brooder stove by a professional writer.

Literary Model

For mothering chicks, a stove has one real advantage over a hen: it stays in one place and you always know where it is. Right there its advantage ceases. In all other respects a hen is ahead of any stove that was ever built. A hen's thermostat is always in perfect order, and her warmth has a curious indefinable quality of sociability, which I believe means a lot to a chick . . . . A hen, moreover, is draft proof. When she gathers her little charges under her feathers, floor drafts are eliminated. A hen has a larger vocabulary than a stove and can communicate ideas more readily— which is desirable even though some of a hen's ideas are flighty and many of her suspicions unfounded. And of course a hen is a good provider and does a lot of spade work which the ordinary stove of today is incapable of. She doesn't have to be shaken down, and red-hot coals never roll out of her on to the dry floor.

From *One Man's Meat* by E. B. White

Think and Discuss Carefully reread the paragraph. Then discuss your answers to the following questions in class.

1. What advantages does a hen have, according to the paragraph?
2. What disadvantages does a hen have, according to the paragraph?
3. Does the writer intend these advantages and disadvantages to be taken seriously? How can you tell?
4. What serious point is the writer trying to make by this comparison?

Follow Up   In these examples, you have seen that comparisons do more than just tell how two related things are alike or different. They also say something important about the things being compared. In the following section, you will learn how to organize a comparison clearly.

Prewriting: Comparison and Contrast

Writing to compare and contrast is a skill you will use often. You might write a sports article, for example, comparing and contrasting your school's football team with its latest opponents. You may put together an explanation comparing and contrasting two television sets to help your family decide which one to buy.

Find the Main Idea   A comparison explains how two related things are alike or different in order to make an important point about them. For instance, the main idea of a comparison between real detectives and movie detectives might be that movies make their routine job seem glamorous and exciting.

Daniel is writing a comparison article for the sports page of his school paper. He is comparing football and baseball. His main idea is that football is more enjoyable on TV, while baseball is more enjoyable when seen in person.

Choose Relevant Features   When you gather information for a comparison paper, keep your main idea in mind. It will help you decide which features are relevant. A feature is a significant point of comparison between two things. Relevant features are ones that help develop the main idea. For example, in a composition that compares New York and Los Angeles as vacation spots, the relevant features might be these: the climate, the hotels and restaurants, the transportation system, the museums, and major entertainment attractions.

Daniel thinks about what he knows about football and baseball for his comparison. He lists the features that seem relevant to his main idea: the speed of the game, the importance of close-ups, the importance of replays, the effects of weather, and the importance of the play-by-play commentator.

Daniel makes the following comparison chart to organize the details. A chart like this might help you plan, organize, and write your own comparison.

Features	Football	Baseball
Speed of the game	Fast-paced action, hard to follow	Slow, suspenseful, easy to follow
Importance of close-ups	Very important, as helmets hide faces	Less important, as players easy to see
Importance of replays	So important they are now official	Less important, as few plays are close
Weather conditions	Played in cold, rain, snow	Warm weather, postponed by rain
Number of players on field	eleven	nine
Importance of commentator	Very important, as formations and plays are complex	Less important, as rules are more familiar

> Maybe I shouldn't include these facts in my explanation. They don't relate to my main idea.

Organize the Comparison One method of organizing a comparison is a subject-by-subject comparison. You discuss all the details about one subject and then discuss all the details about the other. The other method is a feature-by-feature comparison. You compare the weather conditions of football and baseball, and then compare the importance of replays in each sport.

Daniel decides to write a feature-by-feature comparison. His article will have five sections: an introduction; a paragraph comparing the speed of each game; a paragraph comparing the importance of close-ups, replays, and commentary; a paragraph comparing weather conditions; and a conclusion.

Drafting: Comparison and Contrast

In this chapter you have learned to write explanations with effective introductions, well-developed ideas, and convincing conclusions. These skills can also be applied when you write to compare and contrast.

Write the Introduction The opening sentences of a comparison introduce the two subjects to be compared. They also state the main idea. Following are Daniel's opening sentences.

Sports and television are closely linked. Seventy thousand fans might attend a Monday night football game, but millions watch at home on TV. However, some sports are more enjoyable on television than others. Football, for example, is well suited to TV coverage, but baseball is more fun in person.

Use Transitions Transition words and phrases are important in comparisons. They tell the reader whether similarities or differences are being discussed. Some useful words to show similarities are *similarly, likewise, also, in the same way,* and *too.* Some words that show differences are *but, by contrast, on the other hand, unlike,* and *however.* Notice the transitions Daniel uses in the following paragraph.

Watching a football game on TV is a great way to spend a snowy Sunday in December. *Unlike* the fan in the stadium freezing in parka, ski cap, and three pairs of socks, the TV fan is warm and comfortable. On a sunny Sunday in July, *on the other hand,* the best place to be is the bleachers. Who would want to be indoors when it's possible to watch a baseball game and get a suntan at the same time?

Write the Conclusion The last sentences of a comparison restate the main idea and draw a conclusion. Here is part of Daniel's conclusion.

Next time you tune in a football game on TV or head for a box seat at the baseball park, you can be sure you will be enjoying either sport in the best possible way.

Grammar in Action

The comparative form of words will help you write comparisons of two things. The comparative form adds *-r* or *-er* to the word or uses the word *more*.

> Baseball is a *slower* game than football.
> Football is *more* complex.

When you are comparing more than two things, you need the superlative form. The superlative adds *-st* or *-est* or uses the word *most*.

> Golf is the *slowest* sport of all.
> Baseball is the *most* suspenseful game among all
> team sports.

For additional information on the use and forms of comparative words, see pages 516–519 and 520–521.

Revising: Comparison and Contrast

After you have drafted your comparison, you or a peer editor should use the following questions to evaluate your paper. Though a peer editor's comments may serve as a guide for revision, remember that you need to make the final decisions about what needs to be changed.

Revision and Peer-Editing Checklist

1. Is the subject introduced in an interesting way?
2. Is the main idea clearly expressed?
3. Are relevant features compared? Have any important features been ignored?
4. Is the plan of organization logical and easy to follow? Does the paper follow a feature-by-feature or subject-by-subject organization?
5. Are appropriate transition words and phrases used to connect related ideas?
6. Is the conslusion effective?

Writing Activities *Comparison and Contrast*

A   Erin is planning a comparison of big schools (1,000 students or more) and small schools (300 students or less). Her main idea is that big schools have many advantages. Here is the comparison chart she is making. Which features on the chart are relevant to her main idea? Add three features of your own to the chart.

Features	Small Schools	Big Schools
Library	Small collection, limited resources	Large collection, many resources
Building	Few classrooms	Many classrooms
Friends	Everyone knows everyone	You can choose your friends
Teaching	More personal, more teachers	Less personal, large classes
Sports	Less resources, harder to put together good teams, easier to get on a team	More resources, more good athletes, harder to get on a team

B   Review the features on the chart above and the three features you have added. Then use the chart to write your own comparison of big and small schools. Decide your main idea first. Then look over the material and decide which comparison approach is better: subject-by-subject or feature-by-feature.

C   **Writing in Process**   Write a comparison on a subject that interests you. If you need help choosing a topic, see Starting Points (pages 41–53) or Ideas for Writing (pages 655–656). Decide upon a subject with at least two main objects or ideas that are suitable for comparison. Decide whether to use subject-by-subject or feature-by-feature organization. Write an effective introduction. Write a clear explanation with transitions to help the reader follow your points. Write a conclusion that restates the main idea and comes to a decision about the comparison. Finally, revise your explanation, using the guidelines on page 224.

English and Health

You never know when you will be called upon to give first aid. You might be in a restaurant, for example, when one of the people you are dining with gets a piece of food caught in his throat and begins to choke. If you have learned the Heimlich maneuver, you could come to the rescue.

The Heimlich maneuver involves standing behind the victim and placing your arms around his or her waist. You make a fist and place it so that your thumb is against the victim, slightly above his or her navel and below the ribcage. Grab your fist with your other hand and use a quick motion to push your fist into the victim's abdomen with an upward thrust. The motion will force air out of the victim's lungs and blow the object from his or her windpipe.

Four quick back blows   Four quick upward thrusts

Activity

Learning a skill such as the Heimlich maneuver requires studying a clear, step-by-step explanation of the process. You have learned in this chapter about writing to explain a process. Research how you would give first aid for a medical emergency, such as shock, frostbite, or artificial respiration. Write a brief report that clearly and completely explains how the first aid skill is practiced.

Application and Review

A Understanding the Explanation of a Process Read the following list of steps explaining how to measure your heart rate before and then after exercise. Arrange the steps in a logical order, then include them in a paragraph using transitions.

- Run in place for two minutes.
- Find your resting pulse rate by placing two fingers on your neck just below your jaw.
- Start by relaxing for several minutes.
- Multiply the beats by two to get your resting pulse.
- Count the pulse beats you feel for thirty seconds.
- Count your pulse beats again to measure your heart rate after exercise.
- Compare the two rates.

B Recognizing Cause and Effect Read the statements below on city traffic problems. Identify which ones are the causes of the problem and which ones are the effects.

1. It takes fifteen minutes to drive three blocks.
2. There are too many one-passenger cars.
3. The bus and subway system is not well-advertised.
4. Many people are late to work every day.
5. Listening to radio traffic reports, drivers avoid some streets.
6. The highways were originally built for fewer cars.

C Identifying Types of Explanation Read the topic sentences below. Tell which type of explanation each one represents: process, cause and effect, or comparison/contrast.

1. Dentists recommend that their patients follow specific cleaning procedures after every meal.
2. On our shopping trip, we discovered that the most popular brands of basketball shoes differed a great deal in quality.
3. A series of conflicts over taxes led the American colonists to break their ties with England.

12
Persuasive Writing

Dear Senator:
   If you really care about the people in your district, you'll do something about the terrible pollution problem caused by the factories . . .

   This student is trying to convince the senator to clean up a spillover.
   Perhaps you, too, have issues that you feel strongly about and opinions that you want others to accept. How successful you are depends on how well you understand the techniques of persuasion.
   Chapter 12 is an opportunity for you to understand what is involved in writing to persuade. Use this knowledge to write convincingly about the things that matter to you.

1
Analyzing Persuasive Writing

You ask that your allowance be increased, listing for your parents the reasons why you deserve more money. You write an article for the school newspaper warning of the health hazards of smoking. You write to your aunt and uncle to ask them if you can go with them on their trip next spring to Paris. In each instance you are writing to persuade. You have definite opinions, and you hope to persuade others to accept them.

Read and Think Gregory wrote the following letter to the city council after seeing the mayor interviewed on television.

Student Model

Dear Council Members:

Mayor Emmanuel wants the city to sell the vacant Pickering School to industry. I can think of a better use for the school. How about turning it into a teen center?

A teen center would give kids like me a place to go for good, clean fun. One room could be used for recreation, such as table tennis and TV. Another room could be for quiet reading. Arts and crafts could be taught and dancing to records or a band could be allowed on Friday nights.

A center would keep teens busy in a safe, well-supervised program. It would cut down on vandalism. Unlike an industry, it would cause no parking problems, noise, or air pollution.

A center will not mean lost jobs. For every person not hired by business, someone will be needed at the center to supervise or teach. Lost tax dollars will be recovered through rents and admission fees.

Please consider opening Pickering as a teen center. Teens, adults, and the city will all benefit.

Sincerely,
Gregory Holt

Think and Discuss Discuss these questions with your classmates.

1. Gregory writes that a teen center would be a better use for the vacant school than would industry. Is this statement a fact or an opinion?
2. What arguments does Gregory use to support his opinion and persuade the council to adopt his plan?

Read and Think Now read the following opinion by Jack Mc-Garvey. In a computer magazine article, McGarvey complains that classes in cursive (handwriting) always gave him "a wretched time." Only when he learned to type and use a computer keyboard could he really express himself. Cursive, he says, is not as important, as fast, or as attractive as some people claim. Instead, he recommends that young students have the choice of taking a typing class.

Student Model   Good typists are probably more efficient students. And we all know, of course, that efficient students usually earn higher grades than non-efficient ones. Isn't it time, then, to take a hard look at why cursive—rather than typing—is a mandatory part of the curriculum? Besides, word processing technology is speeding ahead at such a rapid rate that right now we may be living in the last days of the pencil-and-paper age. The booting out of cursive and the booting up of computers to teach typing is a timely approach—and a good way to welcome in a new era.

Think and Discuss Read and discuss the following questions.

1. What is McGarvey's opinion of the future of cursive writing?
2. What arguments does he use to support his opinion?
3. What does McGarvey say about good typists? Is this a fact or an opinion?

Follow Up Persuasive writing must express an opinion and then support that opinion. In this chapter you will learn how to persuade others. Your success will depend on how well you target your writing to your audience and how well you present and support your opinions. Remember these goals of persuasive writing as you read the literature selection on the next two pages.

Persuasion in Literature

"Violence—A Useless Direction"

Isaac Asimov

Humankind lived by violence for uncounted thousands of years before history began. There were long ages in which human beings had to (if they could) kill animals for food, sometimes large animals who resented the attempt and resisted.

There came a time when human beings won out over the animal kingdom once and for all. Thanks to humankind's possession of fire and of long-range missile weapons like the bow and arrow, no animal, not even the strongest and most deadly predator, could stand against the human onslaught.

That, however, didn't end the need for tales of violence, for, having run out of other species to pit brain and weapon against, human beings fought other human beings. The skill and emotional drive developed by human beings over long ages of pitting feeble strength against tusks, fangs, claws, horns, and overreaching power was now expended in a civil war to the death, one that has continued to this day.

Through most of history, when a city was taken its inhabitants were quite likely to be killed or enslaved. . . . Under such circumstances, it was important to fight to the death, since one was in any case going to die, or worse, if one lost. So the people, or, at the very least, the warrior class, were constantly fed tales of violence; of heroes who fought against overwhelming odds. . . .

Youngsters had to get used to violence, had to have their hearts and minds hardened to it. They had to be made to feel the glory of fighting against odds and how sweet it was to give one's life for one's tribe, or one's city, or one's nation, or one's king, or one's fatherland, or one's motherland, or one's faith.

Painting a Fortress for the Heart, 1981. Jim Dine.

Opinion
and call
for action

And now it's over! That old-time violence that's got us in its spell must stop! . . . We've got to be rid of violence for the simple reason that it serves no purpose anymore, but points us all in a useless direction. It would appear that human enemies are no longer the prime threat to world survival.

Evidence to
support
opinion

The new enemies we have today—overpopulation, famine, pollution, scarcity—cannot be fought by violence. There is no way to crush those enemies, or slash them, or blast them.

If they are to be defeated at all in their present incarnation, which threatens the whole world and all of humankind, rather than merely this tribe or that region, it must be by human cooperation and global determination. It is that which we had better start practicing. It is with tales of brotherhood and cooperation that we had better propagandize our children.

If we choose not to, and if we continue to amuse ourselves with violence just because that worked for thousands of years, then the enemies that can't be conquered by violence will conquer us—and it will be all over.

Trying Out Persuasive Writing Isaac Asimov felt strongly that our attitude toward violence must change. Think about something that you would like to change. Write a paragraph that explains your opinion. Support your position with facts and reasons.

2
Prewriting: Persuasion

Before you begin your persuasive writing, you must follow five prewriting steps. First, choose an issue. An **issue** is a topic about which people have strong opinions. Second, gather information to support **your opinion** and take notes on your findings. Third, determine your **audience,** the people who will read your writing. Fourth, decide what **form** your writing will take. Finally, **organize your notes** for the best presentation.

Choosing an Issue

Sometimes you will write a persuasive article in response to a situation that troubles or interests you. At other times, however, you will need to search for an issue. By using the gleaning and reflecting skills you learned in Chapter 2, you can think of ideas for a persuasive paper. Are there problems in your school, neighborhood, town, or city that you feel strongly about? What ideas can you think of to improve your county, state, or country? Quickly list as many issues as you can. Then use the following guidelines to choose the one you will write about.

1. The issue should be one on which people disagree.
2. You should be interested in the issue.
3. You should care how other people feel or act about the issue.
4. You should either know about the issue already or be able to find out about it.

Amy chose as her issue: "Should 'street performers' such as musicians, mimes, jugglers, and magicians be allowed on our city streets?" She knew that people, especially businesspeople and homeowners, held different ideas about the issue because she had heard them express their opinions on the radio and television. She had a definite opinion on the question, and she hoped that others would agree with her. She already knew something about the issue and was sure that she could find more information.

Supporting Your Opinion

Use the gleaning techniques you learned in Chapter 2 to gather information about the issue you selected. Talk to your family, friends, and neighbors about the issue. Ask what they think about it and what they like or dislike about it. Read what others have written about the issue in books, magazines, or newspapers. As you read and talk about the issue, take notes. Include facts, examples, and reasons. Enclose the exact words of speakers in quotation marks when they say something you may want to use unchanged in your writing.

Review your notes. Do you still have the same opinion you had before gathering information? Your research may have changed your opinion slightly; you may now see a better solution to the problem, a different angle to talk about. Your research may have changed your opinion completely; you may now wish to argue from the other side of the issue. State in writing the belief you now have and can support with sound arguments. Your statement will be the main idea of your persuasive writing.

Your writing will persuade only if your opinion is supported with logic and evidence. Study the notes you took. Can you find good reasons, facts, examples, and quotations from experts to prove your point? If not, keep digging. Read more, talk more, and take more notes.

Determining Your Audience and Form

Now determine who your audience will be. Use the following questions to analyze your readers and to help you decide what you must do to persuade them.

1. How much do your readers know about the issue? This will tell you how much background information you will need to provide.
2. Do your readers care about the issue? If they do, you will not have to arouse their interest. If they do not, you will have to think of ways to interest them.
3. Will your readers agree with your opinion? If they will, you need only supply arguments that strengthen their own feelings. If they will not, you need to put yourself in their place and offer arguments that will change their minds. If in doubt, assume that the readers will not agree with your opinion.

Amy decided her audience would include anyone who would be affected by street performers: shoppers, homeowners, store-keepers, young children, and students of junior-high and high-school age. Although many people would be interested, most of them would need background information related to the issue.

The next step in writing your own persuasive piece is to determine which form of writing—a letter, a report, a story, an article—will best get your message to your target audience. Amy decided to write a brief article for her school newspaper because she knew it was read by teens, their parents, and even some local businesspeople.

Organizing Your Prewriting Notes

Before you begin writing, you need a plan. Complete a questionnaire like the one that follows to help you plan. Then keep your plan in mind while you write.

Persuasion Questionnaire

1. *Issue:* What is the problem? What is the solution?
2. *Opinion:* How do I feel about the issue? What is the opposing view?
3. *Support:* What facts, examples, quotes, and other information can I use to support my opinion?
4. *Audience:* Who are my readers?
5. *Form:* How can I best reach my audience?
6. *Background:* How much is needed for these readers?
7. *Interest:* Will I have to get readers interested in the issue?
8. *Reasons:* Which reasons will persuade these readers?
9. *Order:* In what order should I present my arguments?

Amy's completed questionnaire looked like this:

1. *Issue:* Should city leaders allow "street entertainment?"
2. *Opinion:* I say yes. Other people think it is not a good idea.
3. *Support:* Use examples from other cities.
4. *Audience:* Junior-high students, parents, and local business-people.

5. *Form:* Article for my school newspaper.
6. *Background:* Many people will not have thought about this issue. I will have to provide background information.
7. *Interest:* Some people probably have an opinion, but others may not be interested. I need to persuade people to write to the city leaders to support my plan.
8. *Reasons:* Street entertainers give a city a special atmosphere. They also help stimulate business. Problems of noise and crowding can be solved by permits.
9. *Order:* Begin with the explanation about the special atmosphere because it is the broadest reason and the one most people can appreciate. Next, talk about the advantages to business. This will appeal to those who might be least likely to want the performers. Last, discuss the use of a permit system to curb noise and crowding. That should eliminate any other objections.

Writing Activities *Prewriting*

A Ben wants to convince the students to vote for Jessica Ming for class president. His notes include the following reasons:

1. She has experience in office. She was vice-president last year.
2. She served well when the class president was sick.
3. She is bright, gets high grades, and has good ideas.
4. She is a natural leader and is always chosen as a team captain.
5. Because students like her, they will work hard for her.

Ben can make a poster, write an article for the school paper, or write a flyer to be given to all students. Choose one form, then fill out a persuasion questionnaire for Ben's project.

B **Writing in Process** Look through *Starting Points: Ideas for Writing* (pages 41–53), glean from newspapers or other sources, or brainstorm for a persuasive writing issue. Research your issue, complete a persuasion questionnaire, and save your notes in a writing folder for later use.

3
Clear Thinking and Persuasion

Before you can begin writing your persuasive piece, you must be sure that your thoughts are clear and are organized logically. Clear thinking nearly always results in clear writing. Because you are starting with a strong opinion, and you hope to convince others to think or act as you do, it is easy to get carried away and to use wording that is unfair or arguments that are not logical.

Judgment Words

Judgment words express opinions and feelings instead of stating facts. Judgment words are often adjectives. Some examples are a *wonderful* solution, a *terrible* plan, an *outdated* idea.

Writing Inside Out

If you have a legal problem and no money for a lawyer, where do you go for help? Meet Nelson Brown. He is a lawyer and community organizer. He works in legal assistance, providing free legal services to low-income people in civil matters such as housing, public aid, and social security. Nelson writes persuasive letters and legal documents for his clients. He also takes government agencies to court in defense of people's rights.

Q. Why did you choose to work in legal assistance?
A. Well, I was very active in the civil rights movement and then in the anti-war movement. Coming out of those experiences, I acquired a strong desire to be involved in

A writer must tell what happened to make the solution *wonderful*, why the plan seemed *terrible*, or why the idea seemed *outdated*. Whenever you read or use judgment words like the following, be sure that there are facts to prove each opinion:

lazy	ambitious	rich	poor	clever
stupid	pretty	ugly	bad	good

Writing Activity *Judgment Words*

Find the judgment word in each of the following sentences.

1. The conditions at the animal shelter are bad.
2. It is essential for everyone to learn a foreign language.
3. Seventeen-year-olds are too immature to vote in elections.
4. Students have been blasting their radios during recess.
5. The Student Council made a ridiculous decision when it cancelled Spirit Week.
6. My brother is too irresponsible to carry a house key.

efforts and struggles for social justice. This seemed to be the kind of law in which I could act consistently with my social values.

Q. What happens when you take a typical case to court?

A. We file a complaint. The state is required to file an answer. Then I have to prepare a brief to argue why the agency made an improper decision. A brief is simply a written argument where I try to persuade the judge the agency messed up. Once I've stated the facts in a logical fashion, then I apply the law to those facts. That involves trying to organize your thoughts so that you state them in as clear and organized a manner as possible.

Q. When you have trouble writing a brief, what do you do?

A. If I'm having trouble thinking it out, if I've got some fragments of the thought, but I don't know how it all fits together, I just start writing and get part of it out. I always start out with an introduction because if I don't have anything else, at least that's a start. Then I try to summarize in a few sentences what my central idea is.

Connotations of Words

A word may have two kinds of meanings. The dictionary definition is its **denotative** meaning. Another type of word meaning is a word's **connotative** meaning. This is the meaning the reader attaches to the word because of the thoughts or feelings it creates.

When you are writing to persuade, always be aware of the subtle meanings your words may be carrying. Most people would rather be called *carefree* than *irresponsible,* or *assertive* rather than *pushy*. *Carefree* and *assertive* have positive connotations; *irresponsible* and *pushy* are negative.

Slanting Writing that uses only facts is **objective**; it does not lean one way or the other. Writing that uses judgment words and connotation to influence the reader is **subjective**. It is called **slanted** writing because it leans toward one side of an issue.

Because persuasive writing calls for you to make the reader believe that your opinion is correct, it will always be somewhat slanted. However, it should also be fair. Given a choice of two words that mean the same thing, you should feel free to choose the word that carries the connotation you want the reader to receive. On the other hand, you should avoid judgment words that cannot be proved by facts, examples, or expert opinion.

Writing Activities Connotation

A In each sentence, find the word or words with a positive or negative connotation. On your paper rewrite the sentence using a neutral word or words.

1. Mayor Adams begged for support in his campaign.
2. The TV newscaster bragged about the awards he had won.
3. Many students at our school are computer illiterates.
4. With Paul as our center, we can slaughter Ridge School.

B Find every example of slanting in the following report. Explain how each example tries to influence the reader. Then rewrite the report so that it has a more objective, factual tone.

> Striking school bus drivers hit the school commit-
> tee with their demands today. First, they want the

committee to waste your tax dollars on twelve luxurious new buses. Second, the drivers are demanding an enormous increase in their plushy retirement benefits. For four long days now, they have halted education in this community.

Generalizing

When you observe something happen over and over, you may begin to see a pattern. Finding such a pattern is called **generalizing**. The pattern itself is a **generalization**. For example, suppose that you notice more and more small cars on the road each year. You might make the following generalization: a lot of people own small cars these days. This conclusion would be a fair and logical statement.

If, however, you said, "Everyone owns a small car these days," you would be guilty of making an overgeneralization. An **overgeneralization** is a statement that is too broad—one that tries to cover all possible cases. The following list gives some words that make generalizations too broad:

always	never	nobody	all the time
everyone	every	everybody	no one

To make a generalization valid, or true, you must **qualify**, or limit, it. When you qualify a generalization, you tell how many cases it applies to. The following are some qualifying words:

sometimes	some	a few	frequently	many
rarely	most	often	infrequently	several

You can make your generalizations more persuasive if you give facts, examples, reasons, and expert opinions. Such evidence will help support a generalization.

Writing Activity *Qualifying Generalizations*

Rewrite each of these faulty, broad generalizations. Use qualifying words to make them more accurate.

1. Computers never make mistakes.
2. No one wants a tax increase.
3. A good education always leads to success.
4. Every new invention changes our lives.
5. She makes mistakes all the time.

4
Drafting

Your persuasion questionnaire is your writing plan. Use that plan and the following guidelines to help write your draft.

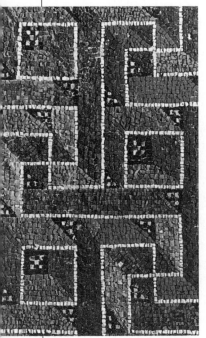

Detail of a
5th century mosaic.
Ravenna, Italy.

Begin effectively Your first sentence or two may be your most important ones. You must "hook" your readers quickly with an idea so interesting they will want to read on. Avoid the boring "I think . . ." opening. Readers won't care what you think, unless you show them what they will gain by reading on.

Present your material in an organized way Choose a plan that makes sense. You might start with your weakest argument and build to the strongest, or move from statements everyone will agree with to controversial statements, or give the opposing point of view and gradually show why it is not sound. Use transition words to move smoothly from point to point.

Provide support Support your opinions with sound reasoning. Use facts, examples, and quotations to prove your points. Do not slant your writing by using judgment words or connotation unfairly. Use generalizations that are not too broad and that are supported by facts.

Conclude effectively Summarize your arguments, restate your opinion, or end with a rewording of your opening sentence. Be sure your readers know how you would like them to feel or think about the issue and what actions you would like them to take.

Amy used her prewriting notes to develop the draft shown on the next page. Her thoughts as she worked are shown in the blue bubbles.

a few musicians and mimes from the local college

~~Some students~~ perform on our streets. They

have become the center of a controversy. Should

street performers be allowed or not?

⌗ How would you like to see a juggler on a

Perhaps you'd enjoy some free music in the midst

unicycle during your lunch period? Many cities *of a hectic day of shopping.*

now benefit from street entertainers, but our city

leaders have yet to decide how to handle the

problem.

Writing Activities Drafting

A You want to convince your principal to approve a class party. Write an effective opening and conclusion for your argument.

B Writing in Process Use the persuasion questionnaire you completed for Activity B on page 237 to help you draft a letter, article, or other form of persuasive writing. Save your draft.

Grammar in Action

Using one sentence pattern too often can make writing boring. Try to provide variety in your sentences by moving phrases and clauses to different positions (see pages 132-140).

When you think of it, stop to appreciate nature.
Stop, when you think of it, to appreciate nature.

Writing Activity How many ways can you write each sentence?

1. Check the labels before buying any product.
2. You should try always to be kind, since you value friendship.

5
Revising and Presenting

When revising your manuscript, ask for the opinion of a class-mate to serve as a peer editor. Have that person try to poke holes in your arguments. What needs improvement? Your peer editor can use the checklist below as a guide for readings.

Plan to read your draft yourself at least three times, checking for different things each time. In that way, you will be able to focus on a few details, and not miss errors that could get over-looked if you tried to check everything at the same time.

On the first reading, check your thinking. That is the most important part of your writing. On the second reading, check the overall content of the writing. Serious flaws in content will make an unconvincing presentation. On the third reading, look for errors of grammar, spelling, and punctuation. Use the following checklist as a guide for your first two readings.

Revision and Peer-Editing Checklist

Thinking

1. *Words:* Are judgment words or connotations fairly used?
2. *Generalizations:* Are they logical and not too broad? Is the reasoning explained?

Content

1. *Opening:* Is the issue stated clearly? Does the opening "hook" the reader?
2. *Body:* Does the draft make the subject interesting? Are the reasons convincing? Is there enough support? Is the writing appropriate for the audience? Will the reader understand the benefits of accepting the writer's ideas?
3. *Organization:* Are the reasons given in the best order? Are the transitions from paragraph to paragraph and sentence to sentence smooth? Are more transitions needed?
4. *Ending:* Are the main points summarized or restated? Will the reader know how the writer wants them to feel, think, or act?

Amy asked a friend to read her writing. Her friend carefully read Amy's work and then met with her to discuss it. Amy's friend politely offered specific, helpful comments, and she followed these guidelines.

1. Use a checklist, such as the one on p. 244, to guide your reading.
2. Draw attention to the positive first. Explain what you liked and why you liked it.
3. Turn negatives into positives. When you find a weak or confusing spot, make specific suggestions for improvement.

Amy used her friend's comments and the checklist on p. 244 to guide her revisions. She found that she was dissatisfied with her second paragraph, which she changed as follows.

Street performers give a city a special feeling.

I need an interesting topic sentence.

A friend recently visited New York City and *she* *emerged from a subway station* told of the excitement she felt as she heard a small *right where* jazz band *was* playing. My uncle tells me that downtown

I need to make my examples more persuasive.

surrounded by cheerful crowds. Boston is full of talented performers. He says that

I need colorful examples.

street performers also bring crowds to Cambridge. You *on summer evenings.* can see all kinds of acts there, *from acrobats to Peruvian flute players.*

When you have written the best piece of persuasive writing possible, proofread it once more and then share it with others. How successful was it in shaping opinion? Could it be improved?

Writing Activities *Peer Editing*

A Choose a peer-editing partner. Then exchange the persuasive writing that you drafted in the Activity on p. 243 with your partner and read each other's work. Use the guidelines on this page as a guide for responding to one another's drafts.

B **Writing in Process** Revise the draft that you evaluated in Activity A. Make revisions based on the comments of your peer editor, but keep in mind that you must make all final decisions.

Crossroads

English and Social Studies

When you see a commercial on television for blue jeans, soda pop, or portable radios, do you ever get the feeling that the actors are speaking directly to you? Are the people on screen near your age? Do they dress, act, and talk like you? If so, then most likely, you are the "target audience" for that commercial. Advertisers are trying to sell that product to people just like you.

Once they decide that you are the target for their product, how do advertisers persuade you to buy it? They start by doing some research about your experiences and buying habits. They might ask questions such as: What products do you need or want to buy? What products have you bought recently? What makes you buy a product? What television shows do you watch regularly?

Companies spend millions of dollars each year asking people questions like these. With this information, the advertisers create a commercial aimed at your needs, feelings, and wishes.

Activity

A company has asked for your help in creating a new product and making a commercial for people your age. Conduct your own research among a group of your friends. Ask questions like those above. Analyze their answers and then invent a product you think they would buy. Create a commercial to sell the product to your target audience. Perform the commercial for your class.

Application and Review

A **Supporting an Opinion** Read the opinion below and the statements that follow it. On your paper, write down all of the statements that can be used as evidence to support the opinion.

OPINION: To be healthy, people should switch to a high-carbohydrate, low-fat diet.

1. Potatoes, pasta, bread, and rice are carbohydrates.
2. Experts, including the American Heart Association and the American Cancer Society, have warned that Americans must change their eating habits to avoid the threats of both disease and early death.
3. Spaghetti tastes great with a light tomato sauce.
4. The average American consumes eight times the daily nutritional requirement of fat (1 tablespoon).
5. Carbohydrates are not fattening.
6. Studies have shown that too much fat in a diet can lead to heart disease and obesity.
7. My next-door neighbor says she feels better on this diet.
8. Jane Brody, a nutrition expert and journalist, writes that the human body is better-equipped to digest grains, nuts, beans, fruits and vegetables than meats and fats.
9. Most carbohydrates taste bland.

B **Writing Effective Openings** Based on the statements you selected as evidence above, write an effective introduction in support of the high-carbohydrate, low-fat diet plan.

C **Identifying Judgment Words** Find the judgment word or words in each of the following sentences.

1. *The Return of It* was an absolutely boring film.
2. During the city council meetings, the mayor blasted the sly tactics of the aldermen on the budget committee.
3. What a wild and preposterous tale the bumbling press agent told!
4. The soothing melodies of Brahms are preferable to the screeching songs of Mick Jagger.

13
Research and
Report Writing

The reporters rush to the scene of the extra alarm fire. Pencils and notebooks in hand, they interview the witnesses, survivors, and firefighters. Then they dash back to the newsroom to file their stories before deadline.

These reporters are using the same skills to gather, organize, and analyze information that you use when you prepare a report. In this chapter you will study the process that will help you prepare effective reports in school and throughout life.

1
Prewriting: Choosing and Limiting a Subject

You may be assigned reports in any of your subjects—science, English, social studies, math, art, or music. It is important that you know how to prepare these reports on your own. Your first step is to choose and limit a subject.

Begin by making a list of subjects that interest you and that you feel would be of interest to your readers. Next, make certain that these subjects do not involve you personally and can be developed from outside sources of information. Subjects such as Navajo sand painting, ocean farming, or termites would meet these requirements. If you find that *you* are the main source of information about the topic you have selected, then you should choose another topic.

Once you have found a general subject, you must then narrow it to an idea that can be developed within the specified length of the report. Which of these subjects do you think would make a good one- or two-page report?

1. The geography of Latin America
2. The first Apollo space flight
3. Our universe
4. Inventions

The second topic is the correct choice. It concerns one particular space flight. The topic is specific enough to be explained in a short, informative report. The first, third, and fourth subjects, however, are much too broad. They would have to be narrowed to be handled in a short report.

To limit a subject, first consider how much information is available on it and how long the report is that you are writing. Then narrow the subject accordingly. You may have to do a little preliminary reading on the subject to make this decision. Try looking at a general encyclopedia article. It will give you an idea of just how large your subject is and may also suggest possibilities for limiting the subject.

One way a writer could limit the broad subject "The Geography of Latin America" would be to concentrate on one particular country. The topic "The Geography of Mexico," for example, might be a good choice for a short composition.

Guidelines for Choosing a Report Topic
1. The subject should require information from outside sources.
2. The subject should be of interest to both you and your audience.
3. The subject should be narrow enough to be developed in a specified number of words, paragraphs, or pages.

Writing Activities *Choosing a Report Topic*

A The following topics are too general to be covered in a short report. Narrow each one so that it is suitable for a one- or two-page paper.

1. Bicycles	14. Exotic plants
2. Thomas Edison	15. Alaska
3. The Civil War	16. Endangered species
4. Pioneers	17. Space flight
5. The Mississippi River	18. American songwriters
6. Mars	19. The desert
7. Japan	20. Science fiction
8. Computers	21. Oceans
9. The Presidency	22. Sports
10. Painting	23. Movies of the 1980's
11. The FBI	24. Heroes
12. Dinosaurs	25. The planet Earth
13. The mail service	26. Language

B **Writing in Process** Turn to *Starting Points: Ideas for Writing* on pages 41-53. Look through the pages for ideas for your report. Add any new ideas to your list. Then choose a topic. Do some general reading on the subject. Narrow the topic to a size suitable for your report. Save your topic in your writing folder.

2
Prewriting: Planning Your Research

Depending on your topic, there may be a great deal of information for you to read, sort through, and record. To make this job easier, take some time to think through a few key points before you begin your research. These points will help you pinpoint the specific kind of information you should look for.

Identifying Your Purpose

The first thing you should consider is exactly what you want to accomplish with your report. In most cases, your purpose will simply be to **inform** your readers. For informative reports, look for facts and details that will provide your readers with the information they need to understand your subject. Listed below are topics for some reports whose purpose would be primarily to inform a reader:

> F.D.R.'s New Deal
> Why stars shine
> Hydroponic gardening

Another purpose of a report is to **compare** and **contrast** one thing with another. Listed below are some topics that have this purpose:

> Galesburg in 1800 and today
> Private schools and public schools
> The Australian Outback and the American Wild West
> Solar and geothermal energy

For this sort of report, begin your research by reading about both topics individually. Look for details that both have in common. Consider how the topics are different. Your report will then be based on these similarities and differences. (For more information on comparison and contrast, see Chapter 11, page 219.)

A third purpose of a report is to **analyze.** When you analyze, you break your topic into smaller parts and examine the parts.

For this sort of report, search for material that will help your reader to draw conclusions about your topic based on an understanding of how the smaller parts are related. Look for details that discuss trends, causes and effects, benefits, and drawbacks. The following topics fit in this category:

> The use of solar energy
> Reasons for food labeling
> How computers are changing our schools

Knowing the purpose of your report will make your search for information easier.

Identifying Your Audience

Whom are you writing for? Will your report be read by other students or is it directed at a different group? Are your readers familiar with the subject, or is it new to them?

The answers to these questions will help you decide how much background you will need to provide. Your purpose and your audience are two of the most important things to remember throughout the writing process.

Understanding Facts and Opinions

A report is made up of facts. A fact is a piece of information that can be shown to be true. Here are some examples of facts:

> The Grand Canyon is in Arizona.
> The population of New York City is eight million.
> There are millions of telephones in the world.

An opinion cannot be shown to be true. It is a statement of how someone *feels* about a subject. Compare these opinions to the facts above.

> The Grand Canyon has the best scenery in the country.
> New York City is too crowded.
> The most important modern invention is the telephone.

When you do your research, concentrate on gathering facts rather than opinions about your topic. (See pages 230-231 and 234-235 for more information on facts and opinions.)

Writing Activities *Working with Facts*

A Assume that you are writing a report on early photography. The purpose of the report is to inform people your.age who are unfamiliar with the topic. Look at the list of statements below. Keeping your subject, purpose, and audience in mind; find the statements that are not appropriate for your report. A statement is not appropriate if it is unrelated to the topic, too technical for the audience, or expresses opinions rather than facts. Write the inappropriate statements on your paper and be ready to tell why you would not use them. Remember that opinions should not be part of a report.

1. Early photographs were not permanent.
2. Early photography was too difficult and complicated to be enjoyable.
3. The first camera was a boxlike device as big as a closet.
4. Color photos are the most interesting.
5. The first camera was used in about 1500.
6. Daguerreotype was the first popular form of photography.
7. George Eastman created one of the most amazing inventions ever seen.
8. Two British scientists produced the first photographic images on paper.
9. In the twentieth century, photography is regarded as a special kind of art.
10. It took eight hours for Joseph Niépce to make the first permanent photograph in 1826.

B Read the following statements. Then decide if the statement fits best in a report to inform, to compare and contrast, or to analyze. Write which type of report you would most likely use the statement in. Be ready to tell why.

1. Every giraffe has its own distinct coat patterns.
2. Both Lincoln and Grant were Presidents in the 1860's.
3. The Missouri River is longer than the Mississippi River.
4. There are several reasons why the city closed the park.
5. The meadowlark is a common North American bird.
6. Determination is one reason why some people are highly successful.

Making a List of Questions

The final step in preparing to do research is to make a list of questions about your topic, ones that you think your readers would want answered. Such questions will help guide you to gather the information that you need.

Carol, who decided on the topic "The Geography of Mexico," listed these five questions:

1. Does Mexico have seasons as the United States does?
2. Does Mexico's climate differ from region to region?
3. What is the overall shape of the country?
4. Does the country have mountains?
5. Does Mexico have any unusual features?

Similar questions will serve as a guide to your own research. Of course, you may find facts as you read that are not covered by these questions. If they fit your subject, purpose, and audience, do not hesitate to use them.

Writing Activities *Planning Questions*

A Choose five of the following report topics. For each, write five questions that need to be answered by using outside sources. You may want to read a brief encyclopedia article on each topic before writing your questions.

1. TV viewing in the average family
2. Sun spots
3. The training of an Olympic gymnast
4. The first World's Fair
5. Energy sources of the future
6. Making pottery
7. The origins of basketball
8. Newspapers in Colonial America
9. Teaching children to swim
10. The National Parks system

B **Writing in Process** Using the final topic you chose for your report in Activity B on page 251, write ten questions that you think need to be answered. Save these questions in your writing folder for a later activity.

3
Prewriting: Gathering Information

To collect all the material you need to write a thorough report, read as much as you can about your subject. You will find most of what you need in the library. However, you should also keep in mind that people can be excellent sources of information. Thus interviewing should also be considered as a way of gathering information.

When using the library to collect information, begin by reading a general encyclopedia article. Then check the card catalog and the *Readers' Guide to Periodical Literature*. These sources will direct you to specific books and magazine articles on your subject. Also consult reference books that generally relate to your subject. (See Chapter 16 for more guidance in using the library.)

Taking Notes

As you look up information on your topic, record the facts you want to use on 3″ × 5″ note cards. Write only one piece of information on each card. At the top of the card, record the title of the book, magazine, or reference article. Also write the page number of the information.

Book

        title   *Solar Energy in Tomorrow's World*

      pages   *pages 50-52*

  information   *Solar cells are being used to capture the sun's energy to power radio stations, highway lights, alarm systems, foghorns and automobiles.*

Magazine Article

title — "Solar Electric Home I"

pages — pages 52-54

information — A Department of Energy project built a house with solar panels that uses solar power for about 80% of its heating and electrical needs.

Encyclopedia Article

title — "Solar Energy"

pages — page 473

information — Because of fuel shortages, people began trying to find ways to harness the sun's energy for heating and cooling homes as well as offices.

As you take notes, be sure that you record the information in your own words and not those of the source. Then the report that you write from the cards will be original. Read the excerpt below. Then see how a student writer summarized a fact about the space shuttle.

A space shuttle orbiter is a reusable vehicle that can be used to launch artificial satellites. The shuttle orbiter also has a compact laboratory in which scientists can conduct a wide variety of experiments.

Student Note Card

U. S. Space Missions

page 67

The shuttle orbiter has a compact laboratory for experiments.

Occasionally, you may want to copy a direct quotation from an expert. If you do, be sure to put quotation marks around it on your note card. Do the same in the report itself and give the source. Your teacher can explain how to do this.

On a separate sheet of paper, list every source that you use. Follow the guidelines below when preparing this list. Notice that the names of authors are given last name first.

Guidelines for Listing Sources

1. For books, give the author, the title, the city of publication, the publisher, and the copyright date.

    Reed, Millard. *Solar Energy in Tomorrow's World*. New York: Julian Mesner, 1980.

2. For magazines, give the name of the author of the article, the title of the article, the name and date of the magazine, and the page numbers.

    Stepler, Richard. "Solar Electric Home I." *Popular Science* Sept. 1981: 52–54.

3. For encyclopedias, give the title of the encyclopedia article and the set's names and year.

    "Solar Energy." *The World Book Encyclopedia*. 1988 ed.

Writing Activities *Taking Notes*

A Assume that you are writing a report on the Ganges River. Write five note cards based on this article from the 1986 edition of *The World Book Encyclopedia*. Make sure that you put the information into your own words.

GANGES RIVER, *GAN jeez*, is the greatest waterway in India and one of the largest in the world. It is most important to the Indians for the part it plays in the Hindu religion. Hindus consider it the most sacred river in India. Each year, thousands of Hindu pilgrims visit such holy cities as Banaras and Allahabad along the banks of the Ganges to bathe in the river and to take home some of its water. Temples line the riverbank, and *ghats* (stairways) lead down to the water. Some pilgrims come to bathe in the water only to cleanse and purify themselves. The sick and crippled come hoping that the touch of the water will cure their ailments. Others come to die in the river, for the Hindus believe that those who die in the Ganges will be carried away to Paradise.

Riverbank scene, Ganges River in India.

The river is an important trade area. Its valley is fertile and densely populated. Some of India's largest cities, such as Calcutta, Howrah, Patna, Banaras, and Kanpur, stand on its banks. New Delhi, India's capital, is on its tributary, the Jumna. But the Ganges is less important commercially than it once was. Irrigation has drained much of its water and steamers can navigate only in the lower part of the river.

The Ganges has its beginning in an ice cave 10,300 feet (3,139 meters) above sea level in the Himalaya Mountains of northern India. The river flows toward the southeast and through Bangladesh for 1,540 miles (2,478 kilometers) to empty into the Bay of Bengal (see INDIA [physical map]; BANGLADESH [map]). Several tributary rivers, including the Jumna, Ramganga, Gomati, Ghaghra, Son, and Sapt Kosi add to the waters of the Ganges. The Brahmaputra River joins some of the branches of the Ganges near its mouth, and together the two rivers form a large delta.

B Writing in Process Use the questions you wrote for Activity B, page 255, to research your subject. Read various sources to find answers to your questions. Take notes for your report on 3″ × 5″ cards or on pieces of paper cut into 3″ × 5″ rectangles. Follow the guidelines given in this lesson for recording information and listing sources. Save your notes to use when you plan and write your report.

4
Prewriting: Organizing Information

Once you have gathered all the information you need, you are ready to organize your notes. You will probably notice that most of your information seems to fall under certain key ideas. One good organizational technique is to divide your note cards into groups. Each group should relate to one key idea.

For her report, "The Geography of Mexico," Carol had note cards with these facts:

> Mexico is a long triangle pointing to South America.
>
> Warm, humid valleys with groves of bananas, guavas, mangoes, mameys, and sapotes
>
> The mountains are steep and high.
>
> Mexico wide at top, narrow at bottom
>
> Paricutín, a new volcano
>
> Strange plants and fruits in the lowlands; hedges of cactus
>
> Some peaks are wild and rugged.
>
> Wet season in summer; dry season in winter
>
> In the dry months, no rain falls.
>
> In the wet months, heavy rains that carry the soil from mountains
>
> One village now lies at the bottom of a lake.
>
> Some mountains are planted in orderly plots.
>
> The geography of Mexico can be beautiful, violent, and unexpected.

Carol found that she could sort her note cards into the following four groups.

Shape

> Mexico is a long triangle pointing to South America.
>
> Mexico wide at top, narrow at bottom

Climate

Wet season in summer; dry season in winter
In the dry months, no rain falls.
In the wet months, heavy rains that carry the
    soil from mountains
Warm, humid valleys with groves of bananas,
    guavas, mangoes, mameys, and sapotes

Mountains and Lowlands

The mountains are steep and high.
Some peaks are wild and rugged.
Some mountains are planted in orderly plots.
Strange plants and fruits in the lowlands;
    hedges of cactus

The Unexpected

The geography of Mexico can be beautiful, violent,
    and unexpected.
Paricutín, a new volcano
One village now lies at the bottom of a lake.

The Order of Information

Once you have sorted your facts, arrange them into a logical order. Many reports are organized in order of importance. Starting with the most familiar information and ending with the least familiar material is another good way to organize. Other reports are best suited to chronological order or spatial order. For example, facts in a report called "The Growth of the Railroads" would be most logical in chronological order.

Making an Outline

Outlining is a good way to organize your notes into a working plan for your report. An outline lays out a framework for a report, showing how the facts should be arranged.

Each group of note cards becomes a major division in the outline. The key idea of the group becomes the division's main heading. It is labeled with a Roman numeral.

Notice, on the next page, how Carol used an outline to structure her report, "The Geography of Mexico."

The Geography of Mexico

I. Shape
  - A. Mexico is a long triangle pointing to South America.
  - B. Mexico is wide at the top and narrow at the bottom.

II. Mountains and lowlands
  - A. The mountains are steep and high.
  - B. Some peaks are wild and rugged.
  - C. Some mountains are planted in orderly plots.
  - D. Strange plants and fruits grow in the lowlands.
  - E. Hedges of round cactus appear in the lowlands.
  - F. There are warm, humid valleys with groves of bananas, guavas, mangoes, mameys, and sapotes.

III. Climate
  - A. Wet in summer, dry in winter.
  - B. In the dry months, no rain falls.
  - C. In the wet months, heavy rains carry the soil from the mountains.

IV. The unexpected
  - A. The geography of Mexico is beautiful and violent.
  - B. Paricutín is a new volcano.
  - C. One village now lies at the bottom of a lake.

Did you notice that Carol arranged her facts in order of familiarity? She began with commonly known information about the shape of the country and ended with less familiar facts about the unexpected in Mexico.

Sometimes after making an outline you will see that you need more facts under a certain heading. Then it's time to return to the library to seek out new sources of information. Also check to see that the order you have chosen works well for your topic. You may want to rework your outline several times.

Below is another outline. The writer divided his topic on gliders into three main groupings. The first is about the parts of the glider. The second tells about flying a glider, and the third group provides information on the history of gliders. Notice that group I is in spatial order and that groups II and III are in chronological order.

Gliders

I. Parts of a glider
    A. Wings
    B. Body
    C. Tail assembly

II. Flying a glider
    A. Launching
    B. Soaring
    C. Landing

III. History of gliders
    A. First gliders
    B. Gliding after World War I
    C. Use of gliders in World War II
    D. Gliding as a sport today

Writing Activities Making a Report Outline

A Sort these facts into three groups under the key ideas of *Awards, Education,* and *Achievements.*

Ben Franklin, Scientist

Invented the lightning rod
Had only two years of schooling
Honorary degrees from two colleges
Invented the fuel-efficient Franklin stove
Given Copley Medal for scientific achievement
Read extensively on many subjects
Was made a Fellow of the Royal Society of London
Proposed several new theories of electricity

B Writing in Process Put the note cards for your own report into three or four related groups. Set aside any unrelated ideas. After you decide on the most logical order, make an outline for your report. Save your outline for the next activity.

5
Drafting:
Using an Outline

A report has three main parts: they are the **introduction,** the **body**, and the **conclusion**.

The Introduction

In Chapter 7, you learned that an introductory paragraph should capture the reader's attention and state the topic or main idea. How well do you think this paragraph introduces the report about Mexican geography?

> I'd like to tell you about the geography of Mexico. Mexico is a very interesting country. Its geography is very interesting, too, because it's so different.

The paragraph is dull and lifeless. Although it introduces the topic, it doesn't catch a reader's attention as the following paragraph does.

> The geography of Mexico is rich and diverse. The country's shape is a long triangle, pointing to South America. In the North it is a wide land, with many miles of cactus country between the Gulf of Mexico and the Pacific Ocean. In the South the country narrows as it meets the Central American states.

The above paragraph not only introduces the topic of the report, it also treats the factual material with a fresh approach. Instead of merely stating that Mexico is wide at its northern border, the writer notes the "many miles of cactus country between the Gulf of Mexico and the Pacific Ocean." With details such as these, she captures the reader's interest in the geography of Mexico.

You probably noticed that the introduction about Mexico uses the first group of facts from the outline. Another way of introducing a topic is with an interesting idea or a general definition. There are still other ways to make an introductory paragraph more interesting. You might, for example, ask a question, state an unusual fact, or tell an amusing anecdote. You might use a quotation that helps to introduce your topic. (For additional information, see pages 119-120 of Chapter 7.)

Grammar in Action

One way to make an introductory paragraph more interesting is to use different types of sentences: declarative, interrogative, imperative, or exclamatory. (See pages 614-615.) Another possibility is to vary the length or complexity of the sentences.

What types of sentences did the writer of the following paragraph use to make his report introduction appealing?

The history of the Statue of Liberty begins with its designer, a Frenchman, Musée Bartholdi. Bartholdi admired America. He wanted to glorify that new republic by building a statue. Did you know that he was influenced by the stone monuments of Egypt? He was also influenced by the Colossus of Rhodes. His mother may even have played a role. Some saw her features in Liberty's face!

Writing Activity Write an introductory paragraph about another national monument. Experiment with sentences of various types and lengths. When reviewing and revising your paragraph, use sentence combining techniques where appropriate. (See pages 132–141.)

Writing Activities *Writing Introductions*

A Decide which of the following are good introductory paragraphs. Then rewrite the other paragraphs to make them interesting introductions to the topic.

1. The first English settlers arrived in India in the early 1600's. They immediately set up colonies. Those long-ago settlements were very interesting.

2. It isn't common for a person to succeed at five careers. But back in the eighteenth century, Benjamin Franklin was respected as an author, statesman, printer, and philosopher. This brilliant man was also a scientist. His scientific inventions astounded the people of his time and gave him a special place in history.

3. I'm going to write a report about solar energy. Most people don't know how it works. This report will explain it and tell what it can be used for. I think you will learn a lot about my topic.

4. For millions of years it glows brightly in the evening sky. Then suddenly, without warning, it fades or falls and disappears. What makes a star die? The answer lies hidden deep within the composition of these heavenly bodies.

B Writing in Process Using your notes from the previous lesson, write the introductory paragraph to your report. Either cover point I in your outline or write a paragraph that uses a new idea to lead into the facts in your outline.

The Body

The body of a report follows the writing plan presented in the outline. Each main division in the outline becomes a paragraph in the body. As in any paragraph, each report paragraph has a topic sentence and contains facts or details that support it. If your outline was well thought out, then each paragraph will be tightly organized.

In the report on Mexico, the introduction covered the first group of facts. The body paragraphs will cover the information listed under the next three headings of the outline.

II. Mountains and lowlands
III. Climate
IV. The unexpected

Now read the introduction and body of Carol's report on Mexico. The version you see is the result of several earlier drafts. Carol followed her outline as she wrote the body paragraphs. The resulting sentences flow together smoothly. Notice, too, the new, catchier title.

Mexico: A Land of Contrasts

Student Model

The geography of Mexico is rich and diverse. The country's shape is a long triangle, pointing to South America. In the North it is a wide land, with many miles of cactus country between the Gulf of Mexico and the Pacific Ocean. In the South the country narrows as it dips toward and meets the Central American States.

Mexico is a country of ups and downs. The mountains are breathtakingly steep and high. Some of the great peaks are wild and rugged, while others are planted in orderly plots so far up that they look like patchwork patterns against the sky. Along the lowlands, the earth grows strange plants and fruits. Cactus plants appear as round as barrels, in great, fierce hedges.

The climate is up and down, too. From a cold mountain road, where pines recall Canadian forests, one may look down on warm, humid groves of bananas, guavas, mangoes, and soft mameys and sapotes. Mexico has a wet season in summer and a dry season in winter. In the dry months no rain falls, and the steep slopes become brown and gray. When the rains come, water pounds the roofs of mud huts like drumbeats and washes down the mountainsides through deep ravines in a rushing roar. The high slopes grow green with grass, and flowers spring out all over them. However, rains carry away soil from the mountains so fast through the ravines that lower slopes do not grow much vegetation. In stark contrast to the lush high slopes, these sparse lower slopes look barren.

Mexico's land is beautiful and at times violent. It is a land of flowers and color, of song and brilliant birds. Snow-topped volcanoes glitter against a sky of vivid blue. Mexico is serene and beautiful, but it can also be unexpectedly violent. Only a few years ago a volcano, called Paricutín, thrust up abruptly through a farmer's field. It quickly buried a village under lava and ashes. A lake now covers the town, and the church spire may be seen by looking straight down into the water from a boat.

Look back at the outline on page 262 to see how the body paragraphs follow the outline. As you write your report, you may find yourself wanting to add, delete, or reorganize information.

Writing Activity *Writing Body Paragraphs*

Writing in Process Write the body paragraphs of your report, following your outline. Make sure that each paragraph has a topic sentence.

The Conclusion

A report, like any other composition, ends with a concluding paragraph. Even though it does not add new information, a conclusion is necessary. It not only ties the report together but also signals "The End" to the reader.

Often the conclusion of a report summarizes the ideas of the report in a new way. Because it often leaves an impression in the reader's mind, the conclusion should be fresh and vivid.

Carol ended her report, "Mexico: A Land of Contrasts," with this concluding paragraph.

> Mexico is truly a land of contrasts. It is a land of mountains and valleys, of hot and cold, of droughts and drenching rains. It is a land of bright green mountains and gray-brown deserts. Above all else, Mexico is a land where one learns to expect the unexpected.

Writing Activity Concluding Your Report

Writing in Process Write the concluding paragraph of your report. Make sure it ties the report together and provides a definite, interesting finish.

The Bibliography

In a report, you must give credit to the outside sources you used. The usual method is to name the sources at the end of the report in a section called the **bibliography.**

Listed below is the bibliography for the report on solar energy. You can see that the sources are listed in alphabetical order, according to the authors' last names or the name of the article when there is no author. When you make a bibliography, follow this form.

Bibliography

Reed, Millard. *Solar Energy in Tomorrow's World.*
  New York: Julian Mesner, 1980.
"Solar Energy." *The World Book Encyclopedia.*
  1988 ed.
Stepler, Richard. "Solar Electric Home I." *Popular
  Science* Sept. 1981: 52–54.

Writing Activity Making a Bibliography

Writing in Process Use the list of sources that you prepared earlier to make a bibliography for your report. Be sure to underline the titles of books and magazines. Also underline the names of encyclopedias. Follow the example given above.

6
Revising and Presenting

When you have finished writing the first draft of the report, study your work carefully. Use the guidelines for revising and proofreading on pages 83–84 to help you improve your writing. Make sure that you have covered your topic thoroughly and presented the information in a clear and lively manner. Rewrite the sections that need work.

Because this is a report, you must add one more step to the revision process: *check your facts*. Make sure all dates, statistics, and other information are correct. Check to see that you have listed your sources accurately.

Once you are finished revising, make a clean final copy. Follow the form your teacher gives you. Use correct grammar, capitalization, punctuation, and spelling. Proofread your final copy.

Your report is now ready to be shared. Perhaps your school newspaper would be interested in your report. You might display your report on a bulletin board or share it with students in another class.

Writing Activities Revising and Presenting

A Read, revise, and proofread the following paragraph from a report about cowboy artists.

Western painting
1890. Charles M. Russell.

The cowboy painter Charles Russell loved the American Indian. In his lifetime, he paint hundreds of pictures depicting the Indians' heroic traditions. among his favorite subjects was a young indian boy who became his lifelong friend. Referring to his friend, and speak about all Indians, he said, This is the only real American. Because of Russell's paintings, every generation will remember the real Americans.

B Writing in Process Read, revise, and proofread your report. Make a final copy. Find ways to share your report.

Speaking and Listening

"Welcome to San Diego's Balboa Park! This magnificent urban park is the home of some of our city's finest museums, theaters, and, of course, our renowned San Diego Zoo. On your left is the Old Globe Theater, where the popular Shakespeare festival is held each summer. Up ahead is the Reuben H. Fleet Space Theater and Science Center, with a dazzling array of scientific exhibits . . . ."

So begins a guided tour of one of San Diego's most popular tourist attractions. Tours like this one, offering an entertaining blend of information and legend, can be found in many different settings: zoos, museums, homes, or cities.

A tour guide is a special type of reporter whose job is to introduce listeners to a particular setting. The best tour guide learns all about the area and shares with the listeners the best of the facts, figures, and folklore. A good tour guide brings color and life to an unfamiliar setting by sharing stories, jokes, and personal experiences.

Activity

Your town or neighborhood is receiving a great deal of publicity because a famous person grew up there. A group of newspaper reporters are touring the area, and you are their tour guide. Put together a tour that shows the group all of the places where the person would have hung out while growing up.

English and Physical Education—Sports

Think about the following names: Kareem Abdul-Jabbar, Pele, Mary Lou Retton, Mary Decker Slaney, Martina Navratilova, and Reggie Jackson. What images come to your mind? Did you picture Olympic gold medals and championship trophies? Did you see grand-slam home runs, Wimbledon trophies, and world titles? If so, you're only seeing half the story because the road to sports stardom is not filled with only glory and championships.

To become champions, these sports heroes had to train hard and long. Many a day, they started early and finished late. Along the way, they wore out a lot of gym shoes, headbands, and sweat socks. And most importantly, they refused to ever give up. For instance, Larry Bird, the basketball star, still spends four to five hours a day during the off-season shooting baskets on the court he built in his backyard.

Sportswriters give you the whole picture of what a sports star's life is like. These writers write about the glory as well as the pain of playing professional sports.

Activity

The local newspaper is running a sportswriter contest. The grand prize is a signed photo of your favorite sports star. To enter, choose a champion of any sport and learn about his or her training and practice routine. Use magazines, newspapers, or books from the library. Write an award-winning report summing up your research.

Application and Review

A Using Note Cards Make a note card for this paragraph taken from page 12 of the article, "The Negro Baseball Leagues," by Craig E. Blohm, in the July 1985 issue of *Cobblestone*.

> The year 1867 saw the first evidence of racial prejudice in baseball. Black players were banned from membership in the National Association of Baseball Players, the game's first league. While a few blacks (The Walker brothers, Bud Fowler, Charley Grant) managed to hold positions on white teams in the years to follow, by 1885, not one black player was left in the major leagues. The era of segregated baseball had begun.

B Preparing an Outline Sort the following facts into three key idea groups: *The Black Leagues, Racial Prejudice,* and *Integration*. Omit any irrelevent facts. Make a report outline.

The Integration of American Baseball

- The turn of the century saw the beginning of Negro baseball with five professional teams.
- In 1947, Jackie Robinson became the first black player in the modern major leagues.
- The owner of the Brooklyn Dodgers, Branch Rickey, established an integration policy.
- The news media ignored the Negro leagues.
- On the road, because of segregated hotels, black players had to sleep at the ball parks or in the buses.
- Buck Leonard was an outstanding player in the Negro Leagues.
- For the first half of this century, baseball was a segregated sport.
- The Civil War ended in 1865.
- "Rube" Foster formed the Negro National League in 1920.
- At first, the black teams played wherever they could rent a field.
- Later, major-league ball parks began hosting Negro baseball games.
- After 1947, other black players, such as Hank Thompson, Willard Brown, and Roy Campanella, began playing in the major leagues.

Resources and Skills

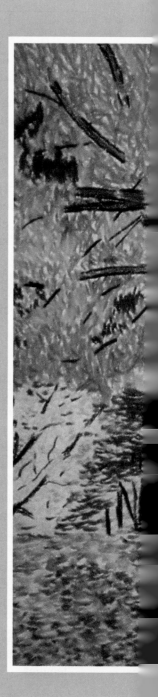

All artists need tools to help them create finished works. A painter needs pigments and brushes. A writer needs a good vocabulary and resource materials. When writers and painters know what tools to use and how to use them, they can create compositions as vibrant and exciting as this painting.

14
Developing Vocabulary Skills

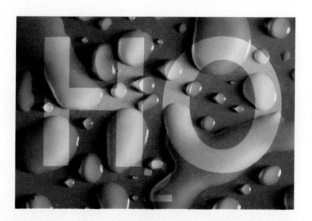

Anyone who has studied chemistry knows that H_2O is the molecular formula for water. It is a symbol that conveys a very specific meaning. Words, too, convey specific meaning. Using words correctly is important. Doing so makes it possible for you to communicate your thoughts and feelings as clearly and accurately as possible.

In this chapter you will study how the English language developed. You will also learn how to make sense of unfamiliar words by using prefixes, suffixes, synonyms, antonyms, and context clues.

1
Bringing New Words into English

Do you know that many of the words you use every day have come directly from other languages? About 85 percent of the words in the English language have been borrowed from such languages as Latin, French, Spanish, German, Italian, Russian, and others. We are still borrowing words from other languages.

Since so many words are borrowed, we need a way to keep track of just where they came from. Dictionary entries, therefore, provide a history of each entry word. This history, or **etymology**, is given in brackets before the definition. Names of languages are almost always abbreviated in the etymology. However, you can find a list of these languages and their abbreviations in the beginning of your dictionary. Sometimes an etymology even provides an earlier meaning of the word. Examine the etymology for the word *chum*.

> **chum** (chum) **n.** [late 17th-c. slang; prob. altered sp. of *cham*, clipped form of *chamber* (*fellow*), *chamber* (*mate*)] **1.** orig. a roommate **2.** a close friend

You would decipher the abbreviations in this etymology as follows: "Probably an altered spelling of *cham*, a clipped form of *chamberfellow* or *chambermate* which meant *roommate*. The word now means 'a close friend.'"

You may have noticed that *chum* is not a borrowed word. It was first used as a slang word in the seventeenth century.

Creating New Words

English-speaking peoples sometimes create words. They may derive them from sounds, from the names of persons or of places, or by combining words. Or, they may form them by shortening existing words. Once a word is created, however, it is not necessarily adopted into the language. Only after it has been used by many people over time does a word become accepted. Then we say that it has passed into standard usage.

Words Derived from Sounds Some words echo or imitate the thing they name. These words are called **echoic words**. Examples are the words *blip, ping,* and *buzz.*

Words Derived from the Names of Persons or of Places Many English words come from the names of persons or of places. Examples include *Ferris* wheel, named after its inventor, George Ferris, and *china,* porcelain dishes originally from China.

Word Combinations Some words are actually combinations of other words. The most common type of word combination is the **compound word**. A compound word is made by joining two or more complete words. Compound words may be closed, such as *eggplant;* open, such as *high rise;* or hyphenated, such as *fly-by-night.* A less common form of word combination, the **word blend**, is a combination of the parts of two words. The word *telethon,* for example, was formed from *television* and *marathon.*

Shortened Forms New words are also formed by shortening existing words. A **clipped form** is taken from a longer word. *Lab* is taken, or clipped, from *laboratory.* Words formed from the initial letter or from parts of a series of words are called **acronyms**. For example, a *quasar* is from *(quas)i stell(ar) radio source,* and is pronounced *kwā′sär.*

Exercise

Write the following words. Next to each word, tell how it entered the English language by writing *borrowed word, echoic word, person's name, place name, compound word, word blend, clipped form,* or *acronym.* Use a dictionary for help.

1. condo   3. hickory   5. cablegram   7. screech   9. bureau
2. NEA   4. byte   6. sunbeam   8. drive-in   10. sequoia

2
Word Building

You have already learned that English words come from other languages, sounds, the names of persons or of places, and longer words. Many of these words we now use as **base words**, meaning words that can stand alone. By adding word parts called prefixes and suffixes to these base words, we create other words. If you know the meanings of these word parts, you can usually figure out the meanings of these additional words. Knowing the meanings of words will help you understand the entire message a writer or speaker is trying to convey.

Word Parts: Prefixes and Suffixes

A **prefix** is a word part that is added at the beginning of a base word to form a new word with a new meaning. Each prefix has a specific meaning, but a prefix cannot be used alone. For example, the prefix *mis-* means "wrong." However, you do not use it to say wrong. You might say, "You *misspelled* that word" because *misspell* means "to spell wrong."

By adding a prefix to a base word, you may sometimes form a word that is a different part of speech than the base word. Usually, however, the addition of a prefix does not form a word with a different function. Examine the chart of prefixes on the following page. Notice that they are divided into four categories: number, place or direction, negative prefixes, and other prefixes. Try to learn these prefixes and their meanings. Knowing them may help you figure out the meanings of unfamiliar words.

A **suffix** is a word part that is added at the end of a base word to form a new word with a new meaning. As with prefixes, each suffix has a specific meaning yet cannot be used alone. *-Ly*, for instance, means "in a certain manner." You do not use it on its own to convey this, however. By adding a suffix you often create a word that functions as a different part of speech than the original base word. The chart on page 282 contains some commonly used suffixes. The chart also shows the parts of speech words usually become when these suffixes are added to them.

Some Commonly Used Prefixes			
Category of Prefix	**Prefix**	**Meaning**	**Example**
Prefixes of Number	**uni-, mono-**	"one" or "having one"	*unicycle, monorail*
	bi-	"twice" or "two"	*bimonthly, bifocals*
	tri-	"three" or "with three parts"	*triangle triathlon*
Prefixes of Position or Direction	**inter-**	"between" or "within"	*international interstate*
	sub-	"under"	*submarine*
	mid-	"halfway"	*midsummer midday*
	trans-	"across"	*transatlantic*
	pre-	"before"	*preheat preschool*
Negative Prefixes	**non-, in-, im-, il-**	"not"	*nonsmoker, independent, impolite, illegal*
	un-, dis-	"not" or "the opposite of"	*uncomfortable, disagree*
Other Prefixes	**mis- re-**	"wrong" "back" or "again"	*misinform replay*

Suffixes are valuable items to know. One clue to the part of speech of an unfamiliar word is its suffix. By learning the suffixes charted on page 282 you can become familiar with the parts of speech usually formed by adding these suffixes. The chart can also help you become familiar with the meanings of these suffixes.

When adding suffixes, follow the spelling rules on page 341.

Some Commonly Used Suffixes			
Part of Speech	**Suffix**	**Meaning**	**Examples**
Noun	-an, -ant, -er, -ian, -ier, -ist, -or	"one who"	*Mexican, defendant, photographer, musician, cashier, pianist, actor*
	-dom, -hood, -ity, -ness, -ty	"state of"	*freedom, brotherhood, humidity, kindness, safety*
Verb	-ify, -ize	"to make"	*intensify, socialize*
Adjective	-able, -ible	"able to be"	*portable, sensible*
	-ful, -ly -ous	"full of"	*truthful, kindly, dangerous*
Adverb	-ly	"in a certain way"	*slowly*

Exercises

A Make three columns on your paper. Label them *Base Words, Prefixes,* and *Suffixes.* Then, for each word, write the base word, prefix, and/or suffix in the appropriate column.

1. repave
2. stillness
3. nonfiction
4. inactive
5. midnight
6. breakable
7. disobey
8. marvelous
9. safely
10. baker
11. unfold
12. director

13. memorize   15. subdivide   17. imperfect
14. misguide   16. beautiful   18. kingdom

B Write on your paper the new words you form by adding the correct prefix from the chart of prefixes to the base words given in parentheses in the following sentences.

1. The (way) train got stuck (way) into the city.
2. The students wore their school (forms) on the (continental) flight.
3. The red, gold, and blue of the (color) flag could be spotted four blocks away.
4. "Our (annual) meetings will be held in January and June," said the secretary in a boring (tone).
5. Joella hopes someday to travel from Mars to Pluto on an (planetary) expedition.

C Write on your paper a new word that functions as the part of speech given in parentheses in the following sentences. Form this new word by adding an appropriate suffix to the italicized base word that is also in parentheses. You may want to refer to the chart on page 282.

1. The (*run*, noun) (*swift*, adverb) crossed the finish line.
2. The (*navigate*, noun) of the plane is not yet here.
3. We had itemized our grocery list so that we could find things (*quick*, adverb) and (*easy*, adverb).
4. Please (*note*, verb) me if you do not see a (*notice*, adjective) improvement in your cold soon.
5. This (*mountain*, adjective) area is both (*beauty*, adjective) and (*bounty*, adjective).

3
Using Precise Synonyms and Antonyms

To be an effective speaker or writer you need to be able to say exactly what you mean. Yet, as you have seen, the English language consists of a huge and growing number of words. Therefore, you need some organized way of searching for words —an organized storehouse of words.

A **thesaurus** is a storehouse of words organized into groups of synonyms and antonyms. **Synonyms** are words with the same or very nearly the same meaning. **Antonyms** are words with the opposite or very nearly the opposite meaning. Instructions given at the beginning of the thesaurus will tell you how to use it. Finding the most precise word to say what you mean requires detective work. However, if you do this work you can become a much more effective writer and speaker.

A single word can provide a great deal of information. For example, you could say, "I walked to the store." However, if you were tired, you might say, "I trudged to the store." In each sentence a single word has a great deal of impact upon the message. Therefore, whenever possible take the time to search through synonyms in the thesaurus to find the most precise word.

A single antonym can help you make your message even clearer. By inserting an antonym, you can emphasize a particular point. For example, you might write, "Try to dance gracefully not clumsily." The contrast between *gracefully* and *clumsily* helps convey a clear image. In a thesaurus entry, antonyms are usually found after all the synonyms have been listed.

Exercises

A For each of the following sentences write a synonym that will be more effective in the sentence than the verb *spoke*. Use a thesaurus or dictionary for help.

1. The famous scientist *spoke* to the students about her recent discovery of a comet.

2. Each person memorized his or her favorite poem and *spoke* it aloud.
3. The angry politician *spoke* for an hour about his opponent's lack of character.
4. "The finalists in the tennis tournament are Andrew Crim and Sally Jefferson," *spoke* the newscaster.
5. The children hidden under the picnic table *spoke* to one another as they waited to be discovered.
6. The cheerleaders *spoke* the cheers in loud, clear voices.

7. The reunited sisters *spoke* happily for hours.
8. Martha *spoke* to everyone for days about the wonderful performance.
9. The lawyer *spoke* while her secretary took shorthand.
10. When he *spoke*, I couldn't understand what he was saying.

B Complete the following sentences by writing on your paper antonyms to the italicized words. You may use a dictionary or thesaurus for help.

1. Amy's complexion is *ruddy* not _____.
2. I'm much more *weary* than _____.
3. Try to be *methodical* instead of _____.
4. He was *troubled* and upset—anything but _____.
5. I don't want a *din;* I want _____.
6. Cora is *graceful;* whereas I am _____.
7. The kittens are *agile,* but their old mother is _____.
8. Colleen would rather do things *spontaneously* instead of

   _____.
9. Andrea is *stubborn,* but her brother Brian is _____.
10. The knife that was so *keen* when new is now _____.

4
Understanding Vocabulary in Context

Context, the words or phrases that surround a word, often helps you determine which meaning of a word an author is using. For example, read the following sentences.

> If we don't plug that leak, the boat will *sink*.
> The *sink* is full of dishes.

In the first sentence, *sink* means "to go under water." In the second, it means "a tub or basin." In each sentence, you can easily tell from the other words around it which meaning of the word *sink* is being used.

The context of a word can also help you discover the meaning of an unfamiliar word. Many times, the context will offer a clue to the meaning of the word. Such a hint is called a **context clue**. In this section you will learn how to use five different types of context clues.

Using Definitions and Restatements

Two common types of context clues are **definitions** and **restatements**. In the same sentence or in a neighboring sentence, an author may define a term or use another word that has the same meaning as the unfamiliar word.

> An *aqueduct* is a pipe or canal designed to carry water.
> *Maize*—a kind of corn—was a staple crop of Central America.

In the first sentence, the word *aqueduct* is defined. Definitions are introduced with key words such as *is, which is, that is, is called, means, which means,* and *in other words.* In the second sentence, the meaning of *maize* is set off by dashes. When a writer presents a definition without using key words to introduce it, the writer is simply restating the meaning of the word. Writers usually set off restatements with a pair of commas, dashes, or the word *or.*

Exercise

Write the meanings of the italicized words from the following sentences.

1. I am *indecisive;* that is, I can't make up my mind.
2. The meeting turned into quite a *fracas,* or uproar.
3. He had a *wan* look, pale and weak, that worried me.
4. In the canyon, we hiked over *pumice,* which is a kind of volcanic rock.
5. The new school seemed like a *labyrinth*—a maze—to me.
6. The canvas is coated with *gesso,* which is a kind of plaster.
7. Carbon monoxide is a *noxious,* or poisonous, gas.
8. We saw a *gnu,* which is a large African antelope.
9. Carl led us on a *devious,* or winding, route home.
10. When I say this is of *paramount* importance, I mean it is of chief importance!

Using Examples

Context clues also come with or as **examples**.

Wheat and other kinds of grain are made into breads.
Most kinds of grain, such as *wheat,* are made into breads.

Neither sentence tells you what wheat is, but both sentences tell you that wheat is a kind of grain. Notice that wheat is itself an example in the first sentence. The following words and phrases are often used with examples: *for instance, for example, like, such as, and other,* and *especially.*

Exercise

Write the meanings of the italicized words from the following sentences.

1. *Perishable* foods, like milk and meat, should be kept cold.
2. Siobhan likes many tropical fruits, especially *mangoes.*
3. The astronomer studies *novas* and other stars.
4. All *arachnids,* such as spiders and scorpions, have four pairs of legs.
5. Most kinds of earthenware, *terra cotta* for example, make beautiful serving dishes.

Using Comparisons and Contrasts

A writer may use a **comparison** to convey the meaning of an unfamiliar word.

> The lawyer's *relentless* questioning of the defendant was like dripping water wearing away rock.

The "relentless questioning" is being compared to "dripping water wearing away rock." Water would have to drip constantly over a long period of time to wear away rock. Therefore, you could conclude from this comparison that *relentless* means "constant" and "for a long time." When writers make comparisons, they usually use the words *like, as, as though,* and *for example.* They may also use synonyms to form comparisons between different kinds of things.

As you have already learned, you can use antonyms to emphasize what you are saying or writing. When you do this, you are forming a **contrast**. When one of these antonyms is familiar and the other is not, you as reader can grasp the meaning of the unfamiliar word from its antonym. In contrasts, key words such as *unlike, but, on the contrary,* and *on the other hand* are often used.

> Your turtle was fast yesterday, but today it seems *sluggish.*

The writer has signaled that *sluggish* is the opposite of fast by using the word *but. Sluggish,* then, must mean "slow" or "slow-moving."

Sometimes contrasts point out the way in which something differs from a group. These sorts of contrasts provide a great deal of information. First, the contrast tells you to which group the thing belongs. Second, the contrast points out a distinguishing feature of the thing—something that makes it different from all or most of the others in that group.

> *Dolphins,* unlike most other mammals, live in water.

This contrast tells you that dolphins are unlike most other mammals. Therefore, you can assume *dolphins* are mammals. It also tells you a way in which dolphins differ from most other mammals: they live in water. From this contrast, then, you learn two important facts about dolphins.

Exercise

Write on your paper the meanings of the italicized words from the following sentences.

1. Some people think Paul is *irrational,* but he has always seemed reasonable to me.
2. The *vibrant* colors of the mural contrasted with the dull, lifeless gray of the street.
3. I was *flippant* about my poor paper; my teacher, however, was very serious.
4. The *putrid* food smelled as though it had been rotting for months.
5. Mom *mollifies* my anger like lotion soothes a sunburn.
6. The *sonnet,* unlike most other kinds of poems, is exactly fourteen lines long.
7. Like other imaginary beasts, the *griffins* and *unicorns* may have had some basis in fact.
8. I don't want to *perpetuate* this problem; on the contrary, I want it over as soon as possible.
9. He was as *aggressive* as a bulldozer.
10. The *rift* between us is deeper and wider than the Grand Canyon.

Inferring

You may be able to understand some words because you have had an experience like the one being described. When you come to a conclusion about something based on what you know or can correctly assume, you are **inferring**. Read the following sentence:

> Jason had such a feeling of *exhilaration* after winning the bowling trophy that he could hardly sleep.

The sentence tells you that *exhilaration* is a feeling. What kind of feeling? It is a feeling that kept Jason from going to sleep. Feelings of sadness, anger, or confusion could keep a person from going to sleep, but you would not connect them with winning a trophy. If you won a prize, you would feel excited. *Exhilaration* must mean "a feeling of excitement and liveliness." You have used your own knowledge as well as the general context of the sentence to determine the meaning of the unfamiliar word.

On occasion you will have to read an entire paragraph to determine the meaning of an unfamiliar word. For instance, try to determine the meaning of *chaotic* from the following example.

> The meeting was *chaotic*. Most members had not yet taken their seats. Many had no minutes from the previous meeting and were running around seeking copies. The chairperson kept calling for order but was ignored. The two candidates scheduled for debate were already arguing in loud voices.

Which of the following is likely to be the meaning of *chaotic: overcrowded, efficient,* or *disorderly? Overcrowded?* It might be. However, if you read carefully, you will have discovered that there is no evidence that too many people are in the room. You will have noted that the people that are there are engaged in different activities, however. You can rule out *efficient* as a meaning because it means "effective" or "producing a desired result without waste." These people are definitely not being terribly efficient. Their common goal is to have a meeting, and yet they are running in different directions and not listening well to one another. *Disorderly?* This word means "lacking order" or "confusing." That certainly describes the meeting. *Chaotic* must mean *disorderly*.

Notice that you could not infer the meaning of chaotic from the sentence in which it appeared or even from just the neighboring sentence. You had to examine the entire paragraph to discover the meaning of the word. Notice also that you figured out this meaning without using the specific kinds of context clues you have learned about previously.

Exercise

Use the general context and your own experience to determine the meanings of the italicized words in the following items. Write on your paper the letter of the correct meaning.

1. Sumi has worn out three pairs of hiking shoes and needs to find a more *durable* kind.
   a. colorful   b. lasting   c. stylish
2. The sudden rainfall *obliterated* everything in front of me; I had to pull over until I could see the road again.
   a. blotted out   b. lighted up   c. damaged

3. Sarah was not *ambulatory* for weeks after her accident, so we got used to going to her house to play games and joke with her.
   a. conscious   b. able to speak   c. able to walk

4. What more can I say to *induce* you to join us? We will pay for your dinner. The movie is supposed to be great. The weather outside is lovely; yet, neither the restaurant nor the theater is far away. Finally, we all want you to come along.
   a. discourage   b. persuade   c. confuse

5. Cory lost a quarter down a grating. First, he tried to reach it with his hand. Then, he tried to get it back by using a long stick with gum stuck to one end. No luck. Finally, he dangled a looped string in the hope of picking up the quarter. After these *futile* attempts, he asked cheerfully, "Can anyone lend me a quarter?"
   a. ineffective   b. successful   c. technological

6. The whole house is *dilapidated*. The roof leaks. Window panes, where there are window panes, are cracked or broken. There is, of course, no hot or cold running water—except for the rainwater that occasionally comes through the roof. Floors sag; doors hang crooked; and wallpaper curls. It isn't a pretty sight or a safe place to live.
   a. under construction   b. run-down   c. repaired

Crossroads

English and Computers

As computers become a fact of everyday life, it is increasingly important for people to become *computer literate*—to learn the vocabulary of computers.

Here are some common computer terms and their definitions:

byte—one character of information, such as a letter or number. Bytes are grouped into kilobytes (1,000 bytes).

floppy disk (also called a diskette)—a flexible magnetic device used for storing information.

hardware—the computer unit, keyboard, monitor, and other machinery used to run a computer.

memory—the computer's ability to store information.

modem—a device to translate computer signals so they can be transmitted over telephone lines.

software—programs that tell the computer hardware what to do.

Activity Read the following advertisement for a computer. Then write a paragraph that explains the computer's features to someone who is not computer literate.

The Orange 2000 PC comes with 640 kilobytes of memory and two floppy disk drives. It can be combined with a full range of hardware, from printers to modems. Software for word processing, home budgeting, and games is available.

Application and Review

A Identifying Word Origins Look up the following words in the dictionary. Write how each word entered the English language.

1. tornado
2. half-truth
3. FORTRAN
4. click
5. delicatessen
6. sabotage
7. sub
8. decal
9. motel
10. bonfire

B Using Base Words, Prefixes, and Suffixes Make two columns on your paper. Label them *Words* and *Definitions*. In the first column, write the italicized words from the following sentences. Then, try to determine the meaning of the words from their base words, prefixes, and suffixes. Write the meanings in the second column. You may refer to a dictionary.

1. Judy is being *unreasonable* and *illogical*.
2. The *tristate* expressway is moving *slowly*.
3. The *violinist* will *reapply* for an orchestra position.
4. Your *likeness* to your mother is *unbelievable*.
5. The *financier* transferred the money *successfully*.

C Recognizing Synonyms and Antonyms Identify the pairs of italicized words as *Synonyms* or *Antonyms*.

1. Jed is an *angular* person, and his cousin is also *bony*.
2. We were *interrupted* once, but then worked *unabated*.
3. The police *released* one prisoner but *retained* the other.
4. Julie *swatted* at the bees and Eva *whacked* at flies.
5. The *furrowed* field was more *rutted* after the rain.

D Using Context Clues Write on your paper the meanings of the italicized words from the following sentences.

1. I got my spade, hoe, and other gardening *implements*.
2. After eating that big meal, I feel *satiated* at last.
3. Draw *concentric* circles—circles with the same center.
4. The ideas were *incontestable*, but Frank argued against them.
5. Tap that glass, and it will sound *plangent*, like a bell.

15
Interviews and Group Discussion

    You probably are not aware of your language skills when you have an ordinary conversation. When you have to conduct an interview or lead a discussion, however, you suddenly become conscious of how well you speak and listen.

    Learning to speak easily and listen carefully will help you in school, in jobs, and in your everyday encounters with other people. This chapter will show you how to improve your speaking and listening skills so you can conduct successful interviews and group discussions.

1
Interviewing Others

An interview is a special kind of conversation in which the purpose is either to gather information or to supply information. An interview gives people the opportunity to exchange questions and answers for a specific purpose. At times when you need to gather information for a report, interviewing a knowledgeable person will be very helpful. At other times, such as when you are applying for a job, you will be the one supplying most of the information.

Although an interview is basically conversational, it is more tightly organized than a casual conversation, because it has a specific purpose. In order to make your interview a successful one, follow these guidelines.

Guidelines for Conducting Interviews

1. Plan the interview carefully.

a. Choose a person who has special knowledge or interesting opinions about the subject on which you are reporting.
b. Make a definite appointment by arranging a time and date that is convenient for the person being interviewed. When you request an interview, be sure to identify yourself and explain why you want the interview.
c. Do some basic research about the subject so you can ask intelligent questions.
d. Prepare clear, specific questions in advance so that you are sure to get the information you need. Avoid questions that would lead to a simple yes or no answer.

2. Make a good impression.

a. Arrive for your interview on time.
b. Introduce yourself and restate your purpose in asking for the interview.
c. Be ready to ask your questions, one at a time. If the person being interviewed just wants to talk about the subject, you may need to save your questions until the end.

d. Be a good listener. Keep your attention on the speaker and what he or she is saying. The person may add some information that you hadn't thought to ask.
e. At the end of the interview, be sure to thank the person.

3. Get the correct facts.

a. Take notes, especially on names and figures. Make the notes brief so that you are not writing continually while the person is talking.
b. If you want to quote the person, be sure to ask permission.
c. Go over your notes as soon as possible after the interview, and write your report while the information is still fresh in your mind.

Exercises

A Write on your paper the answers to the following questions.

1. What are the two general purposes of an interview?
2. When you are being interviewed for a job, what is your main purpose?
3. What is the difference between an interview and a more casual conversation?
4. What should you do before an interview?
5. Why is it a good idea to let the person you interview provide information you did not ask about?
6. Is it polite to take notes during an interview?
7. What are some ways to make a good impression during an interview?
8. What should you record in your notes during an interview?
9. What should you do if you want to quote the person you have interviewed?
10. When should you review your notes after the interview?

B List five purposes for which you might conduct interviews in connection with your classwork or extracurricular activities. Name an appropriate person to be interviewed for each purpose.
Choose one of the interviews you selected and make a list of ten questions as a guide for an interview.

2
Group Discussion

Group discussion is an easy way to find an answer to a problem, to come up with a new idea, or simply to exchange information. This discussion can be either formal or informal, depending on the subject and purpose of the discussion.

There are two basic types of group discussion: **informal group discussion** and **formal group discussion.** It is important that you know which kind of discussion you are involved in, because each has a specific purpose and a certain procedure.

Informal Group Discussion

An informal group discussion usually takes place immediately after a problem or the need for a decision arises. Consider the following situations.

1. Your family has decided to go on a vacation, but each member of your family wants to go to a different place.
2. All the players on your intramural team have to decide on the best day and time to practice.

The best way to resolve these problems is to have an informal discussion. Why? Because you need to exchange your ideas and talk about the pros and cons of each idea for the purpose of arriving at a decision or plan of action that satisfies the group.

Most discussions in which you participate are informal. They usually occur spontaneously, so you don't have to prepare for them. The subjects you discuss are usually those that members of the group know something about from their common knowledge or experience. This is why informal discussions are often organized by the people involved in them.

Sometimes a class or club will break into small informal groups so that everyone will have a chance to express his or her ideas in a shorter period of time. When this method is used, you may need to select a temporary leader to help keep the discussion organized so that your purpose is accomplished.

Informal discussion may seem like a friendly conversation. It is really more organized, however, and has a specific purpose. Here are the characteristics of an informal discussion.

Informal Discussion

Subjects	General knowledge
Preparation	Not required
Organization	Small groups with no audience; a temporary leader may be selected
Purpose	To exchange ideas in order to make a group decision or plan of action

Formal Group Discussion

A formal discussion requires more preparation and organization than an informal discussion does. Consider these topics:

Should space exploration be continued?
Is a college education necessary to achieve success?

You may know something about each of the preceding topics. How much of what you know is only opinion, however, and how much is fact? If you were asked to discuss one of these topics, you would first have to do some research. A formal discussion requires preparation.

Another major difference between the informal and the formal discussion is the subject to be discussed. Generally, the subject of a formal discussion is either assigned to you or is selected by your group according to the needs or interests of the audience.

The formal discussion is also highly organized. One person is selected to be chairperson. The chairperson states the problem or subject, directs the discussion, makes sure that everyone has a chance to speak, and keeps the discussion moving.

Each member of the group has a responsibility to gather information from the many references that are available in the library. Then, the group members freely exchange ideas based on the information they have prepared. In this way, the members of the group and the audience learn more.

Formal Discussion	
Subjects	Assigned or determined by the needs or interests of the audience
Preparation	Very important; researched facts are needed
Organization	A chairperson is selected; discussion is presented in front of an audience
Purpose	To exchange ideas and information in order to inform the audience

Exercises

A For each subject tell whether it would best be discussed *informally* or *formally*. Provide your reasons for each decision.

1. Should schools be air-conditioned?
2. What should be the theme for the spring dance?
3. What are some suggestions for conserving energy?
4. Should school athletes be excused from class for travel to games?
5. Should schools have dress codes?

B Choose one of the subjects in Exercise A and have an informal discussion about it. Write a paragraph describing your discussion. Answer the following questions in your paragraph.

1. Did anyone take over leadership of the group?
2. Was a leader needed? Why or why not?
3. What responsibility did each member have?
4. Did anything slow down the group?
5. What might have improved this discussion?

Listening in Discussions

Good listening is just as important as effective speaking. Whether you are participating in an informal or a formal discussion, you will need to evaluate what is being said, so you can respond to the ideas of others in the group. Good listening is the key to good evaluating. Once you have evaluated what is being said, you will be better able to decide whether you agree with it. You will also find you are better prepared to respond intelligently to it.

The same listening skills are useful to you whether you are listening to one person give a speech or to several people in a discussion. Follow the guidelines given below to improve your listening skills.

1. **Listen for the purpose.** Speakers usually state their purposes in speaking when they begin to talk. For example, "I want to tell you a few things about the new club we're forming." When you keep a speaker's purpose in mind as you listen, you are better able to follow and evaluate the speaker's main points.

2. **Listen for the main points.** Informal discussions are usually less organized than formal ones. The main points in informal discussions may get covered by details and illustrations that are not important to the main subject. Any statement that wanders away from the main subject is a **digression**. For example, if the subject under discussion is where to go on a camping trip, and someone says, "I hope I get a new bicycle this year," this is a digression. It has nothing to do with figuring out where to go. To identify a digression, ask yourself this question, "Is this important to the discussion of the main subject?" If your answer is no, you are listening to a digression.

    In a formal discussion, each speaker has had more time to prepare a presentation. Therefore, the main points are usually well organized. They may even be numbered *first, second, third,* and so on. Or, a speaker may signal a new point by pausing or using a transitional word. For example, "*Next,* we have to figure out how to raise $500." Pay particular attention to any information that is preceded by a transitional word or by a pause.

3. Listen critically to distinguish fact from opinion. As you may recall, **a fact** is a statement that can be proved. **An opinion** cannot be proved. If you mistake an opinion for a fact, you may come to a false conclusion.

Fact   Some people keep young leopards as house pets.
Opinion Leopards make great house pets.

Suppose you mistook the opinion above for a fact? When a speaker in your group introduces a statement with a phrase such as *In my opinion, I think, I believe,* or *I feel,* you can be fairly sure that what follows is opinion.

A particular kind of statement called a **generalization** is usually a statement of opinion. A generalization claims that something is true *everywhere* or *always* or is true of *everyone, everybody, everything,* or *all.* Examine such statements carefully. Some generalizations may be factual, but most are not. A careful speaker will limit a general statement by using words that qualify the statement. *Often, many, some,* and *probably* are some of the words speakers use to qualify statements.

Generalization   The weather is *always* bad on the weekends.
Qualified Statement The weather is *often* bad on the weekends.

Exercise

Listen to a group discussion. This discussion may take place at school, at home, or on television or radio. Then, record the following elements of the discussion.

1. one speaker's purpose in speaking   2. the main points of that person's speech   3. a digression and the main subject from which it wandered   4. an opinion   5. a generalization.

3
Roles of Responsibility

From your own experience in different classes and organizations, you've probably noticed that when one person talks too much, nothing ever gets accomplished. Sometimes a simple discussion turns into an argument and still nothing gets accomplished. For a group discussion to be successful, everyone in the group must accept some responsibility.

When you are a member of either an informal discussion or a formal discussion, you will find that it will be much easier to achieve the purpose of the discussion if the following five roles of responsibility are accepted by members of the group. Each of these roles has a specific purpose.

The Chairperson or Temporary Leader

The role of chairperson or temporary leader carries a lot of responsibility. Each member of the group looks to the chairperson for guidance. The leader must know the subject well, be fair with all members, and see that the purpose of the discussion is accomplished. The chairperson has the following responsibilities:

1. **Starts the discussion by defining the problem or by offering the first bit of information. Look at these examples:**

   "Our purpose is to discuss the importance of using seat belts. There are many areas to consider in this issue, including safety, insurance benefits, government standards, and the results of manufacturers' tests. Barry, will you tell us what information you have gathered about this issue?"

   "If we're going to discuss what gift the student council should buy the school, let's first make a list of things that are needed. I would like to suggest a new and larger trophy case."

2. **Organizes the group into task forces if the subject involves a lot of material or if the group must come to more than one decision about the subject.**

"Andrea will discuss the insurance benefits of using seat belts, Paul will tell us about government standards that must be followed, and David and Sharon will discuss the results of the manufacturers' testing."

"Since we have enough money to buy two gifts and our ideas fall into two main categories, let's divide into two groups to make our final decision."

3. Keeps the discussion on the subject so that time and ideas won't be wasted.

"I think we're talking too much about the performance of individual cars rather than the use of seat belts in those cars. Let's get back to the importance of using seat belts."

"Instead of complaining about what's wrong with the gym, how about some good suggestions for gifts to make it better?"

4. Makes sure that everyone has a chance to talk so that all information and ideas are exchanged.

"Andrea, I think now would be a good time for you to tell us about the insurance benefits people receive when they use seat belts."

"Ed, we haven't heard your ideas yet about what we should buy as a gift. What is your suggestion?"

The Initiator

In an active discussion, everyone should "initiate" new ideas and facts. However, some people may choose to serve only as initiators. The initiator's responsibilities are the following:

1. Offers new ideas for discussion.

"I think we should also consider the safety of a small child in a car seat that has a seat belt."

"My idea is that the student council should buy more typewriters for the library. Everyone could benefit from that gift."

2. Gives additional information to support someone else's idea.

> "The *Newsweek* article I read agrees with your statement that it's just as important for people in the back seat to use seat belts as it is for those in the front seat."

> "I agree with Ann. The library needs more typewriters. It seems they are always taken when my friends and I need to type a report."

The Clarifier

As the clarifier, you help other group members to support their information and to think of new ideas. The responsibility of the clarifier is to stimulate thought, help others to make their ideas and information clear, and to initiate new ideas. By asking key questions and by making suggestions, the clarifier plays an important role. The clarifier has these responsibilities:

1. Asks questions about other people's information.

> "Sharon, how do we know that the test results for that manufacturer reflect the way all seat belts would perform?"

> "A new trophy case might be a good idea, but do you really think it's something the whole school would care about?"

2. Asks for additional information.

> "Paul, do you have more current statistics to prove that the majority of people seriously hurt in car accidents were not wearing seat belts?"

> "We have a lot of good ideas, but do we have to spend all of the money?"

The Summarizer

The summarizer keeps everyone in touch with what's happening during the discussion. When you act as the summarizer, it is important to listen carefully to keep track of the main points that have been made. Take notes and keep the group informed of its progress. The summarizer is responsible for the following:

1. **States main points that have been made so that the group is aware of its progress and what it still has to cover.**

> "So far we have discussed the government regulations for seat belts and the manufacturers' seat belt test results. Now, who has the accident statistics that remain to be discussed?"

> "We know that we have enough money to buy more than one gift, and that we have several good ideas and the approximate price of each. Now we need to make a final decision about what to buy."

2. **Points out areas of disagreement based on information from different sources or different group members. This helps to prevent arguments and helps the group to remember what is really important about the information.**

> "Government regulations state that there should be enough seat belts in every car for the number of people it can hold. Yet, David's research shows us that several manufacturers put only two seat belts in the back seat."

> "Joe says that a new trophy case is a good idea because the whole school is proud of its winning teams. On the other hand, Ann says that the hall is always so crowded near the trophy case that most people don't even bother to look at it."

The Evaluator

The evaluator states the conclusions of the group at the end of the discussion. During the discussion, the evaluator may play another role as well. The evaluator has one responsibility:

State the conclusions of the group at the end of the discussion.

> "The information presented by this group shows that the government, car manufacturers, and insurance agencies are all interested in the safety that seat belts give. The information also proves that if you use a seat belt you are less likely to be hurt seriously in an accident and that you will pay less for insurance. Therefore, using a seat belt is beneficial."

"Our final decision is to buy six new mats for the
gym and two new typewriters for the library."

The more group discussions you participate in, the easier it will
be to see the importance of the five roles of responsibility. You
may find that you are especially good at one role, or you may
want to change roles in different discussions. The five different
roles help the group to achieve the purpose of the discussion.

Exercises

A Read each of the following statements and identify who is
speaking: *the Chairperson or Temporary Leader, the Initiator,
the Clarifier, the Summarizer,* or *the Evaluator.*

1. "What we need to do is to divide into groups to get each
   part of this problem solved."
2. "Do you have more facts to prove that point?"
3. "Our final decision is to hold the Christmas dance on Friday,
   December 18, from 7:30 to 10:00 in the gym."
4. "I would recommend any of Jack London's books for good
   reading, especially *Call of the Wild.*"
5. "The information we have presented shows that our library's
   greatest need is for books about computers."
6. "We have shown that accident rates in the United States
   dropped when the speed limit went down to fifty-five miles
   per hour. Does anyone have data from other countries?"
7. "Dan, can you tell us the source of your information?"
8. "I think we should also consider forming a pep squad to help
   out the cheerleaders."
9. "Marla will discuss the different kinds of activities we might
   want to have at our after school program."
10. "Monica, can you explain more clearly how those statistics
    illustrate your point?"

B With four or five other people, plan a formal discussion to
present to your class. Choose a topic that interests all of you and
that can be easily researched in your school library. Elect a
chairperson and decide what information each person will be
responsible for. Do your research carefully and keep accurate
records of your sources. Present your discussion to the class.

English and Social Studies

TV and radio news shows help you keep up with current events. Perhaps you are following a crucial election campaign or you may just want to find out the baseball scores.

Whatever your interests are, you can benefit from the news shows. Not only do you become better informed, but you also get the advantage of watching and listening to trained, professional speakers. Notice how clearly and precisely newscasters speak. Consider the following report, for example.

> At this moment, there's a fire raging in a chemical factory on the city's east side. The company, Star Chemicals at 1212 May Street, produces chemicals for cleaning fluids.
> Firefighters have not yet gotten the blaze under control, but there have been no reports of injuries. The company's smoke alarms went off immediately, and the thirty-seven employees all fled to safety.

Activity Watch a TV news show tonight. Choose one story. Listen closely to the story. Take notes that answer the questions, *who, what, when, where, why,* and *how.* In addition, watch the newscaster carefully. In your next English class, present a two-minute "news spot" in which you tell the important facts of the story in the way that a newscaster might tell them. Be sure to time yourself as you practice.

Application and Review

A Identifying Types of Discussions Write whether each statement describes *an Interview, an Informal Discussion, a Formal Discussion, None,* or *All.*

1. Usually takes place as soon as a need arises.
2. Is headed by a chairperson.
3. Is usually between two people.
4. Gives people a chance to exchange ideas.
5. Requires participants to be good listeners.
6. Is used when people apply for a job.
7. Is highly organized.
8. Does not require preparation.
9. Can involve only one person.
10. Can best help decide what to name a family pet.

B Listening to Discussions From listening to either an informal or a formal discussion, write one speaker's purpose and main points. Tell whether this speaker used *numbers, transitional words, pauses, none of these,* or *all of these* to introduce main points. Then, write three facts and opinions from the discussion.

C Identifying Roles in Discussions Write whether each statement describes *a Chairperson or Temporary Leader, an Initiator, a Clarifier, a Summarizer,* or *an Evaluator.*

1. Keeps the discussion on the subject.
2. Defines the problem treated in a group discussion.
3. States the group's conclusions.
4. Keeps the group aware of what still needs to be covered.
5. Asks questions about other people's information.
6. Gives information to support someone else's ideas.
7. Points out areas of disagreement based on information from different group members.
8. Asks for additional information.
9. Offers new ideas for discussion.
10. Makes sure everyone has a chance to talk.

16
Library
and
Research Skills

Where can you find an
article on armadillos?
A recording of reggae?
A pamphlet about papaya?
A story by Steinbeck?
A video on vampires?

The library is more than just a collection of books. It is a community resource center filled with a wide range of written, visual, and oral materials. The library can be an invaluable aid for research, studying, or just enjoyment. In this chapter you will learn how to make the most of your library's vast resources.

1
The Library

When you were much younger, you might have written a report on cats strictly from what you knew about them. You might have described a cat you knew and the way most cats tend to behave. A few years after that, you might have written a report on cats based on the facts you'd gathered from an encyclopedia. This report would tell something about the body of a cat, the different breeds of cats that exist, the life cycle of a cat, and how to care for a cat. If, more recently, you wrote a report on this same subject, you might have also turned to almanacs, yearbooks, and periodicals to find interesting facts for your report. The homing instinct of some cats, for example, is so well developed that one cat was able to track its way back to its owner over 1,400 miles away.

A report on cats you might write today would include much more information than a report you might have written as a youngster. In part, this is because you now can make better use of your library. Your growth as a writer and researcher depends, at least in part, on the growth of your ability to find and use the resources available to you at the library.

Sections of the Library

To locate resources efficiently, you need to be familiar with the arrangement of the library. All library book collections are organized into the same basic sections. Review these by studying the chart on the following page.

Sections of the Library

Section	Contents
Catalog	Information about all library books and their locations is filed here. Facts on available non-print materials may be cataloged here too. The information is arranged alphabetically by author, title, and subject and is cataloged on cards, computer discs, or microfilm.
Reference	Reference works that must remain in the library are shelved in this area. These include dictionaries, encyclopedias, almanacs, yearbooks, and atlases. Desks or tables and chairs are often located in the reference area.
The Stacks	All the fiction books and nonfiction books not shelved in a special section, such as the reference section, are shelved here.
Periodical	This section consists of magazines, newspapers, and indexes to them, such as the *Readers' Guide to Periodical Literature*. This area is often part of the general reference section.
Children's	All children's books and reference materials are usually stored together in this section. Frequently, the materials here are listed in a catalog of their own that is kept in this area. Most public and elementary school libraries have a children's section.

A Special Section: Nonprint Materials

In this section you will find collections of recordings, art reproductions, films, filmstrips, projectors, and sometimes even videos. You may also find computers available for public use in this area.

All these items, with the exception of the projectors and computers, are usually listed along with their locations in special catalogs rather than in the card catalog for books. Each of these special catalogs is devoted to a specific kind of collection. One catalog may contain all listings for records, while another is devoted solely to videos, and so on. Most often, these catalogs are kept near the nonprint collections.

Nonprint materials are particularly good for use in classroom presentations. For example, by playing a recording of an old radio show you could involve your classmates in a report on radio shows of the 1930's. Usually you can find some sort of nonprint material related to a topic.

Computers may be useful to you in a variety of ways. You might use a computer program to increase your reading speed and comprehension, to study algebra, or to write an essay or report. Or, you might just relax at the computer by playing a computer game.

Exercise

Write the section of the library where you would find the information necessary to complete each of the following tasks.

1. Find a fairy tale to read to your younger cousin.
2. Get an audiovisual aid for a classroom presentation.
3. Glance through a book by Ray Bradbury.
4. Find all the listings of books by Ray Bradbury.
5. Study an atlas to plan a trip to Dallas, Texas.
6. Glance through a travel book about the American South.
7. Read last month's issue of *Scientific American* magazine.
8. Find out the location of a magazine article that is stored on microfilm.
9. Use a magazine index to find all the magazines that in the last month have printed articles on music videos.
10. Locate a video of your favorite movie.

2
The Classification and Arrangement of Books

Fiction books are usually grouped according to the type of fiction they are: mystery, science fiction, story collection, literature, and so on. Within these groups they are then shelved alphabetically according to the author's last name. Story collections are sometimes shelved by the editor's last name. To find most fiction works, you would simply search the stacks for the letter that begins the author's last name. If the author has written more than one book, you would find the author's works grouped together and then arranged alphabetically by title. Remember, when looking for a title that begins with *A*, *An*, or *The*, look under the first letter of the second word in the title. If two authors have the same last name, the placement of their books on the shelf will be determined first by this last name and then by the alphabetical order of the authors' first names.

The Dewey Decimal System

In most school libraries, nonfiction books are arranged according to the Dewey Decimal System. According to this system, nonfiction books are grouped into ten major categories.

Dewey Decimal System

000–099	General Works (encyclopedias, bibliographies)
100–199	Philosophy (conduct, psychology)
200–299	Religion (the Bible, mythology, theology)
300–399	Social Science (law, education, economics)
400–499	Language (grammars, dictionaries)
500–599	Science (mathematics, biology, chemistry)
600–699	Technology (medicine, inventions, cooking)
700–799	The Arts (painting, music, theater, sports)
800–899	Literature (poetry, plays, essays)—not fiction
900–999	History (biography, geography, travel)

Nonfiction books are grouped into these categories and then into still smaller categories, or subcategories. Even these subcategories are broken down. Look at the subcategories of *History* and the further subdivisions of the subcategory *History of North America* given below.

900	History	970	North America
910	Geography, travel, description	971	Canada
920	Biography	972	Middle America
930	Ancient history	973	United States
940	Europe	974	Northeastern states
950	Asia	975	Southeastern states
960	Africa	976	South central states
970	North America	977	North central states
980	South America	978	Western states
990	Other places	979	States of the Great Basin and Pacific Slope

According to the Dewey system, you would find a book on the California gold rush in the category of *History (900–999)*, the subcategory of *North America (970)*, under the further subdivision *Western states (978)*.

Although biography is also located between 900 and 999 (the exact number for biography is 920), in some libraries there is a special section for biography and autobiography. Books in this section have the label *B* on their spines and are arranged in alphabetical order by the last name of the person the book is about.

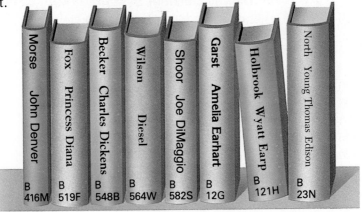

Morse John Denver — B 416M

Fox Princess Diana — B 519F

Becker Charles Dickens — B 548B

Wilson Diesel — B 564W

Shoor Joe DiMaggio — B 582S

Garst Amelia Earhart — B 12G

Holbrook Wyatt Earp — B 121H

North Young Thomas Edison — B 23N

The Library of Congress Classification

Some libraries use another system to classify nonfiction books. It is called the Library of Congress Classification, or LC. By the LC system, all fiction and nonfiction books are arranged into twenty-one major subject categories. Each category is shown by a letter of the alphabet. Every published book is assigned a Library of Congress number, so the LC system is easy for libraries to use. The Dewey system, on the other hand, takes librarians time because they must assign Dewey numbers to each book.

Exercises

A Write on your paper the following fiction titles and authors in the order in which they should appear on the library shelves.

1. *A Tree Grows in Brooklyn,* Betty Smith
2. *A Tale of Two Cities,* Charles Dickens
3. *The Good Earth,* Pearl S. Buck
4. *Lord of the Flies,* William Golding
5. *Lorna Doone,* R. D. Blackmore
6. *Adventures of Oliver Twist,* Charles Dickens
7. *A Wrinkle in Time,* Madeleine L'Engle
8. *East Wind, West Wind,* Pearl S. Buck
9. *Journey to Another Star and Other Stories,* Roger Elwood
10. *Why Corn Is Golden,* Vivian Blackmore

B Use the Dewey Decimal System chart on page 315 to determine the classification numbers between which the following nonfiction books should be found. Write the numbers on your paper.

1. *Skylab, Pioneer Space Station,* Wm. G. Helder
2. *I'm OK—You're OK,* Tom Harris
3. *Inside Jazz,* James Lincoln Collier
4. *The Right to Remain Silent,* Milton Meltzer
5. *Understanding Photography,* George Sullivan
6. *Plays for Great Occasions,* Graham DuBois
7. *Language,* David S. Thomson
8. *Insects as Pets,* Paul Villiard
9. *A Guidebook to Learning,* Mortimer Adler
10. *We, the Chinese,* Deirdre Hunter

3
The Card Catalog

The **card catalog** is a cabinet of small drawers in which cards for all the books in the library are filed alphabetically. There are usually three cards for each book: an author card, a title card, and a subject card. This enables you to find a listing for a book by looking it up in any one of three ways: by the author's last name, the first word of the title, or the subject it is about. Each card contains the same information about the book.

If your library has cataloged these listings on computer files, you can still look up a book in any of those three ways. Computer catalogs often tell if a book has been checked out.

Call Numbers

A **call number,** printed in the upper left corner of every nonfiction listing, tells you where a book is shelved. For nonfiction listings, the call numbers begin with the Dewey Decimal numbers by which the books are arranged in the stacks. If a library uses the Library of Congress classification system, then a Library of Congress letter-number code appears on the card instead of a Dewey number. The next part of the call number is the letter-number code called the **cutter number**. It appears below the Dewey number—or the Library of Congress code. The cutter number helps you narrow your search. Once you have found books that have the same Dewey number, look for the smaller group of books with the same cutter number. From these books you can spot the book you want.

Study the following diagram of a call number.

Call Number: **796.6**
                B225b

Book: *Bicycling*
Author: Nancy Neiman Baranet

Dewey Decimal
Classification Number —— **796.6**
Cutter Number —— **B225b** —— First Letter of Book Title
First Letter of ╱   Author's Assigned Number
Author's Last Name

On some cards you will find an additional code above the call number. This is a letter code that indicates the book is kept in a special section of the library. The following are the most commonly used letter codes and the locations they indicate.

Code	Location Indicated
R or REF	reference section
J or JUV	children's (juvenile's) section
B or BIO	biography section
F or FIC	fiction section
SC	story collection section
SF	science fiction section
MYSTERY	mystery section

At libraries that use the Dewey system, fiction books are shelved simply by the author's last name and therefore do not need call numbers. They have letter codes when necessary.

Guide Cards

These cards are placed in each drawer of the card catalog to help guide you to the correct place in the alphabet for the word you are looking for. They extend above the other cards and have letters or general headings on them.

Author Cards

Imagine you have read one book by John Steinbeck and liked it so much that you want to find another by him. The best place to look is under his name in the card catalog. At a glance you will know all the books by him that your library carries, regardless of whether they are currently on the shelves or out on loan. Furthermore, a card may also give a summary of a book's contents, the date it was published, a listing of its special features (illustrations, maps, etc.), its length, and also its location in the stacks.

If a book has two or more authors, you will be able to find an author card for it under either author's last name. Here is an example of a single author card for *How Things Work*.

Author Card

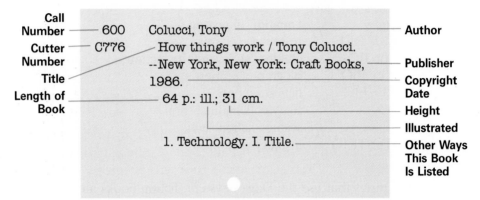

Title Cards

When looking up the title of a book in the card catalog, remember the following two guidelines:

1. If *A, An,* or *The* is the first word in the title, the card is alphabetized by the next word.
2. Abbreviations and numerals are alphabetized as if they were fully spelled out: *Mr.* is *Mister; 100* is *one hundred*; *U.S.* is *United States*.

Here is the title card for *How Things Work*.

Title Card

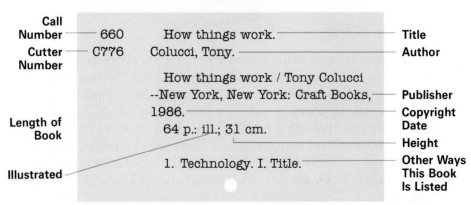

Subject Cards

When you want to find materials on a particular subject, the best approach is to look up the subject in the card catalog. You can find a subject card for *How Things Work* under the heading *Technology,* as in the following example.

Subject Card

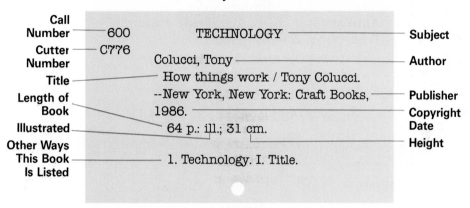

Cross-Reference Cards

When you look up a subject, you may find a card that reads *See* or *See also.* The *See* card refers you to another subject heading in the catalog that has the information you want.

***See* Card**

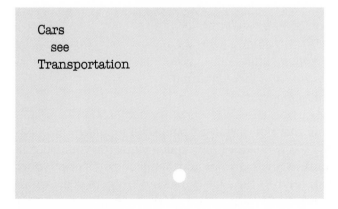

The *See also* card refers you to other subjects closely related to the one you are interested in. This card will help you to find a variety of information on the topic. It will also suggest other topics to you that might be more narrow and therefore easier to research thoroughly. One of these other topics might actually prove to be more interesting than your original subject.

See Also Card

COOKING
see also

Appetizers	Microwave cookery
Barbecue cookery	Salads
Casserole cookery	Sandwiches
Food as gifts	Soups
Frying	

also names of individual foods, e.g., Rice

Exercises

A For each of the following book titles write two subjects under which you might look to find a subject card for that book.

1. *Can Computers Invent Medicines?*
2. *Ethiopian Cooking*
3. *Robots in Industry*
4. *Child Labor Laws*
5. *Spanish Folk Songs*
6. *Are Whales Speaking to Us?*
7. *American History*
8. *Traveling in India*
9. *Nutrition for a Healthy Mind*
10. *Special Olympics*

B Imagine that you have just published a nonfiction book that you wrote. Now create three catalog cards for your book: an author card, a title card, and one subject card. Since your book is nonfiction, refer to the Dewey Decimal System chart on page 315 to assign a Dewey call number. Also, remember to write an appropriate letter code above the call number if one is needed. These codes are listed on page 319. You may make up all the other information.

4
The Reference Section

In the reference section, you are surrounded by the most up-to-date resource materials the library has to offer. The chart below lists some of the most useful resources.

Library Reference Materials

Reference Source	Contents	Examples
Dictionaries	spellings, pronunciations, and meanings of words	*Webster's New World Dictionary*
Encyclopedias	articles on nearly all known subjects	*Encyclopaedia Britannica*
Almanacs and Yearbooks	up-to-date facts, statistics, and un-usual information	*Facts on File, Information Please Almanac*
Atlases	detailed maps and geographical information	*The Hammond World Atlas*
Biographical References	detailed informa-tion about people's lives	*Webster's Biographical Dictionary*
Vertical File	pamphlets, booklets, catalogs, handbooks, and clippings filed by subject	
Readers' Guide to Periodical Literature	listings of articles that have appeared in periodicals (magazines, journals, and newspapers)	

After you have selected the type of reference work you need to use, you may still need to make a choice from several reference works of this kind. For example, you may need to find the almanac that contains the most current statistics. To make the best choice from all those that are available, first examine the publication dates to find the most recently published almanac. This will contain the most current statistics. Then, check the table of contents and/or the index of that almanac to be sure it contains the kind of statistics you are looking for. In general, by comparing the publication date, table of contents, and index of each reference work, you will be able to determine which is the best resource to use.

Excerpt from the *Readers' Guide*

Titan (Satellite) *See* Saturn (Planet)—Satellites	**Cross Reference**
Titanic (Steamship)	
After 73 years, a Titanic find. N. Angier. il map *Time* 126:68-70 S 16 '85	
Americans and French find the Titanic [work of robot vehicle Argo] C. Holden, il *Science* 229:1368-9 S 27 '85	**Author of Article**
Did the ghost of the Titanic appear on U.S. currency? [bank note] E. Rochette. il *Hobbies* 90:77+ N '85	
Discovering the 'unsinkable' Titanic. S. Aikenhead. il *Macleans* 98:52 S 16 '85	**Article Title**
Haunting images of disaster. E. McGrath. il *Time* 126:58 S 23 '85	
How we found Titanic. R. D. Ballard. il map *Natl Geogr* 168:696-719 D '85	**Name of Magazine**
The quest for the Titanic. R. Laver. il *Macleans* 98:44 Jl 15 '85	**Date of Magazine**
The sea gives up a secret. W. D. Marbach. il map *Newsweek* 106:44-6 S 16 '85	
Titanic controversies. W. D. Marbach. il *Newsweek* 106:57 S 23 '85	
A Titanic coup for science [location of shipwreck] il *U S News World Rep* 99:11 S 16 '85	**Illustrated Article**
Titanic weather. D. M. Lundlum. *Blair Ketchums Ctry J* 12:20-1 Ap '85	**Page Reference**
Undersea explorer who found Titanic [R. Ballard] il por *U S News World Rep* 99:9 S 23 '85	
Photographs and photography	
'Deep see' technology makes Titanic find [Argo survey] B. Bower. il *Sci News* 128:182 S 21 '85	**Volume Number**
Titanohematite	**Subject Entry**
Self-reversing minerals make a comeback. S. Weisburd. il map *Sci News* 127:234-6 Ap 13 '85	

Readers' Guide to Periodical Literature

This special index is to periodicals what the card catalog is to books. The unabridged guide lists the articles in over 135 periodicals alphabetically by author and by subject. The abridged, or shortened, guide lists the articles in forty-five periodicals. Study the excerpt on page 324 to review the parts of guide entries. As you may have noticed, most of the information in these entries is abbreviated. A list of abbreviations used in the entries is located in the front pages of each guide.

Exercises

A Write on your paper the best reference source in which to look for the answers to the following questions. Write one of the following: *Dictionary, Encyclopedia, Almanac or Yearbook, Atlas, Biographical Reference, Vertical File, Readers' Guide to Periodical Literature,* or *Periodical.*

1. What language did the word *barbecue* come from?
2. What two seas meet at the northern tip of Denmark?
3. Who was George Gershwin and what were his accomplishments?
4. What fashions for men and women were advertised in the late 1940's?
5. Who were the first two women elected to Congress?
6. What magazine articles has Isaac Asimov written?
7. Who was the founder of our town?
8. What are some general facts about Austin, Texas?
9. What articles have recently been written on gorillas, such as Koko, who use the sign language called Ameslan?
10. How do you pronounce the word *solder*?

B Write the following *Readers' Guide* entry on your paper and label the following parts of this entry: *title, author, magazine, volume, page reference,* and *date of publication.*

> **SALINE, Carol**
> How not to crumble under criticism. il *Redbook*
>   155: 19+ AG '80

Crossroads

English and Geography

Does this phrase sound familiar: "Your notebook could be in Timbuktu for all I know"? Does anyone really know where this place called Timbuktu is? Your library is a good place to find the answer.

There are all sorts of reference materials available at the library that can help you uncover the many mysteries of the globe. Atlases, for example, contain maps of all the different regions of the world. Encyclopedias provide information on just about anything you need to look up, and in the *Guinness Book of World Records* you can find such interesting facts as the world's largest city or the highest mountain. Yearly almanacs give you the most up-to-date facts about a wide variety of topics.

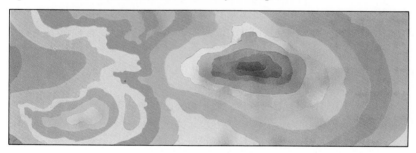

Activity Using a variety of resources (including your librarian), try to find the answers to the following geography questions. Tell which resources provided you with each answer.

1. Where is Timbuktu?
2. What is the most populous city in the world?
3. What is the most populous city in the United States?
4. Which continent is completely surrounded by water?
5. Where is Transylvania, home of Count Dracula?
6. What is the capital city of Canada?
7. Which European country looks like a boot?
8. What is the world's highest mountain?
9. What is the world's longest river?
10. What is the smallest state (in total area) in the United States?

Application and Review

A Identifying and Locating Needed Resources Imagine that a friend intends to give an oral report titled "Trekking in the Himalayas." He has already submitted a draft of this report to his teacher and received the following suggestions for revising it. Now he has come to you for help. For each revision suggestion, name the kind of resource that he will need to use. Then, indicate where this resource is located in the library.

1. Provide a definition of *trekking* and an explanation of where the word comes from.
2. Point out the trekking routes on a map of Nepal and Tibet.
3. Pass around the pamphlets and brochures that some agencies use to advertise the fact they arrange treks.
4. Let the students see photos of the Himalayan region.
5. Add do's and don't's of traveling in this region that recent travelers may have written.

B Understanding Cards in the Catalog Write on your paper an example of an author card, a title card, and a subject card, using the following information.

> Invent your own computer games, published in New York by F. Watts, Dewey decimal number 001.64, cutter number D571i, copyright date 1983, written by Fred D'Ignazio, 225 pages.

C Understanding the *Readers' Guide to Periodical Literature* On your paper, answer the following questions. Refer to the entries from the *Readers' Guide* excerpt on page 324.

1. In what periodical could you find an article about photographing the *Titanic*?
2. How many articles about the *Titanic* include a map?
3. Who wrote the article "The Sea Gives Up a Secret?"
4. What volume of *Newsweek* has two articles on the *Titanic*?
5. What periodical has the longest article on the *Titanic*?

17
Applying Dictionary and Spelling Skills

The Army Corps of Engineers examines core samples of earth before beginning a construction project. Who knows, the engineers may even find petrified pieces of apple core in their samples.

Your dictionary and spelling skills can help you make sense out of words such as *corps* and *core* that sound and sometimes look the same but have different spellings and meanings. To help you get to the core of the many ways words can be used, you will learn dictionary skills and study spelling tips and rules in this chapter.

1
Analyzing Dictionary Entries

A dictionary entry does more than define a word. It shows how the word is divided into syllables, how it is pronounced, where it comes from, and what part of speech it is. Much of the information is given in a type of "shorthand," that is, by abbreviations or symbols. In order to make use of the information, you must be able to understand these devices.

Word Division

In dictionary entries, the entry words are shown divided into their syllables. Some dictionaries use a space between syllables to show this; others use a centered dot.

al ma nac   al•ma•nac

In writing or typing a paper, you sometimes run out of space at the end of a line. If you cannot fit the whole word on one line, you must break the word at the end of a syllable and use a hyphen (-) to show that the word continues on the next line. The dictionary will show you the right place to break a word.

Correct   al-manac; alma-nac
Incorrect   alm-anac; alman-ac

Pronunciation

In a dictionary, the way a word should be pronounced is usually shown through a special respelling that appears in parentheses after the entry word. Not all dictionaries use the same system to show this respelling. The **pronunciation key** in the front of your dictionary shows you how to read the information in your edition. You will find a shortened form of the key at the bottom of most entry pages.

In the sample key on the next page, you will notice that some vowels have special marks above them. These are called **diacritical marks.** They tell you how the vowel should be pronounced. For example, the letter *a* with a horizontal line above it, *ā*, tells you to pronounce that vowel with a long sound as in the word *pay.*

In pronouncing a word with two syllables, you must emphasize one more than the other. The accent mark (′) after a syllable shows you that that syllable is emphasized, or accented. In words with three or more syllables, often two syllables are emphasized. In this case, the syllable shown with the darker accent mark will receive the greater emphasis, or stress.

pen•guin (peŋ′gwin)   dic•tion•ar•y (dik′shə ner′ē)

Exercise

Write the correct pronunciation for each word.

1. closet
2. stubborn
3. friendly
4. ambassador
5. definite
6. surrender
7. rabbit
8. bureau
9. beckon
10. queasy

Definitions and Parts of Speech

Many words have more than one meaning. Use a dictionary whenever you need help deciding which meaning of a word you need. Discovering the intended meaning can often be very important. Look at the trouble Ziggy is headed for if he doesn't know which meaning of *fired* the interviewer is using.

ZIGGY ©1981, Universal Press Syndicate.
Reprinted with permission. All rights reserved.

Many definitions in dictionary entries are followed by a sentence or phrase enclosed in brackets ([ ]) that shows how the word is used. The word is printed in italics. Look at the following examples.

land (land) *n.* [OE. < IE. base *lendh-,* heath] **1.** the solid part of the earth's surface not covered by water **2.** *a*) a country, region, etc. [a distant *land,* one's native *land]* b) a country's people **3.** ground or soil [rich *land,* high *land]* **4.** ground thought of as property [to invest in *land]* **5.** rural or farming regions [to return to the *land]* **6.** *Econ.* natural resources —*vt.* **1.** to put on shore from a ship [the ship *landed* its cargo] **2.** to cause to end up in a particular place or condition [a fight *landed* him in jail] **3.** to set (an aircraft) down on land or water **4.** to catch [to *land* a fish] **5.** [Colloq.] to get or win [to *land* a job] **6.** [Colloq.] to deliver (a blow) —*vi.* **1.** to leave a ship and go on shore [the tourists *landed]* **2.** to come to a port or to shore: said of a ship **3.** to arrive at a specified place [he *landed* in Phoenix after a long bus ride] **4.** to alight or come to rest, as after a flight, jump, or fall [the cat *landed* on its feet]

In addition to having several definitions, a word may function as more than one part of speech. For example the word *heat* can be used two ways. It can be a noun, meaning warmth, or a verb, meaning the act of making warm, as in *I heated the milk.* The dictionary will indicate the parts of speech with standard abbreviations such as the following:

n.	noun	*vt.*	transitive verb
pron.	pronoun	*vi.*	intransitive verb
adj.	adjective	*adv.*	adverb

The word *land,* in the sample entry above, may be used as a noun, a transitive verb, or an intransitive verb. Note that there are several definitions in each category.

The abbreviation *Colloq.* shown in brackets before a definition stands for the word *colloquial* (kə lō′ kwē əl). **Colloquial language** refers to words used in common, everyday speech. Do you understand the colloquial meanings of the word *land* used as a transitive verb?

Dictionary entries also include the inflected endings of words. See the dictionary entry for *bridge* on page 333. *Bridged* and *bridging* are additional forms of *bridge* used as transitive verbs.

Dictionary entries are full of interesting and special information. Notice in the same entry the specialized use of *bridge* in the fields of dentistry and music. This entry also tells you that there is a phrase, *burn one's bridges (behind one)*. This phrase is an **idiom**, which is a specially accepted expression.

Exercise

Refer to the dictionary entry for *bridge,* shown below. Write on your paper the part of speech (abbreviations given on page 332) and the number of the definition that fits the word as it is used in the following sentences.

bridge[1] (brij) *n.* [OE. *brycge:* for IE. base see BROW] **1.** a structure built over a river, railroad, etc. to provide a way across for vehicles or pedestrians **2.** a thing that provides connection or contact /a common language is a *bridge* between cultures/ **3.** *a)* the upper, bony part of the nose *b)* the curved bow of a pair of glasses fitting over the nose **4.** the thin, arched piece over which the strings are stretched on a violin, etc. **5.** a raised platform on a ship for the commanding officer **6.** *Dentistry* a fixed or removable mounting for false teeth, attached to nearby teeth **7.** *Music* a connecting passage —*vt.* **bridged, bridg′ing 1.** to build a bridge on or over **2.** to provide a connection, transition, etc. across /he tried to *bridge* the generation gap/ —**burn one's bridges (behind one)** to commit oneself to a course from which one cannot later retreat —**bridge′a•ble** *adj.*

1. I got angry when I broke the *bridge* of my violin.
2. Her mom went to the dentist to have a *bridge* put in her mouth.
3. The car was stalled on the *bridge.*
4. Music can *bridge* the gap between cultures.
5. The music formed a *bridge* between the cultures of the two countries.
6. She got hit on the *bridge* of the nose by a baseball.
7. The captain of the ship delivered his message from the *bridge.*
8. He broke the *bridge* of his glasses while he was playing basketball.
9. The chorus was the *bridge* between the verses of the song.
10. They *bridged* the gap between them with a hug.

2
Other Parts of an Entry

In addition to defining words, giving their pronunciation, dividing them into syllables, and giving their parts of speech, a dictionary entry usually gives synonyms and word origins.

Synonyms

Synonyms are words with similar meanings. Examples are *wealth* and *treasure, horrible* and *dreadful, strong* and *sturdy.*

Look at the dictionary entry below for the word *command.* After all the definitions for *command,* you will see the abbreviation *SYN.,* followed by seven words in dark type and their meanings. The abbreviation *SYN.* introduces the list of *synonyms.* A list of synonyms is called a **synonymy.**

> **com•mand** (kə mand′) *vt.* [< OFr. < VL. < L. *com-,* very much + *mandare:* see MANDATE] **1.** to give an order to; direct with authority *[the police commanded the thief to halt]* **2.** to have authority over; control *[he commands a large crew]* **3.** to have ready for use *[to command a large vocabulary]* **4.** to deserve and get; require as due *[to command respect]* **5.** to control or overlook from a higher position *[the fort commands the harbor]* —*vi.* to exercise authority; be in control; act as commander —*n.* **1.** an order; direction; mandate
> **2.** authority to command. **3.** power to control by position **4.** range of view **5.** ability to use; mastery *[his command of English is poor]* **6.** *a)* a military or naval force, organization, or district, under a specified authority *b) same as* AIR COMMAND **7.** the post where the person in command is stationed
> *SYN.*—**command,** when it has to do with giving orders, suggests a doing so with the absolute authority of a king, dictator, general, etc.; **order** often stresses the bullying or browbeating of others, and sometimes the use of threats to force others to do as one wishes *[he was ordered to report for duty];* **direct** and **instruct** are both used in connection with management or supervision, as in a business firm, **instruct** perhaps more often stressing the giving of directions clearly and in detail; **enjoin** suggests a directing along with strong warning *[he enjoined them to keep it a secret]* and sometimes involves the prohibiting of some action by legal order; **charge** often involves the giving to someone of some task that should or must be done—see also *SYN.* at POWER

Synonyms, you remember, don't have exactly the same meaning; they have similar meanings, each slightly different from the other. A **synonymy** explains the specific meaning of each synonym listed. Often, it will include examples of how the synonyms are used in phrases or sentences.

A synonymy can help you choose the best word for what you want to say. The word *command* and its synonyms, for example, all have to do with telling someone to do something. There is a big difference, you will agree, between *instructing* a person to do something and *ordering* him or her to do it.

Exercises

A For each of the following words, find two synonyms. Write the synonyms. Then, write a sentence using each to show its specific meaning.

1. comfort	3. method	5. humble	7. effect	9. calm
2. go	4. tell	6. rich	8. lovely	10. fatal

B Find an appropriate synonym to replace the italicized word in each sentence.

1. James ordered me to *stop*.
2. Have you ever seen such a *broad* sidewalk?
3. Some people do not tell their *true* ages.
4. I could not *escape* falling on the ice.
5. The boat moved along in the *fast* current.
6. Jennifer wanted to *help* me in loading the car.
7. She spoke in a low *murmur*.
8. What an *intelligent* solution to our problem!
9. No one *intended* for this to happen.
10. I like to watch the *flash* of neon lights.

Word Origins

Some dictionary entries will include, in brackets, information about the origin of the word. In some dictionaries, this information will appear before the definitions; in others it will appear after all the definitions. Look at the following example.

> **brit•tle** (brit′l) *adj.* [<OE. *breotan,* to break] **1.** easily
> broken or shattered because hard and inflexible

Here, the information about the origin of the word precedes the definition. Within the brackets comes, first, the symbol, <, which means "derived from," or "coming from." Next comes the abbreviation OE., which stands for Old English. The word *breotan*, then, is the Old English word meaning "to break" from which the Modern English word *brittle* has come.

The English language has grown and changed over the centuries, gradually shifting from what is called Old English (OE.) to Middle English (ME.) to Modern English (ModE.). Also, many English words have been borrowed from other languages. Look at the dictionary entry for *base:*

base (bās) *n., pl.* **bas'es** (-əz) [<OFr. *bas* < L. *basis*, BASIS]

The word *base* comes from the Old French (OFr.) word *bas*, which in turn, came from the Latin (L.) word *basis*.

If you need help in reading the information about the origin of words, check the list of abbreviations in the front of your dictionary.

Exercise

Match the Old English words with the Modern English words in the following lists. Write the word pairs on your paper.

Modern English		**Old English**	
1. bear	6. bow	1. yfel	6. betera
2. evil	7. dill	2. bugan	7. ofer
3. nineteen	8. over	3. regn	8. helpan
4. rain	9. help	4. nigontyne	9. beran
5. better	10. bottom	5. dile	10. botm

Early English poem by Thomas Hoccleve with portrait of Chaucer, 1411.

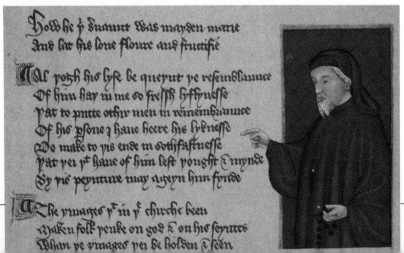

3
Using a Dictionary for Spelling and Writing

The dictionary is one of the most useful reference books you will ever use. It can be especially valuable to you when you are revising and proofreading your writing. (See Chapter 5 for more information on proofreading.) It is at this stage that you want to make certain that you have chosen the best word to express what you want to say—the synonymy will help you here. The dictionary will also help you spell words correctly.

How can you use the dictionary to help spell words? One way is to use the word-finder table in the front of the dictionary. It gives the spellings for different sounds. You can also look up a word that you do know how to spell when you are not sure about the spelling of one of its forms. For example, you can find the plurals of nouns, the comparative and superlative of adjectives and adverbs, and the principal parts of irregular verbs.

Exercises

A Look up the synonyms for the words printed in italics in the following sentences. For each word, write on your paper a synonym that fits the sentence better.

1. They *lifted* the flag on the Fourth of July.
2. The *strange* old house looked like gingerbread.
3. His assignment was to *tell* the results of the survey.
4. The *bright* diamond flashed on her finger.
5. Smiling, she *commanded* her sister to do her homework.

B Write the correct form of the words printed in italics.

1. the correct form—*judgment* or *judgement*
2. the plural of *woman*
3. the correct form—*surprise* or *surprize*
4. the correct form—*irresistable* or *irresistible*
5. the plural of *hero*

4
Spelling Tips and Rules

You can improve your spelling skills without a dictionary too. As you become a better speller, you may find it less necessary to rely on the dictionary.

Good Spelling Habits

1. **Find out what your personal spelling demons are and conquer them.** Keep a list of the words you have misspelled in your schoolwork. Master the spelling of those words.
2. **Pronounce words carefully.** Pronouncing words correctly sometimes helps you spell them correctly. If you spell *helpfully* as *helpfly,* it could be because you are mispronouncing the word.
3. **Get into the habit of seeing the letters in a word.** Often, English spellings do not appear to make sense. By looking at them carefully, you will remember new or difficult words more easily.
4. **Think up a memory device for difficult words.** For example:

   > a**cq**uaint (*cq*) To get a**cq**uainted, I will *seek you* (*cq*).
   > princi**pal** (*pal*) The princi**pal** is my *pal.*
   > princi**ple** (*ple*) Follow this princi**ple**, *please.*

5. **Proofread everything you write.** Read what you've written slowly, word for word. You might even try reading a line in reverse order. Otherwise, your eyes may play tricks on you and let you skip a misspelled word.

A Method of Attack on Particular Words

1. Look at the word and say it to yourself. Say it one syllable at a time. Look at each syllable as you say it.
2. Look at the letters and say each one.
3. Write the word without looking at it.
4. Now check to see if you spelled it correctly. If it is correct, write it two more times.
5. If you made a mistake, note exactly what the mistake was. Then repeat steps 3 and 4 above.

Words Ending in a Silent e

Before adding a suffix beginning with a vowel to a word ending in a silent *e*, drop the *e* (with some exceptions):

amaze + -ing = amazing	love + -able = lovable
create + -ed = created	nerve + -ous = nervous

Exceptions: change + -able = changeable   courage + -ous = courageous

When adding a suffix beginning with a consonant to a word ending in a silent *e*, keep the *e* (with some exceptions):

late + -ly = lately	spite + -ful = spiteful
noise + -less = noiseless	state + -ment = statement

Exceptions: true + -ly = truly   argue + -ment = argument

Words Ending in a y

Before adding a suffix to a word that ends in a *y* and is preceded by a consonant, change the *y* to *i*:

easy + -est = easiest   crazy + -est = craziest

However, when you add *-ing*, the *y* does not change.

worry + -ed = worried   worry + -ing = worrying

When adding a suffix to a word ending in *y* that is preceded by a vowel, you usually don't change the *y*.

play + -er = player   employ + -ed = employed

Words Ending in a Consonant

In words of one syllable that end in one consonant preceded by one vowel, double the final consonant before adding a suffix beginning with a vowel:

dip + -er = dipper	set + -ing = setting
hop + -ed = hopped	drug + -ist = druggist

The rule does not apply to words of one syllable that end in one consonant preceded by two vowels:

feel + -ing = feeling	peel + -ed = peeled
reap + -ed = reaped	heat + -ing = heating

In words of more than one syllable, double the final consonant (1) when the word ends with one consonant preceded by one vowel and (2) when the word is accented on the last syllable:

be•gin′   per•mit′   re•fer′

In the following examples, note that in the new words formed with suffixes, the accent remains on the same syllable.

be•gin′ + -ing = be•gin′ning
de•ter′ + -ence = de•ter′rence

In the following examples, the accent does not remain on the same syllable; thus, the final consonant is not doubled:

re•fer′ + -ence = ref′er•ence
con•fer′ + -ence = con′fer•ence

Exercises

A Write on your paper the new words formed by adding the indicated suffixes to the following words.

1. compete + -ing
2. forty + -eth
3. relate + -ion
4. lazy + -est
5. outrage + -ous
6. drive + -ing
7. happy + -ness
8. argue + -ment
9. apply + -ed
10. joy +-ous

B Write on your paper the new words formed by adding the indicated suffixes to the following words. Indicate the accented syllable with an accent mark (′). If the word has only one syllable, no accent mark is needed.

1. drop + -ed
2. refer + -ing
3. heat + -ed
4. patrol + -ing
5. prefer + -ence
6. drag + -ing
7. control + -able
8. scoot + -er
9. cancel + -ed
10. trim + -ing

Prefixes and Suffixes

When you add a prefix to a word, do not change the spelling of the base word.

dis- + approve = disapprove
ir- + regular = irregular
un- + noticed = unnoticed

re- + build = rebuild
mis- + spell = misspell
over- + ripe = overripe

When you add the suffix -*ly* to a word ending in an *l*, keep both *l*'s. When you add -*ness* to a word ending in an *n*, keep both *n*'s:

careful + -ly = carefully   sudden + -ness = suddenness
final + -ly = finally   thin + -ness = thinness
special + -ly = specially   open + -ness = openness

Special Spelling Problems

Only one English word ends in *sede: supersede.* Three words end in *ceed: exceed, proceed,* and *succeed.* All other words ending in the sound "seed" are spelled with *cede:*

precede   recede   secede   concede

In words with *ie* and *ei* when the sound is long *e* (*ē*), the word is spelled *ie* except after *c.*

I BEFORE *E*

thief   relieve   piece   field   grieve   pier

EXCEPT AFTER *C*

conceit   perceive   ceiling   receive   receipt

EXCEPTIONS:

either   neither   weird   leisure   seize

Exercises

A Correct the misspelled words in the following sentences.

1. The zebra is an unusual speceis.
2. It can be identified by its wierd marks.
3. Its stripes form an iregular pattern.
4. Stripes run verticaly across its sides.
5. Horizontal lines are usualy on its legs.
6. Zebras enjoy the openess of the grassy plains.
7. Their stubborness makes zebras hard to tame.
8. A few trainers do succede in taming them.
9. The zebra's habitat has receeded.
10. It is unecessary, however, to worry about the zebra becoming extinct.

5
Words Often Confused

The following words are often misused and misspelled. Many of these are homonyms. **Homonyms** are words that have the same sound and often the same spelling but differ in meaning.

As you study the following words, notice how their meanings differ. Try to remember which meaning belongs with which word.

accept means "to agree to something" or "to receive something willingly."

except means "to exclude" or "to omit." As a preposition, *except* means "but" or "excluding."

> Did the teacher *accept* your explanation?
> Students who behaved well were *excepted* from the penalty.
> Everyone smiled for the photographer *except* Jody.

capital may refer to "the large letter used to begin the first word in a sentence" or to "the seat of government in a state or country."

capitol refers to "the building where a state legislature meets."

the Capitol is "the building in Washington, D.C., where the United States Congress meets."

> We use *capital* letters to begin such proper names as New York City and Abraham Lincoln.
> Is Madison the *capital* of Wisconsin?
> Protestors rallied at the state *capitol*.
> A subway connects the Senate and the House in the *Capitol*.

des′ert is "a dry, sandy region with little vegetation."

de sert′ means "to leave or abandon."

dessert (note the change in spelling) is "a sweet food, such as cake or pie, served at the end of a meal."

> The Sahara in North Africa is the world's largest *desert*.
> The night guard did not *desert* his post.
> Alison's favorite *dessert* is chocolate cake.

heal means "to make well, to cure."
heel refers to "the back part of a person's foot or of a shoe."

> If the wound is clean, it should *heal* fast.
> When the *heel* of my shoe came off, I walked lopsidedly.

hear means to "to listen to" or "to take notice of."
here means "in this place."

> When the TV is on, we can't *hear* the doorbell.
> The softball team practices *here* on the south field.

hoarse describes "a sound that is harsh and grating; especially a voice."
horse is "a large hoofed animal, used for riding and for carrying loads."

> When I get a cold, I am usually *hoarse* for a week.
> Farm *horses* used to pull plows and do other work that tractors do now.

its is a pronoun that shows possession.
it's is a contraction for *it is* or *it has.*

> Sanibel Island is known for *its* beautiful beaches.
> *It's* great weather for a picnic!

loan refers to "something given for temporary use and expected to be returned."
lone refers to "the condition of being by oneself, alone."

> I gave that shirt to Max as a gift, not as a *loan.*
> The *lone* plant in our backyard is really a scraggly weed.

lose means "to mislay" or "to suffer the loss of something."
loose means "free" or "not fastened."

> That tire will *lose* air if you don't patch it.
> My little brother has three *loose* teeth.

peace means "calm or quiet; freedom from disagreements or quarrels."
piece refers to "a portion or part of something."

> If you want *peace* and quiet, go to the library.
> A *piece* of the scenery crashed onto the stage.

principal describes something "of chief or central importance."
It also refers to "the head of an elementary or high school."
principle is "a basic truth, standard, or rule of behavior."

> Declining enrollment is the *principal* reason for closing the school.
> We will get our diplomas from the *principal*.
> One of my *principles* is a belief in total honesty.

quiet refers to "freedom from noise or disturbance."
quite means "truly" or "almost completely."

> Observers must be *quiet* during the recording session.
> I was *quite* worried when Kevin didn't return.

stationary means "fixed" or "unmoving."
stationery refers to "paper used for writing letters."

> The steering wheel moves, but the seat is *stationary*.
> Rex wrote on special *stationery* that had his name printed on it.

their means "belonging to them."
there means "in that place."
they're is a contraction for *they are*.

> All the campers returned to *their* cabins.
> I keep my coin collection *there* in those folders.
> Lisa and Tammy practice hard, and *they're* becoming very good at soccer.

to means "toward," or "in the direction of."
too means "also, very, or more than enough."
two is the number 2.

> The President flew *to* France for the conference.
> Megan is healthy, and she is happy, *too*.
> *Two* of my friends will be on TV tonight.

weather refers to "atmospheric conditions," such as temperature or cloudiness.
whether helps to express choice or alternative.

> Computers will soon be able to predict the *weather*.
> Val had to decide *whether* to tell the truth or to save Bob from feeling hurt.

who's is a contraction for *who is* or *who has*.
whose is the possessive form of *who*.

> *Who's* going to the recycling center?
> *Whose* parents will drive us to the movie?

your is the possessive form of *you*.
you're is a contraction for *you are*.

> What was *your* time in the fifty-yard dash?
> *You're* heading the canned food drive, aren't you?

Exercise

Write on your paper the correct word, from those given in parentheses, in the following sentences.

1. My brother is trying to (lose, loose) some weight.
2. He bandaged the wound carefully, but it just wouldn't (heel, heal).
3. When you go to the refreshment stand, could you buy me some grape juice (to, too, two)?
4. Margaret couldn't decide (weather, whether) to take Spanish or French.
5. Where did they leave (their, there, they're) coats?
6. Ms. Derwinski has been the (principal, principle) of the school for two years.
7. People are expected to be (quiet, quite) in the library.
8. I think I left my notebook over (their, there, they're).
9. The (Capitol, capital, capitol) of Illinois is Springfield.
10. He was going to (accept, except) an award that evening.
11. Could you turn the radio up so I can (here, hear) it better?
12. (It's, its) almost time for the movie to begin.
13. Dan, will you (lone, loan) me a dollar until tomorrow?
14. Rachel, (whose, who's) my best friend, got a job.
15. (Your, You're) just the person I was looking for.
16. Chris bought her mother a box of (stationary, stationery).
17. He asked his dad if he could have a (peace, piece) of fruit.
18. When I don't get enough sleep, I get (horse, hoarse).
19. The poster was printed in all (Capitol, capitol, capital) letters so people could read it from a distance.
20. The dog frantically searched for (its, it's) bone.

English and Art

   Like writing, art is an important way of communicating ideas
and feelings. Art has a language of its own. To fully understand
art, you need to understand its language. What if you were
entering a poster contest, for example, and you found out that
the poster could be in *pastels* or *gouache*? Would you know the
meaning of these words? If you were invited to the art museum
to see an exhibit of *impressionism*, would you know if you would
be interested in seeing it?

Activity In this chapter you have learned a number of ways to
use the dictionary. Now you can use it to improve your understanding of art. Look up the following art words and list their
meanings. Use some of the words to describe the painting on this
page.

1. perspective	4. abstract	7. pastels	10. realism
2. composition	5. pigments	8. collage	11. monochrome
3. impressionism	6. cityscape	9. tempera	12. relief

Dead End, Jessica A. Brett, Student Artist.

Application and Review

A **Using a Dictionary** Use your dictionary to follow each direction given below.

1. Divide the following words into syllables.
   environment   aluminum   occasional   spectacular
2. Show where you would put an end-of-line hyphen in the following words: barrel   conflict   neither
3. Write the origin of the word *arctic*. When is it capitalized?
4. Show the pronunciation for each of the following words.
   phonograph   neighborhood   absence   muscle
5. Write two sentences using the word *fire* as a different part of speech in each.
6. Write the first meaning given in your dictionary for the word *mark* used as a transitive verb.
7. Write the correct spellings of the following words.
   mouth wash   livingroom   snow storm
8. Write a sentence using a synonym for the word *expect*.
9. Write six meanings for the word *strike*.
10. Write the origins of the words *strength, stress,* and *style*.

B **Spelling Correctly** Write the correct words for the misspelled words in the following sentences.

1. He was nerveous about going to the doctor.
2. The whether is so changable in this area in the spring.
3. Its nice that you have more time for you're sister latly.
4. She was a little worryed about her new job.
5. The drugist just rememberred to fill my prescription.
6. Finaly, she permited him to leave the room.
7. It's ilogical to buy overipe fruit.
8. They were releived to find there coats on the peir.
9. Did you recieve a letter from the principle about the test scores two?
10. Both cars had exceded the speed limit by at least ten miles per hour.

18
Improving Study Skills

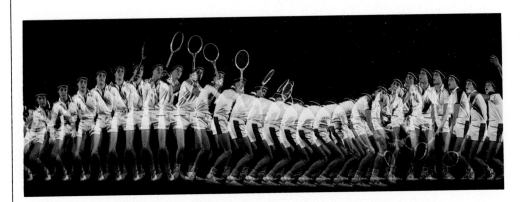

The ball streaks toward you. Will you slam it back—or miss? Skill and practice make the difference in sports as well as in school.

Your chances of doing well at school will increase if you develop and practice good study skills.

This chapter will help you master study skills. You will learn how to make a study plan and take helpful notes. You will be introduced to the SQ3R study method. You will learn how to evaluate sources, use the parts of a book, memorize, and use graphic aids.

1
Preparing to Study

To complete any classroom assignment well, you must understand what your teacher expects. Your teacher will give you oral or written directions. Being able to follow both kinds of directions is important to successfully completing assignments. Look at what happens when this man doesn't follow directions.

Following Directions

To take oral directions well, follow these steps.

How to Follow Oral Directions
1. Concentrate only on what is being said.
2. Notice how many steps are involved.
3. Associate a key word with each step, such as *Read, Answer,* or *Write.*
4. Ask questions to clarify any step you do not understand.
5. Repeat the directions and then write them down.

To fully understand written directions, follow these steps.

How to Follow Written Directions
1. Read all the steps in the directions completely before you start to carry out any steps.
2. Ask questions to clarify any points not covered in the directions.
3. See what materials you will need and assemble them before you begin.
4. Decide on the best order in which to carry out the steps.
5. Reread each step before you perform the task it describes.

Exercise

Use the steps for written directions to follow these directions.

1. Write down the number of letters in your first name.
2. Add to that the number of letters in your last name.
3. Double the result and add your age to it.
4. Omit step three if you are left-handed. Instead, add 25 to the result of step two.
5. Remember, if you are reading the directions correctly, you should be reading all five steps before you begin to follow them. Now, write your name and ignore steps 1–4.

Keeping an Assignment Book

It would be almost impossible to remember every detail of every assignment you are given. Get into the habit of writing down each assignment as soon as you receive it. Record the information in a separate assignment book or in a special section of your notebook. Include the following details about each assignment: subject, the assignment, the date it was assigned, and the date it is due. Look at the following example:

	Subject	Assignment	Date Given	Date Due
◯	History	① Read pp. 210-217	11-8	11-9
		② Book report - Civil War content 300 words. Include summary.	11-8	11-24

Learning to Set Goals

You will continually be balancing daily assignments with more involved, long-term projects. If you organize your time well, however, you will have no trouble completing all of your assignments by their due date. The key to planning your time is learning to set long- and short-term goals.

Every day, determine which assignments have to be completed overnight. Make it your **short-term goal** to complete these. Establish a regular block of time each day for working on these assignments.

Some types of assignments cannot be completed overnight. With such an assignment, finishing the entire project by the due date is your **long-term goal.** Recognize, however, that each long project is made up of several steps. Each of these steps becomes a short-term goal.

It is up to you to identify the smaller steps and decide how much time is needed to complete each one. For instance, suppose you are writing a report on hummingbirds. Your first step will be getting to the library to find your research sources. Then you must read and take notes. Next, you must organize your notes and put them in outline form. After that, you will work on your first draft, and then spend time revising it. Last, you will write your final copy. Obviously, you must plan ahead to allow yourself time to complete each step.

Making a Study Plan

A study plan is simply a way to schedule the various long-term and short-term tasks you have to complete.

To meet your short-term goals, establish a regular block of study time. Add your regular activities to this schedule. The smaller tasks for a long-term assignment must fit into this schedule, too. Look once more at the steps that would be required for the report on hummingbirds previously discussed. Notice how one student fit these tasks into a two-week schedule.

Monday	Tuesday	Wednesday	Thursday	Friday	Saturday	Sunday
Go to library Begin research	Committee meeting	Research	Write up science experiment	Basketball game	Finish research	Organize notes
Begin rough draft	Rough draft	Study for history test	Revise	Sharon's party!	All day trip	Make final copy

2
Using SQ3R to Study

The **SQ3R method** consists of these steps: **S**urvey, **Q**uestion, **R**ead, **R**ecord, and **R**eview. Learn this method by studying these steps in detail:

1. **Survey.** Look over the entire article to get a general idea of what you will be reading. Read the introduction.
2. **Question.** Prepare a set of questions by turning each title and heading into a question. Use any study questions provided by the book or your teacher.
3. **Read** the selection. Look for answers to the questions as you read. Also identify the central thoughts in each section.
4. **Record** the answers to your prepared questions. Make sure you have also understood and recorded any other important points of the selection.
5. **Review** the selection. Read over your notes and look over the main points in the book.

Exercise

Use the SQ3R method to read the following selection. Follow the directions that precede the selection as you study.

1. Survey the selection. What titles and subtitles do you notice? What is the general topic of the selection?
2. Write a set of questions. Read any provided questions.
3. Now read the selection. Find answers to all questions.
4. Record the answers to all questions.
5. Review the main points of the selection.

A Long History

Sources of History All peoples record the events of their past, their *history*. Some records are spoken, and some records are written. However, the records that have survived never tell the whole story. We have to rely on *theory*, a guess based on limited evidence.

Theory Explains the Indian Arrival Many years ago, glaciers covered most of North America. This ice expanded and melted many times before it finally withdrew from the continent. Scientists have developed a theory that animals and people walked from Asia into what is now Alaska during a time when an ice bridge connected Asia and North America. Over many years, these early peoples wandered southward and fanned into eastern areas of both North and South America.

Records of Big-Game Hunters The first Americans hunted large animals called big game. Records of these early life styles exist in the form of stones and bones. Carved bones of now extinct animals have been found in central Mexico. Remains of a bison killed thirty thousand years ago by early Americans have been found in Idaho. The search for more knowledge continues.

Food-Gathering Cultures When big-game hunting declined, early Americans had to find other food sources to survive. The shift from big-game hunting to the use of plants and small animals for food was an important step in the history of early Americans. A new culture based on food gathering reached its broadest development about seven thousand years ago.

Agricultural Societies Over five thousand years ago maize (corn) was first grown from wild plants. In 1948 tiny cobs of domesticated maize were found in caves in New Mexico and Mexico. Also domesticated were beans, chili peppers, sweet potatoes, and other crops. After farming became possible, many American cultures changed from food-gathering to farming societies.

As people began to rely on farming, they had to settle down and live in one place, at least during the planting and harvesting seasons. The settlements around farmlands became villages. Some villages grew to be cities with streets, plazas, and temples.

For Review
1. What is history? How can people learn about the past?
2. Identify three significant changes that occurred in early American history.
3. How did the development of farming lead to the formation of communities on our continent?

3
Taking Notes

Whenever you are studying or listening in class, get into the habit of taking notes. Note taking helps you understand and remember what you read or hear, helps identify the important points in the material, and provides a reference for later study.

Taking Notes as You Read

When you are taking notes during class, doing research, or reading your daily assignments, use a notebook. Divide the notebook into sections for each subject. Put the subject and the date at the top of each page of notes.

Use your own words when taking notes. Develop a set of abbreviations you can use to save time, such as & for *and* and *w/* for *with*. Make sure your notes include all the important points, key words, and definitions you identify as you read.

Taking Notes as You Listen

In a class lecture, you will not be able to write down every word you hear. Therefore, take notes only on major points and key details. Listen for key phrases that tell you what is important: "The main point is . . ." or "What you should remember is . . ." Also listen for clues such as *first, also,* and *furthermore.* The key to note taking is learning to recognize important information.

Using a Modified Outline

One way to take notes quickly and easily is to use a modified outline form. A modified outline breaks information into main headings and related details. Underline each main heading and list the details below it. Use numbers, letters, or dashes to identify details. Look at this example:

Points that affect consumer choices
— Personal taste
— Cost
— Safety

4
Evaluating Sources

When you are doing research on a particular topic, you may find many sources that deal with the topic. You will need to judge which sources are reliable and up to date.

Use these guidelines to evaluate a reference source:

1. **Check the publication date.** Is the material up to date? Look at the copyright date on the page following the title page of a book. Check the cover of a magazine.
2. **Check the credentials of the author.** Is the author an expert in the field? Look at the end of the article or the jacket of the book to find information about the author's work experience and publications.
3. **Separate fact from opinion.** Can the statements made be checked or proved? Are the statements based on actual evidence? Are emotional words used? Might the author be biased for or against the subject for some reason?

Exercise

Assume that you are researching the following subjects. Explain why each source of information below may not be reliable.

1. *Subject* recent improvements in high-speed trains
   Source a science magazine article written by a qualified engineer in 1974
2. *Subject* proper dental hygiene
   Source a new brochure by a manufacturer of hygiene products listing reasons to buy a brand of toothpaste
3. *Subject* Chinese industry
   Source a book by a famous entertainer describing her recent visit to China
4. *Subject* an evaluation of rock music of the 1980's
   Source an interview with a classical pianist
5. *Subject* the effect of TV on recent political elections
   Source a study of the TV debates by presidential candidates published in 1966

5
Types of Reading

The way you read changes with your purpose for reading. Different types of reading are appropriate for different situations.

Fast Reading

Skimming and **scanning** are two types of fast reading. When you survey written material to get a general impression of its content, you are **skimming**. To skim, move your eyes quickly over the entire page or selection. Look for titles, chapter headings, italicized words, and any pictures, charts, or graphs.

Scanning is another type of fast reading. Its purpose is to locate quickly a particular piece of information. To scan, move your eyes rapidly over the page. Look for key words that will help you locate the information you need.

In-Depth Reading

When you want to get the full benefit of a piece of writing, you must use **in-depth reading.** This type of reading calls for careful, thoughtful reading and rereading of paragraphs.

The key to in-depth reading is to look for the topic sentence or main idea of each paragraph. Then notice what method is used to develop that main idea. Did the writer use examples, reasons, details, or comparisons?

Train yourself to notice how the paragraphs relate to each other and to the entire selection. You must be able to tell which paragraphs present main ideas.

Exercise

Follow these directions.

1. Skim the selection on pages 232–233 to determine the main idea of this selection.
2. Read the selection in depth.
3. Scan the selection to find two examples of violence in the life of early man.

6
Memorizing

You need to memorize certain information to use it. For example, you must memorize math formulas so that you can use them whenever you need them. You memorize frequently used phone numbers so that you can dial them from wherever you may be.

Here are some different ways to memorize new information. Use the method that works best for you.

1. **Say the information out loud.** Often, hearing it helps you remember it.
2. **Write the information**. The action of writing sometimes helps imprint things in your memory. Seeing what you have written also helps the material stay in your mind.
3. **Connect ideas.** Connect, or associate, the facts in some way. You might put a list of social studies words in alphabetical order. Historic events would be put in chronological order.
4. **Use memory games.** Try visualizing what you want to remember. Close your eyes and picture the items; to recall the items, visualize the same picture.

   Try making up a sentence using words that start with the first letters of the words you want to memorize. Or, make up a funny name using the first letters of those words. For example, the colors of visible light are red, orange, yellow, green, blue, indigo, and violet, in that order. A funny name often used to help remember the order is Roy G. Biv.
5. **Repeat the information often.** Repeat your list or memory game over a period of days until it comes to mind easily.

Exercise

The following are the countries of Central America. Try to memorize them by making up a funny sentence using words that start with the same first letters as the countries. Then close your book and write as many countries as you can.

Guatemala	El Salvador	Costa Rica	Belize
Nicaragua	Honduras	Panama	

7
Using Graphic Aids

Most of the material you study will include graphic aids. One of the most common graphic aids is the graph.

Reading Graphs

A **graph** is a special type of chart that shows a relationship between sets of number facts. A **circle graph** is drawn like a pie, with each wedge representing a percentage of the whole. A **bar graph** uses the length of separate bars to show relationships. A **picture graph** uses symbols to present information. A **line graph** shows changes in number relationships over time.

To understand any graph, first read the title and headings outside the graph. Follow the bars in the graph below to see which types of work employed the most people in Hamilton.

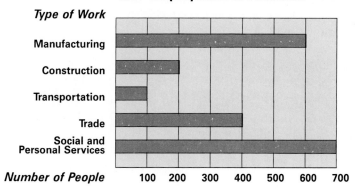

1987 Employment in Hamilton

Drawing Conclusions

Graphs present you with a set of facts. It is up to you to decide what those facts mean. For instance, the graph above can tell you what types of jobs are available in Hamilton and how many people are employed in those jobs. The graph does not, however, give enough information to show future employment trends. When you read a graph, make sure you understand exactly what information it can provide.

English and Science

In our fast-moving world, there are always new scientific discoveries. Researchers turn up exciting information about space, health, energy, medicine, geology, and other areas of science all the time. Keeping up with all the new facts can be difficult.

Right now, you're learning the very skills that can help you keep up with the growing supply of scientific knowledge. Your study skills of skimming, scanning, and note-taking let you simplify the process of reading, hearing, and remembering all these new facts. You can use these skills to create a file of important science information. A quick reading of current newspapers and magazines will tell you about new scientific developments. You can decide which of these recent developments interests you the most. If you list the articles and jot down the important points of each, you will have the beginnings of a useful science file. Such a file will help keep you informed and up to date. You will be better able to participate in science discussions, and you will always be ready with an idea for the next science report or fair.

Activity Begin a science file of your own. Look through newspapers and magazines for one week, and pick out two or three articles that describe a discovery or development in some area of science. Take careful notes and write a brief summary of each article, including the title, source (where you found it), and date.

Application and Review

A Mastering Study Skills Write the answers to each of the following questions.

1. What should you do first when following written directions?
2. What four things should you include when you are recording an assignment?
3. What kind of assignments are short-term goals?
4. What does SQ3R stand for?
5. What do you record when you're using SQ3R?
6. In what situations would you benefit from taking notes?
7. What steps can you take to check the reliability of references?
8. What is the purpose of scanning?
9. What is the purpose of visualizing items?
10. What do you need to make sure of before drawing conclusions from graphs or other resources?

B Understanding Graphs Look at the following graph. The graph was put together by the school carnival committee. Write a conclusion that could be drawn from this set of facts. What kind of publicity was most effective?

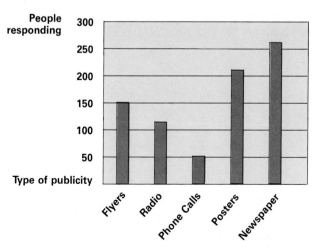

19
Taking
Tests

Just as different recipes require different cooking methods, different tests require different methods of preparation. When you prepare to take a test, you can't just think about the information the test will cover. You must also consider what kind of test it will be.

In this chapter you will learn recipes for successful test-taking.

1
Planning for Tests

"What material will the test cover?" is the question you probably ask when you learn you will have to take a test. An equally important question is, "What type of test will it be?" When you know what type of test you will be taking, you can figure out the best way to prepare. Look at how well one smart lemming prepared for the trial of marching into the sea.

Course or Textbook Tests

Course or textbook tests measure your knowledge of specific topics. The test questions themselves can be of different types. For example, you might be asked to answer objective questions and an essay question on the topic of the Civil War.

To prepare for a course test or a textbook test, you need to study, because the test is based on specific information that you have covered in class. You will be well prepared to study for such a test if you have used the SQ3R study method and taken notes in an organized notebook. Follow these study steps:

1. **Find out what the test will cover.** This will tell you exactly what to study.
2. **Schedule your study time.** Then you can do it a little at a time. Avoid last-minute cramming.
3. **Get organized.** Review your class notes, skim the chapters you have already read, and re-answer your SQ3R questions.
4. **Memorize important facts.** These include names, dates, events, or vocabulary terms.
5. **Rest and relax.** Get plenty of sleep the night before the test. Being rested helps you remember the things you learned.

Standardized Tests

Standardized tests also measure your knowledge, but they are not based on your specific courses or textbooks. Standardized tests try to find out what you have achieved or learned in all your years at school. They often include sections on mathematics, vocabulary, reading comprehension, grammar and language skills, science, and social studies.

You do not study for standardized tests. You already "study" for this kind of test every day that you are in school.

You do have to do one thing to prepare, however—you have to relax. This is important because your mind works better when you are relaxed. One good way to relax is to get plenty of sleep the night before the test.

Exercise

In a paragraph, describe how you actually prepare for a test. You might want to make a list of your study habits first.

Stony Desert. Paul Klee.

2
Types of Test Questions

The main types of test questions include true-false, multiple-choice, matching, fill-in-the-blanks, analogies, short-answer, and essay. The following information will help you learn the best way to approach each type of question.

True-False Questions

True-false questions are statements that are either true or false. Decide whether each example is true or false:

Ⓣ F   1. A quadrangle is a figure with four sides.
T Ⓕ   2. Photosynthesis is the process by which plants lose their color in the fall.
Ⓣ F   3. Africa is a continent.

Certain words in true-false statements are often clues that the statement is false: *all, always, never,* and *none.*

T Ⓕ   *All* countries have mountains.
T Ⓕ   The people of China *always* ride bicycles.

Certain other words frequently are clues that a statement is true: *most, many,* and *usually.*

Ⓣ F   *Most* countries have mountains.
Ⓣ F   The people of China *usually* ride bicycles.

These words do not always mean that a statement is true or false. You must read each statement for yourself. Get all the information it contains. If any part of it is false, then the whole statement is false. Examine the following example and decide which part of it is false:

TⒻ   The earth revolves around its axis in 365¼ days.

The statement is false because the earth revolves around the sun, not its axis, in 365¼ days.

Multiple-Choice Questions

Multiple-choice questions give you three or more possible answers from which to choose. You are usually told to select the best answer from these choices.

A verb is a word that names
    a. a person, place, or thing.
    b. a description.
    (c.) an action or a state of being.

In some questions, one answer choice is partly correct, while another choice is more complete and is also correct. Read all the answer choices, even though you may have already found one that is partly correct. Look at this example:

A verb is a word that names
    a. an action.
    (b.) an action or a state of being.
    c. a person, place, or thing.

In the above example, the first answer, *a. an action,* is partly correct. If you stopped there and chose *a.* as your answer, you would miss *b. an action or a state of being.* Choice *b.* is more correct than choice *a.* because it is the most complete answer. If you had not continued reading, you might have chosen the first choice as your answer. This is why it is important to read all the possible answers.

Sometimes you cannot decide which answer is correct. Then you should start by eliminating the choices that you know are incorrect. If you can eliminate one or two right away, you will have only two or three choices to consider. Study the remaining choices carefully and choose the one that makes the most sense.

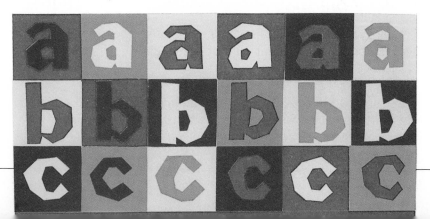

Matching Questions

Matching questions contain two lists. You are directed to match items from one list with those in the other list.

Match the states with their capitals.

California — Springfield
New York — Tallahassee
Illinois — Albany
Florida — Sacramento

To answer more difficult matching questions, first match all the items of which you are certain. This will leave fewer choices.

Fill-in-the-Blanks Questions

These questions are also called *completion* questions. They are statements with words or phrases missing. You are to fill in the missing word or phrase:

1. A _right_ angle has 90 degrees.
2. The capital of Brazil is _Brasilia_.
3. Columbus received support for his voyage to the New World from _Spain_.

Do not spend too much time answering individual fill-in-the-blanks questions. If you cannot think of an answer, continue with the test. Sometimes the answer will occur to you later. First, fill in the answers of which you are certain. Then go back and read over the ones you have left blank. You will probably be able to answer more questions every time you go back and reread the questions.

Analogy Questions

Analogy questions look like fill-in-the-blanks questions, but analogies call for a different kind of thinking:

> *Cow* is to *calf* as *hen* is to _____.

The first two italicized words, *cow* and *calf,* are related to each other in some way. You are to find a word that *hen* is related to in the same way that *cow* is related to *calf.*

Try to make a sentence out of the first pair of words (*cow* and *calf*) that explains the relationship between them.

A *cow* is the mother of a *calf*.

Now take your sentence and substitute the incomplete pair (*hen* and _____) for the first pair.

A *hen* is the mother of a _____.

The correct word to fill the blank is *chick*. Just as a cow is the mother of a calf, a hen is the mother of a chick.

Often analogy questions provide several possible answers.

Hot is to *stove* as *cold* is to _____.
    a. winter   c. refrigerator
    b. ice   d. freezing

Again, try to make a sentence out of the first pair that explains the relationship between them.

A *stove* is an appliance that makes food *hot*.
A _____ is an appliance that makes food *cold*.

The correct answer is *c. refrigerator*. None of the other choices makes sense in the sentence.

Exercise

Write on your paper a sentence that explains the relationship between the first pair of words in each of the following analogies. Make sure that your sentence would also explain the relationship between the second pair of words in the analogy were you to substitute them for the first pair.

1. A *shoe* is to a *foot* as a *glove* is to a *hand*.
2. A *car* is to a *highway* as a *train* is to a *track*.
3. A *lid* is to a *box* as a *roof* is to a *house*.
4. *Fall* is to *winter* as *spring* is to *summer*.
5. A *car* is to *gasoline* as a *human being* is to *food*.
6. A *grape* is to a *raisin* as a *plum* is to a *prune*.
7. A *fish* is to *water* as a *person* is to *air*.
8. *Thorns* are to *rosebushes* as *claws* are to *cats*.
9. *Graphite* is to a *pencil* as *ink* is to a *pen*.
10. A *dictionary* is to *words* as an *atlas* is to *maps*.

Short-Answer Questions

Short-answer questions ask you to write a short answer for each question. Be sure to read the directions first.

Write a complete sentence to answer each question.

1. What bisects a circle into two equal parts?

   The diameter bisects a circle into two equal parts.

2. Who developed the first polio vaccine?

   Jonas Salk developed the first polio vaccine.

3. What five planets are visible to the unaided eye from Earth?

   The five planets visible to the unaided eye are

   Mercury, Venus, Mars, Jupiter, and Saturn.

Write the answer to each question.

1. What plane figure has four sides, but only two that are parallel?

   a trapezoid

2. Who is credited with inventing the working telephone?

   Alexander Graham Bell

3. What does Earth's moon do approximately every 27 days?

   completes its orbit around the earth

In the first set of questions, the directions state that you are to write your answers in complete sentences. In the second set, the directions do not mention using complete sentences; thus, it may be correct to write only words or phrases. You should check with your teacher to be sure.

Essay Questions

Essay questions require that you write a paragraph or more to answer a question. Because you will not have much time or space to answer the question, you must simplify the steps in your writing process. Plan your answer before you write. Identify the purpose of the question by reading it carefully.

1. Contrast the migration patterns of swallows and geese.
2. Explain why some animals are able to blend in with their surroundings.

The first example above asks you to contrast two things. **Contrast** means to tell differences. You would, therefore, write about all the ways the migration patterns of geese and swallows differ. Note that the question does not ask you to write everything about the birds' migration patterns, only the dissimilarities.

The second example question asks you to **explain** something. This means you are to provide the reasons why animals would adapt in order to blend in with their surroundings. You would write everything you knew about this topic.

Other essay questions ask you to compare similar things, list or outline events, discuss ideas, or describe an event or time. Read the questions carefully. List or organize your ideas on scratch paper before beginning to write. Then plan your time so that you can complete each question.

Exercise

Identify each question as a true-false, multiple-choice, matching, fill-in-the-blanks, analogy, short-answer, or essay question.

1. All snakes are poisonous.
2. Describe how snakes shed their skins.
3. In what part of the world do most snakes live?
4. Snakes are
   a) mammals.   b) arachnids.   c) reptiles.   d) rodents.
5. Snakes eat _____.
6. Explain why snakes hibernate in temperate climates.
7. *Legless* is to *snake* as *winged* is to _____.
8. Snakes swallow their food whole because they cannot chew.
9. A snake's skin is dry and smooth.
10. The snake's organ of touch is its _____.

3
Taking a Test

While you are taking a test, use the study and organizing skills you have already learned. Follow these steps during a test:

1. **Skim the test.** See what types of questions the test has and how long it is.
2. **Judge the time.** Read all the directions first. You may decide that you need more time for some sections. A section of essay questions, for example, may take longer than a section of fill-in-the-blanks.
3. **Read all directions carefully.** Ask questions if you do not understand directions. Follow the directions exactly.
4. **Read each test item carefully.** Be sure to read all the choices provided for answers.
5. **Answer easy questions first.** Then go back to harder ones.
6. **Review your answers.** Make sure you have not left out any answers. Change unreadable or confusing answers.

Using Answer Sheets

Standardized tests use answer sheets, as do some course or textbook tests. It is important to use answer sheets correctly because they are usually scored by machines. Therefore, stray marks or answers in the wrong section on the answer sheet will be scored as incorrect answers. Look at these samples. What errors do you see in the second set?

Correctly marked
Part 1

S1	●	ⓑ	ⓒ	ⓓ	ⓔ		8	ⓐ	ⓑ	ⓒ	ⓓ	ⓔ
S2	ⓐ	ⓑ	ⓒ	●	ⓔ		9	ⓐ	ⓑ	ⓒ	ⓓ	ⓔ
1	●	ⓑ	ⓒ	ⓓ	ⓔ		10	ⓐ	ⓑ	ⓒ	ⓓ	ⓔ
2	ⓐ	ⓑ	●	ⓓ	ⓔ		11	ⓐ	ⓑ	ⓒ	ⓓ	ⓔ
3	ⓐ	●	ⓒ	ⓓ	ⓔ		12	ⓐ	ⓑ	ⓒ	ⓓ	ⓔ
4	ⓐ	●	ⓒ	ⓓ	ⓔ		13	ⓐ	ⓑ	ⓒ	ⓓ	ⓔ
5	ⓐ	ⓑ	●	ⓓ	ⓔ		14	ⓐ	ⓑ	ⓒ	ⓓ	ⓔ
6	ⓐ	ⓑ	ⓒ	ⓓ	ⓔ		15	ⓐ	ⓑ	ⓒ	ⓓ	ⓔ
7	ⓐ	ⓑ	ⓒ	ⓓ	ⓔ							

Incorrectly marked
Part 2

S1	●	ⓑ	ⓒ	ⓓ	ⓔ		8	ⓐ	ⓑ	ⓒ	ⓓ	ⓔ
S2	ⓐ	ⓑ	ⓒ	●	ⓔ		9	ⓐ	ⓑ	ⓒ	ⓓ	ⓔ
1	●	ⓑ	ⓒ	ⓓ	●		10	ⓐ	ⓑ	ⓒ	ⓓ	ⓔ
2	ⓐ	ⓑ	ⓒ	ⓓ	ⓔ		11	ⓐ	ⓑ	ⓒ	ⓓ	ⓔ
3	ⓐ	●	ⓒ	ⓓ	ⓔ		12	ⓐ	ⓑ	ⓒ	ⓓ	ⓔ
4	ⓐ	ⓑ	ⓒ	ⓓ	ⓔ		13	ⓐ	ⓑ	ⓒ	ⓓ	ⓔ
5	ⓐ	ⓑ	●	ⓓ	ⓔ		14	ⓐ	ⓑ	ⓒ	ⓓ	ⓔ
6	ⓐ	ⓑ	ⓒ	ⓓ	ⓔ		15	ⓐ	ⓑ	ⓒ	ⓓ	ⓔ
7	ⓐ	ⓑ	ⓒ	ⓓ	ⓔ							

Remember two important things when using an answer sheet:

1. **Keep your place.** Mark the part of the answer sheet that matches the test part you are working on. Make sure you are marking the correct item number as well.
2. **Mark neatly; erase completely.** If your marks go far outside the lines or circles provided, the scoring machine may read them as answers to a nearby item. The machine may also read partial erasures as answers. Erase gently, but completely. Never cross out an answer. Never use a pen.

Tips for Marking an Answer Sheet

These tips may help you mark answer sheets correctly:

1. Read the heading of each section when you start marking it.
2. Quickly check each item number on the answer sheet as you mark it.
3. Fill in only one answer per line.
4. Do not press so hard that your pencil marks go through the paper. Do make heavy, dark marks that show clearly.
5. Practice making marks a few times on scratch paper. Try erasing one neatly without tearing the paper.

Exercise

Write *True* or *False* for each of the following statements.

1. Take as much time as you want on each question in a test.
2. Read the directions only if you cannot figure out what to do by looking at the items.
3. Look over the whole test before starting.
4. Answers should never be changed once you have marked them.
5. Standardized tests' answers are usually scored by machines.
6. It is possible for incomplete erasures to be scored as wrong answers.
7. Answer sheets are always easy to use.
8. Mark answer sheets by pressing as hard as you can with your pencil.
9. The first correct answer choice is usually the best one.
10. Go back over your answers after you have finished a test.

English and Physical Education

Think about the way you studied for your last test. Perhaps you warmed up with a few brainteasers, stretched out your mind with some review questions, strengthened your knowledge by reading, and perfected your skill through practice. If so, you were probably right on track for a test victory.

Just as sporting words can help to describe studying for a test, the test skills you learn in the classroom can help you on the track or playing field. When you get ready for a team tryout or physical fitness test, you need to train your body ahead of time through practice and diet.

Here are a few important tips for smart training:

1. Eat plenty of healthy foods, such as fruit, leafy vegetables, lean meat, and whole grain bread. Avoid foods that are high in sugar, salt, or fat.

2. Get plenty of rest.

3. Always warm up by stretching your muscles before every workout and start workouts slowly.

4. Plan activities that keep your pulse above a normal pace for approximately twenty minutes three times a week such as jogging, swimming, or biking.

5. Pick activities you enjoy. Decide on a way to measure and evaluate your performance.

Activity Create a realistic four-week fitness plan for yourself. Schedule three workouts a week of your favorite sports and exercises. Start out slowly and gradually increase your work. Make a list of healthy fitness foods.

Application and Review

Understanding Test-Taking Skills Write the letter of the best answer for each question.

1. What type of test measures your knowledge of specific classwork?
    a) standardized   c) mathematics
    b) course or textbook   d) multiple-choice

2. How should you prepare for a standardized test?
    a) Study a specific chapter.
    b) Stay up the night before the test.
    c) Do not prepare in any way.
    d) Get a good night's sleep the night before the test.

3. What should you do *first* before a course or textbook test?
    a) Memorize important facts.
    b) Reread chapters in your textbook.
    c) Find out what the test will cover.
    d) Review your class notes.

4. When is a true-false question false?
    a) when any part of it is incorrect
    b) when every fact in it is incorrect
    c) when you disagree with it
    d) when it is stated as a question

5. Which answer is correct in a multiple-choice item?
    a) the first one that has correct information
    b) the one with the most words
    c) the one with the most complete and correct answer
    d) the last one you read

6. What should you do after you have finished the test?
    a) Review your answers.   c) Answer the easy questions.
    b) Judge the time.   d) Ask questions about it.

7. What type of questions are these?
    a) true-false   b) essay   c) analogy   d) multiple-choice

20
Writing Letters and Completing Forms

You have probably had the experience of writing or receiving a letter from a friend. You have also filled out a form at one time or another in your life. Whenever you do either, you are using the writing skills you have studied in this book to provide information to others.

As you grow older there will be different types of letters and forms that you will need to know about. In Chapter 20 you will learn about writing friendly letters and business letters. You also will learn how to fill out forms correctly.

1
Writing Friendly Letters

In a friendly letter, your writing can be casual, just as if you were talking to a friend. The purpose of a friendly letter is to let your friend know what you have been doing and how you feel about what has been happening.

Letter writing is an enjoyable sharing of experiences between friends, but even casual letters need a standard form to keep them organized and easy to read.

Parts of the Friendly Letter

Friendly letters contain five main parts: heading, salutation, body, closing, and signature. Each part has a particular purpose and form.

A Friendly Letter

Heading

316 Laural Road
Bexley, Ohio 43209
October 26, 1988

Salutation

Dear Steve,

I was so glad to get your letter. The pictures are fantastic! I especially like the one of you and Andy in the sailboat. It was a great family reunion. I'm looking forward to the next one.

Body

You'll never guess what I did in school. I actually entered one of my paintings in the art contest -- and it won!

Now I have to get back to the drawing board. Say "hi" to your family for me.

Closing
Signature

Miss you,
Jackie

The **heading** of a letter goes in the upper right corner. It lets the reader know where to reply and includes three lines of information: your street address; your city, state, and ZIP code; and the month, day, and year.

In the **salutation,** or greeting, you say "hello" to your friend. The salutation begins at the left margin. Its first word and other nouns are capitalized, and its last word is followed by a comma. Make the salutation as casual as you wish.

Dear Todd,   Greetings Rebecca,   Hi Buddy,

The **body** of a friendly letter is where you communicate your message. Begin by responding to your friend's letter, and remember to express yourself naturally, the way you speak.

Since you are writing to someone you know well, your writing can be conversational, just as if you were talking. If you write the way you talk, your personality will show through, and your writing will be interesting. Indent each paragraph.

The **closing** is where you say "goodbye." Capitalize only the first word of the closing, align it with the heading, and use a comma at the end. Some closings are standard; others are written to fit specific letters or people. Following are some suggested closings:

Love,   Your friend,   Missing you,

The **signature** in a friendly letter is written below the closing. Only your first name is needed. Always write the signature by hand, even if you have typed the rest of the letter.

Here are some guidelines for writing friendly letters.

Guidelines for Friendly Letters
1. In the first paragraph, make comments about the last letter you received from your friend.
2. Write one or more paragraphs about people and events that interest both you and your friend.
3. Ask questions so that your friend has something to write back about.
4. Use specific words for descriptions and action.
5. Make your handwriting neat and legible.
6. Use the proper letter form.

When you receive a gift, use the friendly letter form to write a thank-you letter. In a thank-you letter, you always want to thank the person for thinking of you, even if the gift was not your favorite.

The friendly letter form is also used for letters of invitation, acceptance, and regret. If you are writing a letter of invitation, be sure to mention what kind of activity you are proposing and when, where, and why it will take place.

Exercises

A Choose one of the following ideas and write about it in a friendly letter. Develop each situation more specifically and use vivid details. Remember to use correct letter form.

1. We bought a puppy last week. It's really cute, but it's always getting into trouble. It's very hard to train.
2. When my brother left for college, he said I could use his stereo. I have set it up in my room. It's a lot of fun.
3. Last weekend I baby-sat for a family with six kids. You wouldn't believe how busy they kept me. What a mess!

B Write a friendly letter to one of your best friends or closest relatives. You may write about events that have actually happened to you, or you may want to use some of those suggested in the following list. Follow the guidelines on page 379. Use your best handwriting.

Student council elections at school
How your cat destroyed your science project

The movie you saw last weekend
How you redecorated your room
Your friend's surprise birthday party
Your recent camping trip

2
Composing Business Letters

To request information, order a product, or complain about a product, you write a business letter. A business letter is written for a specific purpose and requires a different style of writing than a friendly letter. A business letter should be brief, clear, and to the point. It should also follow the correct form.

There are two forms for business letters: block form and modified block form. In **block form,** which is used only when a letter is typewritten, all parts of the letter begin at the left margin, and a line of space is left between paragraphs.

Modified block form is more like the form for friendly letters; the heading goes in the upper right corner, the closing and signature align with the heading, and the paragraphs are indented. Many typed business letters and all handwritten business letters use the modified block form. (*See letter on page 382.*)

Parts of the Business Letter

The parts of the business letter are similar to those of the friendly letter, except that they are written more formally and include one extra part: the inside address.

The **heading** includes the same information as that of a friendly letter. The **inside address** consists of the name and address of the organization to which you are writing.

The **salutation** begins two lines after the inside address and ends with a colon (:). If you are writing to a specific person, use the person's name; for example, *Dear Ms. Gonzales:* If you do not know who will receive your letter, use a general greeting; for example, *Dear Sir or Madam:* or *Ladies and Gentlemen:*

The **body** of a business letter is brief, courteous, and to the point. State clearly the purpose of your letter and any items that you are requesting or that you have enclosed.

The **closing** appears on the first line below the body. Its first word is capitalized, and it ends with a comma. Some common, formal closings are these:

Sincerely,   Yours truly,   Respectfully,

For the **signature,** print or type your name four spaces below the closing; then write your signature in the space.

A Business Letter   (*Modified Block Form*)

Heading	58 Eagle Road LaCrosse, Wisconsin 54601 February 10, 1988
Inside Address	Superintendent of Documents U.S. Government Printing Office Washington, DC 20402
Salutation	Dear Sir or Madam:
Body	I am writing a report about solar energy. I understand that your agency has several publications on this subject. Please send me any free pamphlets about solar energy you have available. Also, please send me your free catalog <u>Selected List of U.S. Government Documents</u>, so I can learn about inexpensive books you may have about solar energy. Thank you for your help.
Closing	Sincerely,
Signature	*Stella Noyes* Stella Noyes

Exercise

Practice writing a letter for one of the situations below. Use the correct business form. (Do not send the letter.)

1. Your uncle has given you his stamp collection. You would like to add to it, but you need more information. Write to *Stamp News,* Box 4066, Anderson, South Carolina 29622.
2. Your family is moving to Texas. To learn about the state, write to Texas Tourism Agency, Dept. NW, Austin, Texas 78711.

3
Addressing Envelopes

When you address an envelope, you want to get the address exactly right, so the letter will get to the right place. Check to make sure all numbers are in the proper order and include the ZIP code. If you do not know the correct ZIP code, ask at your local post office. If you use the two-letter abbreviation for a state, capitalize both letters and do not use a period.

For any business letter, use a business envelope and write the address to which the letter is being sent about halfway down and halfway across the front of the envelope. Place your own address, the **return address,** in the upper left corner.

A Business Envelope

Return Address
Jonathan Caedmon
856 Burke Avenue
Mission, KS 66202

Address
Mr. Lawrence Laski, Store Manager
Heraldica Imports, Inc.
21 West 46th Street
New York, NY 10036

Always be sure the envelope is right-side up before you write on it. For a friendly letter, you may put the return address on the back of the envelope, on the flap.

Exercise

Draw three business envelopes. Correctly address them to the following people. Use your own return address.

1. ms. maria talbot, personnel director, ventura industries, inc., 1700 4th ave., portland, oregon 97201
2. mr. w. l. young, 2600 vista blvd., fresno, california 93717
3. ms. jill fry, hats, ltd., 23 bay rd., lima, ohio 45809

4
Filling Out Forms

As you know, letters are only one way of providing information. Forms are another. You may at some time complete a form to order a product, to apply for a library card, to register for classes, or to do many other things.

Forms are used to collect specific information in an organized way. For instance, one reason you use a form to order a product is to be sure you give all the information the company will need to fill your order.

The T-shirt order form on the following page, for example, asks for your name and address, so the company can mail the shirt to you. It asks for your phone number so the company can call you if there is a question about your order. Other kinds of information often found on forms include telephone numbers of people to call in case of an emergency and the number of years you have been in school.

Here are some guidelines for filling out forms.

Guidelines for Completing Forms

1. Skim the whole form before you write anything on it.
2. Read each part of the directions carefully. Follow any special instructions, such as *Use blue ink* or *Please type*.
3. Collect the information you need to complete the form. For example, if you are applying for a club membership, get names of references and emergency phone numbers. If you are ordering clothing, know correct sizes.
4. Work on the form one line at a time, reading each part of the directions again before you follow it.
5. Write something in every blank. For questions that do not apply to you, write *N/A* (for *not applicable*).
6. Proofread your answers and neatly correct any errors.
7. Make a photocopy of the completed form for your personal records.
8. Mail the completed form to the correct address or deliver it to the correct person.

Cool Cotton, Inc.   **Order Form**

Name _____

Street Address _____

Phone number (including area code) _____

Quantity	Size	Color	Price per shirt	Amount
			$6.95	
			$6.95	
			$6.95	

Colors available are red, green, and blue.	Shipping & Handling	$1.50
	Total Amount	

Sizes available are
XS, S, M, L, and XL.

Mail this order form with your check or money order to:
Cool Cotton, Inc., P.O. Box 342, Spartanburg, SC 29655

Exercises

A Find an order form in one of your favorite magazines for a product you would like to order. Complete the form, following the Guidelines for Completing Forms on page 384. Draw an envelope and write the address on it.

B You are establishing a travel club at your school. Activities will include researching travel destinations and interviewing travel agents about their work. Make up a club application form requesting details about potential club members.

Gooyer Windmill, Amsterdam. Claude Monet.

English and Health

Often, people need help with problems of physical or mental health. Groups like Alateen, for example, help teenagers who have relatives who are alcoholics. The group helps these teenagers cope with their problems. There may be other groups in your area that provide help with such problems as drugs, depression, eating disorders, or other illnesses. The groups listed below help people with health problems.

American Heart Association
7320 Greenville Ave.
Dallas, Texas 75231

National Cancer Institute
Room 10A18, Building 31
National Institutes of Health
Bethesda, Maryland 20705

Clearinghouse on Drug Abuse
Room 10A53, Parklawn Building
5600 Fishers Lane
Rockville, Maryland 20857

Mental Health Association
1800 North Kent St.
Arlington, Virginia 22209

Nutrition Foundation
Suite 300
888 Seventh Ave., N.W.
Washington, D.C. 20006

Alateen
Al-Anon Family Group
1 Park Ave.
New York, New York 10016

down with high blood pressure

Chicago Heart Association

Activity It is helpful to know about the groups that provide support and help for persons with specific illnesses. A good way to find out is by writing a letter to request information. Choose a group you know about or one from the list above. Write a letter asking about the group's work. Once you have received your information, put together a display about the group. Present what you have learned to your class.

Application and Review

A Writing Letters and Addressing Envelopes Answer each of the following questions.

1. What kind of letters are thank-you letters and letters of invitation, acceptance, and regret?
2. Where in your letter should you make comments about the last letter you received from a friend?
3. What information goes in the first line of a heading?
4. What parts of a letter written in modified block form begin at the left margin?
5. For which kind of letter should you use formal language, a friendly letter or a business letter?
6. Should you sign only your first name to a business letter?
7. Which kind of letter uses an inside address?
8. Would you ever put the return address on the back of the envelope for a business letter?
9. What is a standard salutation for a business letter if you do not know who will receive your letter?
10. Where do you put the return address for a friendly letter?
11. What part of a letter includes the date it was written?
12. Which two parts of friendly letters are followed by commas?
13. Does the salutation of a business letter end with a comma?
14. What are the five main parts of a friendly letter?
15. Why should you ask questions in a friendly letter?

B Completing Forms Identify each of the following statements as *True* or *False*

1. Companies use forms to send out information about their specific products.
2. Directions are the same on most forms, so you don't need to read them each time.
3. You should proofread your answers after completing a form.
4. You should fill in every space on a form.
5. All forms should be completed in pencil.

Grammar, Usage, and Mechanics

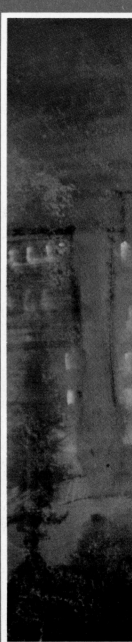

Each art has its own rules, or conventions. Artists, for example, try not to center a subject right in the middle of a painting. The conventions of language are the rules that govern writing. Good writers, like good painters, learn the conventions of their art so they can communicate effectively.

21
The Sentence and Its Parts

A group of soccer players racing aimlessly around a field kicking and heading the ball, do not make a soccer game. Playing soccer requires teamwork.

Similarly, words and phrases thrown carelessly together do not make sentences. The parts of sentences must work together just as a team does. All parts of a sentence must work together for the sentence to express a complete thought.

In this chapter you will study how the parts of a sentence function. You also will learn different ways to structure your sentences.

1
Sentences and Sentence Fragments

> A *sentence* is a group of words that expresses a complete thought; a *sentence fragment* does not express a complete thought.

A complete thought is the clear and entire expression of whatever you want to say. Which of the following groups of words expresses a complete thought?

> 1. Last night a funny thing 2. We were sitting around the dinner table 3. Suddenly, a loud bang

The second group of words expresses a complete thought. It is a complete sentence.

Sentence fragments do not express complete thoughts. Instead, they express incomplete thoughts, which are often difficult to understand. A reader trying to make sense of an incomplete thought is in a spot as bad as that of a penguin stranded on a drifting chunk of ice. Avoid setting your readers adrift in a sea of confusion by always expressing yourself in complete sentences.

"Well, once again, here we are."

Exercises

A Write *S* for each complete sentence and *F* for each sentence fragment.

1. During the relay race
2. A very high wind and then some flashes of lightning
3. Performed on the balance beam
4. A report about car fumes
5. John Glenn, one of America's first astronauts
6. Whose work on the blackboard
7. Told stories to the campers
8. Martha Jane Canary, or "Calamity Jane"
9. The fire engines rushed down the street
10. No one else gave a report on solar energy

B Write *S* for each complete sentence and *F* for each sentence fragment.

1. I saw a TV show yesterday
2. The show was about dolphins
3. Actually a kind of small whale
4. Dolphins are very intelligent
5. Playful animals that seem to enjoy games
6. Under the water in the big tank
7. The dolphins are very entertaining
8. Just for fun
9. Dolphins hear well
10. Because dolphins breathe air and are warm-blooded

c *Write Now* Suppose a friend is telling you an exciting story on the telephone. However, there is a bad connection. It is impossible to hear everything your friend says. Add words to each fragment below to complete the story your friend is telling.

1. all alone in the house
2. a huge crash
3. into the basement
4. rustled behind me
5. I unfortunately

2
Subjects and Predicates

The *subject* of a sentence tells *whom* or *what* the sentence is about. The *predicate* tells what the subject *does* or *is*.

Every sentence has two basic parts: the subject and the predicate. The **subject** tells *whom* or *what* the sentence is about. The **predicate** tells something about the subject.

Subject *(Who or what)*	Predicate *(What is said about the subject)*
Hungry dogs	bark constantly.
My brother	laughed at his own mistakes.

Each sentence expresses a complete thought. Each tells something (predicate) about a person, place, or thing (subject).

One simple way to understand the parts of a sentence is to think of the sentence as telling who did something or what happened. The subject tells *who* or *what*. The predicate tells what was *done* or *happened*. You can divide sentences, then, in this way:

Who or What	Did or Happened
The runner	crossed the finish line.
The car	skidded on the wet pavement.
Liberty	is a national ideal.
Boston Harbor	has become a popular tourist attraction.

Exercises

A Label two columns on your paper *Subject* and *Predicate*. Write the proper words from each sentence in the columns.

1. Gayle made limeade.
2. The Packers will play the Bears on Sunday.

3. The Bronx Zoo had a 250-pound turtle.
4. My parents were fishing off the coast of Nova Scotia.
5. Heavy smoke came from the dingy, red brick chimney.
6. Calligraphy is the art of fine handwriting.
7. I like the poetry of Langston Hughes.
8. Rebecca sailed the boat on the pond.
9. Several passengers stood in the aisle.
10. Rugby is a British team sport similar to American football.

B Write a complete sentence using each group of words below. Add a subject to each predicate. Add a predicate to each subject.

1. monarch butterflies
2. sugar cane
3. huge dinosaurs
4. migrate every year
5. raised money for muscular dystrophy
6. will play intramural hockey tomorrow
7. is the best movie I have ever seen
8. the Astrodome
9. is one of our country's chief exports
10. Black Angus cattle at the Ohio State Fair

c *Write Now* Suppose you are leading an archaeological dig deep in the jungles of Mexico. You make a remarkable discovery. Write a paragraph telling what you find. Underline each subject once and each predicate twice.

3
Simple Subjects and Predicates

A *verb* is a word that tells about action, or that tells what someone or something is. The *subject of the verb* is the most important part of the complete subject.

In every sentence a few words are more important than the rest. These key words make the basic framework of the sentence.

Hungry **dogs**   **bark** constantly.
My **brother**   **laughed** at his own mistake.

The subject of the first sentence is *Hungry dogs*. The key word in this subject is *dogs*. The predicate in this sentence is *bark constantly*. The key word is *bark*. Without this word you would not have a sentence.

The key word in the subject of a sentence is called the **simple subject.** It is the subject of the verb.

The key word in the predicate is called the **simple predicate.** The simple predicate is the **verb.**

Finding the Verb and Its Subject

The verb and its simple subject are the basic framework of every sentence. All the rest of the sentence is built around them. To find this framework, first find the verb. Then ask *who* or *what* before the verb. This will give you the subject.

My brother's car runs well. *Verb* runs
    What runs? car
    Simple subject car

You will be able to tell a fragment from a sentence easily if you keep your eye on subjects and verbs.

Fragment An early frost (What about it? What happened?)
Sentence An early frost *ruined our crops.*

Looking at the Sentence as a Whole

The **complete subject** is the simple subject plus any words that modify or describe it.

EXAMPLE   Hungry dogs bark constantly.

Hungry dogs is the complete subject. What is the simple subject?

The **complete predicate** is the verb plus any words that modify or complete its meaning. What is the complete predicate in the sentence above? What is the simple predicate, or verb?

Diagraming Subjects and Predicates

A sentence diagram is a picture of a sentence. It can help you understand how sentence parts are related. Below is the basic structure of a sentence diagram.

Subject	Predicate
Hungry dogs	bark constantly

The subject and verb are placed on the main horizontal line. Modifiers go on slanted lines below the words they modify.

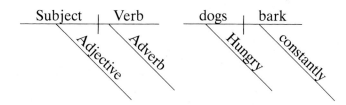

Remember that adverbs may also modify adjectives or other adverbs. Here is how they appear in a diagram.

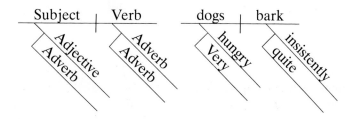

Exercises

A Label two columns *Verb* and *Simple Subject*. Number the columns 1–10. Write the verb and its simple subject for each of the following sentences.

1. A crate of oranges arrived from Florida.
2. The new computer printed our class schedules.
3. A tiny, gray kitten perched itself on our windowsill.
4. The scientist described the search for the *Titanic*.
5. The jubilant crowd rose to its feet.
6. The tall, wiry player sank the basket.
7. The locker next to the library belongs to Miki and me.
8. Maurice Sendak won many awards for his illustrations.
9. The woman in the pin-striped suit is my math teacher.
10. The aluminum cans in those bags go to the recycling center.

B Label two columns *Verb* and *Simple Subject*. Write the verb and its simple subject for each of the following sentences.

1. The kazoo is a six-inch-long musical instrument.
2. Even nonmusical people play the kazoo.
3. Serious kazooists play metal kazoos.
4. Alabama Vest, an American, invented this popular musical instrument.
5. Stores sell over one million kazoos every year.
6. Many people enjoy the sound of kazoos.
7. Four professional kazooists formed a quartet.
8. They call this quartet Kazoophony.®
9. During concerts they wear tuxedos and no shoes.
10. Kazoophony® performs silly songs such as "The 1813 Overture" and "Swine Lake."

C *Proofreading* Copy the following paragraph and correct the errors you find. Pay particular attention to possible sentence fragments.

> The bones of the body. They have several purposes. Bones suport the body. Protect internal organs and allow movement. Without bones, your head and hart would be easily hurt.

4
The Verb Phrase

A *verb* may consist of one word or of several words.

Sometimes the **main verb** in a sentence is used with one or more **helping verbs**. A main verb and one or more helping verbs make up a **verb phrase**.

Helping Verbs +	Main Verb	=	Verb Phrase
might have	gone		might have gone
will	see		will see
are	driving		are driving
could	go		could go

Sometimes the parts of a verb are separated from each other by words that are not verbs. In each of the following sentences, the parts of the verb phrase are printed in bold type. The word in between is not part of the verb phrase.

> I **have** never **been** to a hockey game.
> We **did** not **see** the accident.
> The bus **has** often **been** late.
> The old car **can** sometimes **surprise** us.

Some verbs are joined with other words to make contractions. When naming verbs that appear with contractions, name only the verb. The word *not* and the contraction *n't* are adverbs. They are never part of a verb or a verb phrase.

Contraction	Verb
hasn't *(has not)*	*has*
weren't *(were not)*	*were*
I've *(I have)*	*have*
we'd *(we had* or *would)*	*had* or *would*

Exercises

A Write the verb or verb phrase in each sentence.

1. We have not gone to the lake once this summer.
2. The poem may not have been written by Shakespeare.

3. The buses often arrive late.
4. I have never been to Martha's Vineyard.
5. Daniel Boone did not really wear a coonskin cap.
6. The 747 will arrive at midnight.
7. The hockey team is practicing on the ice until 6:00 P.M.
8. The band is going on a bus trip next week.
9. The package may have been delivered to the wrong house.
10. I am going to a ski lodge next weekend.

B Label two columns on your paper *Main Verb* and *Helping Verbs*. Write the words from each sentence in the appropriate columns.

1. We aren't giving our panel discussion today.
2. I don't really like jazz or rock music.
3. The fire truck had cautiously approached the house.
4. I will read a biography of Martin Luther King, Jr.
5. Pandas can't live without bamboo for food.
6. Our play rehearsal wasn't very successful.
7. Raúl was carefully walking around the fountain.
8. We haven't planted a flower garden this year.
9. My sister and I have already made a rock garden.
10. The counselors had quickly collected the test booklets.

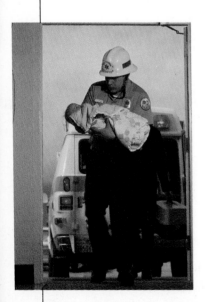

C *Write Now* Suppose you decide to pursue a career as a paramedic. Write a paragraph telling how you would handle a particular emergency. Use helping verbs where appropriate. Refer to a first-aid book or other reference if you wish.

EXAMPLE   I would apply a bandage.

Here are some ideas to get you started:

A young child is stuck up in a tree.
A man has broken his leg.
A woman has cut her arm.
A person is bitten by a dog.

When you are finished, underline each main verb once and each helping verb twice.

5
Sentences Beginning with Here *and* There

When *here* or *there* is the first word in a sentence, the word can be an adverb or merely an introductory word.

Sentences Beginning with There

Many sentences begin with the word *there*. Sometimes *there* is used as an adverb modifying the verb to tell where something is or happens.

> There stood the boy. (The boy stood *there*.)
> There is our bus. (Our bus is *there*.)
> There are the gold coins. (The coins are *there*.)

In other sentences, *there* is only an introductory word to help get the sentence started. It is not necessary to the meaning of a sentence.

> There are some visitors here from China.
> (Some visitors are here from China.)

In diagraming sentences that begin with *there*, decide whether *there* is used as an adverb or simply as an introductory word. When *there* modifies the verb—and is therefore an adverb—place it on a slanted line below the verb. When *there* is an introductory word, place it on a line above the sentence line.

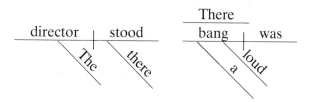

In most sentences beginning with *there*, the subject follows the verb. To find the subject, first find the verb. Then ask *who* or *what*.

Sentences Beginning with Here

In sentences beginning with *here*, the word *here* is always an adverb telling where about the verb.

> Here is your hat. (Your hat is *here*.)
> Here are the keys. (The keys are *here*.)

Exercises

A Write the simple subject and the verb in each sentence.

1. There he goes.
2. Here is the trophy.
3. There are ancient Roman ruins in England.
4. There will be basketball practice tomorrow.
5. Here is the new computer.
6. There I sat.
7. Here are the art supplies.
8. There are fossils in the quarry.
9. There was a sudden pause.
10. There will be earthquakes along the fault lines.

B Write the simple subject and the verb in each sentence. Tell whether *there* or *here* is used as an adverb or as an introductory word.

1. There goes the bus.
2. There is cheesecake for dessert.
3. There will be no school on Monday.
4. Here is the lock for your bicycle.
5. There are many musicals by Rodgers and Hart.
6. There might be a thunderstorm later tonight.
7. There is a swimming meet on Friday.
8. There is the new teacher.
9. There will be a tribute to the coach at the game.
10. Here are several students to see you.

C *Write Now* Suppose that you are leading a tour of your favorite place, such as a museum, a monument, or a zoo. Write a paragraph pointing out the most important features of that place. Begin half your sentences with *here* or *there*.

6
Other Sentences with Unusual Word Order

The subject does not always come at the beginning of the sentence.

The usual order of words in a sentence is *subject-verb*. Writers and speakers often vary the order to make more interesting sentences. You have seen examples of a varied pattern in sentences beginning with *here* and *there*. In questions, too, sentence order is often *verb-subject*:

Are you leaving? (You are leaving?)

Other sentences begin with phrases or adverbs:

Finally the signal came. (The signal finally came.)

To find the subject in a sentence with unusual word order, first find the verb. Then ask *who* or *what*.

Was the concert fun? *Verb* was
Who or *what was?* concert
Subject concert

To diagram sentences with unusual word order, find the verb and its subject. Place them in their usual positions. Then place the modifiers where they belong.

In **imperative sentences**, which state commands or requests, the subject is usually not given. Since commands and requests are always directed to the person spoken to, the subject is *you*. Because the *you* is not given, we say that it is *understood*.

(*You*) Bring me the newspaper.

In the diagram of an imperative sentence, the subject is written in parentheses.

(You)	Wait

Exercises

A Label two columns *Subject* and *Verb*. Write the subject and verb for each sentence below.

1. Hang on!
2. Are there two minutes left?
3. Did you read the article about China?
4. Economy is one advantage of the bicycle.
5. Down the slopes raced the sledders.
6. Down came the rain.
7. Are the Cardinals in the play-offs?
8. There goes the bus.
9. On the porch hung several plants.
10. Have you ever seen an opera?

B Rewrite each sentence below by changing the order of the subject and verb.

1. Are these books due today?
2. Out came the sun.
3. In front of the building stood a statue of Geronimo.
4. Are you going to play croquet?
5. Are you a contestant?
6. On the horizon appeared a beautiful rainbow.
7. Over the speakers came a Beethoven symphony.
8. The children bounded down the street.
9. Into the water dove the dolphin.
10. Along the shore were sleek seals basking and sleeping in the sun.

7
Objects of Verbs

> *Objects of verbs* are words that complete the meaning of a sentence.

Some verbs complete the meaning of spoken or written sentences without the help of other words. The action that they describe is complete.

>   The boys *left*.   We *are going*.

Some verbs do not express a complete meaning by themselves. They need other words to complete the meaning of a sentence.

>   Sue hit _____. (Hit what? Sue hit the *ball*.)
>   Alan raised _____. (Raised what? Alan
>   raised the *window*.)

Direct Objects

The word that receives the action of a verb is called the **direct object** of the verb. In the sentences above, *ball* receives the action of *hit*. *Window* receives the action of *raised*.

Sometimes the direct object tells the *result* of an action.

>   We dug a *hole*.
>   Edison invented the *phonograph*.

To find the direct object, first find the verb. Then ask *whom* or *what* after it.

>   Carlos saw the President.   Anne painted a picture.
>   *Verb* saw   *Verb* painted
>   *Saw whom?* President   *Painted what?* picture
>   *Direct object* President *Direct object* picture

A verb that has a direct object is called a **transitive verb**. A verb that does not have an object is an **intransitive verb**. A verb may be intransitive in one sentence and transitive in another.

>   *Intransitive* We were watching.
>   *Transitive*   We were watching the race.

Direct Object or Adverb?

Many verbs used without objects are followed by adverbs that tell *how*, *where*, *when*, or *to what extent*. These words are adverbs that go with or modify the verb. Do not confuse them with direct objects. The direct object tells *what* or *whom*.

To decide whether a word is a direct object or a modifier of the verb, decide first what it tells about the verb. If it tells *how*, *where*, *when*, or *to what extent*, it is an adverb. If it tells *what* or *whom*, it is a direct object.

> Don worked *quickly*. (*Quickly* is an adverb telling *how*.)
> Sue worked the *problem*. (*Problem* is a direct object telling *what*.)

Exercises

A Label the verb in each sentence *Transitive* or *Intransitive*. To do so, first decide whether the word in italics is a direct object or an adverb.

1. Several guests left *early*.
2. Someone left a red *sweater*.
3. The band plays *often*.
4. The band plays good *music*.
5. I enjoyed *that*.
6. I enjoyed that delicious *soup*.
7. Please return *soon*.
8. Please return my *camera*.
9. Michelle tried *again*.
10. Mark tried the *door* again.

B Write a sentence using each verb below as a transitive verb. Then write a sentence using each verb as an intransitive verb.

1. whistle
2. call
3. fly
4. eat
5. write
6. study
7. dance
8. read
9. sing
10. draw

Indirect Objects

Some words tell *to whom* or *for whom* something is done. Other words tell *to what* or *for what* something is done. These words are called the **indirect objects** of the verb.

> Anne knitted **Kim** a *sweater*. (knitted *for* Kim)
> We gave the **boat** a *coat* of paint. (gave *to* the boat)

In the sentences at the bottom of page 406, the words in bold type are indirect objects. The words in italics are direct objects.

The words *to* and *for* are never used with indirect objects. The words *to* and *for* are prepositions. Any noun or pronoun following *to* or *for* is actually the object of the preposition.

> They baked *me* a cake. (*Me* is the indirect object of *baked*.)
> They baked a cake for *me*. (*Me* is the object of the preposition *for*.)

Diagraming Objects

In a diagram, the direct object is placed on the main line after the verb. Notice that the line between verb and object does not go below the main line. The indirect object is placed below the main line, under the verb.

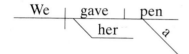

Exercises

A Label three columns *Verb*, *Indirect Object*, and *Direct Object*. Write in the columns the parts that you find in each sentence. After each verb write *Transitive* or *Intransitive*.

1. France sold Louisiana to the United States.
2. We gave our dog a thorough bath.
3. Marta made us a Mexican dinner.
4. Paul waited for me in the park.
5. The students in his English class gave Mr. Bryant a painting for his birthday.
6. The principal gave the co-captains the trophy.
7. The American basketball team won the Olympic gold medal.
8. The sun sparkled on the waves.
9. Pat got a digital watch for Christmas.
10. Brenda hosed the garden.

B Look at the verbs in the following sentences. If the verb has no object, write a sentence using the same verb and an object. If the verb has an object, write a sentence with no object.

> EXAMPLE   An old highway looped around the mining town.
> (In this sentence, the verb *looped* has no object.)
> Bob *looped* the rope twice.
> (Here the verb does have an object: *rope.*)

1. Dad had already packed.
2. Lucy rides her horse in competitions.
3. I cooked all afternoon.
4. The plane left the runway.
5. Alexander painted the garage door.
6. Brazilians speak the Portuguese language.
7. Maria writes elegantly.
8. Jo played the harpsichord in the concert.
9. Stevie Wonder sang on television.
10. Arnetta types quickly and accurately.

Grammar in Action

Objects of verbs help you to express complete thoughts in your writing. Notice the difference in the two sentences below.

Joe cooked.   Joe cooked *me dinner.*

Writing Activity Revise the following paragraph by adding a direct object (DO) or an indirect object (IO) in each blank.

> Tom and Randi bought an old (DO) together. It barely ran, but the engine started. Tom fixed the (DO) first. Then Randi repaired the (DO). Now it would start and stop on command. Then Tom and Randi flipped a (DO). The winner would get the first (DO). Tom won. Randi gave (IO) the (DO) to the car.

8
Predicate Words and Linking Verbs

Linking verbs connect the subject with a word or group of words in the predicate.

Not all verbs express action. A verb may simply say that the subject exists. It may link the subject of a sentence with a word or group of words in the predicate. A verb that simply links the subject with words in the predicate is called a **linking verb**.

> He *is* a doctor.
> They *are* good swimmers.
> She *is* the mayor.
> We *are* students.

The most common linking verb is the verb *be*. This verb has many forms. Study these forms of *be* to make sure that you recognize them:

be	been	is	was
being	am	are	were

The verbs *be, being,* and *been* can also be used with helping verbs. Here are some examples:

might be	is being	have been
could be	are being	might have been
will be	was being	would have been

The words linked to the subject by a linking verb like *be* are called **predicate words**. There are **predicate nouns**, **predicate pronouns**, and **predicate adjectives**.

> Renée is *president*. (predicate noun)
> This is *she*. (predicate pronoun)
> Bill was *happy*. (predicate adjective)

Notice how the subjects and the predicate words in the above sentences are linked by *is* or *was*.

Here are some other common linking verbs:

seem	feel	become	look
appear	taste	grow	sound

Like *be,* these verbs can have various forms *(seems, appears, felt),* or they can be used with helping verbs *(will appear, could feel, might have become).*

> The *music* sounded *beautiful.* (predicate adjective)
> The *plants* grew *taller.* (predicate adjective)
> *I* have become an *expert.* (predicate noun)

Diagraming Predicate Words

In diagrams, the predicate words appear on the main line with subjects and verbs. Note that the line between the verb and the predicate word slants back toward the subject.

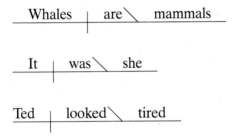

Exercises

A Write the predicate words in the following sentences.

1. Snakes are reptiles.
2. The singing sounded good.
3. This is he.
4. The flowers looked wilted.
5. Has Kathy been sick?
6. The driver was angry.
7. The house seemed empty.
8. Karen felt lonesome.
9. Was it she?
10. Sue became a counselor.

B Label four columns on your paper *Subject, Verb, Direct Object,* and *Predicate Word.* Write in the columns the parts that you find in each sentence.

1. Laser light is important for science and technology.
2. Some powerful lasers can cut metal.
3. Lasers are quite useful in surgery.
4. Laser surgery can mend broken veins.
5. Doctors harness the beam through a thin, flexible glass tube.
6. Scientists first developed the laser in the late 1950's.
7. Lasers are necessary in the communications industry.
8. Some day, lasers may transmit most telephone conversations.
9. A new cane for the blind uses weak laser beams.
10. The beams detect any obstacles.

Grammar in Action

When you write a letter to your friend describing something you did recently, you might want to create a vivid sensory description. You can do this by using linking verbs with predicate adjectives.

EXAMPLES   The apples tasted tart and spicy.
After the game, the players felt hot and tired.

Writing Activity As you know, linking verbs can link three kinds of predicate words to the subject: predicate nouns, predicate adjectives, and predicate pronouns. Using all three kinds of predicate words, write a paragraph describing a walk through the woods on a bright, warm day in early autumn.

9
Compound Sentence Parts

A *compound subject* has two or more parts. A *compound predicate* has two or more parts.

Every part of the sentence you have studied in this chapter can be compound—subjects, verbs, direct objects, indirect objects, and predicate words. Using sentences with compound parts will make your writing more varied and interesting.

If the compound form has only two parts, there is usually a conjunction *(and, or, but)* between them. If there are three or more parts, the conjunction usually comes between the last two of these parts. Use a comma after every part but the last.

Study the following diagrams of sentences with compound parts. The words in italics are the compound sentence parts.

Compound Subjects

Posters, streamers, and *balloons* decorated the room.

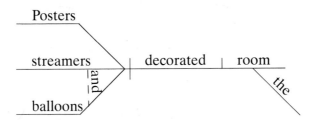

Compound Verbs

The crowd *cheered* and *applauded*.

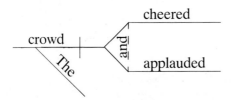

Compound Objects of Verbs

We saw the *President* and his *family*. (direct objects)
The boss showed *Nancy* and *me* the shop. (indirect objects)

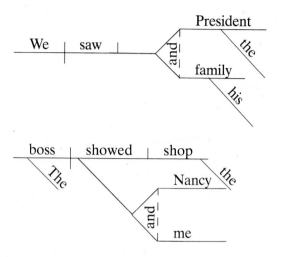

Compound Predicate Words

The winners were *Rebecca* and *Sherry*. (predicate nouns)

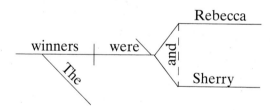

Exercises

A Write the compound parts in each of the following sentences. Then write whether each is a compound subject, verb, object, or predicate word.

1. The water was cool and refreshing.
2. Last weekend we skated and skied.
3. The engine hesitated but finally started.

4. Eisenhower and MacArthur were World War II heroes.
5. Jeff and I washed and waxed the car.
6. We bought posters and banners at the street fair.
7. Did you give Cindy the posters and the flyers?
8. Marla and Robin made hanging planters in shop class.
9. We hung the piñata and the prizes from the ceiling.
10. The gymnasts looked strong but graceful.

B Add words to make a compound of the part noted in parentheses.

1. Jon carried the groceries into the house. *(direct object)*
2. The spaghetti was spicy! *(predicate word)*
3. Did you remember the hamburger buns? *(direct object)*
4. There are modern sculptures in this art museum. *(subject)*
5. The hypnotist's performance was fascinating. *(predicate word)*
6. Mrs. Lopez gave Janelle a bracelet. *(direct object)*
7. The President followed in a long gray limousine. *(subject)*
8. Linda fixed the handlebars. *(direct object)*
9. The Rialto Theater gives students discounts. *(indirect object)*
10. There are ten divers competing in the meet. *(subject)*

Grammar in Action

Compound sentence parts help you combine sentences and avoid repeating phrases.

> I bought celery and onions. I also bought a loaf of bread.
> I bought celery, onions, and a loaf of bread.

Writing Activity Rewrite the following paragraph. Combine sentences by creating compound sentence parts.

> Janette tried out for the basketball team. Beth tried out, too. Carly also tried out. Only Janette made the team. Beth missed the draft by one point. Carly also missed by one point. Carly dribbled the ball well. She passed it well, too. She was weak on guarding. The coach praised Carly for her style.

10
Avoiding Run-On Sentences

A *run-on sentence* is two or more sentences written incorrectly as one.

When two sentences are incorrectly written as one, the result is a **run-on sentence**. Sometimes no punctuation mark is used between run-on sentences. At other times, a comma is incorrectly used.

Incorrect Tony made a pie it tasted great.
Correct   Tony made a pie. It tasted great.

As you can see, a run-on sentence confuses readers. You can avoid run-on sentences by using a period or other end mark to show the reader where each complete thought ends. You will learn another way to avoid run-on sentences in the chapter on compound and complex sentences (*see pages 548–561*).

Exercise

All but three of the following sentences are run-ons. Rewrite the run-on sentences correctly.

1. Jakob and Wilhelm Grimm collected folk tales.
2. "Little Red Riding Hood" is one of their most famous tales, "Snow White" is another.
3. The brothers were afraid that German folk tales would be forgotten, the young men wanted to preserve them by writing them down.
4. The Grimms collected tales between 1807 and 1814, they collected them from farmers in villages.
5. The tales were recorded exactly as they were told.
6. Nineteen of the tales were told by an old spinning woman.
7. The first volume appeared in 1812, it held eighty-six tales.
8. The second contained seventy tales, it appeared in 1815.
9. The Grimms were influenced by German history, they wrote about German myths.
10. The tales involve magic, these stories are about nature.

Linking Grammar & Writing

A Imagine that you are in mission control at NASA head-quarters. You are about to receive a message on your computer screen from an astronaut on another planet. However, there is apparently a malfunction in your system. All you receive are the parts of sentences given below. From these fragments, try to reconstruct the astronaut's description of his or her surroundings. Make each idea a complete sentence.

1. red clouds of gas
2. burning in a haze of steam
3. some unusual plants
4. not plants at all
5. seem to be waving to me

B If you were an inventor, what device would you make that would add happiness to people's lives? Describe your invention and tell how it would bring happiness. After writing about your invention, study each sentence you have written. Underline the subject of each sentence once and the predicate of each sentence twice.

Additional Practice

Part 1 Sentences and Sentence Fragments Label each group of words *Sentence* or *Fragment*. Rewrite fragments to make complete sentences.

1. An hour before serving dinner
2. Cost thirty cents per pound
3. She noticed a tall stranger on the front walk
4. The work of the great American artist Georgia O'Keeffe
5. Before the refrigerator was developed

Parts 2-6 Subjects and Predicates Write the following sentences. Draw a vertical line between the complete subject and the complete predicate. Then put one line under each simple subject and two lines under each verb. Remember to include all helping verbs.

6. The tree's leaves turned a beautiful shade of gold.
7. The mayor delivered a rousing speech to the city council.
8. More than one billion people live in China.
9. In A.D. 79, Herculaneum was buried under layers of lava and mud.
10. Marian will work at her parents' grocery store during summer vacation.
11. Anna will help me with these algebra problems.
12. February is the shortest month of the year.
13. An enormous spider crawled across the living room.
14. José hadn't forgotten the combination to the lock.
15. Barbara and Leanne are not here.

Parts 7-8 Objects and Predicate Words Label four columns on your paper *Verbs, Direct Objects, Indirect Objects,* and *Predicate Words*. Write these parts from each sentence in the correct columns.

16. Henry Aaron hit 755 home runs during regular-season games.
17. Please lend me your hockey stick.

18. Aunt Rhea and Uncle Ralph sent us a postcard from New Zealand.
19. Dr. Christiaan Barnard performed the world's first human heart transplant in 1967.
20. An abacus is a device for making mathematical calculations.
21. Barley is an important ingredient in that recipe.
22. The pork chops look thick and juicy.
23. Call me at home later this afternoon.
24. Elise Wood is a talented jazz flutist.
25. We ate dinner in an excellent Serbian restaurant in Milwaukee.

Part 9 Compound Sentence Parts Add words to make a compound of the sentence part given in the parentheses.

26. The journey across the Great Plains was difficult. (*predicate word*)
27. Helen washed all the dirty clothes. (*verb*)
28. Mr. Collins worked at the school cafeteria for many years. (*subject*)
29. Many people eat turkey on Thanksgiving. (*direct object*)
30. Grandmother gave my brother a savings bond. (*indirect object*)

Part 10 Run-on Sentences All but three of the following sentences are run-ons. Rewrite the run-on sentences correctly.

31. The bricklayer built a wall, it was six feet tall.
32. Mr. Vincent grows a variety of herbs in his garden he uses them in cooking.
33. Mount St. Helens has erupted a number of times.
34. This soup is delicious, can I have another bowl of it?
35. Janna bought a new jacket with the money she earned from baby-sitting.
36. Billy Mills won an Olympic medal in 1864 the movie *Running Brave* tells the inspirational story of his life.
37. The skater gracefully bowed, the crowd applauded her effort.
38. Phil looked very surprised when he found the note on the kitchen table.
39. Mary Paula's photographs won first prize, her drawings also won a prize.
40. Two cups are in a pint four cups are in a quart.

Application and Review

Lesson Review

A Recognizing Sentences and Sentence Fragments Write *S* for each sentence and *F* for each sentence fragment.

1. Because of the driving snow
2. A track was designed and built for the skateboard races
3. A big wave broke over the side of the boat
4. Thousands of people along the parade route
5. Bill's new yellow car out in the driveway
6. A heavy gray sky over the lake
7. The coach explained the basic rules
8. A cheer from the grandstand
9. A helicopter over the traffic jam
10. Pasta and tomato sauce for dinner

B Finding Complete Subjects and Complete Predicates Copy each sentence. Draw a line between the complete subject and complete predicate.

1. Rick caught the ball easily.
2. The atomic submarine surfaced before dawn.
3. A red-tailed hawk circled the field.
4. My uncle uses mulch on his tomato plants.
5. Our janitor was cleaning the basement.
6. A new apartment building was constructed near my house.
7. They unloaded the elephants in the pouring rain.
8. My sister and I went canoeing on Sunday.
9. The tall brunette in the front row spiked the ball.
10. You could hear the crickets outside the cabin.

C Finding Verbs and Simple Subjects Label two columns *Verb* and *Simple Subject*. Number the columns 1–10. Write the verb and its simple subject for each of the following sentences.

1. The chestnut-brown Thoroughbred trotted victoriously.
2. The nest became home for three little mice.

3. The hall outside the cafeteria leads to the music room.
4. One afternoon, a shaggy dog wandered into the gym.
5. The new booklet explains bicycle safety.
6. The landscape by Monet combines tones of blue and green.
7. The slide show on energy conservation explained the importance of natural resources.
8. A friendly dolphin playfully pushed me out of the water.
9. A continuous, heavy snow delighted the skiers.
10. The drought reduced the waterfall to a trickle.

D Finding Main Verbs and Helping Verbs Label two columns *Main Verb* and *Helping Verb*. Number the columns from 1–10. Write the proper words from each sentence in the columns.

1. The television set has broken again.
2. That picture often falls off the wall.
3. The Farmers' Market will open at 7:00 A.M.
4. Paul's old cat does not like children.
5. Chess isn't the fastest game in the world.
6. The sun was barely showing through the clouds.
7. Those plastic dishes will not easily break.
8. My brother and I have frequently had fights.
9. The train doesn't really ride very smoothly.
10. Jan has once again lost the key.

E Finding Verbs and Their Subjects Write the simple subject and the verb in each sentence. Tell whether *there* or *here* is used as an adverb or as an introductory word.

1. Here is the library.
2. There will be band practice in the morning.
3. There is a truck parked in the driveway.
4. There wasn't a cloud in the sky.
5. There was no play rehearsal today.
6. There was no more room in the stadium.
7. There will be a dance next Friday.
8. There sat the box by the bus stop.
9. There were only two commercials during the show.
10. There will be a slight delay before take-off.

F Finding Verbs and Subjects in Unusual Order Number your paper 1–10. Label two columns *Subject* and *Verb*. Write the subject and verb for each sentence.

1. Through the back door of the house the new puppy scampered.
2. Over the hill the motorcyclists raced.
3. Did the rocket misfire?
4. Find the villain.
5. Have you seen the newspaper?
6. Out swarmed the bees.
7. Did you like that book?
8. Onto the field the marching band paraded.
9. Fire this ceramic vase in the kiln.
10. Did you read the editorial in the newspaper?

G Recognizing Transitive and Intransitive Verbs Write the verb in each sentence. Then tell whether it is *Transitive* or *Intransitive*.

1. The telephone rang.
2. The lightning flashed overhead.
3. Paulo scored the first goal.
4. The crowd cheered wildly.
5. Paula lost her wallet.
6. The laundromat charges customers fifty cents.
7. My team won.
8. The newscaster smothered a yawn.
9. Mrs. Brock checked the meter.
10. Steve rose quickly from his chair.

H Finding Predicate Words and Linking Verbs Number your paper from 1–10. Label three columns *Subject, Verb,* and *Predicate Word*. Fill in the parts that you find for each sentence.

1. Nine men were team members.
2. The sky to the west looks strange.
3. The muffins in the oven smell delicious.
4. Green apples are too sour for me.
5. The gulls on the beach were motionless.
6. The apples from the orchard trees were wormy every single year.

7. Their fishing boat looked unstable.
8. From the airplane the toll road appeared empty.
9. Football is a very rough game.
10. The picture on the wall looks lopsided.

I Finding Compound Parts in a Sentence Write the compound parts in the following sentences. Tell whether they are *Compound Subjects, Verbs, Objects,* or *Predicate Words.*

1. Your backstroke is better and stronger.
2. Three monkeys and their trainers were juggling oranges.
3. The high school photography club furnished the doughnuts and cider.
4. Emily and Ken can walk on stilts.
5. A marathon runner must have experience and determination.
6. That Siamese and this Manx are my cats.
7. The roadrunner looked fierce and determined.
8. Laplanders and Finns traditionally hunt reindeer.
9. A landslide uprooted those trees and rocks.
10. The December wind was cold and biting.

J Avoiding Run-on Sentences Rewrite correctly the run-on sentences in the following group. If a sentence does not need to be rewritten, write *Correct.*

1. The train left early we missed it by five minutes.
2. The group of girls had a picnic last Saturday in the park by the fountain.
3. We saw the magic show, the magician did terrific tricks with a set of boxes.
4. Josh lives in a high-rise, his apartment is on the sixty-fifth floor.
5. The wind lifted my kite it stayed high for hours.
6. Lisa hung Impressionist art posters on every wall of her room.
7. Barry rode with Judith on a tandem bike.
8. This is the art museum it has a special exhibit of teen-agers' art.
9. Call me tomorrow I'll be home all day.
10. Meredith took the bus to Yorkville with the other girls on the field hockey team.

Chapter Review

A Finding Sentence Parts Copy each sentence. Label the subjects and verbs. Above direct objects, write *DO*. Above indirect objects write *IO*. Above predicate words write *PW*. Sentence parts may be compound.

1. Workers repaired the elevator.
2. Our street has many deep potholes.
3. Jodi has not been absent this year.
4. There must be an exit.
5. Julie gave me some soap.
6. From the north rumbled the thunder.
7. American space satellites have photographed Jupiter and Uranus.
8. The team has given Gregory and Ryan trophies and certificates.
9. Was Jefferson the President or Vice-President of the United States in 1800?
10. Unexpectedly, the caller was Dr. Robbins.

B Correcting Run-ons and Fragments
contain sentence fragments and run-on sentences. Rewrite the paragraphs, correcting the fragments and run-ons.

> For my social studies project, I am constructing a timetable. Of exploration in American history. My timetable will begin with the landing of Leif Ericson in the year 1000, of course it will include the voyage of Christopher Columbus. The timetable will end with this decade. Covering almost a thousand years.
>
> Events on the timetable will be color-coded. The dates of the journeys of Lewis and Clark will be in blue. Fremont's expeditions west of the Mississippi River in green. Powell's exploration of the Grand Canyon in brown.
>
> I want to show that exploration did not stop after the so-called Age of Exploration, it has continued to the present day. Americans are still exploring. The land and the oceans. As well as space. The next century will see much more American exploration.

22

Using Nouns

A zoo is brimming with people, places, and things named by nouns. There are pandas, gibbons, chinchillas, kangaroos, elephants, reptiles, and amphibians. There are trainers and tourists, cages and amphitheaters, and everywhere, students filled with wonder, laughter, and excitement.

Without nouns it would be impossible to name any of the persons, places, things, and ideas we encounter. In this chapter you will study the different types of nouns and learn how to use them properly in speaking and writing.

1
What Is a Noun?

A *noun* names a person, place, thing, or idea.

All words may be classified into groups called **parts of speech**. **Nouns** are one of the most important of these parts of speech. Read the postcard below. Notice the number of nouns it contains.

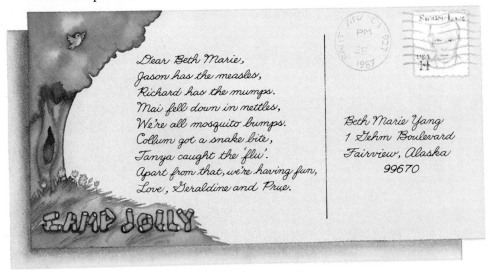

Dear Beth Marie,
Jason has the measles,
Richard has the mumps.
Mai fell down in nettles,
We're all mosquito bumps.
Collum got a snake bite,
Tanya caught the 'flu'.
Apart from that, we're having fun,
Love, Geraldine and Prue.

CAMP JOLLY

Beth Marie Yang
1 Gehm Boulevard
Fairview, Alaska
99670

Nouns name all sorts of things. They name things you can see, such as horses, boats, bats, and footballs. They name things you cannot see, such as feelings, beliefs, and ideas. In the lists of nouns that follow, notice that some nouns are more than one word.

Persons	Places	Things	Ideas
dentist	Spain	magazine	honor
Manuel	home	table	loyalty
columnist	El Paso	tractor	faith
Angelo	New Guinea	book	bravery

In this chapter you will read about nouns. You will learn to recognize the different kinds of nouns. You will also discover how to use these nouns to improve your writing.

Common Nouns and Proper Nouns

There are two kinds of nouns: common nouns and proper nouns. A **common noun** is the name of a whole class of persons, places, things, or ideas. *Student* and *freedom* are common nouns. A **proper noun** is the name of a particular person, place, thing, or idea. Proper nouns always begin with capital letters. *Carlos* and *New Orleans* are proper nouns.

A good way to remember the difference between common and proper nouns is to think of the dog Rex. A *dog* is a common noun, but *Rex* is the name of a particular dog.

"Well, every dog has his day."

Proper nouns are often made up of more than one word. Some examples are *Atlanta Braves* and *Mount Washington*.

Proper nouns are important to good writing. They make your writing more specific and, therefore, more interesting.

> One player had an interesting nickname. Babe Ruth was affectionately known as "the Bambino."

Exercises

A Write the nouns in the following sentences.

1. The ladder may slip on the wet ground.
2. The kit included a hammer, nails, and wood.
3. A computer can store and retrieve information.
4. The diver explored the sunken ship.
5. Truckloads of hay were sent to feed the hungry cattle in the mountains.
6. Our friendship with Milo started in camp last summer.
7. Baseball is sometimes called "the game of summer."
8. The mayor praised Jin for her bravery.
9. Jets streaked across the sky and disappeared.
10. The shop is on the corner of Lake Street and Manor Place.

B Make two columns on your paper. Label one *Common Nouns* and the other *Proper Nouns*. Write each noun in the correct column. Capitalize the proper nouns.

1. One very original writer in america was edgar allan poe.
2. He was born in boston, massachusetts and became an orphan when he was two years old.
3. Among all the jobs poe held were those of editor and critic.
4. Edgar allan poe wrote many poems, including one about a beautiful woman named annabel lee.
5. Poe is sometimes credited with being the first writer of the modern story of suspense.
6. His most famous story of suspense is set in a street called the rue morgue.
7. Another of his stories is about a pendulum.
8. Although poe died in 1849, his poems and stories are still favorites with readers in america and england and other countries around the world.
9. He had great talent for building suspense in a story.
10. Edgar allan poe's works should be listed among our national treasures.

Grammar in Action

Choosing nouns carefully when you write can make the difference between ordinary and interesting writing.

> The governor lives in a huge *house*.
> The governor lives in a *mansion*.

A *huge house* is not very specific, but the word *mansion* gives an immediate picture of the house. Your writing will improve as you learn to use specific nouns.

Writing Activity Write a one-paragraph description of your classroom. As you prepare to write, make a list of ten things you will mention in your description. Use specific nouns in your list; then use these nouns in your paragraph.

2

Forming the Singular and Plural of Nouns

> A *singular noun* names one person, place, thing, or idea.
> A *plural noun* names more than one person, place, thing, or idea.

A noun may be either singular or plural. The noun *shoe* is singular. It stands for only one shoe. The noun *shoes* is plural. It stands for more than one shoe.

Forming Plurals

The first two rules below cover most English nouns. The other five rules deal with words that you use frequently.

1. To most singular nouns, add *-s* to form the plural:

   ropes   boots   books   desks

2. When the singular form ends in *s, sh, ch, x,* or *z,* add *-es:*

   glasses   bushes   coaches   foxes   fizzes

3. When a singular noun ends in *o,* add *-s* to make it plural:

   rodeos   studios   photos   silos   banjos   pianos

   For some words ending in an *o* preceded by a consonant, add *-es.*

   potatoes   heroes   cargoes   echoes   tomatoes

4. When the singular noun ends in a *y* preceded by a consonant, change the *y* to *i* and add *-es:*

   city—cities   lady—ladies   country—countries

   When the *y* is preceded by a vowel *(a, e, i, o, u)*, do not change the *y* to *i*. Simply add *-s:*

   toy—toys   play—plays   day—days

5. For some nouns ending in *f* simply add -*s:*

> beliefs   huffs   wharfs   handkerchiefs

For many words ending in *f* or *fe,* change the *f* to *v* and add -*es* or -*s.* Since there is no rule to follow, these words have to be memorized. Here are some examples of such words:

thief—thieves	elf—elves	life—lives
self—selves	half—halves	calf—calves
loaf—loaves	wife—wives	knife—knives

6. Some nouns have the same form in both the singular and the plural. Memorize these:

deer	salmon	trout	sheep	moose
tuna	cod	pike	bass	elk

7. For some nouns, the plurals are formed in special ways:

child—children	goose—geese	man—men
mouse—mice	ox—oxen	woman—women

Here is a dictionary entry for the word *knife.* Notice that the entry shows the plural, *knives.* Most dictionaries show the plural of a noun if the plural is formed in an irregular way.

> **knife** (nīf) **n.**, *pl.* **knives** [O.E. *cnif:* for IE. base see KNEAD] **1.** a cutting or stabbing instrument with a sharp blade, single-edged or doubled-edged, set in a handle **2.** a cutting blade, as in a machine—**vt. knifed, knif'ing 1.** to cut or stab with a knife ☆**2.** [Colloq.] to use underhanded methods in order to hurt, defeat, or betray—☆**vi.** to pass into or through something quickly, like a sharp knife—☆**under the knife** [Colloq.] undergoing surgery —**knife'like' adj.**

Exercises

A Write the plural of each of these nouns. Then use your dictionary to see if you are right.

1. church	6. dish	11. company	16. baby
2. brush	7. elk	12. watch	17. city
3. elf	8. sheep	13. bookshelf	18. mouse
4. wish	9. fox	14. chimney	19. witch
5. potato	10. tooth	15. lady	20. folio

B Write the plurals of the nouns in italics.

1. Many young *person* think they cannot write *poem*.
2. Many *student* do not read *book* of poetry.
3. Kenneth Koch teaches poetry, and he has worked with *pupil* in *school* in New York.
4. The writing of the *child* astonished the *teacher*.
5. Koch's book about *wish, lie,* and *dream* has many *example* of poetry by young *writer*.
6. Koch said that his inspiration for teaching came from *painting* the *youngster* had made in other *class*.
7. You can learn to write better if you visit art *museum* and *gallery*.
8. There you will see how *artist* have made very ordinary *thing* interesting and beautiful.
9. In writing you use your *sense* to bring to mind the *scene* you are describing.
10. Good writers are constantly aware of their *surrounding*.

C *Write Now* Take inventory of your surroundings. Make two columns on your paper. Head one column *Singular Nouns* and the other column *Plural Nouns*. In the first column, list things you see around you—*pen, book, desk, shoe, shirt,* etc. When you have about twenty items on your list, write their plurals in the second column. Check a dictionary for any plurals that give you trouble.

3
The Possessives of Nouns

> A *possessive noun* shows who or what owns something.

The **possessive noun** may show different kinds of ownership. The noun that follows the possessive noun may be something we own—Carol's essay, Miguel's house. The noun that follows the possessive noun may also be something that is a part of us—our bodies, our emotions: Anna's eyes, Karen's concern.

Forming Possessives

There are three rules for forming the possessives of nouns:

1. If the noun is singular, add an apostrophe and -*s*: Bess's slicker, mother's briefcase, Charles's bike.
2. If the noun is plural and ends in -*s*, add an apostrophe: the Hoffmans' car, students' projects, babies' toys.
3. If the noun is plural but does not end in *s*, add the apostrophe and -*s*: children's books, men's hats.

Exercises

A Write the possessive form of each noun.

1. waitress	8. Jess	15. stereos
2. Max	9. women	16. dresses
3. principal	10. churches	17. county
4. Tracy	11. horses	18. winner
5. Fido	12. birds	19. Pelé
6. boy	13. statues	20. ducks
7. owner	14. Les	

B Write the possessive form of each italicized word.

1. *Farmers* work was made easier by the reaper.
2. The decision was supported by the *students* delegate.
3. *Janine* time broke the *school* record for the 100-yard dash
4. *Darla* sister collected the *class* tests at Ms. *Hires* desk.

5. We spoke to the *teachers* committee about our *club* needs.
6. The actors used the *Parkers* basement for the *farmers* benefit.
7. No one knew Bess or *Lila* address, or *Barry* phone number.
8. The *baby* first steps were recorded in the *cousins* movies.
9. *Mia* cousin painted *Chan grandparents* apartment.
10. *Sandra parents* anniversary party was held at their *son* home.

c *Proofreading* Rewrite the following sentences correctly. Pay particular attention to possessives.

Writers reference books are valued possessions. An authors enclyclopedias, almanacs, and dictionaries are much-needed "tools of the trade." A writer or a students books of grammer are often used to check a rule. For example, what is the rule that governs forming the possessive when the noun is singular. The writer who doesn't rememember the rule has to find it in a reference book. Some writers kept grammar notebooks when they were young. The notebooks are their most valuable possessions now.

Grammar in Action

You use possessives and plurals to make your writing clear and concise. These words, however, have similar forms. Don't use an apostrophe to form a plural.

Incorrect The new car's have great style this year.
Correct The new cars have great style this year.

Keeping plural and possessive forms separate will help you communicate clearly with your readers.

Writing Activity Write a paragraph about a child who has many brothers and sisters and who lives in a large house with an attic. Give the children names and tell about some of their belongings. Use proper nouns and common nouns, including those ending in *-s*.

Linking Grammar & Writing

A Do you dream? Do you dream in black and white or in vivid colors? At times your dreams are influenced by something that has happened to you. Imagine, then, that you have just returned home after seeing your favorite scary movie for the fifth time. You go to bed, fall asleep, and begin to dream. Write a paragraph describing the dream. Be imaginative. Be sure to include common and proper nouns.

B The Carter-Chumley Mansion was closed for years. Now a new owner has restored it and is having a party. The guests include the wealthiest families in the county. Under the crystal chandelier, diamonds and other jewels sparkle. An orchestra plays bright music. Then the clock strikes midnight. The lights go out, and someone screams, "My diamonds! Someone has stolen my diamonds!" The lights come on, and now a woman lies unconscious on the floor. The diamond necklace she was wearing is missing! Others find that their jewelry has been stolen too. You are the detective on the case. Write a report of the missing items. Include common, proper, and possessive nouns. For example, Aunt Jessica's ruby ring might have been stolen from her niece at the party. Include both singular and plural nouns.

C You have heard of wish lists—lists made by people of the things that they want. You are going to write a list of things that you do not want. You may choose items that are practical (a box of the cereal you dislike the most) or outlandish (a pet octopus or a person-eating snail). Head a sheet of paper, "Things I Wouldn't Want If You Gave Them to Me." Then put your imagination to work. Use common and proper nouns, including possessive forms.

Additional Practice

Part 1 Identifying Nouns List the nouns in each sentence. After each noun, tell whether it refers to a person, place, thing, or idea. Capitalize all proper nouns.

1. Some people believe that money can buy happiness.
2. The flag of hungary is red, white, and green.
3. My parents were watching an old movie on television.
4. margaret chase smith was elected to the senate four times.
5. The queen demanded absolute loyalty from her subjects.
6. In mythology, hermes was the messenger of the gods.
7. Doesn't laurel live on main street, about two blocks from city hall?
8. The artist painted with oils on canvas.
9. Irma is a person who has earned my respect and admiration.
10. Cotton, rice, and peanuts are three of the agricultural products of senegal.

Part 2 Singular and Plural Nouns Change each noun in italics to the plural form. Write the nouns on your paper.

11. While unwrapping the gifts, the *child* shrieked with delight.
12. The *illustration* showed how to assemble the bicycle.
13. Father told us that he would have to sell the *calf* at the auction.
14. Ellen wasn't hungry, so she didn't eat the hamburger or the *potato*.
15. The *salesperson* asked the customers if they needed any help.
16. The *tornado* caused a great deal of property damage in our city.
17. After shooting the *deer*, the hunter was arrested for violating the state's game law.
18. The doctor is an expert on the *disease* she is treating.
19. We could see the *ox* pulling the overloaded wagon across the field.
20. I was delighted to be invited to the *party* given by Mr. and Mrs. Lowell.

21. The *coach* said that those who missed practice would not play in the game.
22. After wearing my new shoes all day, I soaked my aching *foot* in warm water.
23. Did you see the enormous *elk* standing at the edge of the forest?
24. The *librarian* had studied library science at Indiana University.
25. The *actor* had to wear a great deal of makeup.

Part 3 Possessive Nouns Write the possessive form of each italicized word. If the italicized word is plural, be sure to use the plural possessive form.

26. Our teacher read one of Robert *Frost* poems to us.
27. The *owners* son collects the rent and takes care of the apartment building.
28. Did you know that an *elephant* tusks are actually teeth?
29. The *woman* hat was decorated with a large feather and some artificial fruit.
30. Jesse *James* older brother, Frank, was his partner in crime.
31. This month the book club will meet at *Kathy father* house.
32. The *knives* blades were quite dull, so we sharpened them.
33. At noon all the *churches* bells began to peal.
34. The police refused to release the *victims* names until their families had been notified.
35. A *dictionary* entries are arranged in alphabetical order.
36. Mr. and Mrs. *Sanders* daughter owns a chain of hardware stores.
37. Did you know that our *neighbors* house is a historical landmark?
38. A rubber *plant* leaves have smooth edges.
39. We visited Abraham *Lincoln* home in Springfield, Illinois.
40. The *trees* roots had damaged the foundation of the house.
41. The *men* basketball team lost an important game.
42. *Lindsay* costume for the play was made by her aunt.
43. The scientists plan to study the *geese* migration route through Minnesota and Wisconsin.
44. *Alice* family often donates canned goods to a neighborhood food pantry.
45. The *coaches* strategy seemed to confuse the other team.

Application and Review

Lesson Review

A Finding Common and Proper Nouns Label two columns *Common Nouns* and *Proper Nouns*. Decide whether the following nouns are common or proper. Write each in the correct column. Capitalize the proper nouns.

1. sun valley, ravine, grand canyon, death valley, pike's peak
2. golden gate bridge, overpass, st. louis arch, brooklyn bridge
3. journalist, senator rosenstein, judge, cardinal bonzano
4. musician, barry manilow, judy collins, guitar, andrés segovia
5. stream, des plaines river, niagara falls, rapids, colorado river
6. intersection, holland tunnel, haggar's corners, highway
7. nation, france, country, united states, scotland, india
8. queen, princess grace, prince charles, queen elizabeth
9. forest, yellowstone national park, westbrook park, woods
10. language, swahili, finnish, travel, spanish, greek

B Forming Plurals of Nouns Write the plural of each of these nouns.

1. tomato
2. donkey
3. auto
4. track
5. ditch
6. wolf
7. shelf
8. party
9. peach
10. foot
11. radio
12. studio
13. scratch
14. cry
15. play
16. toy
17. perch
18. switch
19. leaf
20. deer

C Forming the Possessives of Nouns Write the possessive form as indicated.

1. the horse (plural) mouths
2. Lisa (singular) equipment
3. the child (plural) beds
4. the cat (plural) paws
5. a doctor (singular) appointment
6. the bird (plural) beaks

7. one weather forecaster (singular) prediction
8. the sparrow (singular) wing
9. Ms. Marsh (singular) business
10. the caddy (plural) hours
11. the gull (plural) cries
12. America (singular) resources
13. the pet (singular) owners
14. a bride (singular) bouquet
15. some duck (plural) backs
16. Sara (singular) singing
17. the President (singular) power
18. the moose (singular) antlers
19. the captain (singular) ship
20. Max (singular) shoes

D Finding the Plurals and Possessives of Nouns Write the possessive or the plural form of the italicized noun in each sentence.

1. *Charlie* bike needs a tire.
2. We borrowed *Thomas* snowmobile.
3. Someone gave a hundred *dollar* to the fund.
4. Is *Karl* telephone out of order?
5. Two *class* worked together on the project.
6. There were *clash* between the opposing natural forces.
7. The *ledge* of the windows are rotting.
8. The *box* were stacked one on top of the other.
9. Where is *Perry* share of the apples?
10. The *coach* team rode on a float in the parade.
11. The *lawyers* opening statements were moving.
12. *Francis* new backpack carries all of his books.
13. The *tornado* ripped through the town.
14. Our *team* chances of winning the title are slim.
15. Where did you buy the *kitten* new collar?
16. The band *members* uniforms need to be dry cleaned.
17. Ms. *Keynes* job includes paying the employees.
18. Clarisse went to a party at the *Joneses* house.
19. Oliver broke three *ax* while chopping the wood.
20. Every *reporter* notes are private.

Chapter Review

A Recognizing Common and Proper Nouns Write the nouns in the following sentences. Capitalize all proper nouns.

1. Blind persons use a reading system called braille.
2. The system was invented by louis braille.
3. He became blind as the result of an accident.
4. Another reading system for the blind was invented by charles barbier.
5. Later, braille simplified barbier's system.
6. Braille helps blind people to be independent.
7. Using it, they can read books and can write on a special typewriter.
8. Most publishers have become aware that blind students need aids to help them with their studies.
9. Many books are put on tapes and others are put into braille.
10. Also, many books and magazines are published in large type for people who have partial sight.

B Using Plural and Possessive Forms Correctly Rewrite the following sentences. Correct the errors in the plural and possessive forms.

1. The boss workers were preparing for the days activities.
2. The coachs kept interfering with the umpires decision.
3. We read Dylan Thomas poetry.
4. One of William Shakespeares' plays is about Julius Caesar.
5. The mens' department carries boy's clothing too.
6. The thiefs obviously missed the ladies chain.
7. Scary movies were responsible for the childrens' nightmares.
8. The echos of the fans cheers followed the athletes off the field.
9. The boxs of salmons were gifts from the fishermen's club.
10. Loud pianoes can drown out the choir's soloes.
11. Sophies uncle always carries gum in his coat pocket.
12. People's egoes bruise easily.
13. My mothers' new shoe's look comfortable.
14. The typing classes schedule changed.
15. Harold's copys of the papers got lost.

23
Using Pronouns

Journal   January 15

We had a snow day today! As soon as I heard the news I went back to sleep. In the afternoon a group of us went sledding. It was great fun and we really enjoyed ourselves.

The underlined words in the journal entry above are pronouns. Pronouns take the place of nouns, allowing you to speak and write with greater ease because you do not have to repeat the same nouns over and over again. In this chapter you will study the different types of pronouns and learn how to use them effectively.

1
Personal Pronouns

> A *personal pronoun* is a word that is used in place of a noun or another pronoun.

A **pronoun** is a word used in place of a noun or another pronoun. **Personal pronouns** are used to refer to nouns that name persons or things. They do this in three ways:

1. When the pronoun refers to the person(s) speaking, it is in the **first person**: *I, me, we, our,* and *us,* for example.
2. When the pronoun refers to the person(s) spoken to, it is in the **second person**: *you, your, yours.*
3. When the pronoun refers to some other person(s) or thing(s) that is being spoken of, it is in the **third person**: *he, his, him, she, her, it, they, their, them,* for example.

> The letter was addressed to *me.*
>   (speaker—first person)
> The phone call is for *you.*
>   (person spoken to—second person)
> The boys are looking for *him.*
>   (person spoken of—third person)

The word *it* is called a personal pronoun, even though it is never used in place of a person's name.

Pronouns in the third person that refer to male people are said to be in the **masculine gender**. Pronouns that refer to female people are said to be in the **feminine gender**. Pronouns that refer to things are said to be in the **neuter gender**.

> Bob bought *his* ticket yesterday.
>   (*His* is in the masculine gender.)
> Marie says that book is *hers.*
>   (*Hers* is in the feminine gender.)
> Jill reached for the paddle, but *it* floated out of reach.
>   (*It* is in the neuter gender.)

Animals are often referred to by *it* or *its.*

Exercises

A Write on your paper the pronouns from each of the following sentences.

1. A spotted coat helps the leopard hide from its prey.
2. Snow covered the ball park earlier, but it melted.
3. John and Ginny visited their cousins in Texas.
4. Ken came by and picked up his soccer ball before supper.
5. Many artists built their studios in old warehouses.
6. I wanted to buy a stereo, but it was too expensive.
7. Lucy, will you make enchiladas for the party?
8. The grizzly bear stole our food to feed its cubs.
9. Linda and her best friend are going to New York, and they will compete in a speech contest there.
10. Jay opened the envelope, but he found nothing in it.

B Make two columns on your paper. Label them *Pronouns* and *Nouns*. Write the pronouns from the following sentences in the first column. Write the nouns for which they stand in the second column.

1. Scientists can now fit computer circuitry into a tiny square. They call the square a chip.
2. Mr. Saez held up a chip. It was quite small.
3. Ms. Estes picked up a quartz rock. She explained that silicon comes from quartz.
4. Silicon is important because it is used to make chips.
5. Because of this new technology, many people can now afford their own personal computers.
6. Daryll says that his mother figures out the family budget on her personal computer.
7. The class saw a chip under a microscope. We all thought it looked like the view of a city from an airplane.
8. Tricia said she once saw an interesting picture. It showed an ant carrying a chip.
9. Mr. Saez showed everyone his watch. It was also controlled by a chip.
10. When the chip was first developed, scientists called it the integrated circuit.

2
Reflexive and Intensive Pronouns

Pronouns that end in *-self* or *-selves* are called either intensive or reflexive pronouns.

Reflexive and intensive pronouns are: *myself, yourself, herself, himself, itself, ourselves, yourselves, themselves.*

A **reflexive pronoun** refers back to an action performed by the subject of the sentence. This kind of pronoun is essential for completing the meaning of a sentence.

> Sue gave *herself* a reward. (If you leave out *herself*, the meaning of the sentence is incomplete.)
> Sue judges *herself* too harshly.

An **intensive pronoun** is used to emphasize a noun or a pronoun. It does not add information to a sentence, and it may be removed without changing the meaning of the sentence.

> Rob *himself* baked this apple bread. (If you leave out *himself*, the meaning of the sentence does not change.)
> I *myself* do not agree with your decision to quit the team.

Exercises

A List all the reflexive and intensive pronouns in the sentences. Tell whether each one is reflexive or intensive.

1. You can buy yourself a new pair of jeans.
2. They went home from the game by themselves.
3. The mayor himself presented the award to us.
4. We churned butter ourselves when we lived on the farm.
5. They saw themselves in the newspaper photograph.
6. She did not know the answer herself.
7. I will probably have to complete the project myself.
8. Some people enjoy talking to themselves.
9. He named himself the class king of comedy.
10. If you want to get something done, do it yourself.

B Complete the following sentences with the correct reflexive or intensive pronoun. Identify each as intensive or reflexive.

1. I finished the raking and sweeping _____.
2. You can both see for _____ that the experiment worked.
3. We went to the movies by _____.
4. If you jog, you only compete with _____.
5. Janelle planted the flower bed by _____.
6. They can read for _____ that the game was canceled.
7. I went by _____ to the art exhibit.
8. We treated _____ to concert tickets.
9. Will you take the train to St. Louis by _____?
10. David directed the play _____.

c *Write Now* Rewrite the following paragraph. Add intensive pronouns in three places to make statements more emphatic.

Mount Rushmore Memorial

Gutzon Borglum was the American sculptor who engineered the building of the Mount Rushmore Memorial. Borglum designed the giant stone heads of Washington, Jefferson, Lincoln, and Roosevelt. He supervised much of the work. The stone heads are the height of five-story buildings. Borglum died before the work was completed, but his son finished the project. If you visit South Dakota, you can see the monument.

Grammar in Action

Reflexive pronouns are often misused. When you use a reflexive pronoun, remember that it must refer to a noun or a pronoun that precedes it in the sentence.

Incorrect	Bob and *myself* went running. (*Myself* does not refer to any other noun or pronoun in the sentence.)
Correct	Bob and *I* went running.
Correct	I went running by myself. (*Myself* refers to I.)

3
Indefinite Pronouns

An *indefinite pronoun* is a pronoun that does not refer to a specific person or a specific thing.

Pronouns like *anyone* and *nobody* do not refer to any definite person or thing. They are called **indefinite pronouns**.

Most indefinite pronouns are singular in number. Lists and examples of these pronouns follow.

Singular Indefinite Pronouns			
another	each	everything	one
anybody	either	neither	somebody
anyone	everybody	nobody	someone
anything	everyone	no one	

Neither brought *his* application.
   (Not: Neither brought *their* application.)
Someone left *her* extra pair of shoes here.
Everyone must order *his or her* class ring.

Notice that the phrase *his or her* may be used when the person being referred to could be either male or female.

Do not be confused by phrases that come after singular indefinite pronouns.

Neither of the boys has been a counselor at the camp before. (Although the word *boys* is plural, the indefinite pronoun *neither* is singular.)

A few indefinite pronouns are plural.

Plural Indefinite Pronouns			
both	many	few	several

Both received *their* awards.   Few *are* really worried.

The pronouns *all, some, any,* and *none* may be singular or plural, depending on their meaning in the sentence.

> All of the yogurt *is* gone.   All of the cars *are* here.
> None of the time *was* wasted. None of the nuts *were* left.

Exercises

A Write the indefinite pronouns from the following sentences.

1. Neither of the keys fits the lock.
2. Just a few of my relatives are coming.
3. Some of the Louisiana settlers were French.
4. In the fall everyone rides his or her bike to school.
5. Each of the countries sends two representatives.
6. During the noon hour, anyone can go home to eat lunch.
7. All of the runners were lined up for the race.
8. All of the settlers of Roanoke, Virginia, disappeared.
9. Several of those days last week were scorchers.
10. Both of my brothers work at the theater.

B Make two columns on your paper. Label them *Indefinite Pronouns* and *Verbs*. Write the indefinite pronouns and the correct forms of the verbs given in parentheses in the correct columns.

1. Nobody (know, knows) much about the Loch Ness monster.
2. Some of the Loch Ness visitors (have, has) photographed it.
3. All of the photographs of the monster (is, are) unclear.
4. (Does, Do) everyone know that Loch Ness is a lake in Scotland?
5. Many of the observers (has, have) described the monster.
6. (Has, Have) anyone seen the film of an animal in Loch Ness?
7. Many (believes, believe) some animal does live in the lake.
8. Some (call, calls) it "Nessie, the Loch Ness Monster."
9. All of the pictures (show, shows) a creature with a long neck.
10. Each of the photographs (make, makes) people want more.

C *Write Now* Imagine that you have interviewed your classmates for a newspaper story on the reading tastes of your generation. Write six sentences describing the books, magazines, and newspapers that your classmates like. Use indefinite pronouns.

4

Demonstrative and Interrogative Pronouns

A *demonstrative pronoun* is used to single out one or more persons or things referred to in the sentence.
An *interrogative pronoun* is used to ask a question.

When you speak and write, you often want to point out certain persons and things. You also need to ask questions. There are two kinds of pronouns that are used for these purposes.

The **demonstrative pronouns** are *this, that, these,* and *those. This* and *these* point to persons or things that are near. *That* and *those* point to persons or things farther away.

This is the right road.   *These* belong to Jim.
That is my camera.   *Those* are my boots.

The **interrogative pronouns** are *who, whose, whom, which,* and *what.* They ask questions:

Who rang the bell?   *Which* is your paper?
Whose are those shoes?   *What* did you say?
Whom do you mean?

Exercises

A Write on your paper the correct demonstrative pronouns given in parentheses in the following sentences.

1. (Those, These) are my books over there.
2. (That, This) was Kate on the telephone.
3. (That, This) is my new shirt right here.
4. (These, Those) are Julie's earrings here on the dresser.
5. (This, That) is our house down the block.
6. (That, This) was my brother playing the drums.
7. I have a sore toe from (those, these) shoes I'm wearing.
8. (Those, These) were my cousins you met yesterday.

9. (This, That) was Ryan in the doorway.
10. David, (this, that) is my sister on the stage.

B Make two columns on your paper. Label them *Demonstrative Pronouns* and *Interrogative Pronouns*. Write the demonstrative and interrogative pronouns from the following sentences in the correct column.

1. I have to choose between the silver skates and these.
2. Which of the new TV shows does Rhoda enjoy?
3. This is Jay's cassette player.
4. Who can answer my question?
5. What is everybody waiting for?
6. Which book did Ann choose?
7. Those are hot potatoes!
8. To whom did the caller wish to speak?
9. Which of the shelves does Ernest want painted?
10. Are these the largest shoes in the store?

Grammar in Action

When writing a paragraph, you can use demonstrative pronouns to connect your ideas. Demonstrative pronouns used in this way are called *transitions*.

> The polar bear has a thick coat. The coat keeps it warm.
> The polar bear has a thick coat. This keeps it warm.

Writing Activity Complete the following paragraph, adding demonstrative pronouns to connect the ideas.

> On this desk are some examples of elements we are studying for our science class. _____ are metallic elements right in front of me. _____ at the other end of the desk are nonmetallic. _____ is a sample of carbon over there. Carbon is a nonmetallic element. _____ is a sample of mercury I am holding.

5
The Forms of the Pronoun

A personal pronoun has three forms: the *subject form,* the *object form,* and the *possessive form.*

In English, personal pronouns have three special forms. Like nouns, they have a **possessive form**. In addition, they have a **subject form** and an **object form**.

> *I* own the book. (subject form)
> The owner of the book is *I*. (subject form after linking verb)
> The book belongs to *me*. (object form)
> Where is *my* book? (possessive form modifying a noun)
> The book is *mine*. (possessive form used as predicate pronoun)

Notice that the subject form of a pronoun may be used as the subject of the sentence or as a predicate pronoun. The object form may be used as the direct or indirect object or as the object of a preposition. The possessive form is used to show ownership.

The Subject Form of Pronouns

A personal pronoun is used in the subject form (1) when it is the subject of the sentence or (2) when it follows a linking verb as a predicate pronoun. Here are the subject forms of the personal pronouns:

The Subject Form of Pronouns		
I	you	he, she, it
we	you	they

> *I* agree with Rob. (subject of sentence)
> *She* is not going. (subject of sentence)
> This is *he*. (after linking verb)
> It was *I*. (after linking verb)

The Object Form of Pronouns

A personal pronoun is used in the object form (1) when it is the direct or indirect object of a verb or (2) when it is the object of a preposition, which is a short, connecting word such as *of, for, to, with,* or *by.*

The Object Forms of Pronouns		
me	you	him, her, it
us	you	them

The dog bit *him*. (direct object)
Jack helped *them* with the work. (direct object)
I gave *her* a gift. (indirect object)
The sandwich is for *me*. (object of preposition)

The Possessive Form of Pronouns

The possessive form of a pronoun is used to show ownership. There are two groups of personal pronouns in the possessive form: (1) those used like adjectives to modify nouns and (2) those used like nouns as subjects, predicate words, or objects of verbs or prepositions.

Possessive Forms of Pronouns Used to Modify Nouns		
my	your	his, her, its
our	your	their

my sister	*our* car	*her* mother
his book	*its* wheels	*their* money

Possessive Forms of Pronouns Used Alone		
mine	yours	his, hers, its
ours	yours	theirs

This book is *mine*. (predicate word)
Yours is on the desk. (subject of verb)
I don't see *hers*. (object of verb)
Look at the pictures in *ours*. (object of preposition)

Exercise

Make three columns on your paper. Label them *Subject Form*, *Object Form*, and *Possessive Form*. Write the pronouns printed in italics in the following sentences in the correct column.

1. The hockey stick in the corner is *mine*.
2. Ms. Anderson gave *us* several problems for homework.
3. *I* gave *you* the schedule.
4. *They* were taking *her* to dinner.
5. *He* brought *them* the gifts.
6. *We* have been watching *him*.
7. Cindy couldn't find *her* basketball.
8. Where is *my* Astros hat?
9. Did *you* take *her* picture?
10. The third one in the front row is *she*.

c *Proofreading* Proofread the following paragraphs. Then rewrite them correctly.

In our science class, us wrote reports on animals of the world. My group and me did research on lions. We learned some interesting things about the majestic beasts.

Lions, the most fearsome of all the big cats, are aslo the most social. The live in groups called *prides*. Between ten and thirtyfive lions live in a pride. They're are usually only a few males in the pride. The job of the male is to protect the group and it's hunting area. Any animal that approaches here's his loud roar. Several females do the hunting. They provide the pride with it's food. As fierce as lions are, life in the pride is usually calm. The lions spend most of there time aslep, as cubs run around and play. Occasionaly a female will wake up to take care of his cubs or the cubs of other lions.

6
Pronouns in Compound Subjects and Compound Objects

Use the same pronoun in a compound subject or a compound object that you would use if the pronoun stood alone.

You seldom make mistakes when you use one personal pronoun by itself. You would never say, "Give *I* the pencil."

Trouble arises when two pronouns or a pronoun and a noun are used together in compound sentence parts. Would you say, "Brian and me built a radio" or "Brian and I built a radio"?

Have you heard people say "between you and I"? Does this sound right? Should it be "between you and me"? Let's look at some sentences with pronouns correctly used in compound parts.

> *Terry and she* went to the rink. (compound subject)
> We visited the *Browns and them*. (compound direct object)
> Leo gave *Sue and me* a job. (compound indirect object)
> The package was for *Jack and me*. (compound object of preposition)

Read the sentences above a second time. This time drop out the noun in each compound part. For example, read "*She* went to the rink." Each sentence will sound right and sensible to you.

Whenever you are in doubt about which form of the pronoun to use in a compound sentence part, drop out the noun. Read the sentence with just the pronoun, and you will usually choose the correct form.

If there are two pronouns in the compound part, read the sentence for each pronoun separately.

> Mrs. Huber will call for (she? her?) and (I? me?)
> Mrs. Huber will call for *her*.
> Mrs. Huber will call for *me*.

Remember to use only *I, we, he, she,* or *they* as predicate pronouns after forms of the verb *be.*

The current president is *she.* The new president will be *I.*

Exercises

A Write the correct pronouns given in parentheses from the following sentences.

1. Dawn and (her, she) will bring the peanuts.
2. Can you give Sandy and (we, us) some advice?
3. Gayle and (her, she) are trying out for cheerleading.
4. The doorman gave Al and (I, me) a pass.
5. Leave the canoe and oars with Jeff and (him, he).
6. Anna researched John Glenn and (him, he) for her report.
7. Jeff lives between (them, they) and (I, me).
8. (Her, She) and I are the newspaper editors.
9. Some famous painters were Georgia O'Keeffe and (her, she).
10. Have you heard about Joel and (they, them)?

B All but one of the following sentences contain an error in pronoun use. If a sentence is correct, write *Correct.* If there is an error, write the sentence correctly.

1. My parents and me are going to the ice show tonight.
2. Paul and them started a baseball team.
3. The telephone call must be for either you or she.
4. Everyone had enough except Janet and she.
5. The packages were divided evenly between Tanya and I.
6. Charles and me found dozens of arrowheads on the lake bed.
7. Ms. McGowan made sandwiches for Meg and I.
8. The police officer gave Alex and I directions.
9. Peggy and Linda sat next to Lauri and I at the concert.
10. The helicopter kept circling around Pete and me.

C *Write Now* Imagine that you are showing a movie of a trip you have taken. Using at least five of the following groups of words, write a short description of the movie.

1. my family and me
2. they and I
3. her and me
4. a friend and I
5. me and them
6. he and they

7
Using Who, Whom, *and* Whose

> The words *who, whom,* and *whose* may be used as *interrogative pronouns* to ask questions.

Who, whom, and *whose* are often used to ask questions. When that is their function, they are called **interrogative pronouns**. *Who* is the subject form. It is used as the subject of a verb. *Whom* is the object form. It is used as the direct object of a verb or as the object of a preposition.

> *Who* told you that story? (*Who* is the subject of *told*.)
> *Whom* did you meet? (*Whom* is the object of *did meet*.)
> To *whom* did you go? (*Whom* is the object of the
>   preposition *to*.)

Whose is the possessive form. Like other possessives, it can modify the noun: *Whose bike* is missing? When it is used without a noun, it may be the subject or object of a verb.

> *Whose* house is that? (*Whose* modifies *house*.)
> *Whose* did you use? (*Whose* is the object of *did use*.)
> *Whose* are those boots? (*Whose* is the subject of *are*.)

Exercise

Write *who, whom, or whose* for these sentences.

1. _____ blue and gold notebook is this?
2. _____ did you invite?
3. _____ painted the *Mona Lisa*?
4. _____ do you know in Alaska?
5. To _____ did the shortstop throw the ball?
6. _____ are these people?
7. I don't know _____ plaid scarf this is.
8. For _____ shall I ask?
9. _____ wore the red socks?
10. _____ will be voted the most valuable player?

8
Possessive Pronouns and Contractions

A possessive pronoun never has an apostrophe; a contraction always has an apostrophe.

A **contraction** of a pronoun and a verb is formed by omitting one or more letters from the verb and inserting an apostrophe to show where the letters are left out.

it + is or has = it's   they + are = they're
you + are = you're   who + is or has = who's

Some possessive pronouns sound like contractions. Because the words sound alike, they are sometimes confused.

Possessive Pronouns	Contractions
its	it's
your	you're
their	they're
whose	who's

Incorrect   The groundhog saw it's shadow.
Correct   The groundhog saw its shadow.

Correct   You're (You are) late for your appointment.
Correct   They're (They are) planning to show their slides.
Correct   Who's (Who is) the boy whose coat you are wearing?

There are two simple rules to follow to make sure that you use possessive pronouns and contractions correctly:

1. When you use one of two words that sound alike, ask yourself whether it stands for one word or two words. If it stands for two words, it is a contraction and needs an apostrophe.
2. Never use an apostrophe in a possessive pronoun.

Remember that in certain types of writing, such as reports and business letters, you should not use contractions. Contractions are acceptable, however, in written dialogue and in informal writing, such as friendly letters.

Exercises

A Write on your paper the correct words given in parentheses in the following sentences.

1. The theater gave free passes to (it's, its) staff.
2. (Whose, Who's) bike is chained to the tree?
3. (You're, Your) idea might work.
4. (They're, Their) taking pictures of Jupiter.
5. (Whose, Who's) going to the Ridgetown Fair?
6. (They're, Their) saying that (its, it's) not theirs.
7. (Who's, Whose) the sculptor of the *Venus de Milo*?
8. (Their, They're) picking up (their, they're) uniforms now.
9. Have you made up (you're, your) mind?
10. (Who's, Whose) cottage is that next to the stream?

B Write on your paper the correct words given in parentheses in the following sentences. If the word is a contraction, write the words it stands for.

1. (It's, Its) twenty miles from this town to Omaha.
2. (Whose, Who's) the fastest runner in the world?
3. The tiger hid in the bush until it saw (it's, its) prey.
4. "(Your, You're) hired," said the store manager to Jesse.
5. The spectators couldn't believe (they're, their) eyes.
6. (Who's, Whose) the author of *Moby Dick*?
7. (Who's, Whose) red gym shoes are those?
8. Bring (your, you're) camera and a roll of color film.
9. (Your, You're) not in the right line for tickets.
10. (Their, They're) arriving by helicopter.

C *Write Now* Suppose a family from Mars has moved in next door. Write a dialogue that you might have about your new neighbors. Use at least six of the following words: *it's, you're, they're, who's, its, your, their, whose.*

9
Special Pronoun Problems

> When using phrases like *we girls* and *us boys,* decide on the correct pronoun by dropping the noun and saying the sentence with the pronoun only.

In certain situations, you may find it difficult to decide which pronoun is the correct choice. Here is some information that will help you decide which pronoun to use in some of those situations.

We *and* Us *Used with Nouns*

When you use phrases like *we girls* and *us boys,* you must be sure that you are using the correct form of the pronoun. You can tell which pronoun to use by dropping the noun and saying the sentence without it:

Problem   (We, Us) girls will be at Jan's house.
Correct   We will be at Jan's house.
Correct   We girls will be at Jan's house.

Problem   Will you call (us, we) boys?
Correct   Will you call us?
Correct   Will you call us boys?

Using the Pronoun Them

The word *them* is always a pronoun. It is always used as an object of a verb or preposition.

> We found *them* here. (direct object of verb)
> The whole audience likes *them*. (direct object of verb)
>
> We gave *them* the award. (indirect object of verb)
> Sue handed *them* some plates. (indirect object of verb)
>
> We have never heard anything from *them*. (object of preposition *from*)
> We have lost every football game to *them*. (object of preposition *to*)

Using **Those**

You have already learned that *those* can be used as a demonstrative pronoun (page 444). Sometimes, however, *those* is used as an adjective. An adjective is a word that modifies a noun or a pronoun. If a noun appears immediately after it, *those* is probably an adjective. Used without a noun, *those* is a pronoun. *Those* is a pronoun in the first sentence below:

> *Those* are cardinals. (subject of verb)
> *Those* birds are cardinals. (adjective modifying *birds*)

Exercises

A Write on your paper the correct pronouns given in parentheses in the following sentences.

1. Will you go to the beach with (us, we) girls?
2. (We, Us) scouts would like to sponsor a canoe trip.
3. (Them, Those) portraits look very old.
4. (We, Us) players are going to the Knicks–Bulls game.
5. Will you call for (we, us) boys on the way home?
6. Who piled all (them, those) boards up?
7. Would you like to sit with (us, we) girls at the play?
8. Most of (us, we) boys will help paint the bleachers.
9. You won't need all of (them, those) pencils.
10. (We, Us) students held a pep rally yesterday.

B Write *P* or *A* on your paper to indicate whether *those* is a pronoun or an adjective in each of the following sentences.

1. *Those* are copies of the Statue of Liberty.
2. The original is much larger than *those* statues.
3. *Those* spikes on the crown look like sun rays.
4. *Those* are the words of poet Emma Lazarus at the base.
5. *Those* words have become famous.
6. *Those* flowing robes are made of copper.
7. Did you know that *those* fingers are eight feet long?
8. *Those* are lights inside the torch.
9. *Those* burn brightly all night, every night.
10. Freedom and liberty—*those* are the things represented by the Statue of Liberty.

10
Pronouns and Their Antecedents

The *antecedent* of a pronoun is the noun or another pronoun for which the pronoun stands.

A personal pronoun, you remember, is used in place of a noun. This noun is the word to which it refers. The noun usually comes first, either in the same sentence or in the sentence before it. The noun for which a pronoun stands is called its **antecedent**.

> We waited for *Kay*. *She* was making a phone call.
> (*She* stands for *Kay*. *Kay* is the antecedent.)
> The men had taken off *their* coats.
> (*Their* stands for *men*. *Men* is the antecedent.)

Pronouns may be the antecedents of other pronouns:

> Does everyone have *his* books?
> (*Everyone* is the antecedent of *his*.)
> Do you have *your* music lesson today?
> (*You* is the antecedent of *your*.)

Pronoun and Antecedent Agreement

A pronoun must agree with its antecedent in number. Here the word *agree* means that the pronoun must be the same in number as its antecedent. The word *number* here means *singular* or *plural*. The pronoun must be singular if the word it stands for is singular. It must be plural if the word it stands for is plural. Pronoun–antecedent agreement will make your writing and speaking clearer.

> The runners took *their* places.
> (*Runners* is plural; *their* is plural.)
> The scientist told of *her* early experiences.
> (*Scientist* is singular; *her* is singular.)
> Everybody brought *his* or *her* own records.
> (*Everybody* is singular; *his* and *her* are singular.)

Notice that the last example on page 456 uses the pronouns *his* and *her*. When the antecedent refers to both males and females, you may use either the masculine pronoun or the feminine and masculine pronouns together.

Exercises

A Write the antecedents of the personal pronouns printed in italics in the following sentences.

1. George Washington wore a wig in *his* portraits.
2. You usually bring *your* own towel to the pool.
3. The box isn't pretty, but the paper around *it* is.
4. Everyone on the team had tears in *her* eyes.
5. Both arrived without *their* applications.
6. Everyone thinks *you* can do the job, Sarah.
7. The Liberty Bell has a crack in *it*.
8. Mr. Patimkin weaves *his* own fabrics.
9. The cast members took *their* places.
10. The old store had *its* entrance boarded up.

B Write the correct pronouns given in parentheses in the following sentences.

1. Has everyone taken (his, their) turn?
2. If anyone wants to be a doctor, tell (him or her, them) to do volunteer work in a hospital.
3. Few were able to finish (his, their) work.
4. Many of Rembrandt's paintings have lost (its, their) original colors.
5. Somebody has left (his or her, their) wallet on my desk.
6. Everyone had a chance to state (their, her) opinion.
7. All of the contestants had (his, their) entries ready.
8. Nobody expects to hear (his, their) own name on the radio.
9. Neither of the actors could remember (his, their) lines.
10. Each of the students explained (his or her, their) collage.

C *Write Now* Invent a new backyard game for four players. Use a net, a ball, and a paddle. Write a paragraph explaining how to play the game. When you are finished, make sure each pronoun agrees with its antecedent in number.

Linking Grammar & Writing

A Imagine that you are a reporter for a local newspaper. Write a news story about something that might have occurred in your area. For example, your story may be about a major fire or a heroic rescue. The story may be made up or true. Remember that a news story provides the following information: *who, what, when, where, why,* and *how.*

B Imagine that you are the new president of a major television network. Write a speech telling what your goals are. Use at least ten of the following indefinite pronouns in your speech:

another	either	nobody	both
anybody	everybody	no one	many
anyone	everyone	one	few
anything	everything	somebody	several
each	neither	someone	some

Make sure that each time you use an indefinite pronoun, other pronouns and verbs agree in number with the indefinite pronoun.

C Write a fan letter to one of your favorite performers. Ask the performer to send you and your friends some autographed photos of herself or himself. In your letter, use the phrases *we fans* and *us fans* at least two times each. Also use at least two compound personal pronouns *(myself, ourselves, yourself, yourselves, himself, herself, itself, themselves)* in your letter.

Additional Practice

Parts 1-2 Personal Pronouns List each pronoun in the following sentences. Label each one *Personal, Reflexive,* or *Intensive.*

1. The mayor herself called each campaign worker to express her appreciation.
2. The children were afraid to go into the dark house by themselves.
3. Our cat caught a mouse, killed it, and then left it behind our piano.
4. Walter Mondale ran for President of the United States in 1984, but he lost the election to Ronald Reagan.
5. What are you planning to cook for yourself tonight?
6. The new Cambodian students tested themselves to prepare for the entrance examination.
7. Rattlesnakes do not always rattle before attacking their prey.
8. Hercules himself could not lift my suitcase.
9. She finished the chores herself and then helped me with my work.
10. Martina Navratilova and Chris Evert walked off the tennis court by themselves.

Parts 3-4 Other Types of Pronouns List each pronoun in the following sentences. Label each one *Indefinite, Demonstrative, Interrogative,* or *Personal.*

11. Neither of the punishments fits the crime.
12. That is a building designed by Andrea Palladio.
13. Whom do you plan to invite to your birthday party?
14. Someone drove across our front lawn, leaving deep ruts in it.
15. Without a doubt, this is the best chili I have ever tasted.
16. Whose shoes left black heel marks on the floor?
17. In tropical areas, people use palm trees for building their homes.
18. Several of my friends are planning to paint houses next summer.
19. Which do you prefer, rock or country and western?
20. Who wrote the Declaration of Independence?

Parts 5-7 Pronoun Forms Seven of the following sentences contain an error in pronoun use. If a sentence is correct, write *Correct*. If there is an error, write the sentence correctly.

21. My mother and me heard Maya Angelou speak at the convention.
22. Mr. Henderson decided to give his concert tickets to Paul and he.
23. Kevin's science report is about marsupials; ours is about amphibians.
24. Whom left these roller skates on the stairs?
25. Let's keep this news between you and I.
26. The person who can give you information about the computer system is she.
27. Samuel Adams, Paul Revere, and him are considered great patriots.
28. The children watched the news report about she and they.
29. Whose gloves are these, yours or hers?
30. The Secretary-General of the United Nations was him.

Parts 8-10 Other Pronoun Problems Write the correct words given in parentheses in the following sentences.

31. Did you see the newt shedding (its, it's) skin?
32. Both of my sisters set (her, their) hair every morning.
33. (We, Us) boys all think that Michael Jordan is a great basketball player.
34. (Them, Those) chemicals are harmful to humans.
35. (They're, Their) rushing to finish (their, they're) work.
36. Can someone help (we, us) unload the car?
37. The birds collected twigs for (its, their) nests.
38. Has anyone lost (their, her) keys?
39. (You're, Your) going to be surprised by the movie's ending.
40. (We, Us) jockeys have to keep our weight down.
41. (Who's, Whose) responsible for the ticket sales?
42. (Their, They're) planning a party for their parents.
43. The guide warned (us, we) girls not to stray from the path.
44. Either Bob or Nate will have to share (his, their) book.
45. (Its, It's) not easy to be a gracious loser.

Application and Review

Lesson Review

A Finding Pronouns Make two columns on your paper. Label them *Pronouns* and *Nouns*. Write the pronouns from the following sentences in the first column. Write the nouns for which they stand in the second column.

1. Mike said he would set the dinner table.
2. There's no stamp on the envelope. It must have come off.
3. One rancher drove his jeep ten miles out on the range.
4. There's the box. Its lid has a picture of a cornfield.
5. Brad and Joe said Scott could use their tent.
6. Claire and Joy put their baseball equipment into the car.
7. Mr. Hernandez attached his trailer to the back of the van.
8. Two archaeologists told how they had discovered the ruins.
9. Sue and Jill missed the bus, and they got caught in the rain.
10. There's the tree where Megan snagged her kite.

B Using Reflexive and Intensive Pronouns Write the correct reflexive or intensive pronoun to complete each of the following sentences. Then identify the antecedent for each reflexive or intensive pronoun. (If the pronoun *you* is understood, write *you*.)

1. The boys decorated the gym by (pronoun).
2. Julie cleaned the fish (pronoun).
3. I moved the plants (pronoun) so that they wouldn't get damaged.
4. Evan, please help (pronoun) to more salad.
5. The majorette usually led the parade (pronoun).
6. Rob made dinner (pronoun).
7. Why doesn't Janet try out for the team (pronoun)?
8. We watched (pronoun) on the TV screen.
9. Ken, Rachel, and Jill painted the scenery (pronoun).
10. A lion cub sunned (pronoun) on the rock.

C Finding Indefinite Pronouns Make two columns on your paper. Label them *Indefinite Pronouns* and *Verbs*. Write the indefinite pronouns from the following sentences in the first column. In the second column, write the correct form of the verbs given in parentheses.

1. Some of the girls (look, looks) like good hockey players.
2. Several (of the foreign exchange) students (come, comes) from South America.
3. Everything in the boxes (is, are) wet.
4. None of those stars to the west (set, sets) before 10 P.M.
5. Each of the divers (perform, performs) twice.
6. One of those tires (has, have) a slow leak.
7. Somebody always (forget, forgets) the money.
8. (Are, Is) anybody coming?
9. No one in the caves (wander, wanders) away from the guide.
10. Both of us (know, knows) the way around the swamp.

D Finding Demonstrative and Interrogative Pronouns Make two columns on your paper. Label them *Demonstrative Pronouns* and *Interrogative Pronouns*. Write the pronouns from the following sentences in the correct column.

1. How did Kirk get these out of the water?
2. What is the correct answer?
3. This is the lost suitcase.
4. Why would Bill bring these to a picnic?
5. Whom did the speaker ask?
6. Who let the cat out of the bag?
7. Carry those over there.
8. Pete is buying this as a present.
9. What's that by the rock pile?
10. To whom was the check sent?

E Using Personal Pronouns Write the correct pronouns given in parentheses in the following sentences.

1. Was it (he, him) who won the trophy?
2. It was (she, her) who painted that picture.
3. The workers demanded (their, theirs) pay immediately.
4. (We, Us) organized the pep assembly.

5. Strong winds blew the shack over on (it, its) side.
6. We thought it was (he, him) who made the announcements.
7. The manager gave (me, I) tickets to the movie.
8. Caryl and (me, I) are going to the shopping mall.
9. Jack wanted you to bring (your, yours) along.
10. Please give these music books to (she, her).

F Using Pronouns in Compound Subjects and Compound Objects Write the correct pronouns given in parentheses in the following sentences.

1. (He, Him) and Sally set up the Ping-Pong table.
2. Did you meet John and (they, them) at the exhibit?
3. A waiter showed Mrs. Ryan and (she, her) to a table.
4. (She, Her) and (me, I) were digging for clams.
5. They gave Ted and (we, us) just ten minutes to get ready.
6. My father packed Ken and (me, I) a lunch.
7. Barb waited fifteen minutes for Mr. Kopp and (they, them).
8. Bob and (us, we) had to mow and rake the lawn.
9. The setter came to Greg and (he, him) right away.
10. The lifeguard warned Patty and (we, us) about the undertow.

G Using Interrogative Pronouns Write the correct interrogative pronouns given in parentheses.

1. (Whom, Who) came in second?
2. (Who, Whose) was the best answer?
3. (Who, Whom) left her sunglasses on the counter?
4. To (whom, who) are you giving the macrame hanger?
5. To (who, whom) did Scott give the folder?
6. (Whom, Who) knows how to get to the airport?
7. (Whose, Whom) phone number is that?
8. (Who, Whom) did the coach choose for the starting line-up?
9. (Whom, Who) let the dog out of the house?
10. (Who, Whom) are these posters for?

H Using Possessive Pronouns and Contractions Write on your paper the correct words given in parentheses.

1. (It's, Its) too early.
2. The panther boxed (its, it's) cub's ears.

3. (Who's, Whose) team do we play next week?
4. (Your, You're) appointment with the dentist is for tomorrow.
5. Tim and Fay said that (they're, their) report was on bicycle safety.
6. (Whose, Who's) got the relish?
7. (It's, Its) Monday and it's (you're, your) turn to cook.
8. (Their, They're) ready for takeoff.
9. (It's, Its) (your, you're) coat.
10. (They're, Their) always late starting the meeting.

I Using Pronouns Write on your paper the correct words given in parentheses in the following sentences.

1. The coach handed the trophy to (me, myself).
2. (Them, Those) are too big.
3. The principal presented (we, us) students with diplomas.
4. (Them, Those) are the boxes that we need.
5. (Us, We) girls got special recognition for our efforts.
6. (Them, Those) are the posters to be hung in the cafeteria for the dance.
7. (Them, Those) are the shops that are open late.
8. Would you like to go to the show with (us, we) girls?
9. (Us, We) players protested the decision.
10. It is lunch time for (we, us) workers.

J Finding the Antecedents of Pronouns Write on your paper the antecedents of the pronouns printed in italics in the following sentences. If the pronoun *you* is understood, write *you*.

1. The paramedics entered the fiery building with all *their* equipment.
2. Chris's coat had a tear in *it*.
3. Phil fixed *his* back tire.
4. Vicki's yard has a fence all around *it*.
5. Mrs. Kohl was knitting a sweater for *her* granddaughter.
6. Bring *your* gym clothes for the intramural game tomorrow.
7. Bandit looked at *his* dog dish and walked away from it.
8. Lara and Pete told *their* parents about the band concert.
9. Susie brought *her* tape recorder.
10. The swallows always make *their* nests in the barn.

Chapter Review

A Finding Pronouns Make six columns on your paper. Label them *Personal, Reflexive, Intensive, Indefinite, Demonstrative,* or *Interrogative.* Write the pronouns from the following sentences in the correct column.

1. We photographers will explain backlighting to everyone.
2. Eric is building a soapbox derby car himself.
3. Of the two kickers, neither scored a point during the playoff game.
4. What is this?
5. Whom have you invited to your Cinco de Mayo celebration?
6. Our landlord is painting the building by himself.
7. Nikola is visiting his grandparents in Yugoslavia.
8. Both of us read the same review of the movie.
9. The group is donating its money to famine relief in Africa and Asia.
10. These are my slides of Mount Fuji.

B Using Pronouns Write on your paper the correct pronouns given in parentheses in the following sentences.

1. (She, Her) and (I, me) finished our jigsaw puzzle before anyone else.
2. (Who, Whom) designed the costumes for the play?
3. Somebody left (her, their) bicycle in the alley behind the swimming pool.
4. (Us, We) students are grateful for the help of senior citizen volunteers.
5. (Them, Those) are the cheerleaders who left (her, their) megaphones on the bench.
6. The baby chimpanzee could barely hold on to (its, it's) mother.
7. (Who, Whom) do you prefer to listen to, Beethoven or Chopin?
8. (Your, You're) going to be late for (your, you're) next class.
9. The school librarian showed (we, us) boys the new microfilm equipment.
10. Will (they, them) debate you and (we, us)?

Cumulative Review

A Identifying Complete Sentences Write whether each group of words is a *Sentence*, a *Run-on*, or a *Fragment*.

1. Wore a strange costume for the play.
2. Snakes shed their skins, their bodies grow too large for their own skin.
3. Whales are mammals, not fish.
4. The stranger took off his gloves, his hands glowed in the darkness of the room.
5. Put the chickens in the barn, they'll freeze outside.
6. Who invented spoons?
7. Millions of individual grains of sand on the beach.
8. Became a separate country after World War I.
9. Another name for Great Britain.
10. The Erie Canal was built in New York.

B Identifying Nouns Write all the nouns in each of the following sentences. Capitalize the proper nouns.

1. A recent avalanche on mount evans caused little damage.
2. One of the greatest artists in spain was pablo picasso.
3. "I value your loyalty," said king arthur.
4. Who lives in the old house on twenty-eighth street?
5. The red sox from boston played in the world series.
6. The carpenter brought her tools up to the roof.
7. Thick gray clouds covered the sky over the city.
8. Some people call denver "the mile high city."
9. Gil took a boat down the mississippi river.
10. Tall weeds grew by the side of the road.
11. Some people dream in color every night.
12. The noise in the garage was deafening.
13. In england, queen elizabeth lives in a palace.
14. Many earthquakes strike the islands of japan.
15. The fireplace added warmth and beauty to the room.

C Identifying Pronouns Make six columns on your paper. Label them *Personal, Reflexive, Intensive, Indefinite, Demonstrative,* and *Interrogative.* Write all the pronouns from the following sentences in the correct columns.

1. Some of us like to work by ourselves.
2. Who was the sixteenth president of the United States?
3. Everyone enjoyed that movie.
4. Does anybody know the score?
5. Dave bought himself a desk.
6. All of the trees were damaged by the force of the hurricane winds.
7. Which of the photographs is hers?
8. You should try to change a tire yourself.
9. She wrote out a check and signed her name.
10. What is the scientific name of the inchworm?
11. The house itself is on a small hill.
12. Neither of the swimmers set a record.
13. Whose are these?
14. Bess named her dog after herself.
15. That is my turtle hiding in its shell.

D Combined Review Write whether the italicized part of each of the following sentences is a *Proper Noun,* a *Common Noun,* a *Verb,* a *Verb Phrase,* or a *Pronoun.*

1. The *iris* is the colored part of the eye.
2. *Jackson Hole* is an exciting place to visit in the state of Wyoming.
3. Lewis and Clark *explored* the Missouri River.
4. *What* are the colors of light?
5. The locomotive *was stalled* on Track 3.
6. Tonight's meeting about water pollution will be held at *Farnum Auditorium.*
7. The Industrial Revolution was an important period in *history*.
8. *This* is a magazine article about Sacagawea, the Native American trail guide whose name means Birdwoman.
9. The Missouri River *floods* its banks frequently.
10. *Do* fish *close* their eyes while sleeping?

24
Using Verbs

The pitcher <u>pauses</u> and <u>nods</u> . . . . . click/flash!
He <u>winds</u> up and <u>stretches</u> . . . . . click/flash!
He <u>hurls</u> his first pitch . . . . . click/flash!

Like a good photograph, a verb can capture the
excitement of a scene. Without verbs, it would be
impossible to describe a pitcher throwing a strike or
even to say that a pitcher exists.

No sentence can be complete without a verb. In
this chapter you will learn about the two types of
verbs, action verbs and linking verbs. They are the
words that add movement, activity, and life to your
sentences.

1
What Is a Verb?

> A *verb* expresses an action, states that something exists, or links the subject with a word that describes or renames it.

When you speak or write, you use two kinds of verbs. These are **action verbs** and **linking verbs**.

Action Verbs

Some verbs express actions: Sam *clung* to the rope. The action may be one that you cannot see: Kate *needed* help.

Whether you can see the action or not, an action verb says that something is happening, has happened, or will happen.

Linking Verbs

A few verbs do not tell about an action. They may state that someone or something exists, or they may link the subject with a word or words that describe or rename the subject.

> I *am*. (says that someone exists)
> The sky *looks* gloomy. (links subject with description)

These verbs are called **linking verbs** because they can be used to connect, or link, the subject with some other word or words that describe it.

Linking Verbs			
be (am, are, is, was,	look	smell	seem
were, been, being)	appear	taste	sound
became	feel	grow	remain

Some linking verbs can also be used as action verbs.

Linking Verbs	Action Verbs
The melon *looked* ripe.	Annie *looked* at the melon.
The corn *grew* tall.	The farmer *grew* corn.

Exercises

A Write the verbs from the following sentences.

1. That potato soup smells delicious.
2. The florist appeared at the door with flowers.
3. Sherry looked in the attic.
4. The people of the village grow rice.
5. Vito remained healthy all winter.
6. Clovis smelled the smoke first.
7. Angela became the new class president.
8. The first wrestler pinned his opponent in ten seconds.
9. The music grows very loud at the end of the piece.
10. I knew all the answers on the test.

B Make two columns on your paper. Label them *Action Verbs* and *Linking Verbs*. Write the verbs from the following sentences in the correct column.

1. Queen Christina ruled Sweden from 1632 to 1654.
2. As a child, she seemed quite studious.
3. She was also wild and tomboyish.
4. Sometimes she appeared in men's clothes and a man's wig.
5. This shocked most people of her day.
6. While Queen, she brought peace to Sweden.
7. The arts were more popular during her reign as well.
8. Between 1644 and 1654, the Swedes established several colleges.
9. Foreign scholars, such as the French philosopher Descartes, became members of Christina's court.
10. Then, in 1654, Christina willingly gave the crown to her cousin Charles Gustavus.

C *Write Now* Imagine that you have discovered a strange new fruit. Write a paragraph to describe the fruit. Use each of the following verbs in your paragraph. Use one of these verbs twice: once as an action verb and once as a linking verb. Then, study the verbs in your paragraph. Underline the action verbs once and the linking verbs twice.

tasted   smelled   felt   looked

2
Verb Phrases

> A *verb phrase* consists of a main verb and one or more helping verbs.

A **verb phrase** consists of more than one verb. It is made up of a **main verb** and one or more **helping verbs**.

Helping Verbs	Main Verb	Verb Phrases
had	gone	had gone
might have	gone	might have gone
must have been	gone	must have been gone

Some verbs, such as *do, have,* and *be,* can be used either as main verbs or as helping verbs. Here are their forms:

do	have	be	is	were
does	has	am	was	been
did	had	are		

The examples below show how they can be used:

Used as Main Verbs	Used as Helping Verbs
Can you *do* this job?	I *do know* your sister.
Who *has* my key?	Faith *has seen* the telescope.
Where *were* you?	The boys *were camping.*

Helping Verbs		
can	shall	will
could	should	would
may	might	must

Sometimes helping verbs and main verbs are separated by words that are not verbs.

I *did* not *make* that noise.
Mac *musn't see* the gifts.
Will we *surprise* him?
We *have* certainly *worked* hard at this.

Exercises

A Make two columns on your paper. Label them *Helping Verbs* and *Main Verbs*. Write the parts of the verb phrases from the following sentences in the correct column.

1. We are going to the circus tomorrow.
2. Can Manny and Liza come to the baseball game with us?
3. The snow must have fallen all night.
4. Colleen and I have not skated at the new roller rink.
5. The hot air balloons had landed in the stadium.
6. After the concert, we are going to a restaurant.
7. My sister is running in the marathon.
8. The reporters have asked many difficult questions.
9. In May, my parents will have been married for fifteen years.
10. Haven't you already seen the camels at the zoo?

B Write on your paper the following sentences, completing them with one or more helping verbs.

1. Mopeds _____ designed for economical transportation.
2. A moped _____ go up to thirty miles per hour.
3. _____ moped drivers need a special license?
4. In many states, licenses _____ not required for moped drivers.
5. However, moped drivers _____ observe traffic regulations.
6. Motor scooters _____ become more popular than mopeds.
7. You _____ pedal a moped to start it.
8. You _____ easily start a scooter by just pressing a button.
9. Scooters _____ travel quite far on little gasoline.
10. Scooters _____ repaired more easily than most mopeds.

C *Write Now* Imagine that you want to get a job as counselor at a summer camp for boys and girls ages six to twelve. Camp activities include games, sports, nature walks, and crafts. In applying for this job, you must write a paragraph saying why you think that you would be a good counselor. Write this paragraph. List the activities that you could lead and skills that you could teach. Be clear and specific.

3

The Principal Parts of the Verb

The many forms of the verb are based on its three *principal parts:* the *present,* the *past,* and the *past participle.*

The form of a verb can be changed in a number of ways in order to show the time of an action. These forms, called *tenses,* are based on the three **principal parts** of the verb: the *present,* the *past,* and the *past participle.*

Regular Verbs

For all **regular verbs**, the past and past participle are spelled alike. They are made by adding *-d* or *-ed* to the present form. The past participle is used with a helping verb.

Present	Past	Past Participle
add	added	(have) added
divide	divided	(have) divided

The spelling of many regular verbs changes when *-d* or *-ed* is added. (See Chapter 17 for a review of spelling rules.)

knit + –ed = knitted	pay + –d = paid
hurry + –ed = hurried	lay + –d = laid
try + –ed = tried	say + –d = said

Exercise

Make three columns on your paper. Label them *Present, Past,* and *Past Participle.* Write the principal parts of the following regular verbs in the correct column.

1. worry	6. help	11. rob	16. fry
2. sob	7. pass	12. like	17. flip
3. pay	8. end	13. rap	18. push
4. carry	9. slip	14. scurry	19. vary
5. grab	10. use	15. rub	20. glow

Irregular Verbs

Hundreds of verbs follow the regular pattern of adding -*d* or -*ed* to form the past and the past participle. Verbs that do not follow this pattern are called **irregular verbs**. There are only about sixty frequently used irregular verbs. For many of these, the past and the past participle are spelled the same. They present few problems.

> buy   bought   (have) bought
> make   made   (have) made

For a few irregular verbs, like *hit* and *shut*, the three principal parts are spelled the same. They offer no problems. Most verb problems come from irregular verbs with three different forms. For example, the irregular verbs *throw* and *ring* have three different forms:

> throw   threw   (have) thrown
> ring   rang   (have) rung

If you are not sure about a verb form, look it up in the dictionary. If the verb is regular, only one form will be listed. If the verb is irregular, the irregular form or forms will be listed.

Common Irregular Verbs

Present	Past	Past Participle	Present	Past	Past Participle
begin	began	(have) begun	lay	laid	(have) laid
break	broke	(have) broken	lie	lay	(have) lain
bring	brought	(have) brought	ride	rode	(have) ridden
choose	chose	(have) chosen	ring	rang	(have) rung
come	came	(have) come	rise	rose	(have) risen
do	did	(have) done	run	ran	(have) run
drink	drank	(have) drunk	see	saw	(have) seen
eat	ate	(have) eaten	sing	sang	(have) sung
fall	fell	(have) fallen	speak	spoke	(have) spoken
freeze	froze	(have) frozen	steal	stole	(have) stolen
give	gave	(have) given	swim	swam	(have) swum
go	went	(have) gone	take	took	(have) taken
grow	grew	(have) grown	throw	threw	(have) thrown
know	knew	(have) known	write	wrote	(have) written

Practice Pages on Irregular Verbs

Irregular verbs can cause problems in writing as well as in speaking. Pages 475–485 provide practice in the correct use of some irregular verbs.

How well do you use these verbs? The exercise below will tell you.

If the exercise shows that you need more practice with certain verbs, your teacher may ask you to do the exercises on pages 475–485. For each verb there are many sentences that will help you to "say it right," "hear it right," and "write it right."

Exercise

Write on your paper the correct form of the irregular verbs given in parentheses.

1. The play (began, begun) at eight o'clock.
2. The gate had been (broke, broken) long ago.
3. Who (bring, brought) these posters to class?
4. Has everyone (chosen, chose) a topic for his or her report?
5. Jack had (came, come) home after the debate.
6. Rob has always (did, done) a great job.
7. The camels have not (drank, drunk) water for miles.
8. Someone had (ate, eaten) all the raisins.
9. Tina has (given, gave) a report about U.S. Customs Department regulations.
10. Everyone had (went, gone) home by then.
11. That tree has (grew, grown) several feet this year.
12. The team (known, knew) all of the defensive plays.
13. The sun had (rose, risen) early.
14. We (run, ran) the relay races on the indoor track.
15. Bill (seen, saw) two deer.
16. The audience (sang, sung) the chorus of the song.
17. The President has (spoke, spoken) to the reporters.
18. The thief had (stole, stolen) several appliances.
19. We had (swam, swum) in the ocean before.
20. Have you (took, taken) pictures of your new baby brother?
21. Terry (threw, thrown) the Frisbee to Darcy.
22. Eric has (write, written) a short story.

Say It Right   Hear It Right

A Say these sentences over until the correct use of *began* and *begun* sounds natural to you.

Begin
Began
Begun

1. Bill began his work.
2. Have you begun yet?
3. He began yesterday.
4. I have begun.
5. Mary began writing.
6. I began reading.
7. We had begun to hike.
8. We began humming.

B Say these sentences over until the correct use of *broke* and *broken* sounds natural to you.

Break
Broke
Broken

1. Pam broke the school record.
2. No one else has broken it.
3. The car broke down in Ohio.
4. Dennis broke the window.
5. Dan had broken the mug.
6. Steve broke his ankle.
7. The mirror was broken.
8. I have broken my watch.

Write It Right

Write on your paper the correct form of the verbs given in parentheses.

1. Has the movie (began, begun) yet?
2. Yes, it (began, begun) ten minutes ago.
3. I haven't missed that series since it (began, begun).
4. Have you (began, begun) your new book yet?
5. We (began, begun) our day playing tennis.
6. The people (began, begun) to leave the scene of the accident.
7. Jody has (began, begun) to mow the lawn.
8. I have (broke, broken) the can opener.
9. Now that it's (broke, broken), we'll need to replace it.
10. The clock is (broke, broken) beyond repair.
11. The car had (broke, broken) down on the road.
12. Someone has (broke, broken) into the storeroom.
13. The heat wave (broke, broken) all records for July.
14. Sara (broke, broken) the record for the hundred-yard dash at the track meet on Friday.
15. If he has (broke, broken) the seal on that package, it can't be returned.

Say It Right   Hear It Right

Bring
Brought
Brought

A Say these sentences over until the correct use of *bring* and *brought* sounds natural to you.

1. Did you bring the map?
2. Sam brought an atlas.
3. Did Mike bring the radio?
4. Yes, he brought it.
5. What did Suzi bring?
6. She has brought the food.
7. Claire had brought a guitar.
8. I wish I'd brought napkins.

Choose
Chose
Chosen

B Say these sentences over until the correct use of *chose* and *chosen* sounds natural to you.

1. Have you chosen a book?
2. No, I haven't chosen one.
3. Rob chose his.
4. What has he chosen?
5. He chose a biography.
6. Renée had chosen a novel.
7. Ginny chose a book to read.
8. Trina chose a book on sports.

Write It Right

Write on your paper the correct form of the verbs given in parentheses.

1. Patti (bring, brought) home a puppy yesterday.
2. Please (bring, brought) the typewriter in to the shop to be repaired.
3. Have you (bring, brought) in the mail?
4. Did you (bring, brought) the book I wanted to read?
5. I have (bring, brought) the clothes in off the line.
6. Did you (bring, brought) sleeping bags for our weekend camping trip?
7. We have (bring, brought) plenty of food.
8. Have you (bring, brought) all the books you borrowed back to the library?
9. Our club (chose, chosen) a new treasurer.
10. Who was (chose, chosen)?
11. Have you already (chose, chosen) a new president for the class?
12. Yes, we have (chose, chosen) our president.
13. Ella has (chose, chosen) that dress.
14. Which plant have you (chose, chosen) to buy?
15. I (chose, chosen) this one.

Say It Right   Hear It Right

A Say these sentences over until the correct use of *came* and *come* sounds natural to you.

Come
Came
Come

1. Nathan came to the meeting yesterday
2. Your packages have come.
3. They all came together.
4. The mail came late.
5. Joe came to lunch early.
6. He has come early before.
7. Janelle should have come to practice.
8. Hasn't Doug come home?

B Say these sentences over until the correct use of *did* and *done* sounds natural to you.

Do
Did
Done

1. I did my chores.
2. Sue has not done hers yet.
3. Amy has done two sketches.
4. Did you do this sculpture?
5. Doug has done his job.
6. Tom did the dishes tonight.
7. Have you done any hiking?
8. Ron did nothing to help.

Write It Right

Write on your paper the correct form of the verbs given in parentheses.

1. Peter has (came, come) to the game with us.
2. He had (came, come) with us before.
3. My parents (came, come) to our play.
4. Summer has finally (came, come).
5. The coach (came, come) to see me in the hospital.
6. The sailboat (came, come) toward us.
7. We have (came, come) to the parade in Centerville every Fourth of July.
8. Jonathan has (did, done) a beautiful painting.
9. He (did, done) it with oil paints.
10. Rosa and I (did, done) the French horn and bassoon duet together.
11. Have you (did, done) your essay?
12. I (did, done) it last night.
13. We (did, done) our work and went skating.
14. Pablo had (did, done) the organizing for the program.
15. He (did, done) a better job of research on this paper than anyone else.

Say It Right   Hear It Right

Drink
Drank
Drunk

A Say these sentences over until the correct use of *drank* and *drunk* sounds natural to you.

1. Who drank the milk?
2. Liz must have drunk it.
3. We have drunk all the tea.
4. We drank it all?
5. Maya drank lemonade.
6. Who had drunk it?
7. Al drank orange juice.
8. I have drunk goat's milk.

Eat
Ate
Eaten

B Say these sentences over until the correct use of *eat, ate,* and *eaten* sounds natural to you.

1. Have you eaten yet?
2. Yes, I have eaten.
3. Jenny ate quite early.
4. Did you eat at noon?
5. When did you eat dinner?
6. We ate at six o'clock.
7. Last night we ate outside.
8. José had eaten with us.

Write It Right

Write on your paper the correct form of the verbs given in parentheses.

1. The kittens (drank, drunk) all the cream.
2. We (drank, drunk) the lemonade and went back to work in the yard.
3. Have you ever (drank, drunk) coconut milk?
4. No, I have never (drank, drunk) coconut milk.
5. The patient (drank, drunk) the medicine.
6. Dad has not (drank, drunk) coffee for a month.
7. All the iced tea has been (drank, drunk).
8. The oranges have all been (ate, eaten).
9. Which one of you has (ate, eaten) all the oranges?
10. Have you ever (ate, eaten) nectarines?
11. Yes, I have (ate, eaten) them.
12. We (ate, eaten) dinner at the Spaghetti Factory.
13. Carl and I had (ate, eaten) dinner with our grandparents before the party.
14. Mary had (ate, eaten) before we got home.
15. Pam and Sal (ate, eaten) half the watermelon with no help from us.

Say It Right Hear It Right

A Say these sentences over until the correct use of *give, gave,* and *given* sounds natural to you.

Give
Gave
Given

1. Who gave you that hat?
2. It was given to me by Joe.
3. Joe has given it away.
4. I have given him a book.
5. Did he give his pen away?
6. I have given her two pens.
7. Dick gave me his puzzle.
8. I had given him a model.

B Say these sentences over until the correct use of *went* and *gone* sounds natural to you.

Go
Went
Gone

1. Who went skating?
2. Pete has gone home.
3. Julie went to the park.
4. Has she gone alone?
5. Janice went downstairs.
6. Hasn't she gone yet?
7. Everyone has gone home.
8. They went an hour ago.

Write It Right

Write on your paper the correct form of the verbs given in parentheses.

1. Jerry has (gave, given) up playing baseball.
2. We have always (gave, given) toys to the orphanage.
3. Maria (give, gave) me a compliment.
4. Pete has (gave, given) two recitals this year.
5. Nancy (give, gave) her brother a sweater.
6. Have you (given, gave) that album away?
7. Our team (give, gave) our rivals a beating.
8. The spacecraft (went, gone) around the earth many times before it landed.
9. Another spacecraft has (went, gone) into orbit around the moon.
10. We (went, gone) to Disneyland last summer.
11. The Petersons have (went, gone) to New York for a week of sight-seeing.
12. My sister has (went, gone) to France to study French.
13. Have you ever (went, gone) skiing?
14. Judy has (went, gone) to Florida for spring vacation again this year.
15. Hasn't Ellen (went, gone) to the planetarium?

Say It Right   Hear It Right

Grow
Grew
Grown

A Say these sentences over until the correct use of *grew* and *grown* sounds natural to you.

1. Mr. Olaf grew apples.
2. He has also grown pears.
3. The weeds have grown.
4. They grew tall.

5. The fall air grew cold.
6. It has grown warm again.
7. The child had grown tired.
8. Have you ever grown herbs?

Know
Knew
Known

B Say these sentences over until the correct use of *knew* and *known* sounds natural to you.

1. I knew the results.
2. I have known Jim for years.
3. Who knew the answers?
4. Bret knew the answers.

5. I knew the answers, too.
6. Have you known Jo long?
7. Who knew the date?
8. I had known the date.

Write It Right

Write on your paper the correct form of the verbs given in parentheses.

1. Les has (grew, grown) faster than his cousin has.
2. What have you (grew, grown) in your garden?
3. We have (grew, grown) lettuce and tomatoes.
4. Sandy had (grew, grown) beans and peppers in his yard.
5. The beans have (grew, grown) quite tall.
6. Jean (grew, grown) strawberries in her garden.
7. Alan has (grew, grown) too tall to wear his old baseball uniform.
8. The sapling (grew, grown) into a beautiful tree.
9. How long have you (knew, known) the Bernsteins?
10. We have (knew, known) them for a long time.
11. Had you (knew, known) before that winter vacation was extended?
12. Some things are (knew, known) with certainty.
13. I (knew, known) you were coming to visit us at the farm yesterday.
14. Very few others (knew, known) that.
15. Lou has never (knew, known) anyone who could juggle as well as you do.

Say It Right   Hear It Right

A Say these sentences over until the correct use of *rose* and *risen* sounds natural to you.

Rise
Rose
Risen

1. The sun has risen.
2. It rose at 6:15.
3. The river rose rapidly.
4. It has risen before.
5. The road rose sharply.
6. Becka rose early today.
7. The kite rose swiftly.
8. Jo had risen from her seat.

B Say these sentences over until the correct use of *ran* and *run* sounds natural to you.

Run
Ran
Run

1. Bill ran a race.
2. He had never run faster.
3. He ran twenty kilometers.
4. The race was run in Seattle.
5. Ed ran quickly.
6. Have you run the relay?
7. I have never run faster.
8. Pam ran a marathon.

Write It Right

Write on your paper the correct form of the verbs given in parentheses.

1. The audience had just (rose, risen) for the anthem when it began to rain.
2. The official has (rose, risen) to a high rank.
3. The moon (rose, risen) over the mountain.
4. Why hasn't the dough (rose, risen)?
5. The crowd (rose, risen) to cheer the players.
6. The divers had (rose, risen) to the surface.
7. The temperature has (rose, risen) to 35 degrees centigrade.
8. That calculator is (ran, run) by solar energy.
9. The students (ran, run) the bazaar last year.
10. They had never (ran, run) it before.
11. We (ran, run) for shelter when the tornado alert sounded.
12. Have you ever (ran, run) in a relay race?
13. Our air conditioner (ran, run) for twenty-four hours when it was so hot last week.
14. Janice has (ran, run) in the ten-mile Fourth of July race for two years.
15. The thieves (ran, run) when the burglar alarm went off and the police arrived.

Say It Right   Hear It Right

**See
Saw
Seen**

A Say these sentences over until the correct use of *saw* and *seen* sounds natural to you.

1. Have you seen Dan?
2. Yes, I saw him.
3. Ted has seen him, too.
4. Maureen saw him Sunday.
5. I saw that movie.
6. Have you seen it?
7. We saw it Saturday.
8. Nora hasn't seen it yet.

**Sing
Sang
Sung**

B Say these sentences over until the correct use of *sang* and *sung* sounds natural to you.

1. Craig sang a solo.
2. He has sung it before.
3. The tenor sang softly.
4. Lori also sang a solo.
5. She had never sung one.
6. Has she sung an aria?
7. The birds sang loudly.
8. The violin had sung sadly.

Write It Right

Write on your paper the correct form of the verbs given in parentheses.

1. Have you (saw, seen) my glasses anywhere in the living room?
2. It's the best show I have ever (saw, seen).
3. Judy (saw, seen) the sunrise over the mountain from her window.
4. Penny (saw, seen) her friends at the library.
5. I have (saw, seen) both raccoons and chipmunks in our backyard.
6. In the mountains Art (saw, seen) wild horses.
7. Jack had (saw, seen) the Bolshoi Ballet.
8. Our chorus (sang, sung) to the patients at the hospital.
9. We (sang, sung) a medley of show tunes.
10. We had (sang, sung) them before.
11. Our quartet (sang, sung) my favorite song at the state competition.
12. They had (sang, sung) last year, too.
13. Has Phil ever (sang, sung) in the choir?
14. The choir has (sang, sung) in many cities.
15. Had Jean (sang, sung) the alto or soprano part?

Say It Right   Hear It Right

A Say these sentences over until the correct use of *spoke* and *spoken* sounds natural to you.

Speak
Spoke
Spoken

1. Jan spoke to us yesterday.
2. She had spoken to us before.
3. Manny spoke first.
4. Has Liz spoken yet?
5. No, she hasn't spoken.
6. Terri spoke slowly.
7. She hadn't spoken before.
8. She spoke rather well.

B Say these sentences over until the correct use of *stole* and *stolen* sounds natural to you.

Steal
Stole
Stolen

1. Who stole the money?
2. Two gangsters stole it.
3. Why had they stolen it?
4. Have they stolen before?
5. When was it stolen?
6. It was stolen yesterday.
7. They stole it at noon.
8. They stole it wearing masks.

Write It Right

Write on your paper the correct form of the verbs given in parentheses.

1. Dr. Wagner has (spoke, spoken) to me about a job in her office.
2. I have (spoke, spoken) to my parents about it.
3. Everyone in the class has (spoke, spoken) at least once.
4. Rita hasn't (spoke, spoken) to me about her plans yet.
5. Jean has not (spoke, spoken) a word.
6. Our group (spoke, spoken) on energy consumption.
7. I had already (spoke, spoken) to Frank about the surprise when Mary arrived.
8. The coach (spoke, spoken) at our sports banquet.
9. Someone has (stole, stolen) our spare tire.
10. Why has someone (stole, stolen) it?
11. Lou Brock has (stole, stolen) many bases in major-league baseball.
12. He (stole, stolen) 938 bases in his baseball career.
13. Ty Cobb had (stole, stolen) the most bases until Brock broke his record in 1977.
14. The thief (stole, stolen) three oil paintings.
15. We know why he might have (stole, stolen) them.

Say It Right   Hear It Right

Swim **A** Say these sentences over until the correct use of *swam*
Swam and *swum* sounds natural to you.
Swum
1. I swam in the pool.   5. Mark swam ten laps.
2. Have you swum there?   6. They had already swum there.
3. Kelly swam all day.   7. Linda has swum thirty laps.
4. We swam in the lake.   8. I swam at Walden Pond.

Take **B** Say these sentences over until the correct use of *took*
Took and *taken* sounds natural to you.
Taken
1. Paula took a walk.   5. Who took these pictures?
2. Steve took one, too.   6. Gene took them.
3. Gwen has taken his bike. 7. He has taken lots of them.
4. Craig took the bus.   8. We took a helicopter ride.

Write It Right

Write on your paper the correct form of the verbs given in
parentheses.

1. Beth (swam, swum) at a very early age.
2. We haven't (swam, swum) much until now.
3. Our team (swam, swum) in the state meet.
4. During vacation, Sally (swam, swum) every day.
5. Have you (swam, swum) in the new pool?
6. Tanya has (swam, swum) there many times.
7. Chuck became ill when he (swam, swum) in the icy water of the lake.
8. Our team has often (swam, swum) in the 200-meter medley relay.
9. I have never (took, taken) a ride on an elevated train.
10. It (took, taken) us an hour to drive downtown.
11. Wilma had (took, taken) pictures before we arrived.
12. We (took, taken) potato salad with us.
13. Ms. Miller has (took, taken) our guest speaker to the airport to catch a flight to Toronto.
14. It has (took, taken) me a long time to get here.
15. I have never (took, taken) that kind of medicine before.

Say It Right   Hear It Right

A Say these sentences over until the correct use of *threw* and *thrown* sounds natural to you.

Throw
Threw
Thrown

1. Who threw the ball?
2. Carrie threw it.
3. Have you thrown it?
4. Bruce hasn't thrown it.
5. I threw the paper away.
6. Haley threw the door open.
7. Lee has thrown the list away.
8. Chris threw a fast pitch.

B Say these sentences over until the correct use of *wrote* and *written* sounds natural to you.

Write
Wrote
Written

1. I've written my paper.
2. Have you written one?
3. I wrote a letter.
4. Mat hasn't written yet.
5. Who has written to you?
6. Paul wrote to me.
7. Donna has written a speech.
8. They wrote the script.

Write It Right

Write on your paper the correct form of the verbs given in parentheses.

1. The captain had already (threw, thrown) the cargo overboard.
2. The runner was (threw, thrown) out at home plate.
3. The quarterback (threw, thrown) a touchdown pass.
4. I had just (threw, thrown) cold water over my face.
5. The athlete (threw, thrown) the discus expertly.
6. I have (threw, thrown) those old magazines away by mistake.
7. Have you ever (threw, thrown) a horseshoe?
8. That novel was (wrote, written) by Mark Twain.
9. Jim has (wrote, written) several humorous poems.
10. Melinda (wrote, written) to her friend.
11. Have you (wrote, written) your composition for class tomorrow?
12. I've (wrote, written) the first draft.
13. Our class has (wrote, written) letters to the governor of the state.
14. Last year we (wrote, written) to the mayor.
15. Why haven't you (wrote, written) that letter yet?

4
Verb Tenses

Different forms of the verb are used to show the time of an action or of a state of being. These forms are called the *tenses* of the verb.

A verb has different forms, called **tenses**, to indicate whether an action takes place or a condition exists in the present, past, or future. To indicate time differences, the spelling of the present form of the verb may change, or the present form may be used with a helping verb.

1. The spelling of the present form of the verb may change: *walk, walked; run, ran.*
2. A helping verb may be used: *will creep, has crept, had crept; will stop, has stopped, had stopped.*

A verb has six tenses: three simple tenses and three perfect tenses.

The Simple Tenses

The **simple tenses** are the most common tenses of the verb: present, past, and future. You use these tenses most often in your speaking and writing. Using the tenses correctly helps your reader or listener understand clearly what you mean.

The **present tense** places the action or condition in the present time. The present tense of any verb is usually spelled the same as the name of the verb (the *infinitive*) but without the word *to*: *run, go, walk.*

The **past tense** places the action or condition in the past. The past tense of a regular verb is formed by adding *-d* or *-ed* to the present form: *walked, placed.* The past tense of an irregular verb is shown by a change in spelling within the word: *shine, shone; swing, swung.*

The **future tense** places the action or condition in the future. The future tense is formed by using the words *shall* or *will* before the present form: *shall run, will go.*

The Perfect Tenses

Sometimes you want to show that an action was completed or that a condition existed before a given time. In that case, use one of the perfect tenses.

The **perfect tenses** are formed by using *has, have,* or *had* before the past participle. They are formed as follows:

Present Perfect   have run, has run
Past Perfect   had run
Future Perfect   shall have run, will have run

Exercises

A Make two columns on your paper. Label them *Verbs* and *Verb Tenses*. Write the verbs from the following sentences in the first column. Write their tenses in the second column.

1. How many games have the Bengal Tigers won?
2. Tourists hunt for diamonds in Arkansas mines.
3. Will the frost kill the oranges?
4. By Thursday, Elise will have arrived in Vienna, Austria.
5. At fourteen, Tracy Austin competed at Wimbledon.
6. Bernard has hiked to Image Lake many times before.
7. In Minnesota, the leaves will all have fallen by now.
8. The construction crew will complete our new school soon.
9. This pottery class ends in two weeks.
10. For days, Ricardo had practiced his lines for the play.

B Write on your paper the form of the verb given in parentheses in the following sentences.

1. An elephant (present of *have*) the largest ears of any animal.
2. It also (present of *possess*) the keenest sense of smell.
3. In a day, an elephant (future of *consume*) as much as five hundred pounds of food.
4. These peaceful animals (future of *protect*) a sick or wounded elephant by forming a circle around it.
5. In parts of Africa, elephants (present perfect of *eat*) all the available foliage.
6. Some African elephants (present perfect of *live*) to be over eighty years old.

7. Most elephants (future of *reach*) only fifty or sixty years of age.
8. By the time an elephant is full-grown, it (future perfect of *come*) to weigh about ten thousand pounds.
9. One calf that (past perfect of *weigh*) over two hundred pounds at birth grew to an amazing size.
10. People (present perfect of *hunt*) elephants for over twenty thousand years.

Grammar in Action

A story that is told or written in many different tenses can confuse the reader. Consider the following excerpt from the travel column in a local newspaper:

> Slowly and carefully we climbed the rocks. Every time we <u>look</u> back, the lake <u>seems</u> farther away. Long after we were exhausted, we <u>keep</u> climbing. Finally, at dusk, we <u>reach</u> the top. Then we <u>learn</u> about the stairs on the other side of the hill.

To prevent confusion, tell and write stories for the most part in one tense. Occasionally, you might write a sentence in the future tense *(will go)* or in one of the perfect tenses *(had gone, have gone, will have gone)*. In general, however, use either the past or the present tense in telling or writing a story.

Writing Activity Rewrite the paragraph given above. Be sure to make each underlined verb match the tense of the rest of the paragraph.

5
Progressive Verb Forms

> The *progressive form* of the verb shows continuing action.

Sometimes we tell the time of an action like this:

> I *am* talking. (instead of I *talk*)
> I *was* talking. (instead of I *talked*)

We use a form of the verb *be* plus the **present participle,** a verb form that ends in *-ing*. A verb phrase made up of one of the forms of *be* and a present participle is called a **progressive form**.

The progressive form of a verb shows continuing action. For instance, "I am talking" shows that my talking is going on right now, whereas "I talk" shows that I can or do talk. Here are the progressive forms of *talk* that are used with *I*:

> I am talking.   I have been talking.
> I was talking.   I had been talking.
> I shall (will) be talking.   I shall (will) have been
>   talking.

Have you ever noticed that radio sportscasters sometimes use the present progressive when broadcasting a sports event? They do this because the present progressive shows action as it is occurring.

> "The ball *is flying* out into center field. It*'s going*. It*'s going*. It*'s gone!*"

The present progressive conveys the excitement of action that is going on in the present. Use it in your writing when you want to convey action as it is occurring.

Exercises

A Write each verb from the following sentences.

1. The Kleins are growing vegetables without chemicals.
2. Nicole was talking to Ms. O'Shea about the exhibit.

3. Julio will be running for treasurer of the German Club.
4. We were feeding the ducks and geese this morning.
5. The storm front is moving sixty miles per hour.
6. I have been sanding this battered old desk.
7. Sam and my brother had been out fishing early today.
8. My grandparents are staying at our house.
9. Next fall I will be playing on the soccer team.
10. Rita has been knitting sweaters in her spare time.

B Rewrite each of the following sentences, changing the verbs to a progressive form.

1. Before the statewide competition, Kurt practiced his gymnastic routine every day.
2. Sharona and Jim went to the grocery store for milk.
3. Leon will play professional basketball some day.
4. They had wrapped their fine trophies in soft towels.
5. From space probes, scientists learn more about our solar system every day.
6. Some fans have waited in line all night for tickets to the opening game.
7. According to the weather forecast, it will rain for the next three or four days.
8. I will talk to my counselor about my class schedule on Friday.
9. On May 5, we will have lived in New Mexico for seven years.
10. I collect toys, books, photographs, and souvenirs for my time capsule.

C *Write Now* Imagine that Mr. Peabody and his Way Back Machine can take you to any time and place. Go to a time and place where an important event is occurring. This can be back to a historical moment that you have read or heard about. It can be forward to an important future event that you imagine will take place. In a paragraph, describe the event. Use the present tense and progressive forms of the verbs.

6
Active and Passive Verb Forms

When the subject of the sentence performs the action, the verb is *active*. When the subject of the sentence receives the action or expresses the result of the action, the verb is *passive*.

One of the interesting things about our language is that it allows us to express ideas in a wide variety of ways. The form of a verb may be changed to express many different times. There is another way you can use verbs to say exactly what you mean.

Suppose that a window has been broken. If you know who broke it, you can say something like this:

My little brother broke the window yesterday.

Now suppose that you don't know who broke it or that you do not want to say who broke it. You can then say this:

The window was broken yesterday.

In the first sentence, the subject says who performed the action. The verb of this sentence is **active**. In the second sentence, the subject says what received the action. The verb of this sentence is **passive**. The word *passive* means "acted upon."

The passive form of a verb consists of some form of *be* plus the past participle.

Only transitive verbs, those that take objects, can be changed from active to passive.

Active	**Passive**
Mike has made tea.	The tea has been made by Mike.
Elsa draws the cartoons.	The cartoons are drawn by Elsa.

Exercises

A Rewrite these sentences, using the passive form of the verbs.

1. Mr. Harvey cleaned the rug.
2. The digital scoreboard shows the scores and time.

3. Those children fed the ducks.
4. Mary Ann Evans used the pen name George Eliot.
5. The wind blew the storm out to sea.
6. The professional golfer scored a hole in one.
7. The lawyer will appeal the judge's decision.
8. Timmy delivered the papers at five o'clock in the morning.
9. Regina has done all the yard work.
10. Belinda has found a robin's nest.

B Rewrite the following sentences, changing the active verbs to passive verbs and the passive verbs to active verbs.

1. Many folk songs were written by Bob Dylan in the 1960's.
2. The Potter's Wheel also sells ceramic supplies.
3. Frank Johnson sold corn at the Farmers' Market.
4. The money was earned by the Girls' Club.
5. Roberta will frame the picture.
6. The final goal was scored by our team.
7. The last page of the novel will surprise you.
8. Our teacher just quoted Mark Twain.
9. Water cannot damage my new watch.
10. The baseball was blown out of the park by the wind.

Grammar in Action

One way to keep your reader's interest is to use active verbs. When you proofread your writing, change passive verbs to active verbs as often as you can. You may need to add details to the sentence in order to give the active verb a subject:

> The horse has been ridden across the desert.
> The fleeing fugitive rode the horse across the desert.

Writing Activity Imagine that you are a detective investigating a robbery at an art museum. You have no suspects. Write a paragraph using only passive verbs to describe the robbery. Then imagine that the criminal confesses. Rewrite the paragraph, changing the passive verbs to active ones. Use the criminal's name: Art Theefe.

7
Troublesome Pairs of Verbs

Several pairs of verbs cause confusion. These include *sit* and *set, lie* and *lay, let* and *leave, rise* and *raise, may* and *can*, and *learn* and *teach*.

These pairs of verbs cause trouble because they are similar in meaning and often similar in appearance.

Using Sit *and* Set

Sit means "to rest in a seated position." The principal parts of the verb *sit* are *sit, sat, sat*. Example: *Sit* in the car.

Set means "to put or place." The principal parts of the verb *set* are *set, set, set*. Example: *Set* the box down.

Using Lie *and* Lay

Lie means "to rest in a flat position." The principal parts of the verb *lie* are *lie, lay, lain*. Example: Fido *lies* at the foot of my bed at night.

Lay means "to put or place." The principal parts of the verb *lay* are *lay, laid, laid*. Example: *Lay* the blankets here.

Using Let *and* Leave

Let means "to allow or permit." The principal parts of the verb *let* are *let, let, let*. Example: *Let* us help you.

Leave means "to depart" or "to allow something to remain where it is." The principal parts of the verb *leave* are *leave, left, left*. Example: *Leave* your coats here.

Using Rise *and* Raise

Rise means "to move upward." The principal parts of the verb *rise* are *rise, rose, risen*. Example: The elevator *rises* fast.

Raise means "to move something upward" or "to lift." The principal parts of the verb *raise* are *raise, raised, raised*. Example: Please *raise* the flag.

Using May *and* Can

May refers to permission or possibility. *Might* is another form of this word. The verb *may* has no past participle. *May* and *might* are used as helping verbs.

      May we go to the pool?   We *might* go to the pool later.

Can refers to ability. *Could* is another form of this word. The verb can, meaning ability, has no past participle. *Can* and *could* are used as helping verbs.

      Yes, you *can* go to the pool.
      You *could* have gone to the pool yesterday.

Using Learn *and* Teach

Learn means "to gain knowledge or skill." The principal parts of the verb *learn* are *learn, learned, learned.* Example: I *learn* a lot about nature from public television programs.

Teach means "to help someone learn" or "to show how or explain." The principal parts of the verb *teach* are *teach, taught, taught.* Example: Nature programs *teach* me a lot.

Exercises

A Write the correct verb given in parentheses.

1. The geyser (rose, raised) at least thirty yards in the air the last time it spouted.
2. (Let, Leave) the lasagna to bake in the oven for at least forty-five minutes.
3. Take off those wet shoes and (sit, set) them by the fire to dry.
4. The kindergarten teacher (lain, laid) her students' pictures out on the table to dry.
5. Liza (lay, laid) the blanket she had made for her mother across her mother's favorite chair.
6. Before the parade started, Consuelo and George (rose, raised) the banner.
7. (May, Can) Geraldo really do backward somersaults, back flips, and handsprings?
8. Jennifer would like to know if she (might, can) use your telephone to call home.

9. My brother Emanuel (learned, taught) me how to juggle.
10. Will you (let, leave) Ginny play baseball with you?

B Choose the correct verb form given in parentheses. Write it on your paper.

1. We usually (sit, set) on the porch steps and talk about the news of the day.
2. The sun (sat, set) well before nine o'clock.
3. (May, Can) I see the bicycle that was advertised as being for sale?
4. (May, Can) you play classical guitar?
5. Sam (sat, set) the mysterious brown package on the table and then studied it from across the room.
6. (Learn, Teach) me not to bellyflop when I dive, will you?
7. The work was so hard that Ray (might, could) not do it in just one hour.
8. Rosanna (learned, taught) her parrot to say, "I know I'm cute."
9. The audience (rose, raised) and applauded the jazz pianist's incredible performance.
10. Frank and Joe (lay, laid) the carpeting in our living room yesterday and will install the upstairs carpeting today.

c *Proofreading* Proofread the following paragraph about a science teacher who is being nominated for the honor of Teacher of the Year. The paragraph is from a composition written to support the nomination. Rewrite the paragraph correctly. Watch especially for errors in verb choice.

> I taught about the greenhouse effect this year from my teacher Mr. Palazzo. Mr. Palazzo explained how the greenhouse effect might rise the temperature on earth. If the temprachure were to raise a few degrees, this might cause trouble. Glaciers would start melting. After that happened, the oceans would slowly raise and flood large areas of land. Many people would be forced to leave those areas Mr. Palazzo also learned us that this was are problem. We cannot let it for somone else to solve.

Linking Grammar & Writing

A Imagine that you are a young doctor without much experience. You are now in the South American jungle trying to cure a patient who has a rare tropical disease. However, you are not having much success. You cannot even find a description of the disease in any of your medical books. Therefore, you have decided to write a world-famous specialist in tropical diseases. One paragraph of your letter should detail your patient's symptoms. Write this paragraph. Be sure to include a description of how your patient looks, sounds, and feels. Then, underline all the linking verbs.

B Imagine that in her last letter, your French pen pal asked, "What is peanut butter?" In one paragraph, write a description of peanut butter for your pen pal. You may want to tell her how it is made, how it is eaten, and how it tastes. Use the present tense.

C Imagine that you are on an archaeological dig in Egypt when an entrance to a previously undiscovered tomb is found. You rush to the entrance. In a paragraph, describe everything that happens and everything you experience from the moment that you arrive at the entrance to the tomb. As much as possible, use the present progressive forms of the verbs.

Additional Practice

Parts 1-2 Identifying Verbs List the verbs and verb phrases in the following sentences. Identify each main verb as an *Action Verb* or *Linking Verb*. Then underline all helping verbs.

1. Our next-door neighbor's dog barked all night long.
2. Throughout the volleyball game, Janet was spiking the ball.
3. The President of the United States is also the Commander-in-Chief of the armed forces.
4. Monica had written a long letter to her pen pal in Australia.
5. Many adults are now collecting old teddy bears.
6. Jack has already spent most of his money.
7. Queen Elizabeth I ruled England for more than four decades.
8. She was the daughter of Anne Boleyn and King Henry VIII.
9. His trumpet solo has never sounded better.
10. The asphalt driveway felt hot and sticky.

Parts 3-5 Verb Forms On your paper write the form of the verb given in parentheses in the following sentences.

11. Joan (present perfect of *live*) on Maple Street all of her life.
12. The artists (present progressive of *work*) on a sculpture of Susan B. Anthony.
13. John (future of *enter*) his giant pumpkin in the country fair.
14. Leslie (future progressive of *ride*) a bus to her new junior high school.
15. The football game already (past perfect of *begin*) when we arrived.
16. The reporter (present of *write*) his articles on a word processor.
17. After this race, the runner (future perfect of *compete*) in three marathons.
18. Ransom E. Olds (past of *build*) the world's first automobile factory.

19. Last night Anne and I (past progressive of *study*) for our history test.
20. The waters surrounding Nova Scotia (present of *contain*) lobsters, cod, and scallops.

Part 6 Active and Passive Verbs Rewrite the following sentences, changing active verbs to passive verbs and passive verbs to active verbs.

21. Pikes Peak was discovered by Zebulon Montgomery Pike in 1806.
22. Gwendolyn Brooks wrote the poems "The Children of the Poor" and "The Explorer."
23. Natalie took the cans and bottles to the recycling center.
24. The San Francisco 49ers were narrowly defeated by the Chicago Bears.
25. Freezing destroys most of the B vitamins in bread.
26. That portrait was painted by Gilbert Stuart.
27. The basketball tournament was won by Central Junior High School.
28. The film explained the dangers of cigarette smoking.
29. The Statue of Liberty was designed by Frederic Auguste Bartholdi.
30. The drought caused higher food prices.

Part 7 Choosing the Right Verb Write the correct form of the verb in parentheses.

31. (Can, May) I borrow your catcher's mitt?
32. The cat (lay, laid) in front of the fire all afternoon.
33. Please don't (set, sit) your books on the kitchen counter.
34. A helium balloon (rises, raises) because helium is lighter than air.
35. (Leave, Let) me help you carry those groceries.
36. The experience (learned, taught) me to be more careful.
37. Can't you (sit, set) and visit for a while?
38. Greyhounds (can, may) run very swiftly.
39. (Let, Leave) your books on the desk.
40. The builder (lay, laid) the blueprints on the table.

Application and Review

Lesson Review

A Identifying Verbs Make two columns on your paper. Label them *Action Verbs* and *Linking Verbs*. Write the verbs from the following sentences in the correct column.

1. The air smells clean and fresh after that storm.
2. The first wrestler pinned his opponent to the mat in only a few seconds.
3. A beautiful rainbow appeared magically across the dewy meadow.
4. Our dog is a German shepherd.
5. I finished my social studies assignment in class this morning.
6. After school Erica and I ride our bicycles through the park.
7. The yearbook staff sold peanuts and popcorn at the football games last season.
8. The speaker for the assembly sounds interesting.
9. The weekend at the amusement park was fun.
10. Ms. Bauer grows cantaloupe and watermelon in her garden.
11. The train whistle startled the sleepy stationmaster.
12. Eli is an expert gardener.
13. Maxie seems a lot more cheerful today.
14. Mr. Song works at the Korean embassy.
15. Is this a picture of you?

B Identifying Verb Phrases Make two columns on your paper. Label them *Helping Verbs* and *Main Verbs*. Write the parts of the verb phrases in the correct column.

1. Where did you buy those socks?
2. Don't take the dog out in the rain.
3. I should have been the villain in the play.
4. Are Jody and Basil standing in line for hockey tickets?
5. You might have told me the news earlier.
6. The wind must have blown down the antenna.

7. Can you read the sign?
8. We have decorated the school lobby for the holidays.
9. Do you like this kind of weather?
10. Shall I make banana nut bread for Friday?
11. Jayne has studied ballet for three years.
12. Tomorrow, Mindy will give us a tennis lesson.
13. Jean and Jim are flying to Ireland.
14. Would you bring me a glass of milk, please?
15. You should never ride your bicycle so carelessly.

C **Using Irregular Verbs** Write on your paper the correct form of the verb given in parentheses.

1. We had never (saw, seen) such a sight!
2. The plumber (did, done) the work in our upstairs bathroom extremely quickly.
3. I have (knew, known) Clark all my life.
4. Our science class (grew, grown) different plants for a botany experiment.
5. Leslie (spoke, spoken) sharply to the cat.
6. We have (went, gone) to that restaurant before.
7. My aunt has (gave, given) me a birthday present every year.
8. Peter (drank, drunk) every drop of milk from the carton in the refrigerator.
9. I have only (ate, eaten) such a big meal one other time in my life.
10. The nurse (took, taken) my temperature.
11. I have (written, wrote) many letters to our local newspaper.
12. Slowly, Dora (swum, swam) across the peaceful lake.
13. Have you (began, begun) your term paper yet?
14. The pond (froze, frozen) last night.
15. Miguel (grew, grown) three inches taller over the summer.

D **Recognizing Verb Tenses** Make two columns on your paper. Label them *Verbs* and *Verb Tenses*. Write the verbs from the following sentences in the first column. Write their tenses in the second column.

1. Have you subtracted correctly?
2. The water temperature will be a mild 72 degrees Fahrenheit.

3. My sister and I flew to Alaska.
4. Walter Payton is a great football player.
5. Will the new school have a darkroom?
6. The movie will have already begun.
7. We had waited in line for over an hour.
8. That boat doesn't look seaworthy.
9. Will you take a message for me?
10. I liked that Agatha Christie book a lot.
11. Have you ever seen the Mississippi River?
12. By late afternoon the game will have ended.
13. Our plane will land in Seattle at 3:30.
14. Hailstones rattled against our window.
15. I had never met Jackie before Sunday.

E Using Progressive Verb Forms Rewrite the following sentences, using the progressive forms of the verbs.

1. Paul ate the melon.
2. Have you watched the Olympic games?
3. Mrs. Levy directs the junior high band.
4. Amanda and Evie could help us with the garden.
5. Tyler has worked here since July.
6. I have saved my money for a new ten-speed bike.
7. Marla collects newspapers for the neighborhood recycling center.
8. The children slept soundly throughout the storm.
9. The sea lions basked in the sun.
10. I have helped my father at his office for the past several days.
11. The whole team stands on the sidelines.
12. My family has gone to Canada every summer.
13. I had skated all afternoon.
14. I will see you tomorrow.
15. Tony tumbled down the small, snowy hill.

F Using Active Verb Forms Rewrite the following sentences, changing the verbs from the passive to the active form.

1. The football was caught by Stacey.
2. Consumer education is taken by everybody at our school.

3. The radio station was called immediately by about one hundred people.
4. The school bus was delayed by a flat tire.
5. This mural was designed and painted by my two sisters.
6. Sunspot activity will be recorded by this computer.
7. The ice rink was covered by snow.
8. The photographs were developed by Juan.
9. That house was built by my grandfather and grandmother.
10. Wheat and corn are grown by Ross's uncle.
11. The morning aerobics program is led by Mr. Thomas.
12. Each evening our campsite was visited by three portly raccoons.
13. As usual, a tempting Italian meal will be prepared by my Uncle Emelio.
14. *The Three Musketeers* was written by Alexandre Dumas.
15. Wasn't that lovely landscape painted by Vincent van Gogh?

Choosing the Correct Verb Write on your paper the correct verb given in parentheses.

1. (Let, Leave) Craig build the model airplane by himself.
2. (Raise, Rise) the shelf about another inch on the left side and it will be even with the right.
3. Dan (raised, rose) his glass of orange juice to drink a toast to his sister's wedding.
4. I saw the shovel (lying, laying) out in the rain.
5. (May, Can) I use your pencil?
6. Would you (sit, set) the geraniums on the windowsill?
7. The tool box is (lying, laying) on the workbench in the shed.
8. Jamie certainly didn't (learn, teach) Laura to rollerskate like that.
9. How our coach can just (sit, set) on the bench so calmly is beyond me!
10. I am (learning, teaching) how to hem these trousers.
11. Yesterday, I (lay, lie) on the beach for two hours.
12. Will you (learn, teach) me how you throw a curve?
13. Mr. Davis felt dizzy and went to (lay, lie) down.
14. Will the entire class please (rise, raise)?
15. (Leave, Let) my bicycle alone!

Chapter Review

A Recognizing Verbs Write on your paper the *Action Verbs* and *Linking Verbs* from the following sentences.

1. The morning air felt damp.
2. The runner removed the stone in her shoe.
3. A small plane out over the ocean appeared on the radar screen.
4. The baby cried loudly.
5. Celeste plays the trumpet in the Greenville High School Band.
6. The milk definitely tastes sour.
7. We waited impatiently in the doctor's waiting room.
8. The sky had seemed perfectly cloudless.
9. The cook has been sounding the bell every night at six o'clock.
10. Debbie rode her prize-winning horse in the junior competition.

B Using Verbs Write on your paper the correct form of the verb given in parentheses.

1. By tonight we will have (eaten, ate) a huge turkey dinner.
2. Has anyone (wrote, written) to the mayor?
3. Janean has (bring, brought) in slides from her trip to Mexico last summer.
4. How long have you (knew, known) about the contest?
5. Scientists have barely (begun, began) their exploration of space.
6. The children have (sat, set) in the hot sun on the beach too long.
7. Ms. Butler has (let, left) us publish our own class newspaper.
8. Rip Van Winkle had (lain, laid) on the ground for twenty years.
9. (May, Can) my fingers move as fast as yours move on the typewriter keys?
10. Our math teacher has (taught, learned) us many computer terms.

25
Using Modifiers

The racers pedal <u>quickly</u> toward the finish line. The <u>first</u> racer under the wire will hold up one arm <u>victoriously</u>. Who will win the <u>silver</u> trophy?

Without the underlined modifiers, the sentences above would be lifeless and not very informative. Modifiers—adverbs such as <u>quickly</u> and <u>victoriously</u>, and adjectives such as <u>first</u> and <u>silver</u>—are words that describe or clarify nouns, pronouns, or verbs. They can make the difference between boring statements and sparkling ideas. This chapter explains how you can use modifiers to add color and precision to your writing and speaking.

1
What Are Modifiers?

Modifiers are words that make other words more precise.

Nouns and pronouns help us name and identify things and people in the world around us. Verbs help us make statements and ask questions about things and people. **Modifiers** provide additional information about nouns, pronouns, and verbs. Modifiers help us describe what we have seen and heard:

Carlos wore a *yellow cotton* shirt.
The jet roared *faintly* in the distance.
Three mice scurried out of sight.

In addition, modifiers help us state how we feel about things and people:

Dan was *very angry* about the *bad* decision.
Holly likes *only funny* movies.
Ron swam *happily* in the *clean, cool* water.

As the examples above show, modifiers add color and detail to speaking and writing. They make dull, lifeless sentences vivid.

Remember, to change something slightly is to *modify* it. We can modify a house by adding an extra room or by enclosing a porch, but it remains the same house. Similarly, we can modify the meaning of a word by adding or changing a word that describes it.

Which bicycle ad would get your attention?

Ten-speed bicycle. $65.
Sleek, red, ten-speed bicycle, *excellent* condition. $65.

Both ads could be for the same bicycle, but the second sounds more attractive because modifiers are used to appeal to your senses. The image you have of the bicycle is made more precise by the addition of the words *sleek, red,* and *excellent.*

We have already studied nouns, pronouns, and verbs in detail. In this section we will study two kinds of modifiers—adjectives and adverbs.

2
Adjectives

An *adjective* is a word that modifies a noun or pronoun.

What is the difference between these sentences?

Rain fell.
A cold, hard rain fell.

The difference is in the descriptive words that tell what kind of rain fell. These words are **adjectives**. They modify nouns or pronouns.

Some adjectives tell *how many* or *what kind* about the words they modify.

Jim found *twenty* pennies.   Nan bought a *new* coat.
We have had *little* rain.   *Yellow* flags mean caution.

Some adjectives tell *which one* or *which ones*.

These pens work better.   *My* kite flies well.
Her jacket looks warm.   *That* door sticks.

Proper Adjectives

Proper adjectives are adjectives formed from proper nouns. They are always capitalized.

an American dollar   the Spanish language
a Norwegian sardine   a British custom
the French flag   an Oriental rug

Predicate Adjectives

Sometimes a *linking verb* separates an adjective from the word it modifies. An adjective that follows a linking verb and that modifies the subject is called a **predicate adjective**. (See page 468 for information about linking verbs.)

Everyone was *quiet.*   Phil seemed *upset.*

Jenny feels *ill.*   Porcupines are *prickly.*

505

Pronouns Used as Adjectives

As you learned on page 444, the words *this, that, these,* and *those* can be used as demonstrative pronouns. When used alone, they are pronouns. When followed by a noun, they are adjectives telling *which one* or *which ones.*

> *These* are my sunglasses. (pronoun)
> *These* problems are easy. (adjective modifying *problems*)
> *That* answer is wrong. (adjective modifying *answer*)

The words *my, your, her, his, its, our,* and *their* are possessive pronouns, but they can also be classified as adjectives. These modifiers tell *which one* or *which ones.*

> *My* mother works at home; *your* mother commutes.
> *Her* coat is blue; *his* coat is brown.
> *Our* team plays on Saturdays; *their* team plays on Sundays.

Exercises

A Write the adjectives from the following sentences.

1. The baby birds opened their mouths.
2. That hat costs ten dollars.
3. The new glue was sticky.
4. This bottle can hold my Dutch tulips.
5. The American tourists were tired after the long trip.
6. The huge gray mansion was famous for antique furniture.
7. The little girl looked sad as her new balloon blew away.
8. The furry cat felt smooth and soft under my rough hand.
9. The fans cheered as their team won the final match.
10. The small, brown puppy nestled against me.

B Write the adjectives from the following sentences. After each adjective, write the word it modifies.

1. Vincent van Gogh was a Dutch painter.
2. Many fine galleries in major cities exhibit his colorful works.
3. Different shades of blue paint make his work distinctive.
4. *The Starry Night* is one famous painting by van Gogh.
5. In that painting, the dark sky is filled with brilliant stars.
6. The night sky moves like a stormy sea.
7. The dark city below the sky is quiet and peaceful.

The Starry Night, 1889, Vincent van Gogh.

8. Van Gogh studied Oriental painting.
9. Japanese art influenced his painting of peasant women washing clothes in a river.
10. He showed the simple tasks of everyday life in that picture.

Grammar in Action

You can use adjectives to create either a positive or negative impression on your reader. Changing the adjectives can change the meaning of a sentence completely.

> The *empty* room felt *spacious* and *airy.* (positive)
> The *deserted* room felt *cavelike* and *musty.* (negative)

Writing Activity Change all of the positive adjectives in the following paragraph to negative ones. Notice how the meaning changes.

> The bright sun woke the campers at dawn. They got up from their comfortable sleeping bags and poked their cheerful faces out the tent flap into the delightful warmth of summer. It was going to be another lovely day.

3
Articles

A, an, and *the* are special adjectives called *articles*.

The is a special kind of adjective known as the **definite article**. It is used to refer to a particular thing.

> Please buy me *the* book. (a particular book)

A and *an* are also special adjectives. They are called **indefinite articles**. They refer to any item in a category.

> Please bring me *a* book. (any book)
> Please give me *an* apple. (any apple)

We use *a* before a word that begins with a consonant sound (*a* book, *a* cap, *a* dog). We use *an* before a vowel sound (*an* apple, *an* egg, *an* olive). The first sound of a word, not the spelling, makes the difference. This means that we say *an honest person,* but we say *a house.*

All articles are adjectives. We use *the* with both singular and plural nouns, but we use *a* and *an* only with singular nouns.

the books	the book	a book
the honors	the honor	an honor

Exercise

Write the correct article from those given in parentheses.

1. (A, An) elephant supposedly has a good memory.
2. (A, The) best book on that shelf is *Treasure Island.*
3. That is (a, an) heavy chair.
4. I have (a, an) hunch you're right.
5. Joe was wearing (a, an) orange T-shirt.
6. We had (a, an) history test this week.
7. All of (a, an, the) honors went to people from our class.
8. Don't use (a, an) onion in that recipe.
9. Each of us had to do a report on (a, an) event in history.
10. Tracy made (a, an) honest effort to meet the deadline.

4
Adverbs

An *adverb* modifies a verb, an adjective, or another adverb.

In order to make our meaning clear, vivid, and complete, we often have to tell *how, when, where,* or *to what extent* something is true. **Adverbs** are used for this purpose.

Adverbs Used with Verbs

Adverbs that modify verbs tell *how, when, where,* or *to what extent* an action happened.

Study the following list of adverbs:

How?	When?	Where?	To What Extent?
secretly	then	nearby	too
quickly	later	underground	very
sorrowfully	afterward	here	quite
hurriedly	finally	there	extremely

Now use some of the adverbs above in this sentence:

The pirates buried their gold.

Afterward, the pirates hurriedly buried the gold.

You can see what a great difference adverbs make. They can make the meaning of the verb *buried* clearer and add vividness and completeness to the sentence.

Adverbs Used with Adjectives or Other Adverbs

In addition to modifying verbs, adverbs can also modify adjectives and other adverbs. Notice the italicized adverbs in the following sentences:

Niki was happy.   Rena spoke slowly.
Niki was *extremely* happy.   Rena spoke *too* slowly.

On the next page are some adverbs that can be used to modify adjectives or other adverbs:

Frequently Used Adverbs		
very	nearly	so
just	somewhat	more
quite	rather	most

These adverbs all tell *to what extent* something is true. You can see how useful adverbs are in making adjectives or other adverbs clearer, more complete, or more vivid.

Forming Adverbs

Many adverbs are made by adding *-ly* to an adjective:

neat + -ly = neatly   bright + -ly = brightly

Sometimes the addition of *-ly* involves a spelling change in the adjective:

easy + -ly = easily (*y* changed to *i*)
full + -ly = fully (*ll* changed to *l*)

Many words, like *soon* and *quite,* can be used only as adverbs:

The bell will ring *soon.*
This footprint is *quite* recent.

Some other words, like *early* or *fast,* can be used either as adverbs or as adjectives:

Bill arrived *early*. (adverb)
He ate an *early* breakfast. (adjective)

Dana can run *fast*. (adverb)
She is a *fast* runner. (adjective)

Exercises

A Write on your paper the adverbs from the following sentences.

1. The doctor has just left.
2. We finished the lesson on Greenland quite recently.
3. That cyclist was too tired to keep riding.
4. That movie was quite informative.
5. The pounding stopped almost immediately.
6. The usher greeted us cordially at the door.

7. The flooding has been very heavy this fall.
8. Our canoe drifted lazily down the river.
9. The summer rain fell extremely heavily.
10. The newspaper is always careful about its editorials.

B Write the adverbs from the following sentences. Beside each adverb write the word it modifies.

1. Egyptians were highly successful in preserving their dead.
2. The bodies, or mummies, were very carefully saved.
3. First, Egyptian embalmers painstakingly removed the brain.
4. The intestines were often stored in jars.
5. The heart and kidneys generally remained inside the body.
6. Egyptians believed that the dead person would soon need these organs.
7. The body was covered with a special substance and was then dried gradually.
8. Finally, the embalmers rubbed the body with oils and spices and intricately wrapped it in fine linen.
9. The extremely dry Egyptian climate preserved the mummy.
10. This very elaborate process sometimes took seventy days.

Grammar in Action

We use adverbs to help verbs create a vivid picture. Notice that you can form a clear image in your mind of the action described in the second sentence below.

Dull   The farmers ate lunch.
Vivid   The farmers ate lunch *greedily*.

Writing Activity Use some of the adverbs in the list on page 509 to help you write a paragraph describing an imaginary visit with your favorite television character. Describe the visit and your feelings about it. Use adverbs in addition to the ones in the list if you wish. Use enough adverbs to make the paragraph interesting, but be careful not to use too many.

5
Adjective or Adverb?

> An *adjective* modifies a noun or pronoun. An *adverb* modifies a verb, an adjective, or another adverb.

Study the following sentences. Which sentence sounds right?

Our debate team won *easy*.
Our debate team won *easily*.

The second sentence is the correct one. An adverb *(easily)* should be used, not an adjective *(easy)*.

When you are not sure whether an adjective or an adverb should be used, ask yourself these questions.

1. *Which word does the modifier go with?* If it goes with an action verb (like *won* in the sentences above), it is an adverb. It is also an adverb if it goes with an adjective or another adverb. If it goes with a noun or pronoun, it is an adjective.

2. *What does the modifier tell about the word it goes with?* If the modifier tells *when, where, how,* or *to what extent,* it is an adverb. If it tells *which one, what kind,* or *how many,* it is an adjective. In the sentences above, the modifier tells *how* our team won; it must therefore be an adverb.

Exercises

A Write the adjectives and adverbs from the following sentences. Next to each write the word it modifies. Do not write articles.

1. Two white puppies scampered carelessly through the flowers.
2. The commuter trains were very late.
3. Red and blue paper hung decoratively on the stage.
4. The new fish are too big for the aquarium.
5. They paid the bill quite promptly.
6. That new wallpaper is too dark for this small room.
7. The suspect answered the questions rather cautiously.
8. The American ambassador spoke openly and honestly.

9. The enormous football player was quite graceful.
10. The two swimmers dived very quickly into the cold pool.

B Write on your paper the correct form of the modifiers given in parentheses. Tell what word is modified and whether it is an adjective or adverb.

1. The athlete ran an unusually (slow, slowly) race.
2. America has explored space (enthusiastic, enthusiastically).
3. Debbie's drawings were (real, really) good.
4. The leaves turned very (quickly, quick) this year.
5. George Washington's troops (brave, bravely) faced many hardships.
6. Our spaniel puppy peered (cautious, cautiously) around the sofa.
7. Ted appeared at the door (prompt, promptly) at eight.
8. The ice was made (rough, roughly) by the skate blades.
9. Each of your bones contains a (delicate, delicately) balance of proteins and minerals.
10. Dad prepared a (delicious, deliciously) chicken for our dinner.

c *Write Now* Suppose you have just made a long train trip across your home state. Write a paragraph or two describing the journey. You might tell about the things you saw, the people you met, and the adventures you had. Use five adjectives and adverbs to make your description colorful and precise.

Adverbs and Predicate Adjectives

You remember that a predicate adjective appears after a linking verb and modifies the subject. Notice the predicate adjectives in the sentences below:

> The lens is clear. (*clear* modifies *lens*)
> The sky became cloudy. (*cloudy* modifies *sky*)
> The nectarine tastes good. (*good* modifies *nectarine*)
> The pillow felt soft. (*soft* modifies *pillow*)

You also remember that in addition to the forms of *be,* the following words can be used as linking verbs: *become, seem, appear, look, sound, feel, taste, grow,* and *smell.*

Sometimes these verbs are used as action verbs. When they are used as action verbs, they are followed by adverbs, not adjectives. The adverbs modify the verbs and tell *how, when, where,* or *to what extent.* The problem of choosing an adjective or adverb form is often most difficult when these verbs are used.

Look at the following sentences to see when adjectives are used and when adverbs are used:

Linking Verbs with Adjectives	Action Verbs with Adverbs
The *cloth* felt *smooth.*	Jane *felt* her way *slowly.*
The *melon* tasted *good.*	We *tasted* the melon *eagerly.*
The *dog* appears *sick.*	A stranger *appeared suddenly.*
The *water* looks *green.*	Bob *looked up.*
The *horse* grew *tired.*	The plant *grew fast.*

If you are uncertain about whether to use an adverb or adjective after a verb like *sound, smell,* or *look,* ask yourself these questions:

1. Can you substitute *is* or *was* for the verb? If you can, the verb is probably a linking verb, and the modifier is probably an adjective.
2. Does the modifier tell *how, when, where,* or *to what extent*? If it does, the modifier is probably an adverb.

Good *and* Well

The meanings of *good* and *well* are very much alike, but they are not exactly the same. Study the following sentences:

Incorrect   The team played *good.*
Correct   The team played *well.*

Good is always an adjective and modifies nouns or pronouns. Never use *good* to modify a verb; use *well. Well* can be used as either an adjective or an adverb, depending on the situation.

When used as an adjective, *well* usually refers to a person's health. For example, "I feel *well*" means "I feel healthy." Remember that "feeling good" refers to being happy or pleased.

Exercises

A Write the correct form of the modifiers given in parentheses.

1. The ice looked (thick, thickly).
2. This water tastes (bitter, bitterly).
3. All of the gymnasts did fairly (good, well).
4. At the start of the game we played (cautious, cautiously).
5. Both teams played (good, well) in the second half.
6. John was sick, but now he's (good, well) again.
7. Press (firm, firmly) on the button.
8. The sandpiper darted (quick, quickly) across the beach.
9. The band looks (good, well) in its new uniforms.
10. The music sounded (strange, strangely).

B Write the correct form of the modifiers given in parentheses. Then tell whether the word is an adjective or adverb.

1. Stretch your muscles (good, well) before running.
2. Gwen glided (smooth, smoothly) over the water.
3. I remained (good, well) all winter long.
4. Those yellow roses smell (good, well) and look delightful.
5. Those people were talking rather (loud, loudly).
6. Carol's idea sounded (reasonable, reasonably) to everyone.
7. The tomatoes are growing (slow, slowly).
8. The bird was perfectly (good, well) after its wing healed.
9. The lake became calm (prompt, promptly) after the storm.
10. The band sounds (loudly, loud) to me.

C *Write Now* Suppose you have been invited to a party given by a visitor from a foreign country. The party includes a dinner at which food from that country is served. Write a paragraph about the party, telling about the food and how everyone (including you) liked it. Use the words *good* and *well* at least once. Also include either the adjective or the adverb form of at least three of the words below and tell which form you used.

quiet	quick	tasteful	smooth
spicy	hot	cool	colorful

6
Adjectives in Comparisons

Use the *comparative form* of an adjective to compare two things. Use the *superlative form* of an adjective to compare more than two.

Comparing people and things is one way of learning about the world. We say, "This new calculator is like a mini-computer. Of course, it is *smaller* and *more portable*."

The Comparative

If we compare one thing or person with another, we use the **comparative form** of the adjective. It is made in two ways:

1. For short adjectives like *neat* and *happy*, add *-er*.

   neat + er = neater   happy + er = happier

2. For longer adjectives like *particular* and *careless*, use *more*.

   more particular   more careless

Most adjectives ending in *-ful* and *-ous* also form the comparative with *more*.

   more beautiful   more ambitious
   more hopeful   more curious

The Superlative

To compare a thing or a person with more than one other of its kind, we use the **superlative form** of the adjective.

   This is the *best* dinner I have ever tasted.
   Pat is the *smartest* person I know.
   This is the *most interesting* book I have ever read.

We make the superlative form of adjectives by adding *-est* or by using *most*. For adjectives where we add *-er* to form the comparative, we add *-est* for the superlative. For those that use *more* for the comparative, we use *most* for the superlative.

Notice how the adjectives in the chart below change forms according to those simple rules.

Adjective	Comparative	Superlative
high	higher	highest
big	bigger	biggest
friendly	friendlier	friendliest
strong	stronger	strongest
agreeable	more agreeable	most agreeable
expensive	more expensive	most expensive
careful	more careful	most careful

There are three things to remember in using adjectives for comparison:

1. Use the comparative to compare two persons or things. Use the superlative to compare more than two.

   Comparative This car is *wider* than that one.
   Superlative This car is the *widest* one I have ever seen.

   Comparative George is a *faster* runner than Bill.
   Superlative George is the *fastest* runner of all the players on the team.

2. Do not leave out the word *other* when you are comparing something with everything else of its kind.

   Incorrect New York is larger than any American city. (This sentence says that New York is not an American city.)
   Correct New York is larger than any *other* American city.

   Incorrect Claire runs faster than any girl in her class. (Is Claire a girl?)
   Correct Claire runs faster than any *other* girl in her class.

3. Do not use both *-er* and *more* or *-est* and *most* at the same time.

   Incorrect Diamonds are more harder than jade.
   Correct Diamonds are *harder* than jade.

   Incorrect Diamonds are the most hardest of all minerals.
   Correct Diamonds are the *hardest* of all minerals.

Irregular Comparisons

We form the comparative and superlative of some adjectives by changing the words as shown in the chart below.

Adjective	Comparative	Superlative
good	better	best
well	better	best
bad	worse	worst
ill	worse	worst
little	less *or* lesser	least
much	more	most
many	more	most
far	farther	farthest

Exercises

A Write the correct form of each adjective given in parentheses.

1. Of the two paintings that one was (bad).
2. His flower arrangement was (good) than any other in the shop.
3. Laredo, Texas, is one of the (hot) American cities.
4. When I was writing my social studies paper, the dictionary was (helpful) to me than the almanac.
5. These shelves are (high) than those over there.
6. She had (little) time than usual.
7. This is the (difficult) question of all.
8. The double play is (hard) than any play in baseball, except the triple play.
9. The (funny) thing happened yesterday when I was walking backwards down the sidewalk.
10. My house is (far) from school than any other student's house.

B Study each of the following sentences. If a sentence contains an error, rewrite it correctly. If it is correct, write *Correct*.

1. Marcy felt more good than she had felt since last week.
2. The Amazon is the longer of all the South American rivers.
3. What is your favoritest color?

4. Ralph knows the computer better than any other student in our school.
5. Today is the most warmest day of the summer.
6. That was the worstest movie I have ever seen.
7. Our new dog is much friendlier than our old dog.
8. Hawaii is farther from Florida than any state in the U.S.
9. It was even more surprisinger when I won the contest.
10. Of the two plants, the fern is the healthiest.

c *Write Now* Suppose you are a reviewer for your town newspaper. Write a paragraph comparing two restaurants, movies, plays, or concerts. Use at least five comparative adjectives.

Grammar in Action

Comparison and contrast can be an effective way to organize compositions or reports. You can use adjectives to help you compare things or people when you use this form.

> Stephen A. Douglas was *more famous* than Abraham Lincoln at one time, but Lincoln was a *better* speaker.

Be careful to use the correct form of the adjective for the kind of comparison you are making.

Writing Activity Write a paragraph comparing Abraham Lincoln and Stephen A. Douglas at the time of their debates in 1858. Use the characteristics in the following lists. Use as many comparative and superlative adjectives as you can.

Douglas	Lincoln
popular senator	unknown lawyer
school educated	self-educated
born in New England	born in Kentucky
deep voice	high, penetrating voice
heavy set	gangly
five feet four inches tall	six feet four inches tall
known as "The Little Giant"	known as "The Railsplitter"

7
Adverbs in Comparisons

Use the *comparative* form of an adverb to compare two actions. Use the *superlative* form of an adverb to compare more than two actions.

Adverbs are used to compare one action with another. We say, "This engine runs well, but that one runs *more smoothly*." Or we say, "Julie planned her exhibit *more carefully* than any other student in the class." Adverbs have special forms or spellings for use in making comparisons, just as adjectives do.

The Comparative

When we compare one action with another, we use the **comparative** form of the adverb. The comparative form is made in two ways:

1. For short adverbs like *soon* and *fast*, add *-er*.
   We called *sooner* than you did.
   Kim can sew *faster* than Peg.

2. For most adverbs ending in *-ly*, use *more* to make the comparative.
   Bill acted *more quickly* than Jeff did.
   The water flowed *more rapidly* than before.

The Superlative

When one action is compared with two or more others of the same kind, we use the **superlative** form of the adverb.

All of the joggers ran near the water, but that one ran
   nearest.
Of the three boys, Scott speaks Spanish the *most fluently*.

The superlative form of adverbs is formed by adding *-est* or by using *most*. Adverbs that form the comparative with *-er* form the superlative with *-est*. Those that use *more* for the comparative use *most* for the superlative.

Notice how the following adverbs change forms:

Adverb	Comparative	Superlative
long	longer	longest
rapidly	more rapidly	most rapidly
clearly	more clearly	most clearly

There are three things to keep in mind when you use the comparative and superlative forms of adverbs:

1. Use the comparative to compare two actions and the superlative to compare more than two.

   Comparative It rained *harder* today than yesterday.
   Superlative   Of all the players, Terry tries the *hardest*.

2. Do not leave out the word *other* when you are comparing one action with every other action of the same kind.

   Incorrect Tara runs faster than any student in school.
   Correct   Tara runs faster than any *other* student in school.

3. Do not use both *-er* and *more* or *-est* and *most* at the same time.

   Incorrect Bob went home more sooner than you did.
   Correct   Bob went home *sooner* than you did.

Exercises

A Write the comparative and superlative forms of these adverbs.

1. fast
2. wildly
3. hard
4. happily
5. closely
6. long
7. bravely
8. slowly
9. recently
10. naturally

B Nine of these sentences contain errors in the use of adjectives. If a sentence is correct, write *Correct*. If there is an error, rewrite the sentence so it is correct.

1. We drove more carefully there than on any road.
2. Vacation ended more soon than we had expected.
3. I pedaled the faster ever to school this morning.

4. These photographs were trimmed more better than those.
5. That fish jumped more higher than any other in the pond.
6. This recipe is the more consistently successful of all.
7. I ran most hardest near the end of the race.
8. I can exercise more easily with music than without it.
9. Sam jumped more longer than any other athlete.
10. Of all the constellations, I saw the Big Dipper more clearly.

c *Write Now* Imagine that you held an animal olympics for pets. Write a paragraph telling which animals won awards in five different categories. Use the comparative or superlative form of an adverb in each sentence of your paragraph. For example, "Polly imitated a human voice more realistically than any other parrot."

Grammar in Action

Sometimes adverbs are more informative than adjectives. Compare the following sentences.

Joe is an excellent speaker.   Joe speaks loudly and clearly.

Did you notice how much more informative the second sentence is? It actually conveys the way Joe speaks by using an action verb, *speaks*, and adverbs, *loudly* and *clearly*. To show an action, use an action verb and one or more adverbs.

Writing Activity Supply adverbs to complete the following revisions of sentences. Write the new sentences on your paper.

1. The rooster looked proud. The rooster strutted _____.
2. I am a good writer. I write _____ and _____.
3. Those acrobats are great! Those acrobats fly _____ through the air and yet catch each other _____.

Now, look through *Starting Points* on pages 41-53. Find a topic for an action-packed paragraph. Write the paragraph using vivid and precise action verbs and adverbs.

8
Special Problems with Modifiers

Use *modifiers* according to rules for their use, not according to the way you hear them used in everyday conversation.

We sometimes write things the way we hear them. This can cause mistakes in writing, because spoken English is less formal than written English. Here are some common adjective and adverb problems to watch for.

Them *and* Those

Them is always a pronoun. It is used only as the object of a verb or as the object of a preposition.

Those is an adjective if it is followed by a noun. It is a pronoun if it is used alone.

> We heard *them* in the night. (pronoun)
> *Those* books are lost. (adjective modifying *books*)
> *Those* are our gifts. (pronoun)

The Extra Here *and* There

How often have you heard someone say, "This here book" or "That there window"? The word *this* includes the meaning of *here*. The word *that* includes the meaning of *there*.

Saying *this here* is like repeating your name every time you say *I* or *me*: "Please pass me, Pat Smith, the milk."

Kind *and* Sort

Kind and *sort* are singular. Use *this* or *that* with *kind* and *sort*. *Kinds* and *sorts* are plural. Use *these* or *those* with *kinds* and *sorts*.

> I like *this kind* of juice.   *Those sorts* of games are fun.

The Double Negative

Negative words are such words as *no, none, not, nothing,* and *never.* A **double negative** is the use of two negative words together when only one is needed. Good speakers and writers take care to avoid the double negative.

Incorrect We do*n't* have *no* more tape.
Correct We do*n't* have *any* more tape.

Incorrect Jack did*n't* win *nothing* at the fair.
Correct Jack did*n't* win *anything* at the fair.

Incorrect She has*n't never* gone there.
Correct She has*n't ever* gone there.

In the sentences above, the first negative is a contraction for *not.* When you use contractions like *haven't* and *didn't,* do not use negative words after them. Instead, use words such as *any, anything,* and *ever.*

> The club *hasn't any* new members.
> We *couldn't* hear *anything.*
> We *haven't ever* seen an eclipse.
> The band *can't* play *any* popular songs.

Hardly, barely, and *scarcely* are often used as negative words. Do not use them after contractions like *haven't* and *didn't.*

Incorrect We could*n't hardly* breathe.
Correct We *could hardly* breathe.

Incorrect They ca*n't barely* talk.
Correct They *can barely* talk.

Exercises

A Write the correct modifier given in parentheses.

1. We chose (those, those there) designs for our National Library Week posters.
2. Do you like (this, these) sort of cheese sandwich for your lunch?
3. (Them, Those) are my favorite photographs of our trip to the Grand Canyon.
4. Our dog won't eat (them, those) biscuits.

5. These (kind, kinds) of dogs live a long time.
6. I always buy (that there, that) kind of bread to make peanut butter sandwiches.
7. (Them, Those) are bear tracks.
8. We watched (them, those) as they played.
9. These (sort, sorts) of arguments are pointless.
10. (This, This here) computer needs to be fixed before anyone else tries to learn about the new program.

B Six of these sentences contain errors in the use of modifiers. If a sentence is correct, write *Correct*. If there is an error, rewrite the sentence so it is correct.

1. The girls couldn't scarcely believe their ears when the teacher announced they had won a trip to Disney World.
2. Bryan hasn't had no piano lessons since he broke his arm at the picnic.
3. We have no more time.
4. The movers couldn't hardly lift the heavy box.
5. There isn't no time for games.
6. Marguerita couldn't find the stamps.
7. Ms. Ryan won't let nobody use the power tools unless they wear safety goggles.
8. We couldn't find the volleyball net.
9. Nobody could have had more fun.
10. We had plenty of newly picked apples from the orchard, but Ellen didn't want none.

C *Proofreading* The following paragraph contains some common errors in the use of modifiers. It also has a number of other kinds of errors. Copy the paragraph and correct the errors you find. Pay particular attention to modifiers.

This here cookbook doesn't give no good directions. I want to cook baked chiken, and there is not one recipe for it here. That meens I will have to ask my sister. she said I shouldn't not overheat the oven, or the chicken would brun. If I can't raech my sister, Perhaps I'll cook somethin else. That there recipe for boiled frog legs looks good.

Linking Grammar & Writing

A Suppose you are a newspaper editor whose job is editing the reviews of entertainment writers. Edit the following review of a concert to make the writing more colorful and specific. Add vivid, precise adjectives and adverbs. Replace overused or weak modifiers with strong ones. You may add details.

> Stevie Wonder gave a good show last night. He is a good musician. Last night he sang and played well. As he sang, he moved his head from side to side. He swayed in time to the beat of his songs. He used his hands to encourage the audience to sing along. He tapped his feet. And, of course, Wonder used his voice to express emotions. Seeing Stevie Wonder in person is a good experience.

B There are advantages and disadvantages to having certain kinds of pets. Write a one-page comparison of the experiences likely to be encountered by the owner of a huge guard dog and the owner of a Chihuahua.

Be sure to use both adjectives and adverbs in their comparative forms. For example, "A nervous little Chihuahua is a funnier sight than a surly guard dog, but running alongside a powerful dog is certainly more exciting than begging a Chihuahua to come out from under the porch."

Additional Practice

Parts 1-4 Identifying Modifiers Identify all adjectives and adverbs in the following sentences. After each modifier, write the word it modifies. Do not include articles.

1. Dorothy Parker was famous for her witty comments.
2. Diane had a sore throat and a bad cough.
3. Gazelles run swiftly and gracefully.
4. I was quite frightened by the strange noises.
5. Yesterday my parents and I took a long, relaxing stroll through the woods.
6. Last summer Rob earned four hundred dollars.
7. Do you feel somewhat better now?
8. The Bruins easily defeated the Eagles in the championship game last night.
9. That book contains many Greek and Roman myths.
10. I welcomed my dear friend joyfully.

Part 5 Choosing the Correct Modifier Write the correct form of the modifiers given in parentheses. Identify the correct form as an adjective or adverb and tell what word it modifies.

11. The accident was George's fault, and he feels very (badly, bad) about it.
12. Mary Cassatt was a (really, real) talented artist.
13. Christina felt (good, well) about being elected president of the Spanish club.
14. The students said that the milk tasted (sour, sourly).
15. Most foods can be cooked more (quick, quickly) in a microwave oven than in a conventional oven.
16. After eating an entire pizza, I did not feel very (well, good).
17. Dave can run more (quick, quickly) than any other student in his class.
18. The constellation Cassiopeia can be seen (easily, easy.)
19. Golden Delicious apples are usually sweet, but this one tastes (tart, tartly).
20. The child spoke so (softly, soft) that no one could hear her.

Parts 6-7 Adjectives and Adverbs in Comparisons All of the following sentences contain errors in comparisons. Write each comparison correctly.

21. *Citizen Kane* is the most famous of the two movies we saw.
22. Allen lives more farther from town than Jason does.
23. Of all the clowns in the circus, that one has the more ridiculous costume.
24. California has the largest population of the two states.
25. The new secretary, Mr. Herman, types more quickly than any secretary in the office.
26. Did you know that the Nile is the world's most long river?
27. Our neighbor to the south moved in most recently than our neighbor to the north.
28. China has a more larger population than any other country in the world.
29. Kerry can mow the lawn more quicker than Pam.
30. Of all the job applicants, she is the less qualified.
31. Which country is closest to the United States, Costa Rica or Panama?
32. An elephant can run more faster than most other animals.
33. Of all the students in our science class, Christine works harder.
34. Lara's victory showed that she was a more better runner than Katie.
35. Grandfather said the picture reminded him of the most happiest day of his life.

Part 8 Special Problems with Modifiers Write the correct modifier given in parentheses.

36. (These, This) kinds of toys are dangerous.
37. (This, This here) restaurant serves delicious food.
38. The candidate doesn't have (no, any) chance of winning.
39. Ernest Hemingway wrote all of (those, them) books.
40. (That, Those) sort of thing really makes me angry.
41. It was raining so hard that the driver (could, couldn't) scarcely see the road.
42. (Them, Those) birds fly south every winter.
43. This dictionary doesn't list (any, no) word origins.
44. Would you please close (that there, that) door?
45. Sabrina hasn't (ever, never) been to Disney World.

Application and Review

Lesson Review

A Finding Adjectives Write the adjectives. After each adjective, write the word it modifies. Do not write the articles.

1. A blue van was parked next to the large mobile home.
2. The Chicago library has a wonderful display of dolls.
3. The tiny gray kitten rested on our roof.
4. Those old trucks clattered noisily down our alley.
5. Very few books are as long as this one.
6. That woman is very funny.
7. An English movie became popular in the United States.
8. The new American policy caused widespread concern.
9. The music on the radio was too loud.
10. The automatic door was controlled by an electric eye.

B Finding Adverbs Write on your paper the adverbs and predicate adjectives from the following sentences. Write the word each adverb or predicate adjective modifies.

1. The students walked quickly down the hall.
2. The runner jumped joyfully at the end of the race.
3. The two Dalmatians were too loud.
4. Now that they've been washed, my jeans finally feel soft.
5. The paramedics moved extremely quickly through the crowd.
6. Some people were very happy after the gentle rain.
7. Nearly forty kegs of nails split open on the highway.
8. We left precisely at 8:15 P.M.
9. The children anxiously awaited the clown's arrival.
10. The cyclists looked totally drained after the grueling race.

C Choosing Modifiers Write on your paper the correct form of the modifier given in parentheses.

1. The afternoon passed (slow, slowly).
2. The guards moved (quick, quickly) up the basketball court.

3. You play tennis quite (good, well).
4. The music was (quiet, quietly) in the doctor's office.
5. That tar smells (awful, awfully).
6. Ellen didn't feel (good, well) after her race.
7. Her word is always (good, well).
8. The desktop feels (smooth, smoothly).
9. The operator answered (angry, angrily).
10. My new sewing machine works very (good, well).

D Using Modifiers in Comparisons Eight of these sentences contain errors in the use of modifiers. If there is an error, rewrite the sentence so it is correct. If a sentence is correct, write *Correct*.

1. This lemon is more sour than others I've eaten.
2. This album is more better than those two.
3. They weren't the carefullest house painters I've seen.
4. May is the most nice month of the year.
5. These are the healthiest plants I've ever seen.
6. Her apartment is more smaller than mine.
7. Rita plays soccer better than any student in her class.
8. That was the worstest mistake I ever made.
9. Helen Hayes is one of the very bestest actresses.
10. This novel was more easier to read than the one I read last.

E Avoiding Special Problems with Modifiers Nine of these sentences contain errors in the use of modifiers. If there is an error, rewrite the sentence so it is correct. If a sentence is correct, write *Correct*.

1. The coaches couldn't hardly believe the final score.
2. Them there look dangerous.
3. I've eaten so much I can't eat no more.
4. Them belong to Roberto and Denise.
5. Brian couldn't catch those.
6. Them cattle haven't scarcely moved off the road.
7. That sort of behavior could get a player benched.
8. Meredith hasn't had no breakfast.
9. Them runners couldn't barely finish the race.
10. My typewriter doesn't need no repairs.

Chapter Review

A Finding Modifiers Write each sentence on your paper. Underline each adjective once and each adverb twice. Then draw an arrow from each modifier to the word it modifies. Do not underline articles.

1. The new director of the choral society requires absolutely perfect attendance at all rehearsals.
2. We were very nervous about the philosophical questions on the test.
3. That runner in the outside lane runs most gracefully.
4. The English lavender soap always makes me sneeze.
5. Yesterday rain fell steadily, but the sun has finally appeared.
6. This Oriental rug looks beautiful in your bedroom.
7. I hit the ball much farther than Cass did.
8. Any lie can grow to unexpected proportions quite rapidly.
9. Mona brought my Spanish book back immediately.
10. Those raspberries taste much sweeter than these grapes.

B Using Modifiers All of the following sentences contain errors in the use of modifiers. Rewrite each sentence so it is correct.

1. Which island is largest, Hawaii or Oahu?
2. Lyle considers this invitation an high honor.
3. In March at the equator, does the Pacific Ocean feel as coldly as the Atlantic Ocean?
4. This here pencil is more sharper than any pencil on my desk.
5. Patty works serious on her homework, and she does good in her classes.
6. The temperature rose steadily, and we all felt much too warmly.
7. Hardly no one has a difficulter job than Murray.
8. This is the most quietest room in the house but also the most hot.
9. That there sort of bird is the unusuallest I have seen.
10. There isn't no reason why those kind of computer should perform bad if programmed correctly.

26
Using Prepositions, Conjunctions, and Interjections

How do the underlined words change the meaning of the following sentences?

> *I drove <u>on</u> the highway.*
> *I drove <u>under</u> the highway.*
> *I drove <u>off</u> the highway.*

The underlined words are prepositions. They are little words that can make a big difference in the meaning of a sentence. Prepositions and also conjunctions link words, ideas, and sentences.

In this chapter you will learn more about prepositions and conjunctions. You will also learn how to use interjections to add emotion and emphasis to your writing.

531

1
Prepositions

A *preposition* is a word that relates its object to some other word in the sentence. The noun or pronoun after the preposition is the *object of the preposition*.

Connectives are words that are used to join together two or more other words or groups of words. **Prepositions** are one important kind of connective. They show relationships between the noun or pronoun following the preposition and another word in the sentence. Notice the prepositions in the following sentences:

> The plane flew *into* the storm.
> The plane flew *around* the storm.

In the first sentence, *into* connects the verb *flew* with *storm*. *Storm* is the noun following the preposition and is called the **object of the preposition**. *Into* points out the relationship between *flew* and *storm*. In the second sentence, *around* connects *storm*, its object, with the verb *flew*. It points out a different relationship between *flew* and *storm*. You can see that *into* and *around* join parts of each sentence. Like all prepositions, they make clear a certain relationship between the words that they connect.

Now look at the prepositions in the following sentences:

> My sister is the person *at* the counter.
> My sister is the person *behind* the counter.

You can see that *at* and *behind* join parts of each sentence. They describe the relationships between *person* and *counter*. Simply changing the preposition from *at* to *behind* changes the meaning of the sentence. A person at a counter is probably a customer; a person behind a counter is more likely to be a clerk.

On the next page is a list of words often used as prepositions. Most of these prepositions tell *where*. Others show a relationship of *time*. Still others show such special relationships as *reference* or *separation*. Study these prepositions and see if you can tell the relationship that each of them shows between words.

Words Often Used as Prepositions			
about	beneath	in	past
above	beside	inside	since
across	between	into	through
after	beyond	like	to
against	but (except)	near	toward
along	by	of	under
among	concerning	off	until
around	down	on	up
at	during	onto	upon
before	except	out	with
behind	for	outside	within
below	from	over	without

Exercises

A Write the prepositions from the following sentences.

1. The library will hold the book until tomorrow.
2. The runners ran down the avenue and through the park.
3. A plane made an emergency landing in the cornfield.
4. During the night we were awakened by thunder.
5. After the play, we're going to Mike's house.
6. The city of Denver is concerned about air pollution.
7. The actors gathered around the director for instructions.
8. The seal sits happily on the rock in the sun.
9. The city was without power for several hours.
10. In the science classroom there are many books on wildlife.

B Write prepositions that correctly complete each sentence.

1. In July we are going _____ Florida _____ a visit.
2. The Student Council meets _____ school _____ Friday.
3. A sky-writing plane flew _____ the field _____ the game.
4. The bicycle shop is located _____ Green Bay Road.
5. _____ the island _____ Oahu, we visited the beach.
6. The dog ran _____ the stairs and _____ the house.
7. Walter Payton dazzled the crowd _____ the Coliseum _____ a 93-yard run.

8. We rode a tram ———— the top ———— the mountain.
9. Nan likes skiing ———— forests and ———— open fields.
10. The market ———— the village is ———— the clock.

Preposition or Adverb?

Many words used as prepositions can also be used as adverbs. A preposition never appears alone. It is always followed by its object, a noun or a pronoun. If the word in question has a noun or pronoun following it, it is probably a preposition. If it is not followed by a noun or pronoun, it is probably an adverb.

> The ball flew *over* the base. (preposition)
> They asked me to come *over*. (adverb)
>
> Betty ran *down* the street. (preposition)
> Ted put his books *down*. (adverb)

Exercises

A Make two columns on your paper. Label them *Prepositions* and *Adverbs*. Write the italicized words from the following sentences in the first column if they are prepositions. Write them in the second column if they are adverbs.

1. Janice turned *around*.
2. There is a new shopping center *near* our house.
3. Mother went *into* her room to lie *down*.
4. The light bulb burned *out*.
5. The horses trotted *around* the ring.
6. All local traffic was allowed *through*.
7. Pete threw his old track shoes *away*.
8. The boomerang flew *across* the backyard.
9. The doctor is *in*.
10. The circus parade just went *past*.

B Make two columns on your paper. Label them *Prepositions* and *Adverbs*. Write the prepositions from the following sentences in the first column. Write the adverbs in the second column.

1. Have you ever been to a gymnastics meet before?
2. Before a gymnastics meet, the athletes stretch their limbs, necks, and backs.

3. When the gymnast jumps to the bar, a spotter stands below.
4. When the gymnast jumps off the equipment, this is called the dismount.
5. Balance beam performers seldom use spotters during meets.
6. In the balance beam competition, performers sometimes fall.
7. Floor exercises are carefully planned and performed to music.
8. Some gymnasts vault over the horse, a tall padded block with sturdy legs.
9. Others swing on the rings.
10. In some meets, each gymnast performs different routines.

Grammar in Action

Often an adverb can be replaced by a preposition and object. The change can make the sentence clearer and more specific. Consider the following examples:

> If you need me, I'll be walking *around*.
> If you need me, I'll be walking *through the park*.

> Did Kelly come *by* last night?
> Did Kelly come *to your house* last night?

Writing Activity Write a short paragraph describing a visit to a haunted mansion. Use adverbs instead of prepositions. For example, you might say *I peered in* or *I snooped around*. Then rewrite the paragraph changing adverbs to prepositions with objects. Do the changes improve your sentences?

2
Prepositional Phrases as Modifiers

A *prepositional phrase* consists of a preposition, its object, and any modifiers of the object. A prepositional phrase can modify a noun, a pronoun, or a verb.

A modifier can be a single word or a group of words. A **phrase** is a group of words that belongs together but lacks a subject and verb. Phrases are used as modifiers in these sentences:

The bears hibernated *during the long winter*.
The player *in the blue jersey* sank the next basket.

A **prepositional phrase** consists of a preposition, its object, and any modifiers of the object.

Preposition	Modifiers	Object
during	the long	winter
in	the blue	jersey

Prepositional phrases can modify nouns, pronouns, or verbs. A phrase that modifies a noun or pronoun is an **adjective phrase**. A phrase that modifies a verb is an **adverb phrase**.

Remember that adverbs tell *how, where, when,* and *to what extent*, about verbs. Adverb phrases tell the same thing.

Regina found a box *of marbles*. (adjective phrase modifying the noun *box*)
Roberta walked *into the room*. (adverb phrase modifying the verb *walked*)

Often you will find two prepositional phrases in a row. Sometimes the second phrase is an adjective phrase modifying the object of the first phrase.

Cory put the powder <u>into the can of paint</u>.
(*Into the can* tells where the powder was *put*.)
(*Of paint* modifies *can*. It tells *which can*.)

Diagraming Prepositional Phrases

To diagram a prepositional phrase, place the preposition on a slanted line below the word modified. Then put the object of the preposition on a horizontal line connected with the slanted line. Other words in the phrase are placed on slanted lines below the object of the preposition.

EXAMPLE   The girl *with the red hair* plays *in the band.*

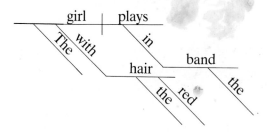

Sometimes two or more nouns or pronouns are used as objects in a prepositional phrase.

EXAMPLE   Put spices *on the potatoes and squash.*

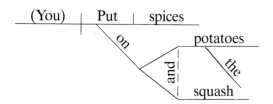

Exercise

Make three columns. Label them *Adjective Phrases, Adverb Phrases,* and *Words Modified.* Write the prepositional phrases from the following sentences in the correct column. Write the words they modify in the third column.

1. The passengers on the jet were served a special dinner of steak and baked potatoes.
2. The five huge oak trees in back of our school are very old and tall.
3. Are you going to the store down the street?

4. Jane took these photographs with a wide-angle lens on her camera.
5. The monkey ran from the sound of humans.
6. Kent walked through the park by the lake every day last summer.
7. I enjoyed my work at the animal clinic.
8. On Tuesday Jennifer took the social studies test on Russia.
9. A mola is a picture made from layers of fabric.
10. We rôde a tram to the top of the mountain.

Grammar in Action

Prepositions can help make relationships between ideas clear. Be careful, though, not to string too many prepositions together. Move some of the prepositions elsewhere in the sentence or divide your sentence into two or more sentences.

Preposition String	The mother robin sat *in* her nest *in* the birch tree *in* the yard *with* her babies.
Prepositions Moved	In the birch tree in the yard, the mother robin sat with her babies.
Sentence Divided and Changed	In our yard is a birch tree. In it, a mother robin sat in a nest with her babies.

Writing Activity Rewrite the following sentences by moving prepositional phrases and dividing sentences.

The scuba divers in their wet suits slid into the water near the boat with the yellow flag with the blue emblem. They launched an orange warning buoy before their plunge to the wreck under the surface of the murky water.

3
Conjunctions and Interjections

A *conjunction* is a word that connects words or groups of words.
An *interjection* is a word or short group of words used to express feeling.

A conjunction is another kind of connecting word you can use in your writing and speaking. Unlike prepositions, conjunctions do not have objects. Like prepositions, however, they show a relationship between the words they connect.

Coordinating Conjunctions

To connect single words or similar parts of a sentence that are of equal importance, we use **coordinating conjunctions**. The most common coordinating conjunctions are *and, but,* and *or.*

> Lucy *and* Roger came to the party. (connects subjects)
> Todd will call his father *or* mother. (connects direct objects)
> The canister smelled spicy *but* damp. (connects predicate adjectives)
> The cabin is by the lake *and* near the road. (connects prepositional phrases)
> We can't see, *but* we can hear. (connects sentences)

Correlative Conjunctions

A few conjunctions are used in pairs. Such conjunctions are called **correlative conjunctions**.

Correlative Conjunctions	
both . . . and	not only . . . but also
either . . . or	whether . . . or
neither . . . nor	

Notice how correlative conjunctions are used in the following examples:

> *Both* the chorus *and* the orchestra will perform.
> *Either* you *or* I have made an error.
> *Neither* the bench *nor* the table had been painted.
> We need *not only* nails *but also* a hammer.
> Will we go *whether* it rains *or* snows?

Interjections

An **interjection** is a word or short group of words used to express strong feeling. It can be a real word or merely the representation of a sound.

Interjections can express surprise, joy, longing, anger, or sorrow. An interjection that expresses very strong emotion is often followed by an exclamation point. An interjection that expresses mild emotion is usually followed by a comma.

> *All right!* We made the semi-finals.
> *No way!* I'm not riding that roller coaster.
> *Oh,* now I understand.
> *Listen,* I should get back to work.

Exercises

A Find the conjunctions in the following sentences and write them on your paper.

1. The clowns and magicians wore colorful clothing.
2. Neither freezing rain nor poor visibility delayed the flight.
3. Can Eric play music by Chopin or Brahms on the piano?
4. Either the yearbook staff or the newspaper staff will sell refreshments at the home football games.
5. We had barbecued chicken but not hamburgers.
6. Cynthia wants to be a veterinarian or a pediatrician.
7. Marcia and I are going either to the water polo match or to the indoor tennis match.
8. Neither Henry nor Cheryl was at the game today.
9. The San Diego Zoo and Disneyland were the highlights of my trip to California.
10. Stan can't decide whether to play baseball or basketball.

B Find the *Conjunctions* and *Interjections* from the following sentences and write them on your paper.

1. Neither the coaches nor the timekeepers knew the score.
2. Both badminton and volleyball require a net on the court.
3. Hurry! Here comes our train for Philadelphia and New York.
4. We collected not only money but also canned goods.
5. Racquetball requires both speed and endurance.
6. I hope neither sleet nor hail falls today.
7. The guide dog led Bill down the street and to the store.
8. Alex and Blanca stayed for dinner.
9. Does anyone care whether we have fish or chicken?
10. Oh, here comes Emilio now.

C *Proofreading* Rewrite the following paragraph correctly. Improve it by combining two pairs of sentences.

> Every student from the school was at the furst foot ball game of the seasen. It was very exciting. Our team won. Vince returned a kickoff down the feild for a touchdown james threw six touchdown passes. The final score was sixty-four to ten. wow.

Grammar in Action

Conjunctions help us link ideas together, but they can also cause confusion. When you write, be careful not to use too many conjunctions in one sentence. Also be careful not to join more than two sentences with a conjunction.

Awkward   James asked Nora to the movie and they chose a horror movie and they came out looking green.

Better   James asked Nora to the movie, and they chose a horror movie. They came out looking green.

Writing Activity Suppose that you have discovered an odd reptile. Write a paragraph describing all the things this reptile likes to do. Use at least five conjunctions in your paragraph.

Linking Grammar & Writing

A Think of a game that you like to play. It could be a board game, a word game, or a sport. Write a simplified set of directions that another person could follow to play the game properly. Give as many specific directions as you can, such as "Choose one of the five pieces from the box," "Place the ball in the middle of the field," or "Draw one card from the pile at your left." Then, circle every prepositional phrase you have used.

B What do you and your best friend have in common? Write a one-page essay telling what interests, attitudes, abilities, and dislikes you share. In addition to using the coordinating conjunctions *and, but,* and *or,* use at least three of the following pairs of correlative conjunctions:

both . . . and
either . . . or
neither . . . nor
not only . . . but also
whether . . . or

C Have you heard of these superstitions?

Don't walk under a ladder.
Don't step on a crack in the sidewalk.
If you spill salt, throw some extra salt over your shoulder.
A broken mirror means seven years of bad luck.
Finding a four-leaf clover will bring you good luck.
Seeing a white horse in a pasture means your wishes will come true.

Make up five superstitions of your own. Be sure to make up consequences as well. For example, "If the point on your pencil breaks during a test then your hair will turn gray within twenty-four hours." Write your superstitions in the "if . . . then" format, and underline all of the prepositions you use.

Additional Practice

Part 1 Prepositions Make three columns on your paper. Label them *Prepositions, Objects of Prepositions,* and *Adverbs*. Write the prepositions from the following sentences in the first column. Write the objects of prepositions in the second column, and the adverbs in the third column.

1. Geraldine Ferraro ran for Vice-President of the United States in 1984.
2. The new student stood in the center of the room and looked around.
3. The cat was scratching at the door, so Ted let him inside.
4. The mystery is not solved until the last scene of the play.
5. The officer stopped traffic and let the ambulance through.
6. Did you know that part of the U.S.S.R. is in Asia, and part is in Europe?
7. Eileen turned around and saw a red fox running across the field.
8. A ferret is a member of the weasel family.
9. The hailstones left small dents in the car's finish.
10. Our last-period gym class will be held outside.
11. The piccolo is a kind of flute.
12. I had never before been so frightened.
13. My little sister and her friends play jacks on the front stoop of our house.
14. Many Americans were unemployed during the Great Depression.
15. The due date of your report is near, so you should get started.

Part 2 Prepositional Phrases Write the prepositional phrases from the following sentences. Label them as *Adjective Phrases* or *Adverb Phrases*. Then write the word or words that each phrase modifies.

16. The antenna on our roof helps us get a better picture on our television set.

17. During the summer we swim in Lake Michigan.
18. The O'Reillys served a dinner of lasagna, tossed salad, and Italian bread.
19. During the American Civil War, members of the same family sometimes fought against each other.
20. The nurse stayed at the patient's bedside throughout the night.
21. Harry Carney played in Duke Ellington's band for many years.
22. The girl with the long, blond hair is my cousin.
23. Sheila will run in the relay race.
24. The towering tree on the left is a linden.
25. The dentist's office is in the building on the corner.
26. Woody Allen wrote the script for the movie.
27. Do you think you'll be coming to my party?
28. A famous artist drew the illustration on the book's cover.
29. Margaret Mead traveled around the United States giving lectures.
30. The flowers on that plant are quite fragrant.

Part 3 Conjunctions and Interjections Write the conjunctions and interjections in the following sentences.

31. Ms. Cunningham could not decide whether to accept the job offer or refuse it.
32. Oh, can I help you?
33. Both Haiti and the Dominican Republic are located in the West Indies.
34. My mother wanted to study art, but she did not have enough money to go to art school.
35. Wow! Did you see the goalie block that slap shot with his hand?
36. Thomas Jefferson sent Meriwether Lewis and William Clark to explore the northwestern part of the United States.
37. Say, do you know how to reduce a fraction to its lowest terms?
38. Ouch! You just stepped on my toe.
39. Honshu, Shikoku, Hokkaido, and Kyushu are Japan's four major islands.
40. Neither Margaret nor Rosemarie wanted to sing in the choir this year.

Application and Review

Lesson Review

A Identifying Prepositions Write the prepositions from the following sentences.

1. The story of the big race will be in the newspaper sports section tomorrow.
2. Used car trade-ins are accepted at almost all automobile dealerships.
3. On our doorstep after the storm we found a lost puppy with blue eyes and a long tail.
4. The new shopping mall near the school will soon be open for business.
5. Dale and I went to the Twelfth Street Bakery for some bagels.
6. We rode the subway from Brooklyn into Manhattan and then to Queens.
7. During August you can't get into that restaurant on a Friday without a reservation.
8. The complete list of contest winners will be announced in just a few minutes.
9. The black-and-white photographs in the display case were taken by Sue and Richard.
10. Rafferty High School is located up the hill beyond the municipal building.

B Using Prepositional Phrases as Modifiers Make three columns. Label them *Adjective Phrases*, *Adverb Phrases*, and *Words Modified*. Write the prepositional phrases from the following sentences in the correct column. Write the words they modify in the third column.

1. Look in the drawer with the brass handle.
2. Please give Francine a cheese and tomato sandwich with lettuce.

3. The plants and flowers in the greenhouse need watering today.
4. The Canadian history books on the table were borrowed by my brother.
5. Arturo will clean the aquarium in the living room and the bird cage on the porch.
6. On our class trip, we visited Abraham Lincoln's home in Springfield, Illinois.
7. The Statue of Liberty was a gift to the United States from France.
8. The hikers leaped over the small stream.
9. The elevator ride to the top of the Sears Tower takes about fifty-four seconds.
10. A huge bale of hay fell from the wagon.

C Recognizing Conjunctions and Interjections Make two columns on your paper. Label them *Conjunctions* and *Interjections*. Write the conjunctions from the following sentences in the first column. Write the interjections in the second column.

1. Last Saturday, Kathy and I went cycling and bowling in Germantown.
2. Neither Bob nor Jeff has a catcher's mitt of his own for the game today.
3. Astonishing! My five-year-old cousin can play both the guitar and the banjo.
4. "Checagou," or "land of stinking onions," is the Native American name originally given to the city of Chicago.
5. They went to the planetarium last weekend, but we went to the zoo.
6. Wow! The length of every marathon race is 26 miles and 385 yards.
7. Both Wisconsin and Mississippi were named by the Chippewa tribe of Native Americans.
8. "Ouisconsin" means "grassy place," and "mici zibi" means "great river."
9. Oh, don't worry about Helen and me.
10. Neither my parents nor my brothers and sisters can answer all my questions.

Chapter Review

A Using Prepositional Phrases as Modifiers Make three columns on your paper. Label them *Adjective Phrase*, *Adverb Phrase*, and *Word Modified*. Write the prepositional phrases from the following sentences in the correct column. Write the words they modify in the third column.

1. We stumbled over the abandoned bicycles in the alley.
2. Jeffrey rode his scooter through the mud.
3. People who run with untied shoelaces risk stumbling.
4. The Grand Canyon was created by the current of the Colorado River.
5. Nicole leaned against the fence for support.
6. We can't tolerate three days in a row without a ray of sunshine.
7. Before lunch Jerry will enter the data into the computer in the learning center.
8. David got a haircut before his interview with the manager.
9. Rebecca took scuba diving lessons at the public pool near her house.
10. During the storm the puppy hid under the bed.

B Recognizing Conjunctions and Interjections Make two columns on your paper. Label them *Conjunctions* and *Interjections*. Write the conjunctions from the following sentences in the first column. Write the interjections in the second column.

1. Achoo! The ragweed and pollen have made all my allergies act up.
2. Mom likes not only roses but also tulips.
3. Neither Harvey nor Cindy could give directions to Professor Quigley.
4. Denise raked and mowed the lawn this afternoon.
5. Everyone read the assignment, but no one understood it.
6. Ahh! This warm bath feels great to my sore muscles.
7. I like buying new pens and pencils for school every fall.
8. Oh no, I forgot to mail this letter.
9. Do you prefer this salad or that one?
10. I don't care whether we go to a movie or a play.

Cumulative Review

A Using Verbs Write the correct form of the verb given in parentheses.

1. I haven't missed the new comedy show since it (began, begun).
2. My little sister has (grew, grown) two inches recently.
3. We (wrote, written) him a letter today.
4. In gym class yesterday, we (ran, run) the mile.
5. Some of the kids (lay, laid) down on the grass.
6. "Rise and shine, everyone!" Mrs. Lee (sang, sung) out.
7. Tracy has (broke, broken) the girls' diving record.
8. We had (swam, swum) the length of the pool.
9. When I finished, she (threw, thrown) me a sweater.
10. After the game, we (ate, eaten) dinner at my house.
11. We (sit, sat) for an hour and talked about school.
12. Last week, raccoons (stole, stolen) food from our garbage cans.
13. Our neighbor, Mr. Higgins, (rang, rung) our doorbell to tell us about the accident.
14. The squirrels have (gave, given) us a mess to clean up!
15. We can't (let, leave) our bikes unlocked again.

B Identifying Modifiers Make two columns on your paper and label them *Adjectives* and *Adverbs*. Write all the adjectives and adverbs from the following sentences in the correct columns. Do not write articles.

1. The photographer quickly snapped three pictures.
2. The movers very slowly pushed the heavy piano up a steep ramp onto a truck.
3. The chemistry laboratory has too little equipment.
4. Artists very often make frames for their pictures.
5. Many immigrants move to a new country for a better life.
6. Eddie feels much worse today.

7. Shana could barely see a wide smile in the dim light.
8. Those newspapers are the best sources of information about the current movies.
9. Tony was really surprised at his fourteenth birthday party.
10. "Play a little louder," the conductor told the players.
11. The brick was too thick for the small saw.
12. The time passed very slowly during the final exam.
13. Harold likes crispy and spicy chicken.
14. The play seemed too long.
15. Denise experiments with new recipes often.

C Identifying Prepositions, Conjunctions, and Interjections

Write whether each italicized word in the following sentences is a *Preposition*, a *Conjunction*, or an *Interjection*.

1. Steel is made *from* iron *and* other raw materials.
2. *No,* I want *neither* the red socks *nor* the green socks.
3. *Help!* My finger is stuck *inside* the pipe.
4. Is Cyd's family moving *to* Rhode Island *or* Delaware?
5. *Before* the war, the colonists *and* the Indians were friends.
6. Roosevelt fought *in* Cuba *during* the Spanish-American War.
7. The water sports *at* camp included *not only* skiing *but also* swimming *and* boating.
8. *"Yes,"* I looked *under* the stairs and *on* the porch."
9. Saturn's rings revolve *around* it *like* moons.
10. Trees *and* bushes hid the sun *from* view.

D Combined Review
Write the correct word or phrase given in parentheses in each of the following sentences.

1. Has the last inning (began, begun)?
2. Which is (taller, tallest), the tree or the house?
3. Marge bought both apples (and, or) oranges.
4. "I'm here!" Andrew answered (loud, loudly).
5. Neither the rake (or, nor) the hoe can be found.
6. Everyone has (gone, went) on the field trip.
7. The picnic will be held whether it rains (nor, or) shines.
8. Both the students (saw, seen) the correct answer.
9. What is the (more valuable, most valuable) gem?
10. Julia has accidentally (taken, took) the wrong locker.

27
Using Compound and Complex Sentences

A complex work of art is something that becomes more interesting each time you look at it. Intricacy and variety are what make it fascinating.

The same applies to sentences. Too many simple sentences sound stilted. If you mix them up with compound and complex constructions, however, your writing becomes flowing, intricate, and interesting.

In this chapter you will learn how to write compound and complex sentences so that you can add variety and richness to your writing.

1
Compound Sentences

> A *compound sentence* consists of two or more simple sentences joined together.

Sometimes two simple sentences are so closely related in thought that you can join them together. You can join them by using a coordinating conjunction—*and, but,* or *or.* Two or more simple sentences joined together are called a **compound sentence**.

> We washed the car. Mom took us for a ride.
> We washed the car, **and** Mom took us for a ride.

Compound sentences are useful, but they must be written carefully. Two sentences should be combined to form one sentence only if the ideas they express are closely related. If the ideas are not closely related, the resulting sentence may not make sense.

Incorrect Jim painted the barn, and he is nineteen.
Correct Jim painted the barn, and John fixed the roof.

Punctuating Compound Sentences

When you write a compound sentence, use a comma before the conjunction. The comma tells your reader where to pause. Without a comma, compound sentences can be quite confusing:

Confusing I painted the chair and Liz painted the table.
Better I painted the chair, **and** Liz painted the table.

The first sentence might cause someone reading quickly to think that the writer had painted both the chair and Liz. The comma prevents this confusion.

Sometimes you can join the parts of a compound sentence with a semicolon (;) instead of with a comma and a conjunction.

> It snowed heavily all night; classes were canceled the next day.
> The whistle blew; the game was over.

Never join simple sentences with a comma alone. A comma is not powerful enough to hold the sentences together.

Incorrect	The symphony was over, we went home.
Correct	The symphony was over, and we went home.
Correct	The symphony was over; we went home.

Remember these two ways to join simple sentences.
1. Join them with a comma and one of the conjunctions *and, but,* or *or.* Place the comma before the conjunction.
2. Join them with a semicolon when there is no conjunction. Place the semicolon at the end of the first sentence.

Compound Sentences and Compound Verbs

A simple sentence with a compound verb looks and sounds very much like a compound sentence. There are two important reasons for knowing how compound verbs differ from compound sentences: (1) They must be punctuated differently. (2) Sometimes you can improve your writing by changing a compound sentence to a simple sentence with a compound verb.

Compound Sentence	The students rose to their feet, and they applauded.
Simple Sentence	The students rose to their feet and applauded.

You remember that a simple sentence has one subject and one predicate. The simple sentence in the example above has one subject: *students.* It has two verbs or one compound verb: *rose* and *applauded.* Both verbs have the same subject: *students.* In the compound sentence, each verb has its own subject: *students rose* and *they applauded.* Whenever both subjects of a compound sentence refer to the same person or thing, you can often make your writing more concise by making a simple sentence with a compound verb.

Diagraming Compound Sentences

When you diagram a compound sentence, you show one simple sentence above another. Join the sentences with a dotted line and a "step" for the conjunction.

EXAMPLE The boys explored the cave, but they found
         nothing.

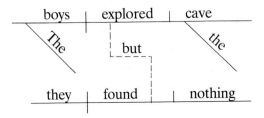

Exercises

A Join the following sentence pairs to make compound sentences. Some pairs are not related and should not be joined. Use correct punctuation and appropriate conjunctions.

1. Amelia Earhart first worked as a school teacher. She later became a famous airplane pilot.
2. We are going to the planetarium tomorrow. We will see a Sensurround movie there.
3. Tanya and I were playing checkers. I prefer chess.
4. You can bring potato salad. I can bring macaroni salad.
5. Teddy Roosevelt was a dynamic President. He encouraged the construction of the Panama Canal.
6. Clara climbed up the rope. Her gym teacher watched.
7. Sam finished his homework. He enjoys history most.
8. We can go to the movie tonight. We can go to a play.
9. There are 2,000 species of roses. Some roses have only five petals.
10. Rhode Island has a forty-nine mile coastline. It is nevertheless the smallest state in the Union.

B Write on your paper the following sentences as simple sentences with compound verbs. Punctuate each correctly.

1. Ellen plays volleyball, and she runs track.
2. Volleyball teams compete in winter, and they play indoors.
3. A volleyball court is 60 feet long, and it measures 30 feet wide.
4. Volleyball is a team sport, and it requires cooperation.
5. Players practice teamwork, and they work on other skills too.

6. They drill serves, and they practice setting the ball.
7. Team members also do aerobics, and they run a mile a day.
8. Sometimes the players get rough, and they drill spikes.
9. Jo spikes the ball well, and she serves it even better.
10. Volleyball is fun, and it provides good exercise.

c *Proofreading* Proofread and revise the following paragraph. Combine simple sentences to make compound sentences to improve the "flow" of the paragraph.

> The Santa Ana wind blows accross the San Bernardino Valley in Octber. It makes people uneasy. People say they are more burglaries then.
> They say there are more violent crimes committed then. Is there something eval in the wind. Does the wind just spark people's imaginations?

Grammar in Action

Writers often make the mistake of trying to string too many ideas together in one sentence. For example, notice that the first sentence below drags on and is difficult to follow. The second sentence is much clearer and more interesting.

> Nine of us stood close together and we stood on the porch and we posed for the picture and we laughed and we talked happily.

> Nine of us stood close together on the porch, and we posed for the picture. We laughed and talked happily.

Writing Activity Write a paragraph about a talent you wish you had. Tell how you would use this talent and how it might change your life. Use a variety of sentence structures in your writing.

2
Complex Sentences

A *complex sentence* is a sentence that contains one *main clause* and one or more *subordinate clauses*.

Before you can know what a complex sentence is, you need to know about clauses. A **clause** is a group of words that contains a verb and its subject. There are two types of clauses: main clauses and subordinate clauses.

Main Clauses

A clause that can stand as a sentence by itself is a **main clause**. A compound sentence contains two or more main clauses. That is because it contains two or more simple sentences. Each of those simple sentences is a main clause.

Jane hit the ball, and it flew into the bleachers.

In the example above, *Jane hit the ball* and *it flew into the bleachers* are both main clauses. All clauses in compound sentences are main clauses. They can stand as simple sentences. That is why they are sometimes called **independent clauses**.

Subordinate Clauses

Some clauses do not express a complete thought, so they can not stand by themselves. These clauses are called subordinate clauses. Read these examples:

       s.   **v.**   **s.**   **v.**
If the mail has come   When the door opened

       s.   **v.**   **s.**   **v.**
While you were out   After the rain stopped

None of these clauses express a complete thought. Each one is a sentence fragment that leaves you wondering, *then what?* Now, cover the first word in each of these clauses. What happens? Each clause now expresses a complete thought.

You can see that the words *if* and *when* are important. They *subordinate* the groups of words they introduce and are called **subordinating conjunctions**. They introduce **subordinate clauses**.

Words used frequently as subordinating conjunctions are listed in the box below.

Words Often Used as Subordinating Conjunctions			
after	because	so that	whatever
although	before	than	when
as	if	though	whenever
as if	in order that	till	where
as long as	provided	unless	wherever
as though	since	until	while

Now you have the information you need to understand a complex sentence. A **complex sentence** is a sentence that contains one main clause and one or more subordinate clauses.

Main Clause	Subordinate Clause
We left	before you came.
We were on the lake	when the storm began.

Avoiding Sentence Fragments

When a subordinate clause is used by itself, as if it were a sentence, it is a **sentence fragment**. A subordinate clause must be joined by a main clause to form a sentence.

Fragment   When you arrive
Complex Sentence When you arrive, come in the back door.

Exercises

A Write the subordinate clauses from the following sentences. Underline the subject of each clause once and the verb twice.

1. Before practice begins, the team always runs laps.
2. Although the heat was on, the room was cold.
3. Stop and see us when you return from Thailand.
4. I put the goggles in my bag so that I wouldn't forget them.
5. Were you home when Elena called?
6. The water was warmer than I thought.
7. Because whales are warm-blooded, they are mammals.

8. Whenever we are in Philadelphia, we visit the Liberty Bell.
9. Although Denver is on flat land, the city is still nearly a mile above sea level.
10. We can't start the game until the field is drier.

B For each sentence, write on your paper *Simple*, *Compound*, or *Complex* to show what kind of sentence it is.

1. Most people associate robots with science fiction, but today robots are found in everyday life.
2. A robot is programmed like a computer.
3. A robot can move and do work, and some robots can even sense changes in their environment.
4. When it senses a change, the robot will respond.
5. Both traffic lights and room thermostats are robots.
6. Whenever the temperature in a room falls below a certain point, the thermostat responds by turning on the heat.
7. The automatic pilot system of an airplane is a robot and can control the plane from takeoff to landing.
8. Industrial robots are used when the work required is too hazardous for a person.
9. They can pick up very hot pieces of metal or work in a room filled with harmful gases.
10. Robots have not been in existence for very long, but experts say they will become more and more common.

c *Write Now* Suppose you are founding a new community. What rules will you need to make life pleasant for everyone? Write ten laws, each stated in a complex sentence. Use different subordinating conjunctions from the list on page 555.

HAPPINESS, IDAHO
POPULATION 132

3
Types of Subordinate Clauses

Subordinate clauses may be used in sentences as adjectives, adverbs, and nouns. Then they are called *adjective clauses, adverb clauses,* and *noun clauses.*

Complex sentences can be used to add variety to your writing. They can also make your writing more interesting.

Original   The mysterious stranger rode up the dark lane.
Revised   The mysterious stranger, **who was carrying a glowing object,** rode up the dark lane.

A subordinate clause as in the second sentence above can act as an adjective, an adverb, or a noun in a complex sentence.

Adjective Clauses

An **adjective** is a word that modifies a noun or pronoun. An **adjective phrase** is a phrase that acts as an adjective. An **adjective clause** is a subordinate clause that acts as an adjective. Remember, a clause has a subject and a verb; a phrase has neither.

Adjective   Mike carried the *apple* box.

Adjective Phrase Mike carried the box *of apples.*

Adjective Clause Mike carried the box *that held the apples.*

An adjective clause usually comes immediately after the word it modifies, as in the following examples:

I know the cave *that you are talking about.*

Ms. Peters is the one *who asked about you.*

The train, *which had been stopped,* was delayed an hour.

Relative Pronouns and Adjective Clauses

Adjective clauses are sometimes introduced by subordinating conjunctions. More often, however, adjective clauses begin with the words *who, whom, whose, that,* or *which.* These words relate the subordinate clause to the word it modifies in the main clause. When used this way, *who, whom, whose, that,* and *which* are called **relative pronouns**.

Relative Pronouns

who   whom   whose   that   which

A relative pronoun relates the adjective clause to a noun or pronoun in the main clause. It also acts as the subject, object, or predicate pronoun of the verb in the adjective clause. It may also be the object of the preposition in the clause.

This is the tree *that was struck by lightning.*
    (*That* is the subject of *was struck.*)

Is Carl the student *whom you met?*
    (*Whom* is the object of *met.*)

Angela is the magician *of whom we were speaking.*
    (*Whom* is the object of the preposition *of.*)

Jon is the musician *who won the contest.*
    (*Who* is the subject of *won.*)

Diagraming Adjective Clauses

Write the adjective clause on its own line below the line for the main clause. Then draw a dotted line from the word that introduces the subordinate clause to the word in the main clause that the adjective clause modifies.

EXAMPLE   Bruce is the person who won the debate.

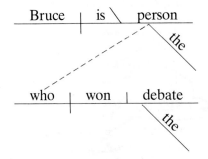

EXAMPLE   Jo is the guitarist to whom we were listening.

```
Jo  |  is  \  guitarist
                 \  the
                   \
we  |  were listening
              \  to
               \
                whom
```

Exercise

Make two columns on your paper. Label them *Adjective Clauses* and *Words Modified*. Write the adjective clauses from the following sentences in the first column. Write the words they modify in the second column. Underline the subject of each adjective clause once and the verb twice.

1. The family that owns the snowmobile lives in the house next door.
2. Burt, who was still awake, smelled the smoke and woke everyone.
3. This is the student whose book was lost.
4. This is the cookbook that has the best recipes.
5. The mayor is a woman whom I admire.
6. Our team, which lost the tournament last year, gets the silver cup.
7. We couldn't find anyone who had seen the accident.
8. We saw the picture that won the contest.
9. It was one of those days when everything went wrong.
10. Your camera is in the closet where we keep the skates.

Adverb Clauses

An **adverb** is a word that modifies a verb, an adjective, or another adverb. An **adverb phrase** is a prepositional phrase used as an adverb. An **adverb clause** is a subordinate clause used as an adverb. Adverbs, adverb phrases, and adverb clauses all tell *where, when, how,* or *to what extent* about the words they modify. In addition, an adverb clause may tell why.

Adverb   Pam sat *down*.

Adverb Phrase   Pam sat *in the rocking chair*.

Adverb Clause   Pam sat *where she would be comfortable*.

An adverb clause contains a subject and a verb, like any clause. It is always introduced by a subordinating conjunction. (See the list of subordinating conjunctions on page 555.)

Diagraming Adverb Clauses

Write the adverb clause on its own line below the line for the main clause. Then, draw a dotted line from the adverb clause to the word it modifies in the main clause. Place the subordinating conjunction on the dotted line.

EXAMPLE   Whenever we arrive on time, we surprise her.

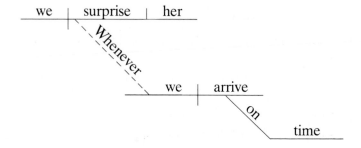

Exercise

Write on your paper the adverb clauses from the following sentences. Underline the subject of each clause once and the verb twice. Then label the subordinating conjunction *SC*.

1. When we arrived in Tokyo, it was cold.
2. We traded our dollars for yen before we left the airport.
3. We traveled with a translator to the small villages, because we did not speak Japanese.
4. We ate plenty of rice because the farmers grow it in rural Japan.
5. If you like fish, you'll be happy in Japan.
6. Although we were tourists, we adjusted quickly to the Japanese life style.

7. We read a guidebook as we waited for a train.
8. When the train stopped in the station, many Japanese students poured onto the platform.
9. We stayed close together as the train approached.
10. Because the trains are so clean, tourists photograph them.

Noun Clauses

Remember that nouns can be used as subjects, as objects of verbs, as predicate words after linking verbs, and as objects of prepositions. A **noun clause** is a clause used as a noun.

A noun clause can be used in any way that a noun is used. Noun clauses do not modify anything because nouns are not modifiers. The following sentences show ways in which noun clauses can be used:

Subject   *What we wanted* was permission to attend the baseball game.

Object   We saw *that you were in a hurry.*

Object of Preposition   Give the clothes to *whoever can use them.* (The clause is the object of the preposition *to.* Notice, however, that *whoever* functions as a subject within the clause.)

Predicate Noun   The answer to our question was *what we had expected.*

A great many noun clauses are introduced by *that* or *what.* Some are introduced by *whatever, whoever,* and *whomever.* Other noun clauses are introduced by *who, whose,* and *whom.* Still others are introduced by *where, when,* and *how.*

You cannot tell the kind of clause from the word that introduces it. You can tell the kind of clause only by the way it is used in a sentence. If the clause is used as a noun, it is a noun clause. If the clause is used as a modifier, it is an adjective clause or an adverb clause.

Wherever he went was a mystery. (noun clause as subject)
No one knew *where we hid.* (noun clause as object)

He left pieces of paper *wherever he went.* (adverb clause)
This is the cave *where we hid.* (adjective clause)

Diagraming Noun Clauses

Diagram a noun clause on a bridge at the place where the clause is used in a sentence. Place the word that introduces the clause on a horizontal line above the clause.

The diagram below shows a sentence with a noun clause as its subject.

    EXAMPLE   That she wasn't coming was certain.

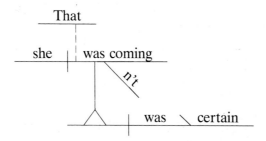

The sentence diagramed below has a noun clause used as the object of the verb. Notice that the part of the diagram that shows the noun clause closely resembles a diagram of a simple sentence.

    EXAMPLE   Donna could see who was coming.

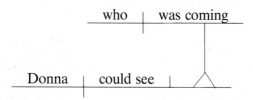

The sentence diagramed below has a preposition with a noun clause used as the object of the preposition.

    EXAMPLE   We were surprised by what happened.

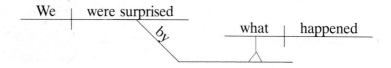

Exercises

A Write the noun clauses from the following sentences. Underline the subject of each clause once and the verb twice.

1. I was just thinking about what you said.
2. Show this card to whoever is at the door.
3. Paula didn't know where Kevin was going.
4. Where we will go on our class trip hasn't been decided.
5. Whoever finds the watch will receive a reward.
6. Why they chose me is a mystery.
7. We wondered who would buy a pink car.
8. Sally knows where the supplies are.
9. Sign the papers for whoever needs them.
10. How you finish so quickly is beyond me.

B Write the following sentences and underline the subordinate clauses. Then tell what kind of clause you underlined (*Adjective Clause, Adverb Clause,* or *Noun Clause*).

1. Can you study while the radio is playing?
2. Before the snowball hit him, Jeff ducked.
3. The plane that leaves at seven shows a feature movie.
4. The experiment that you propose is not possible.
5. Someone said that we would have a holiday tomorrow.
6. My father lived in Montana when he was young.
7. We arrived when Carol was speaking.
8. Is this the book that you want?
9. We did not know who the man was.
10. I do not know why the dog is sick.

C *Write Now* Read a newspaper story about a recent event in your community, or choose a story from your school paper. Make a list of ten verbs that describe the action in the news story. Then write five sentences using those verbs. Be sure you do not copy sentences from the story. Write two complex sentences, two compound sentences, and one simple sentence with a compound verb.

Linking Grammar & Writing

A Writing that contains only simple sentences is choppy and often dull. Rewrite the paragraphs below, changing some simple sentences to compound or complex sentences whenever you can. Use a variety of coordinating conjunctions, subordinating conjunctions, and relative pronouns.

> Last week was a terrible week in our house. We were all sick. Mom and Dad came home from work Monday. Mom and Dad both had upset stomachs. They couldn't get out of bed. I had to bring them everything. I had to make dinner for my sister and me. I had to help my sister with her homework.
>
> Tuesday, Mom and Dad felt better. They were still weak. They couldn't take me to my meeting. A neighbor drove me. During the meeting, I felt sick. I was in bed for four days.

B Certain short sayings, called *aphorisms*, offer advice about how you should conduct your life.

> People who live in glass houses shouldn't throw stones.
> If at first you don't succeed, try, try again.
> If you can't say something nice about a person, don't say anything at all.
> When the going gets tough, the tough get going.

Notice that these aphorisms are in complex sentence form. Write five of your own short sayings, using complex sentences.

Additional Practice

Part 1 Using Compound Sentences Join related sentence pairs to make compound sentences. Use correct punctuation and appropriate conjunctions. Three pairs of sentences are not related and should not be joined.

1. I went to the beach with my friends. We played volleyball.
2. Marie Curie won Nobel Prizes in chemistry and physics. She was born in Poland.
3. Mr. Miguez paid his bills. He balanced his checkbook.
4. I spent two hours studying for the test. I still did not pass it.
5. Redwood trees are related to giant sequoias. Redwoods grow in central California.
6. We can shovel the snow now. We can wait to see if it melts.
7. My mother bought an electric typewriter. She never owned one before.
8. February usually has twenty-eight days. During leap years it has twenty-nine.
9. Frank cooked dinner. Penny washed the dishes.
10. You can rake the leaves. Don't burn them.

Part 2 Complex Sentences Write the subordinate clause in each of the following sentences. Then underline the subject of the subordinate clause once and the verb twice.

11. Don't forget to turn off the lights before you leave for school.
12. The car would not start because the battery was dead.
13. Would you like a magazine to read while you wait?
14. The news media follow the candidate wherever she goes.
15. If my grades do not improve, I will have to quit the basketball team.
16. Let's go to the concert early so that we can get good seats.
17. Although I have read many of Shakespeare's plays, I have never seen one performed.

18. Dad likes to relax in his favorite chair after he finishes the day's work.
19. Arizona was a territory before it became a state.
20. You make the salads while I broil the steaks.

Label each of the following sentences *Simple, Compound,* or *Complex.*

21. The American Legion is an organization of war veterans.
22. Kathy had planned to study for the test this morning, but she overslept.
23. We will be at the airport when your plane lands.
24. Although ants are small, they are extremely strong.
25. We can go to a restaurant for dinner, or we can order a pizza.
26. The Gallaghers own a plumbing repair service.
27. Bulbs can be planted as long as the ground can be worked.
28. Dennis spent many hours at the library in town.
29. The baker made the muffin batter, and then he spooned it into the muffin pans.
30. If you want to ride with us, be at my house at 7:00 A.M.

Part 3 Types of Subordinate Clauses Write the following sentences and underline the subordinate clause. Then tell what kind of clause you underlined (*Adjective Clause, Adverb Clause,* or *Noun Clause*).

31. Everyone knew that I didn't make the team.
32. The mayor fell asleep while the speeches were being given.
33. This is the salesperson who sold me the computer.
34. Lyndon Johnson was a teacher before he became President.
35. The woman who is holding the microphone is a reporter.
36. The kite that is stuck in the tree is mine.
37. Elizabeth Kenny was a nurse who treated polio patients.
38. Whoever broke the window will have to pay for it.
39. Let's listen to the news while we eat dinner.
40. We learned that Angora goats have silky wool coats.
41. The coat that fell off the hook is mine.
42. That book, which won many awards, did not interest me.
43. You should tell the guests where they should sit.
44. They called your number when you were out of the room.
45. We saw Okefenokee Swamp, which is in Georgia and Florida.

Application and Review

Lesson Review

A Recognizing Compound Sentences Write the following sentences. Underline each subject once and each verb twice. Then label each sentence *Simple* or *Compound*.

1. The key was on the table; I hung it on the hook by the back door.
2. Carlos patched and cleaned the sail of the boat every spring.
3. I threw the trash into the basket, but I didn't notice all the newspapers.
4. Maple trees lined and shaded the street in front of the high school.
5. Out-of-town newspapers come in at noon, and Candice buys one on her way home.
6. A wind started about lunchtime and blew hard for the rest of the day.
7. I finished my supper quickly and went outside with my glove and ball.
8. Jose looked toward the source of the noise and then pointed.
9. Joan and Tom planted and fertilized each little tree in the garden.
10. It rained all afternoon; my sister and I stayed in and played chess.

B Recognizing Complex Sentences Write the following sentences. Underline each subject once and each verb twice. Then label each sentence *Simple, Compound,* or *Complex.*

1. The shutters and doors of the house flapped and banged in the wind.
2. Karen groomed four horses, but she didn't have time for the fifth.
3. The tide had come in so that the beach by the pier was under water.

4. Although the bus was full, the driver had not yet started the engine.
5. Our class collected aluminum cans and took them to the recycling center.
6. When Steven opened the kitchen door, two dogs rushed into the warm house.
7. The traffic helicopter flew over the park; that's its usual route.
8. I like short stories, but I really enjoy long, detailed mystery novels.
9. We did not leave the stadium until we were sure of the final score.
10. Provided that it does not rain, we will swim at the public pool this afternoon.

C Recognizing Clauses Make two columns on your paper. Label them *Subordinate Clauses* and *Kinds of Clauses*. Write the subordinate clauses from the following sentences in the first column. In the second column, write *Adjective Clause, Adverb Clause,* or *Noun Clause* to show what kind of clause each is. Then, underline the subject of each clause once and the verb twice.

1. If the shelf is too low, move it up.
2. Whoever wins the regional tennis finals goes to the state meet.
3. Ben Franklin, who invented bifocals, the electrical generator, and the Franklin stove, was a famous statesman.
4. The postcards that you sent us from South America arrived today.
5. When the trumpet fanfare began, members of the audience returned to their seats.
6. How this sewing machine works is what Abraham would like to know.
7. Many of us did not agree with what the speaker said.
8. Maurita said that her report was about Renaissance painters.
9. Peter, who had just finished the marathon, looked very tired.
10. Lauren hurt her ankle as she was jumping the hurdles at the track meet.

Chapter Review

A Recognizing Compound and Complex Sentences Write *Simple, Compound,* or *Complex* to show what kind of sentence each of the following is.

1. The Girl Scouts are selling cookies, and the Boy Scouts are selling popcorn.
2. While Jeremy has braces on his teeth, he cannot chew gum.
3. The final basket was scored as the buzzer rang.
4. When we have steak for dinner, Dad bakes potatoes.
5. The firefighters rescued the child, and everyone cheered.
6. Whomever you choose for your team must complete an entry blank.
7. Maureen brushes and flosses her teeth twice every day.
8. Troy wears glasses, and he looks very good in them.
9. The assignment that Mr. Henderson gave us will take hours.
10. Terri is training seriously for the gymnastics competition; she practices three hours every day.

B Recognizing Clauses Make three columns on your paper. Label them *Adjective Clauses, Adverb Clauses,* and *Noun Clauses.* Write the subordinate clauses from the following sentences in the correct column.

1. Martin Luther King told the world that he had a dream.
2. *Bartlett's Familiar Quotations,* which is a valuable reference book, has a 600-page index.
3. Since the pipes were insulated with asbestos, the building was declared unsafe.
4. The elevator that carries people to the top of the Sears Tower in Chicago travels at about twenty miles per hour.
5. No one could tell me what Susan's arrival time would be.
6. Because she wanted a car, Gina saved her money.
7. Lewis Carroll, who was a mathematics professor, wrote *Alice's Adventures in Wonderland.*
8. How the team lost is beyond my comprehension.
9. Iris will help whoever cannot solve the equation.
10. Miguel joined the debate team because he wants to be a lawyer.

28
Understanding Subject and Verb Agreement

When we encounter things that do not quite make sense, like a dog wearing a sweatshirt and shades, or students wearing costume parts, the effect can be humorous.

When we encounter sentences that are not quite right, however, the effect can be confusing. When the subject and verb of a sentence do not agree, the sentence as a whole will not work well.

In this chapter you will study how to make sure subjects and verbs agree in number in the many types of situations you will encounter in your writing.

1
Making Subjects and Verbs Agree in Number

> The subject and verb in a sentence must agree in number.

When a word refers to one thing, it is **singular**. When it refers to more than one thing, it is **plural**. **Number** refers to whether the word is singular or plural.

A verb must agree in number with its subject. A singular subject takes a singular verb. A plural subject requires a plural verb.

To find the subject of a sentence, first find the verb. Then ask *who* or *what* before it. Keep this questioning pattern in mind, and you will have no trouble with agreement, even when words come between the subject and its verb.

> One of the players is my sister.
> (*Is* is the verb. Who is? One. *One* is the subject.)

Notice in the examples below that the third person singular of the verbs ends in *s*. Plural verbs, however, do not end in *s*.

Singular	Plural
The bird *sings*.	The birds *sing*.
She *listens*.	They *listen*.

Interrupting Words and Phrases

Watch for phrases that lie between the verb and its subject:

One of the eggs *was* broken.   The *pens* on sale *are* red.

The subject of the verb is never found in a prepositional phrase. In the two sentences above, the nouns *eggs* and *sale* cannot be subjects.

Other phrases can also divide subject and verb. Common examples are phrases beginning with the words *with, together with, including, as well as, along with,* and *in addition to.*

The *principal,* in addition to the teachers, *is* here.

Exercises

A Write the correct form of the verbs given in parentheses. Make sure the verb agrees with the italicized subject.

1. The second *store* past the post office (sell, sells) tapes.
2. The *captain*, along with the crew, (scan, scans) the sky.
3. Several *pages* in this book (is, are) missing.
4. The *drawings* on display (was, were) done by students.
5. The *bus* with our opponents (arrive, arrives) at three.
6. *Rules* for the contest (is, are) on the cereal box.
7. *Calls* by officials sometimes (anger, angers) fans.
8. A *shutter,* with slats missing, (flaps, flap) in the wind.
9. *One* of my front teeth (are, is) loose.
10. A *bus* to downtown stores (leave, leaves) every hour.

B Make two columns on your paper. Label them *Subjects* and *Verbs*. Write the subjects from the following sentences in the first column. In the second column, write the correct form of the verbs given in parentheses.

1. The doctor, together with her staff, (are, is) here every Monday.
2. The edges of the playing field (was, were) rimmed with ice.
3. My jacket, as well as my shoes, (is, are) wet.
4. Each of the homerooms (display, displays) artwork.
5. Antique cars like that (cost, costs) thousands of dollars.
6. Our request for money and provisions (was, were) granted.
7. The club, including Terry and Chris, (meet, meets) today.
8. The players on the baseball team (like, likes) their coach.
9. The doors on the house (was, were) painted blue.
10. Kate, along with Gabe, (go, goes) to tennis lessons.

C *Write Now* Imagine a club or group you would like to start. Write a one-paragraph description of the club or group. Describe the requirements for membership. In your description, include at least four interrupting phrases. Here are some suggestions:

as well as . . .   along with . . .
including . . .   in addition to . . .

Reread your paragraph. Be sure that subjects and verbs agree.

2
Compound Subjects

Compound subjects joined by *and* take a plural verb.
When subjects are joined by *or* or *nor,* the verb agrees
with the part nearer to it.

Compound subjects joined by *and* take a plural verb regardless of the number of each part. Consider these examples:

> The truck and the trailer *were* badly damaged.
> Trucks and trailers *are* forbidden from the far left lane.

When the parts of a compound subject are joined by *or* or *nor,* the verb agrees with the nearer part. Read the following sentences:

> Either Mom or the boys *have* come home.
> Neither the boys nor Mom *has* called.
> Either the musicians or their leader *has* your music.

Exercises

A Write on your paper the correct form of the verbs given in parentheses.

1. Al and Ken (hasn't, haven't) finished repairing their car.
2. Either the coach or the co-captains (call, calls) time.
3. Both winter and summer (is, are) mild here.
4. Either a raccoon or some dogs (has, have) raided the garbage.
5. The evening news and the late edition (report, reports) the sports results of the day.
6. Neither the tent nor the sleeping bags (arrive, arrives) until tomorrow.
7. Both the tugboats and the ferry (dock, docks) here.
8. Corrine and I (am, are) arriving on the noon bus.
9. Neither my gym shoes nor my baseball uniform (need, needs) laundering.
10. Tom and I (refuse, refuses) to disagree with our coach.

B Make two columns on your paper. Label them *Compound Subjects* and *Verbs*. Write the compound subjects from the following sentences in the first column. In the second column, write the correct form of the verbs given in parentheses.

1. Death Valley and Mount Whitney (is, are) in California.
2. Neither Illinois nor Indiana (have, has) mountain ranges.
3. Both Alabama and Kentucky (provide, provides) caves for spelunking.
4. Kyle's mother and father (love, loves) the coast of Maine.
5. Neither Tina nor Maria (want, wants) to leave Boston.
6. Jason and Stacy (visit, visits) the St. Paul winter carnival.
7. Both the Space Center and the Alamo (is, are) in Texas.
8. The badger and the deer (is, are) animals of Wisconsin.
9. Either Arizona or Nevada (is, are) a good place to retire.
10. Montana and Idaho (has, have) widely scattered populations.

Grammar in Action

Incorrect subject–verb agreement can confuse your readers and listeners. Consider these examples:

Incorrect   The latches on the gate *is* broken.
Correct   The latches on the gate *are* broken.

Notice how important subject–verb agreement is for clarity. Someone might misunderstand the incorrect example and think the *gate* is broken, since *gate* and *is* are both singular. In the correct example, the plural verb *are* refers to *latches*.

Writing Activity   Rewrite the following paragraph. As you write, edit the paragraph so that each verb agrees with its subject.

> The passengers on the ferry huddles in the cabin to escape the heavy rain. The sounds of the motor makes them think that the boat might be about to stall. The sight of houses on the island look so comforting, as huge drops of rain continues to fall.

3
Indefinite Pronouns

Some *indefinite pronouns* are singular and some are plural. A few can be either singular or plural.

Study the chart of indefinite pronouns below. Then study the examples that follow. Notice that interrupting words do not change subject–verb agreement.

Indefinite Pronouns

Singular			Plural
another	either	nobody	both
anybody	everybody	no one	few
anyone	everyone	one	many
anything	everything	somebody	several
each	neither	someone	

Singular	Plural
Everybody *has* a job.	Several *have* already phoned.
Neither of us *is* ready.	Both of the dogs *are* collies.

The words *some, all,* and *most* may be either singular or plural. They are singular when they refer to a singular word and plural when they refer to a plural word or words.

Singular	Plural
All of the *park* is dusty.	All of the *guests* are here.
Most of the *work* seems easy.	Most of the *books* are new.

Exercises

A Write on your paper the correct form of the verbs given in parentheses.

1. Another of those talk shows (begin, begins) tonight.
2. Many of Debbie's friends (were, was) in the choir.
3. Most of the barn (need, needs) a new coat of paint.

4. Someone (has, have) my notebook.
5. Some of the bread (look, looks) moldy.
6. No one in the class (was, were) absent from school this morning.
7. Several of the reporters (use, uses) that news service.
8. All of the students (are, is) asked to complete this personal health form.
9. All of the class (go, goes) to the safety assembly.
10. Each of the band members (rent, rents) a uniform.

B Make two columns on your paper. Label them *Subjects* and *Verbs*. Write the subjects from the following sentences in the first column. In the second column, write the correct form of the verbs given in parentheses.

1. Few of nature's attacks (cause, causes) as much destruction of life and property as a major earthquake.
2. Some of the thousands that occur each year (pass, passes) unnoticed, however.
3. Many of the largest earthquakes (is, are) beneath the sea.
4. No one among us nonscientists ever (feel, feels) them.
5. Some of the biggest quakes (have, has) been reported in ancient writings.
6. One of the strongest earthquakes ever (was, were) recorded in Alaska in 1964.
7. Each of the big quakes (leaves, leave) deep scars on the earth.
8. Most of the world's major earthquakes (have, has) occurred along a line known as the "earthquake belt."
9. Each of the nations along this line (pay, pays) close attention to seismologists' reports.
10. Almost all of the world's earthquake activity (occurs, occur) in regions that border on the Pacific Ocean.

4
Other Problems of Agreement

The pronouns *he, she,* and *it* are used with the verb *does.*
All other personal pronouns are used with *do.*
   In sentences beginning with *here, there,* and *where,* the
subject comes after the verb.

Agreement with Forms of *Do* The verb form *does* calls for a
singular noun, and *do* calls for a plural noun. However, agreement of *do* with pronouns is not so simple. The forms *does* and
doesn't are used with *he, she,* and *it*. The forms *do* and *don't* are
used with all the other personal pronouns.

He *doesn't* swim well.
She *does* like you.
It *doesn't* look good.

I *don't* dance.
We *do* know your cousin.
You *don't* agree, do you?
They *do* not often visit us.

Here, There, Where In sentences beginning with *here, there,* and
where, the subject comes after the verb. Find the subject to
check the number of the verb.

Here *is* your ticket.
Where *is* the projector?

There *are* the keys.

Exercises

A Write on your paper the correct form of the verbs given in
parentheses.

1. It (doesn't, don't) look as if the rain will stop soon.
2. Where (was, were) she taking those packages?
3. Here (is, are) the team's tube socks and T-shirts.
4. There (go, goes) that car alarm again.
5. That idea (doesn't, don't) appeal to me.
6. Where (is, are) the Seven Wonders of the World?
7. Here (is, are) all the sheet metal that I could find.
8. He (doesn't, don't) want to go apple-picking at the farm with
   our 4-H club.

9. Where (are, is) all the deer in that zoo?
10. Here (are, is) one of your gloves.

B Write on your paper the correct form of the verbs given in parentheses.

1. It just (doesn't, don't) make sense.
2. There (are, is) many reasons for the growth of a city.
3. There (was, were) few skiers on the chairlift.
4. Jeanne and I (do, does) plan to study tonight.
5. Here (is, are) the diamonds our baseball teams always use.
6. She (doesn't, don't) like camping in the Rockies.
7. I (does, do) not know which assignment to choose.
8. Where (is, are) the paintings by Georgia O'Keeffe?
9. There (seem, seems) to be less traffic than usual.
10. Here (are, is) some flowers from my grandparents' garden.

C *Proofreading* Proofread the following paragraphs. Then re-write them correctly. Check especially for errors in subject–verb agreement.

You have probaly heard of the "Seven Wonders of the World." There is realy more than one list of the "Seven Wonders," however. You probably does know that the ancient world had its list of wunders. You does agree that the magnificent pyramids in Egypt were an ancient wonder. There were also the light-house of Alexandria in Egypt. Babylon was known for its Hanging Gardens, built by King Nebuchadnezzar II. Does you know any of the other wonders of the ancient world?

There is other lists of wonders One is the "Seven Wonders of the Natural World." Do you know any of these? Mount Everest is one, and the Grand Canyon is another. You may have heard of the "Seven Won-ders of the Modern World." Three of these wonders are in North America. These is the Golden Gate Bridge, the Empire State Building, and the Alcan Highway. What places do the Alcan Highway con-nect? What body of water do the Golden Gate Bridge cross? Where are the Empire State Building?

Linking Grammar & Writing

A Read the Bill of Rights in an encyclopedia. Working with a partner, write your own bill of rights for the school of your dreams. This list will have three sections.

First, one of you will list ten students' rights, beginning each with an indefinite pronoun. Some suggested beginnings for the list of student rights follow:

> Each of the students . . .
> Many of the students . . .
> All of the students . . .

At the same time, the other will draw up a list of ten rights for teachers. Like the students' rights, each of the teachers' rights should begin with an indefinite pronoun. (See the list on page 574 for more suggestions.)

Finally, both of you will add a list of five items that state common rights of both students and teachers. Use phrases beginning with words such as *with*, *including*, *as well as*, and *in addition to*.

Diego Rivera mural

B Some of the most-loved books have taken readers to imaginary lands. Alice visited Wonderland and went Beyond the Looking Glass. Gulliver visited Lilliput, among other places; Meg Wallace travels through space and time in *A Wrinkle in Time*; and many have visited King Arthur's court in stories and verse.

Imagine that you find yourself in another land, perhaps even another time. Describe the people (or creatures) there. How do they look? talk? behave? How do they treat each other? In what kind of houses do they live? Or do they live in houses at all? Do they have cities? What do they eat? In your description, use some of the indefinite pronouns listed in the box on page 574. Be sure that all your verbs agree with their subjects.

Additional Practice

Part 1 Agreement in Number Make each of the following sentences singular or plural as directed. Write the correct choices of the words in parentheses on your paper.

1. (One, Both) of my brothers (work, works) in the building trades. *Plural*
2. The (shrubs, shrub) growing next to the house (need, needs) trimming. *Singular*
3. The (skirt, skirts), as well as the jackets, (is, are) made of wool. *Singular*
4. My (neighbor, neighbors) (teaches, teach) at the local community college. *Plural*
5. The (insects, insect) (try, tries) to escape from the spider's web. *Plural*
6. (He, They) (work, works) at a florist's shop after school. *Singular*
7. The (stork, storks) (have, has) strong wings and long legs. *Plural*
8. (Both, Neither) of the doors (was, were) locked. *Singular*
9. My (aunt, aunts), in addition to my grandparents, (is, are) visiting us. *Singular*
10. (Most, One) of the students (goes, go) home for lunch. *Plural*

Part 2 Agreement with Compound Subjects Write the correct form of the verbs given in parentheses.

11. Illinois, Kansas, and Ohio (is, are) in the Midwest.
12. The teachers and the principal (attend, attends) the school board meeting.
13. Neither the college nor the high schools (have, has) a hockey team.
14. Mother and I (am, are) collecting food and clothing for needy people.
15. Neither the cucumber plants nor the pepper plant (has, have) any flowers.
16. Either Ms. Schwartz or Mr. Allie (is, are) in charge of the fair.

17. The gopher, the porcupine, and the rat (is, are) rodents.
18. Claude Monet and Edgar Degas (was, were) part of a group of French painters called impressionists.
19. Either your sister or your brother (has, have) your baseball glove.
20. Neither the windows nor the door (is, are) open.

Part 3 Agreement with Indefinite Pronouns Make two columns on your paper. Label them *Simple Subjects* and *Verbs*. Write the simple subjects from the following sentences in the first column. In the second column, write the correct form of the verbs given in parentheses.

21. Each of the actresses (want, wants) the part.
22. Several of the stamps in that collection (are, is) rare.
23. Most of the discussion (was, were) about last night's storm.
24. Nobody (makes, make) me laugh like Jackie Gleason did.
25. Each of the countries (are, is) a signer of the Warsaw Pact.
26. One of the children (have, has) German measles.
27. Someone (leaves, leave) fresh flowers on my doorstep each morning.
28. Some of the boards (have, has) rusty nails sticking out of them.
29. One of Robin Hood's followers (were, was) Little John.
30. Neither of the boxers (hear, hears) the bell.

Part 4 Other Problems of Agreement Write on your paper the correct form of the verbs given in parentheses.

31. She (doesn't, don't) like music videos.
32. Where (is, are) the Native American artifacts?
33. There (was, were) a police officer directing traffic into the ballpark.
34. Here (are, is) the lumber for repairing the fence.
35. It (doesn't, don't) matter if you are a little late.
36. There (is, are) thousands of mystery writers in our country.
37. Here (is, are) one of the names that you requested.
38. She (doesn't, don't) agree with her friend.
39. Where (is, are) Libya and Algeria located?
40. There (was, were) only a few cars on the highway.

Application and Review

Lesson Review

A Making Verbs Agree with Their Subjects Write on your paper the correct form of the verbs given in parentheses.

1. The sandbars in the Mississippi (cause, causes) accidents.
2. Some sections of the city (has, have) no bus service.
3. Three students' paintings, including mine, (was, were) chosen to compete in the state fair.
4. That lady in the gray sweatsuit (jog, jogs) five miles.
5. The new books in the library (is, are) on a special shelf.
6. The answers to the exercise (is, are) in the back of the textbook.
7. The evidence on these films (looks, look) convincing.
8. The photographers on the yearbook staff (is, are) Jeffery and Patti.
9. The price of the German binoculars (are, is) too high.
10. Our team, including the coach and the cheerleaders, (take, takes) the bus from here.

B Using Verbs with Compound Subjects Write on your paper the correct form of the verbs given in parentheses.

1. Neither the fenders nor the license plate (was, were) dented.
2. The principal and the teachers (organize, organizes) a student-faculty softball game every year.
3. Either my alarm clock or the clock in the family room (is, are) wrong.
4. If school is canceled, the principal or one of the secretaries (telephone, telephones) the radio station.
5. Both Chico and his brother (was, were) there.
6. Neither porcupine quills nor skunks (stop, stops) our hunting dog Rusty.
7. Either Sean or his grandparents usually (pick, picks) up the mail each day.

8. Yogurt and frozen yogurt (come, comes) in a variety of interesting flavors.
9. Both the fire department and city hall (has, have) tours for school groups.
10. Either a van or a truck (suit, suits) our purpose.

C Using Verbs with Indefinite Pronouns Write on your paper the correct form of the verbs given in parentheses.

1. Some of these stamps (don't, doesn't) stick.
2. Several of the entrants (wasn't, weren't) ready.
3. Not one of the radio stations (has, have) publicized our school fair.
4. Most of the time (was, were) wasted.
5. Everything on the two bottom shelves (belong, belongs) to my brother David.
6. All of the fenceposts (has, have) snow on them.
7. Anything made of metal (was, were) immediately magnetized.
8. Both of the gas pumps (is, are) working.
9. Nobody in the bleachers (cheer, cheers) louder than our Pep Club members.
10. Most of our art supplies (come, comes) from school.

D Choosing the Correct Verb in Special Cases Make two columns on your paper. Label them *Subjects* and *Verbs*. Write the subjects from the following sentences in the first column. In the second column, write the correct form of the verbs given in parentheses.

1. Where (is, are) the fire trucks?
2. Here (is, are) the newspaper story about the eclipse.
3. There (goes, go) the runners.
4. Sam (doesn't, don't) ever stop reading.
5. Here (is, are) the photographs that Heather picked out.
6. Where (is, are) the envelopes for these letters?
7. There (isn't, aren't) any time to waste.
8. (Don't, Doesn't) the *Orient Express* run any more?
9. Here (is, are) your tickets for the carnival.
10. She (doesn't, don't) know how to do the butterfly stroke.

Chapter Review

A Choosing the Correct Verb Write on your paper the correct form of the verbs given in parentheses.

1. Each of the crossing guards (wears, wear) a bright yellow slicker when it rains.
2. A staple or several paper clips (is, are) needed to keep the papers together.
3. One of the pipes above the lockers (leak, leaks).
4. The President, together with a group of senators, (is, are) holding a press conference.
5. Each of the pages in the review sections (contain, contains) a practice test.
6. Neither Alexander nor Michelle (want, wants) to be on the baseball team.
7. Most of the assignments (require, requires) library research.
8. Everyone in the laboratory (is, are) careful around the flammable liquids.
9. Where (is, are) the fire exits?
10. It (doesn't, don't) ever get cold enough here for ice skating.

B Choosing the Correct Verb Write on your paper the correct form of the verbs given in parentheses.

1. Neither of those pencils (has, have) an eraser.
2. Kim, as well as both of her sisters, (has, have) a weekend baby-sitting job.
3. Few of the families in our area (belong, belongs) to the community center.
4. Either the coach or the team members always (thank, thanks) the cheerleaders for their support.
5. One of the car doors (is, are) frozen shut.
6. Both Bill Cosby and Lily Tomlin (is, are) delightfully funny comedians.
7. There (isn't, aren't) enough sandwiches for everyone.
8. The words in the glossary (help, helps) me understand the story.
9. (Don't, Doesn't) anybody know how to run the projector?
10. Here (is, are) all the information you will need.

29
Using Verbals

First one domino fell, <u>knocking</u> over the next one in line. Then the <u>clicking</u> and <u>clattering</u> increased as they all began <u>to fall</u>, one after another, in a rush of <u>tumbling</u> dominoes.

In addition to the parts of speech you have learned about already, there are three other kinds of words—infinitives, participles, and gerunds. They are called verbals. As the example above shows, verbals add movement and interest to sentences. This chapter explains how you can use verbals to make your writing more varied.

1
Infinitives

An *infinitive* is a verbal that usually appears with the word *to* before it. *To* is called the *sign of the infinitive*.

You have learned that there are eight parts of speech: nouns, pronouns, verbs, adverbs, adjectives, prepositions, conjunctions, and interjections. In addition, the English language contains three other kinds of words: infinitives, participles, and gerunds. These words are called verbals.

A **verbal** is a word that is formed from a verb but acts as another part of speech. In this chapter you will study all three kinds of verbals. You will learn how they can add interest and variety to spoken and written sentences.

The infinitive is the easiest verbal to recognize. An **infinitive** is a form of a verb that usually appears after the word *to*. *To* is called the **sign of the infinitive**.

> to go   to see   to run   to walk

The word *to* is also used as a preposition. It is a preposition if it is followed by a noun or pronoun that is its object. It is the sign of the infinitive if a verb follows it.

> We went *to the park.* (prepositional phrase)
> We wanted *to swim.* (infinitive)

Because infinitives are formed from verbs, they are like verbs in several ways. Infinitives may, for example, have objects. They may also be modified by adverbs. The infinitive with its objects and modifiers is an **infinitive phrase**. The italicized groups of words in the sentences below are infinitive phrases.

> Chris learned *to run a lathe.*
>   (*Lathe* is the direct object of the infinitive *to run.*)
> We tried *to give the dog a bath.*
>   (*Dog* is the indirect object, and *bath* is the direct object of *to give.*)
> You will need *to work fast.*
>   (*Fast* is an adverb modifying *to work.*)

The Split Infinitive

In an infinitive phrase, a modifier is sometimes placed between the word *to* and the verb. A modifier in this position is said to split the infinitive. Usually, a split infinitive sounds awkward and should be avoided in writing and speaking.

Awkward Ann expects to *easily* win.
Better Ann expects to win *easily*.

Uses of Infinitives

Infinitives and infinitive phrases can be used in three ways: as nouns, as adjectives, and as adverbs. You remember that nouns are used as subjects and objects of verbs. Infinitives and infinitive phrases can be used as subjects, as objects, and in other ways that nouns are used.

Subject *To leave early* is sometimes impolite.
  (*To leave early* is the subject of *is*.)
Object Sue wanted *to leave*.
  (*To leave* is the object of *wanted*.)

Infinitives and infinitive phrases can also be used as modifiers. If the infinitive or infinitive phrase modifies a noun or pronoun, it is used as an adjective. If it modifies a verb, adjective, or adverb, it is used as an adverb.

Adjective The catcher is the player *to watch*.
  (*To watch* modifies the predicate noun *player*.)
Adverb Tickets for the big game are hard *to get*.
  (*To get* modifies the predicate adjective *hard*.)
Adverb Rick went *to see the doctor*.
  (*To see the doctor* modifies the verb *went*.)

Exercises

A Make four columns on your paper. Label them *Subjects*, *Adjectives*, *Adverbs*, and *Direct Objects*. Write the italicized infinitives and infinitive phrases from the following sentences in the correct column.

1. Mr. Lee wants *to explain the new procedures to the staff*.
2. Pam came *to join us for lunch*.

3. *To finish this project Monday* is my assignment.
4. We tried *to remember the address.*
5. Amy has someone *to help her.*
6. Do you want *to play tennis after school?*
7. The vet came *to see our horses.*
8. *To read all the plays by Shakespeare* is my goal.
9. Bill ran down the stairs *to get a flashlight.*
10. Nellie has homework *to do.*

B Make four columns on your paper. Label them *Subjects, Adjectives, Adverbs,* and *Direct Objects.* Write the infinitives and infinitive phrases from the following sentences in the correct column.

1. To clean my room is my plan for the afternoon.
2. I want to give you the good news.
3. Rebecca has a key to open the darkroom.
4. We went to visit my grandparents.
5. My brother plans to cook dinner for all of us.
6. To read your notes is very difficult.
7. That table is too heavy to lift by yourself.
8. I have learned to speak Spanish at school.
9. Our class chose three topics to write about.
10. The field is too wet to play our game.

C *Proofreading* Proofread the following paragraph. Then rewrite it, correcting any errors. Pay particular attention to the placement of modifiers in infinitive phrases.

Janice loves learn new skills, so she often takes night classes at her local college. This sumer she learned how to properly canoe. She wanted to also take a self-defense class, but the class was full. In the winter she hopes to learn cross-country skiing quickley. Than she will be able to go on a ski trip with her friends in Febuary.

2
Participles

A *participle* is a verbal that always acts as an adjective.

You have learned that one of the principal parts of a verb is the past participle. The **past participle** is formed by adding -*d* or -*ed* to the present tense: *walk, walked.* The past participles of irregular verbs do not follow this rule and have to be learned separately: *bring, brought; ring, rung.*

There is another kind of participle, called the present participle. A **present participle** is formed by adding -*ing* to the present tense of any verb: *walk, walking; bring, bringing.*

Participles may be used as parts of verb phrases: *had turned, am singing.* When used as verbals, however, both past and present participles always function as adjectives. A participle modifies either a noun or a pronoun.

Smiling, Jan accepted the award.
(*Smiling* is a present participle modifying the noun *Jan.*)

Delayed, he rushed up the steps.
(*Delayed* is a past participle modifying *he.*)

Because participles are formed from verbs, they can have objects and be modified by adverbs. The participle with its objects and modifiers forms a **participial phrase**.

Turning the pages, Barb learned new facts.
(*Turning the pages* is a participial phrase modifying Barb; *pages* is the object of the participle *turning.*)

Turning suddenly, Jean bumped into Ms. Wood.
(*Turning suddenly* is a participial phrase modifying *Jean; suddenly* is an adverb modifying the participle *turning.*)

Completely exhausted, the swimmer crawled out of the pool.
(*Completely exhausted* is a participial phrase modifying *swimmer; completely* is an adverb modifying the participle *exhausted.*)

Exercises

A Write the participles and participial phrases from the following sentences.

1. Exhausted, the runners crossed the finish line.
2. Moving effortlessly, the skaters danced across the ice.
3. Crossing the old bridge, she passed the old store and stable.
4. Watch for the gravel truck leaving the quarry.
5. You may find this alarming news.
6. Hidden by the bushes, the cat silently watched us.
7. Clutching the receiver, Ruth listened intently.
8. The movers left the couch sitting in the hallway.
9. Emil forgot the paperback book lying on the table.
10. Breathing deeply, Nan bent her knees and lifted the box.

B Make two columns on your paper. Label them *Participles and Participial Phrases* and *Words Modified*. Write the participles and participial phrases in the first column. Write the words they modify in the second column. If the understood *you* is the word modified, write *you* in the second column.

1. You should be careful putting together a computer.
2. A broken monitor is useless.
3. A disk drive, knocked out of alignment, will not work.
4. Attach a cord connecting the monitor to the computer.
5. Assured of the correct kind of electricity, you can plug the computer into the wall.
6. A spike protector protects the computer from electrical surges coming through the wire.
7. A computer placed on a flat desktop is easiest to use.
8. Place the keyboard in front of the computer, leaving space to insert disks.
9. Do not leave the computer collecting dust in a corner.
10. Good care will keep your computer running for a long time.

C *Write Now* Imagine that you have traveled in a time machine to the American Revolution. Your parents have just come home from a town meeting. Write a paragraph about what they tell you they learned at the meeting. Use at least two participial phrases.

3
Gerunds

A *gerund* is a verbal that is used as a noun.

A **gerund** is a verb form used as a noun. Adding *-ing* to the present form of a verb creates a gerund. Gerunds can be used in all the ways nouns are used: subjects, objects, predicate words.

> *Swimming* is good exercise.
> (*Swimming* is a gerund, the subject of *is*.)
> Karen likes *riding*.
> (*Riding* is a gerund, the object of *likes*.)
> The time for *wrestling* has been changed.
> (*Wrestling* is a gerund, the object of the preposition *for*.)

Because gerunds are formed from verbs, they can have objects and can be modified by adverbs. Because they are used as nouns, they can also be modified by adjectives and by prepositional phrases. A **gerund phrase** consists of a gerund with its objects and modifiers. Look at the following examples of gerund phrases:

> *Riding a horse* scares Kitt.
> (*Riding* is a gerund; *horse* is the object of *riding*.)
> *Running uphill* is difficult.
> (*Running* is a gerund; *uphill* is an adverb modifying *running*.)
> *Careful reading* requires concentration.
> (*Reading* is a gerund; *careful* is an adjective modifying *reading*.)
> *Cycling in city traffic* is frustrating.
> (*Cycling* is a gerund; *in city traffic* is a prepositional phrase modifying *cycling*.)

Gerund or Participle?

Both the gerund and the present participle are created by adding *-ing* to the present form of the verb. How can you tell whether the word is a gerund or a participle? It depends on how the word is used in a sentence. When it is used as a modifier, it is a participle. When it is used as a noun, it is a gerund.

Walking is good exercise.

(*Walking* here is a gerund, the subject of *is*.)

Walking fast, we overtook the others.

(*Walking* here is a participle modifying *we; fast* is an adverb modifying *walking*.)

Exercises

A Make three columns on your paper. Label them *Subjects, Direct Objects,* and *Objects of Prepositions*. Write each gerund and gerund phrase from the following sentences in the correct column.

1. Danielle enjoys skydiving.
2. Cleaning the attic was not my idea of a good time.
3. My uncle specializes in abstract painting.
4. The summer adventure trip features rafting down the Colorado River.
5. Putting on a play requires teamwork.
6. Skating on the lake in winter is fun.
7. That dog specializes in digging.
8. Last summer, Joe learned the sport of fencing.
9. Driving to Alaska was a long, interesting experience.
10. Clare likes walking in the rain.

B Make three columns on your paper. Label them *Gerunds and Gerund Phrases, Participles and Participial Phrases,* and *Words Modified*. Write the verbals from the following sentences in the correct column. In the third column, write the words modified by the participles and participial phrases.

1. In 1849, there was a rush of settlers moving west.
2. Responding to news about gold, 80,000 people packed all of their possessions and journeyed to California.
3. Many of the settlers and their families got to California by sailing.
4. Panning for gold was their new occupation.
5. Sifting through river water, prospectors sought their fortunes.
6. The key to success was finding the right spot.
7. Discovering gold was every California newcomer's dream.
8. However, few were successful at finding gold there.

Prospectors find gold by washing ore in a process called "cradling."

9. Looking for gold, some miners went into the mountains.
10. Some prospectors trampled farms, stealing cattle.

Grammar in Action

Sometimes you can join two related sentences with a verbal. Remove the subject of one sentence and make its verb a verbal.

> Dan arrived today. He helped with the party.
> Dan arrived today to help with the party. (infinitive)

> The rain came down hard. It washed away the new seeds.
> The rain came down hard, washing away the new seeds.
>   (participle)

> Kim rode carelessly. He hit a fence.
> Riding carelessly, Kim hit a fence. (participle)

Writing Activity Rewrite the following paragraph using verbals to combine sentences where possible.

> Yesterday, Michele decided something. She signed up for a creative writing class. Her first assignment was to write a tale she had heard as a child. She thought back to when her family lived in Bombay. Michele remembered many fascinating stories she had been told there. She wrote down some story ideas. That made her feel enthusiastic about the class.

Linking Grammar & Writing

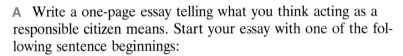

A Write a one-page essay telling what you think acting as a responsible citizen means. Start your essay with one of the following sentence beginnings:

> Acting as a responsible citizen means . . .
> To act as a responsible citizen, I must . . .
> Acting as a responsible citizen, I . . .

Use as many verbals as you can in your essay. Underline all of the verbals you have used.

B Compare two hobbies that you might be interested in trying. Some possibilities are skateboarding and sledding, reading and keeping a diary, playing folk music on a guitar and studying classical piano. Write about the good points and the bad points of each hobby. Also write about similarities and differences between the two hobbies. Use each kind of verbal as you write.

C Imagine that today is January 1. Make a list of ten resolutions concerning one area in which you hope to improve during the coming year. You might want to focus on improving an athletic skill, raising your grades, or being a more agreeable family member. For example, you might write "I resolve to run three miles every day." Use infinitives as subjects, objects, and modifiers.

Additional Practice

Part 1 Infinitives Write each infinitive and infinitive phrase from the following sentences and tell whether it is used as a *Subject, Adjective, Adverb,* or *Direct Object.*

1. My parents and I plan to take a canoe trip.
2. Crop dusters are used to spray farmers' fields with chemicals.
3. Mrs. White always has interesting stories to tell.
4. To forget the song's words is an embarrassment for a professional singer.
5. You must study to get a good grade on the test.
6. My brother's French class wants to visit France next summer.
7. The store was very crowded, and I could not find anyone to help me.
8. To become a documentary film maker is Marcy's ambition.
9. Katy tried to call you last night.
10. To direct foreign policy is the duty of the President of the United States.

Part 2 Participles Each of the following sentences contains a participle or participial phrase. Write the participle or phrase in each sentence. Then write the word that it modifies.

11. Who left the orange juice sitting on the kitchen counter?
12. A dripping faucet can send gallons of water down the drain.
13. Delighted, Mr. Wozniak accepted the trophy on behalf of his volleyball team.
14. Last night, a person dressed in a gorilla suit came to our front door.
15. Weeping, the boy told his mother about the accident.
16. Hearing the announcer's voice, she realized that it was her uncle.
17. Our coach, pacing along the sidelines, seemed annoyed and frustrated.
18. The written word has enormous power.
19. Singing the national anthem, we all felt proud to be Americans.

20. The golden eagle swooping down on its prey was a magnificent sight.
21. The wooden bridge spanning the river is old and in need of repair.
22. Excited, the children rushed to get into line for the roller coaster ride.
23. Walking on the moon in 1969, Neil Armstrong earned a place in history.
24. Protected by metal armor, the soldiers mounted their horses and charged into battle.
25. Hit by a severe earthquake in 1906, San Francisco lay in ruins.

Part 3 Gerunds Make three columns on your paper. Label them *Gerunds and Gerund Phrases, Participles and Participial Phrases,* and *Words Modified.* Write the verbals from the following sentences in the correct column. In the third column, write the words modified by the participles and participial phrases.

26. Working at home, I don't have to spend time commuting to an office.
27. Jogging is beneficial to the respiratory and circulatory systems.
28. Following the trail, the bloodhounds led the police to the criminals' hideout.
29. Gardening is one of the most popular hobbies in the United States.
30. Experimenting with a new medicine, the scientist discovered dangerous side effects.
31. Running in the halls is prohibited at our schools.
32. The citizens meeting at city hall will complain about taxes.
33. Paula likes playing chess, checkers, and other board games.
34. Struggling against fatigue, the runners paced themselves.
35. Some people feel that bullfighting is a cruel sport.
36. Seeking relief from the heat, the girls decided to spend the afternoon at the pool.
37. Some doctors recommend skating to strengthen weak ankles.
38. Our family enjoys watching old movies.
39. The wilting flowers were badly in need of water.
40. Brisk walking has recently become a popular form of aerobic exercise.

Application and Review

Lesson Review

A Finding Infinitives and Infinitive Phrases Make four columns on your paper. Label them *Subjects, Adjectives, Adverbs,* and *Direct Objects.* Write the infinitives and infinitive phrases from the following sentences in the correct column.

1. We hope to visit Washington by train this summer.
2. To satisfy their curiosity is impossible.
3. Alisha went to watch the game.
4. We plan to go to the movie with our friends on Sunday afternoon.
5. I still have a couple of windows to wash.
6. We were just starting to eat the other half of the watermelon.
7. Jill arrived to help us with the fundraiser.
8. Andy is teaching us to float.
9. To go around the bridge takes too long.
10. Wendy had laundry to do.

B Recognizing Participles and Participial Phrases Make two columns on your paper. Label them *Participles and Participial Phrases* and *Words Modified.* Write the participles and participial phrases from the following sentences in the first column. Write the words they modify in the second column.

1. Jogging along the path, Ken felt invigorated.
2. Speaking quietly, the librarian explained the reference book to me.
3. Look at the cat carrying the kitten in its mouth.
4. Racing wildly, the horses crossed the finish line at the same time.
5. Elated, Beth told us the news.
6. The outboard motor purchased ten years ago still worked well.

7. Cleaning the garage, John found some dusty old newspapers.
8. Snorting and kicking, the pinto refused to wear a saddle.
9. Walking slowly, Laura and her friend watched the purple and orange sunset.
10. The tape recorder made in Korea had every possible feature.
11. Heather had seen Mike walking across the field.
12. Tod, jogging in place the whole time, told us his story without any pauses.
13. Lurching from side to side, the train slowed to a stop.
14. Exhausted from the effort of the climb, the hikers sprawled on the ground for a nap.
15. The music playing on the speakers overhead suddenly became very loud.

C Identifying Gerunds and Gerund Phrases Make three columns on your paper. Label them *Subjects, Direct Objects,* and *Objects of Prepositions*. Write the gerunds and gerund phrases from the following sentences in the correct column.

1. Finishing the last question on the test caused everyone to sigh with relief.
2. Jim and Jean talked about going to the game.
3. Debbie enjoyed painting the kitchen.
4. Have you forgotten about mowing the lawn?
5. In a basketball game, quick thinking is essential to victory.
6. I'm tired of rushing around town.
7. Robin and her family began traveling through California.
8. Walking is good exercise and a healthy habit.
9. Running up the hill was the most difficult part of the race.
10. Please stop playing your radio on the bus.
11. Performing in front of all those people made Therese feel nervous and excited.
12. Practicing the cello is Paulo's favorite pastime.
13. Will you ask Mr. Weeks about driving us to the theater?
14. This new computer program makes learning about math easier and more fun.
15. Many people enjoy writing stories about their own experiences or about imaginary experiences.

Chapter Review

A   Identifying Verbals   Make three columns on your paper. Label them *Infinitives and Infinitive Phrases, Participles and Participial Phrases,* and *Gerunds and Gerund Phrases.* Write the verbals and verbal phrases from the following sentences in the correct column.

1. I need to change the battery in my watch.
2. Gasping for breath, the runner commented on the Boston Marathon.
3. Look for the letter from Erica arriving in today's mail.
4. Reading that book changed my outlook on life.
5. The rain, driven by a gusty wind, ruined the billboard.
6. Physics is an important subject if you plan to be an engineer.
7. Using a calculator during the test is not permitted.
8. Skiing can be an excellent form of exercise.
9. Our dog Lucky, devoted to my mother, barks as soon as Mom enters the building.
10. To develop his leg muscles, Chris rides a bike to school instead of taking the bus.

B   Identifying Verbals and Their Uses   Make four columns on your paper. Label them *Infinitives and Infinitive Phrases, Participles and Participial Phrases, Gerunds and Gerund Phrases,* and *Functions.* Write the verbals and verbal phrases from the following sentences in the correct column. Write the functions of these verbals and verbal phrases in the fourth column (*Subject, Direct Object, Object of Preposition, Adjective* or *Adverb*).

1. Eating too much before bed may cause a restless night.
2. My parents grounded me for losing my bus pass again.
3. Completely frustrated, the small child began to cry.
4. Andy tired himself out by playing basketball.
5. Everyone rose to cheer the victors.
6. Kevin wanted to catch the train.
7. I enjoy looking at fossils.
8. Uncooked, certain foods can cause serious intestinal illness.
9. To get the most out of aerobic exercise is his goal in this class.
10. The batter ducked to avoid the pitch.

Cumulative Review

A **Recognizing Compound and Complex Sentences** Label each sentence *Simple, Compound,* or *Complex.*

1. Sharlene hopped and skipped all the way home.
2. The Aztecs lived in Mexico, and the Incas lived in Peru.
3. When the bell rang, Colin ran to the door.
4. Barb should turn off the light when she comes home.
5. At one time barbers were surgeons who bled patients.
6. My dog often barks at strangers, but he does not bite.
7. The trapeze artist flew through the air and landed on one foot on the high wire.
8. Was your aunt a sergeant or a colonel in the army?
9. Thoreau went to Walden Pond so that he could live alone with nature.
10. Toys that have sharp points are dangerous for children.

B **Recognizing Subject–Verb Agreement** Write the correct form of the verbs given in parentheses in the following sentences.

1. The climate of the Great Lakes (is, are) often harsh.
2. Jacob Grimm, along with his brother Wilhelm, (was, were) famous for writing fairy tales.
3. An indentured servant in the thirteen colonies (were, was) under contract for seven years.
4. The insects in the back yard (buzz, buzzes) constantly.
5. A lamp, as well as two vases, (were, was) broken by the vibrations from the airplane overhead.
6. Each of the pipes (carry, carries) water from the street into a different house.
7. Neither karate class nor piano lessons (is, are) available on Tuesday afternoon.
8. The old mixer and a new blender (sits, sit) side by side.
9. Neither of the lizards (is, are) poisonous.
10. Here (is, are) the cat with all her new kittens in tow.

C Identifying Verbals Label whether each italicized verbal is an *Infinitive or Infinitive Phrase,* a *Participle or Participial Phrase,* or a *Gerund or Gerund Phrase.*

1. The king decided *to raise taxes.*
2. *Holding the vine in one hand,* Tarzan swung to a tree.
3. *Dancing* is Montgomery's favorite pastime.
4. *Walking to school* takes thirty minutes.
5. Stan went next door *to borrow some milk.*
6. Doesn't everyone like *playing?*
7. The magician, *closing her eyes,* guessed my weight.
8. The two thieves were caught in the act of *robbing a store.*
9. *To win the pennant* is our goal.
10. The *running* water soon became cold.
11. Florida is a good place *to grow palm trees.*
12. I can hear the popcorn *popping already.*
13. *Totally exhausted,* the pony walked to the stable.
14. Lee was praised for *saving the swimmer's life.*
15. Two boys went to the costume party *dressed as radios.*
16. I hope you learn *to sing that song by Friday.*
17. Anne has a picture *to copy.*
18. The salmon, *caught on a rock,* could not swim upstream.
19. *Hissing furiously,* the snake moved its head toward me.
20. *Sewing* is a difficult and precise skill.

D Combined Review Write the following paragraph on your paper and correct any errors you find. Watch for sentence fragments and run-on sentences. Also make sure the subject–verb agreement is correct.

Baseball and softball is similar sports. Both are played on a diamond both use bats and balls both have nine innings with three outs each. Some differences, though. Baseball is a nationwide spectator sport in the United States softball is a nationwide participation sport. Some softball players does not even use gloves and softball is sometimes played with ten players instead of nine. Baseball—overhand and sidearm pitching; softball—underhand pitching.

30
Capitalization

Suddenly Old Faithful erupts in a great mass of hissing steam, throwing a stream of water one hundred feet into the air. Perhaps anything that spectacular ought to be capitalized!

This "rule" may not be the best way to determine where capital letters are needed. Old Faithful and Yellowstone National Park, where she is found, are both capitalized because each is the name of a particular place or thing.

This chapter will help you learn the many different rules of capitalization. It will explain these rules and show you how to apply them in your writing.

1
Proper Nouns and Proper Adjectives

Capitalize *proper nouns* and *proper adjectives*.

A **common noun** is the name of a whole group of persons, places, things, or ideas. A **proper noun** is the name of an individual person, place, thing, or idea. A **proper adjective** is an adjective formed from a proper noun. All proper nouns and proper adjectives are capitalized.

Common Noun	Proper Noun	Proper Adjective
person	Charles Dickens	Dickensian
country	Spain	Spanish
city	Paris	Parisian

There are many different types of proper nouns. The following rules and examples will help you solve the problems in capitalizing proper nouns and proper adjectives.

Names and Titles of Persons

Capitalize the names of persons and also the initials or abbreviations that stand for those names.

J. R. R. Tolkien	John **R**onald **R**euel Tolkien
Ella **T.** Grasso	Ella **T**ambussi **G**rasso
T. S. Eliot	**T**homas **S**tearns Eliot

Capitalize titles used with names of persons and capitalize the initials and/or abbreviations that stand for those titles. Capitalize the titles *Mr., Mrs., Ms.,* and *Miss*.

Rev. M. R. Eaton	**S**enator Smith	**D**r. Patricia Ryan
Mr. Ralph Lee	**M**rs. A. L. Mark	**M**s. J. Rita Marconi

Do not capitalize titles used as common nouns.

Your appointment with the doctor is next Thursday.
The vice-president writes the company brochures.

Capitalize titles of people in unique positions whose rank is very important, even when the titles are used without proper names.

> The **P**resident of the United States
> The role of the **V**ice-**P**resident in foreign affairs

Family Relationships

Capitalize such words as *mother, father, aunt,* and *uncle* when these words are used as names.

> Did you know that **M**other taught **D**ad to swim?
> When is **A**unt Sonja arriving?

Note that when the noun is modified by a personal pronoun, the noun is not capitalized.

> My **a**unt called five minutes ago from the airport.
> Tina resembles her **m**other and her **f**ather.

The Pronoun I

Capitalize the pronoun *I*.

> Is Richard taller than **I**?
> May **I** borrow your bike to go to the store?

The Deity

Capitalize all words referring to the Deity, to holy books, and to religious scriptures.

God	the **L**ord	the **B**ible
Allah	the **A**lmighty	the **B**ook of **E**xodus
Jesus	**K**rishna	the **K**oran

Capitalize personal pronouns referring to the Deity.

> God spoke to **H**is prophets.
> They prayed to **H**im for guidance.

Exercises

A Write the following sentences, using correct capitalization.

1. My mother told me i had a doctor's appointment.
2. The new french teacher is a parisian.

3. He came from france to study english in america.
4. We spent the summer with dr. costello and her family.
5. The first book of the bible is the book of genesis.
6. Please take this message to the principal, lynn.
7. I wish my sister and i were going to camp this summer.
8. Among the names for god are jehovah and the almighty.
9. Would you direct me to mr. holchak's office?
10. Did aunt rose drive tad and maria to the concert?

B Write the words in the following sentences that are not capitalized correctly. Use correct capitalization.

1. There are seven cities in the united states named springfield; the largest is in massachusetts.
2. Our country is sometimes described as a jeffersonian democracy.
3. The new student is toshio kitagawa. His sister is mieko.
4. Their home is kyoto, japan, where their grandparents live.
5. The *city of new orleans* is a train.
6. Which cairo do you mean, the one in egypt or the one in illinois?
7. The first woman to be appointed to the united states supreme court was sandra day o'connor.
8. For breakfast, i had a spanish omelet and texas chili.
9. p.t. barnum was famous for "the greatest show on earth."
10. Was dwight d. eisenhower our thirty-fourth president?

c *Write Now* Imagine that you could travel to any place you wished. Where would you go? Write a description of the place you would like to visit. Include the names of places of interest you would visit there. Be sure to capitalize correctly.

2
Geographical Names

Capitalize major words in geographical names. Also capitalize names of sections of the country but not compass directions.

Following are examples of geographical names:

Continents	Africa, Australia, Antarctica
Bodies of Water	the Pacific Ocean, Puget Sound, the Columbia River, Hudson Bay, the Straits of Magellan, Lake Michigan
Land Forms	the Mississippi Delta, the Cape of Good Hope, the Mojave Desert, the Atlas Mountains, Pikes Peak
Political Units	Los Angeles, Commonwealth of Puerto Rico, First Congressional District, Utah, the Azores, Great Britain
Public Areas	Badlands National Monument, Grant Park, Shawnee National Forest, the Battery, the Black Hills
Roads and Highways	Oregon Trail, Lincoln Highway, Route 23, 34th Avenue, Riverside Freeway

Directions and Sections

Capitalize the names of sections of the country and proper adjectives derived from them.

> Industrial production was high in the North.
> The first English settlements were along the East Coast.
> The Southwest is our fastest-growing region.
> Princeton University is in the East.

Do not capitalize directions of the compass or adjectives derived from them.

> They flew east then north.   We took an eastern route.
> The frontier moved westward.   The north winds are cold.

Exercises

A Write the following phrases, using correct capitalization.

1. at yosemite national park
2. capri in the bay of naples
3. the sixth street overpass
4. siberia in the soviet union
5. north of youngstown, ohio
6. asia and africa
7. on the amazon river
8. on the sahara desert
9. one of the wisconsin lakes
10. the trans-canada highway

B Write the following sentences, using correct capitalization.

1. For the pioneers, the journey to the west was hard.
2. Many wagon trains left from independence, missouri.
3. Some trains headed northwest on the oregon trail.
4. Some headed southwest on the santa fe trail.
5. The mormon trail began in nauvoo, illinois.
6. The trail ended in salt lake city, utah.
7. The push to settle the west took its toll of the pioneers.
8. Settlers crossed the great plains and the rocky mountains.
9. At the donner pass in 1846, many were trapped by snow.
10. On the oregon trail, disease took many lives.

Grammar in Action

Capitalization is important when you're writing about places. A capital letter alerts your reader to the fact that you're talking about a particular place and not a general category of places.

The kamaran islands are in the red sea.

Since there are no capital letters in the above sentence, you don't know if *kamaran* and *red sea* are the names of actual places.

Writing Activity Imagine you are an explorer who has discovered a lost city. Write an account of the city, naming it. Name a nearby lake, a park, a municipal building, roads, and highways. When you have finished, check your capitalization.

3
Names Relating to Organizations, History, and Time

Capitalize the names of:
- organizations
- institutions
- historical events
- documents
- periods of time
- days
- months
- holidays

Organizations and Institutions

Capitalize all the important words in the names of organizations and institutions, including their abbreviations.

Oakwood High School   Children's Hospital
New York University   **NATO**

Do not capitalize such words as *school, college, church,* and *hospital* when they are not used as the names of specific institutions.

the band at our school
each local church

Events, Documents, and Periods of Time

Capitalize the names of historical events, documents, and periods of time.

Battle of Hastings   Treaty of Paris   Age of Discovery
the Civil War   Magna Charta   Prohibition

Months, Days, and Holidays

Capitalize names of months, days, and holidays, but not the names of seasons.

March   Friday   Independence Day
summer   Thanksgiving   New Year's Day

Exercises

A Write the words in each sentence that should be capitalized. Use correct capitalization.

1. In 1898, the treaty of paris ended the spanish-american war.
2. The enrollment at pulaski high school increased this year.

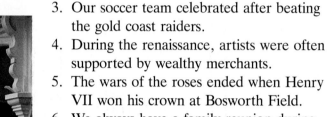

3. Our soccer team celebrated after beating the gold coast raiders.
4. During the renaissance, artists were often supported by wealthy merchants.
5. The wars of the roses ended when Henry VII won his crown at Bosworth Field.
6. We always have a family reunion during memorial day weekend.
7. Last spring, I visited Washington, D.C. and saw the declaration of independence.
8. At river dell high school, our football team's colors are black and gold.
9. In 1779, a group of settlers in Tennessee drew up an agreement called the cumberland compact.
10. The league of women voters organized a white elephant sale.

B Write the following sentences, using correct capitalization.

1. The treaty of ghent in 1814 ended the war of 1812.
2. Patients from all over the country are flown to the mayo clinic in Minnesota.
3. My father has a ucla T-shirt that he wears when he watches college football.
4. Sometimes we go to church on st. patrick's day.
5. During winter vacation, I plan to study italian.
7. The leaves will be at their peak of color by columbus day.
8. My great-grandfather fought in France during world war I.
9. From the mid-1960's on, television regularly brought viewers battle scenes from the vietnam war.
10. The democratic party has more registered voters in our state than the republican party.

4
Languages, Peoples, Courses, Transportation, and Abbreviations

Capitalize the names of:
- languages
- races
- nationalities
- courses
- religions
- transportation

Capitalize abbreviations:
- B.C.
- A.D.
- A.M.
- P.M.

Languages, Races, Nationalities, and Religions

Capitalize the names of languages, races, nationalities, religions, and the adjectives derived from them.

Spanish   Puerto Rican   German   American
Oriental   Christianity   Buddhism   French

School Subjects

Do not capitalize the names of school subjects unless they are languages or unless a course name is followed by a number.

Algebra I   social studies   World History II

Ships, Trains, Airplanes, Automobiles

Capitalize the names of ships, trains, and aircraft. Capitalize brand names of automobiles.

Santa Fe Chief   *Apollo 17*   Hawk Sport Wagon
Spirit of St. Louis   *Delta Queen*   *Old Ironsides*

Abbreviations

Capitalize the abbreviations *B.C., A.D., A.M.,* and *P.M.*

The Olympic Games may have started in 776 **B.C.**
The date of the Norman Conquest is **A.D.** 1066.
Does the class start at 8:00 **A.M.** or 8:00 **P.M.**?

Exercises

A Write the words in each sentence that should be capitalized. Use correct capitalization.

1. The *orient express* is the name of a famous train.
2. The mysterious car was a shiny black glitz.
3. After I learn more french, I want to visit Quebec.
4. I registered for ancient history 101 and social studies.
5. Charles Lindbergh's plane was the *spirit of st. louis*.
6. In 44 b.c. Julius Caesar was assassinated.
7. The *queen elizabeth* was docked in New York.
8. The u.s.s. *constitution* was nicknamed *old ironsides*.
9. The Wars of the Roses began in england in a.d. 1455.
10. The prophet muhammad founded the religion of islam.

B Write the following sentences, using correct capitalization.

1. Today there are russian jews, haitians, and salvadorans who want to come to the United States.
2. Most natives of Brazil speak portuguese.
3. Last year I took algebra I; now I'm taking geometry.
4. In a.d. 1066, the normans of France conquered the english.
5. Many asians speak english, but most americans don't speak asian languages.
6. The latin-based languages are french, italian, and spanish.
7. When europeans first settled in North America, there were a great many indians in present-day Mexico.
8. My sister is taking a yoga class, and I am enrolled in a class called modern american poetry 101.
9. The egyptian queen Nefertiti was the wife of a pharaoh who ruled from 1367 to 1350 b.c.
10. Someday I'd like to take a class in the russian language.

C *Proofreading* Copy the following paragraph, correcting each error you find. Be sure to capitalize correctly.

> In our social studies class, we talked about native americans living on resurvations. We also discussed the impact of the industrial revolution on europeans. Mr. Deemer's social studies 102 is my favorite class.

5
First Words

Capitalize the first word in sentences, most lines of
poetry, quotations, outline entries, and the closings of
letters. Capitalize the first word and all important words
in the greetings of letters and titles.

Sentences

Capitalize the first word of every sentence.

Turn at the corner and drive two blocks to Ellis Avenue.
I thanked Mike for reminding me about the parade.

Poetry

Capitalize the first word in most lines of poetry.

Sometimes in modern poetry, the lines of a poem do not begin
with capital letters. The following poem shows the traditional
style for capitalization of poetry.

Go roll a prairie up like cloth,
Drink Mississippi dry,
Put Allegheny in your hat,
A steamboat in your eye—
And for your breakfast, buffalo
Some five and twenty fry.
                    Anon.

Quotations

Capitalize the first word of a direct quotation.

Ralph Waldo Emerson said, "Hitch your wagon to a star."

Do not capitalize the first word of the second part of a divided
quotation unless it starts a new sentence.

"I know," he said, "that what you say is true."
"That's true," he said. "You have known it all along."

Letters

Capitalize all the important words in the greeting of a letter.

Dear **M**s. **Y**ang: **D**ear **D**r. **M**artino: **D**ear **M**rs. **C**ostello,
Dear **S**ir: **D**ear **M**adam: **D**ear **B**eth and **A**my,

Do not capitalize the words *or* or *and* in a greeting.

Dear **S**ir or **M**adam: **D**ear **M**r. and **M**rs. **M**artin:

In the closing of a letter, capitalize only the first word of the phrase.

Yours very truly,   **S**incerely yours,

Outlines

Capitalize the first word in each entry of an outline.

  I. **I**mprove your handwriting.
      A. **F**orm letters carefully.
          1. **W**atch *a, e, r, l,* and *t.*
          2. **H**old pencil correctly.
      B. **S**pace your words evenly.

Titles

Capitalize the first word, the last word, and all important words in the titles of books, poems, short stories, articles, newspapers, magazines, plays, motion pictures, works of art, television programs, and musical compositions.

Articles (the words *a, an,* and *the*), conjunctions, and prepositions are not usually considered important words. However, note that an article, a conjunction, or a preposition used as the first or last word of a title must be capitalized.

Book	*The **G**ood **E**arth*
Story	"**A G**ame of **C**atch"
Play	*The **M**iracle **W**orker*
Magazine	***S**ports **I**llustrated*

Exercises

A Write the following phrases, using correct capitalization.

1. a poem about lincoln entitled "o captain! my captain!"
2. a subscription to *national geographic*
3. very sincerely yours,
4. an actor in *fiddler on the roof*
5. a quotation that began, "no one can make you feel inferior"
6. dear mr. and mrs. cummings:
7. was asking me if I had read the poem "hiawatha"
8. said, "we'll go before lunch."
9. took us to see an old movie, *modern times*
10. yours truly,

B Write correctly the words that should be capitalized.

1. the poem begins, "he would answer to 'Hi'."
2. The second part of my outline will read: A. red ants.
3. "i'm going to be late," Janet said. "please hurry."
4. we think *the call of the wild* is jack london's best book.
5. he began the letter, "dear ms. shehan:"
6. Robert Frost wrote "the death of the hired man."
7. the letter ended, "sincerely yours, elena."
8. my parents saw *the wizard of oz* when they were young.
9. "there it goes," said father, "into its mouse hole."
10. the morning paper is the *herald tribune*.

Grammar in Action

Using direct quotations can make your writing lively and interesting. Compare these two statements:

Joe said that white water rafting was exciting.
Joe said, "White water rafting was so exciting!"

Writing Activity Ask several friends to express their opinions on an issue that is important to them and to you. Write five sentences in which you quote these opinions. Capitalize correctly.

Linking Mechanics & Writing

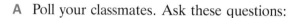

A Poll your classmates. Ask these questions:

1. What is your favorite musical group?
2. May I quote you on that?

Be sure to quote each person exactly in your notebook. Try to have variety in the answers. If two persons like the same group, ask for a second choice or even a third choice so you can get a variety of opinions.

Gather the data and then show the results by listing the groups and the comments on the bulletin board, with an appropriate heading. Is the capitalization correct?

B You are reading the newspaper, and you see an ad from a famous musical group. They need a person to manage their next concert tour. Imagine that you got the job. Think about where the group might go to perform. Write out an itinerary for the tour. Include the cities on the tour, the travel dates and times, the names of hotels, and the places of interest you might like to visit during your time off. Include the names of any holidays that will occur during the tour. Be as creative as you wish and be sure to capitalize correctly.

Additional Practice

Parts 1-5 Using Capital Letters Write the words that should be capitalized in the following sentences. Change small letters to capital letters. Write *Correct* for those sentences that are correct.

1. Neptune and pluto are the planets that are farthest from us.
2. I read an article about miniature horses in *national geographic*.
3. Jesus was betrayed by judas iscariot, one of his disciples.
4. Mr. and Mrs. j.b. Dawes own acme manufacturing, inc.
5. "Let's go to Dolphin lake and feed the ducks," said Mary jane.
6. Bolivia was named after simónbolívar, who helped the country win its independence from Spain.
7. The fire station is at the corner of Douglas Lane and fifth street.
8. One of William Shakespeare's most famous plays is *romeo and juliet*.
9. The Bill of Rights consists of the first ten amendments to the united states constitution.
10. My little sister's favorite cartoon character is mighty mouse.
11. John F. Kennedy wrote *profiles in courage* and *why england slept*.
12. Ms. Eastwood recently became the principal of Westlake Junior high school.
13. In 1979, Margaret Thatcher became great Britain's prime minister.
14. Shel Silverstein wrote a poem called "Where the sidewalk ends."
15. Ms. Istad's ancestors were norwegian and irish.
16. Muslims believe that the Prophet muhammad was the messenger of God.
17. Columbus's ships were named the santa maria, the niña, and the pinta.
18. Henry David Thoreau said, "time is but the stream I go a-fishing in."

19. Olivia buys most of her clothes at a department store in downtown Fairfield.
20. We are having chicken and spanish rice for dinner.
21. Rosh Hashana and yom kippur are two important Jewish holidays.
22. My grandparents moved to Scottsdale, Arizona.
23. The battle of the coral sea was fought in May of 1942.
24. *Main street* is one of the most famous books written by Sinclair Lewis.
25. Kareem Abdul-Jabbar attended ucla and played on its basketball team.
26. "Come to my house after school, " said Carla. "we can study for the algebra test together."
27. Sacramento is the capital of California.
28. My mother usually takes the 8:00 a.m. train to her job downtown.
29. have you ever read *Johnny Tremain* by Esther Forbes?
30. Dutch and french are the official languages of Belgium.
31. This regional cookbook includes a section on southern cooking.
32. New year's day fell on a monday that year.
33. "i would like to go horseback riding this afternoon," said Linda, "but I have to baby-sit for my neighbor's children."
34. On our vacation we visited the grand canyon, as well as several other tourist attractions.
35. The children who live next door attend a roman catholic school.
36. A local television station is airing reruns of "mr. ed," a program about a talking horse.
37. Pennsylvania, new Jersey, and new York are the middle Atlantic states.
38. The Andersons live three blocks south of the grain elevator.
39. Joan Sutherland, the great opera singer, was born in sydney, australia.
40. In social studies class we are learning about Buddhism and Hinduism.
41. Traffic can only move west along that street.
42. Regina is the largest city in saskatchewan, a province in Canada.
43. Did you ever read *the Diary of a young Girl* by Anne Frank?
44. Her father asked, "have I met your new friend?"
45. The fourth of July celebrates our nation's independence.

Application and Review

Lesson Review

A Capitalizing Proper Nouns and Adjectives Write the words that should be capitalized. Use correct capitalization.

1. martin luther king, Jr., received the nobel peace prize.
2. i look like mom, but i have my father's brown eyes.
3. The poet hilda doolittle was known by her initials, h.d.
4. In peru and mexico, indian civilizations once flourished.
5. Is aunt theodosia dad's favorite sister?
6. warren burger was chief justice of the supreme court.
7. Shall I send an invitation to mr. and mrs. albert g. schill?
8. A famous polish army officer was named tadeusz kosciuszko.
9. In boston there is a very large catholic population.
10. The bible tells of the israelites' escape from egypt.

B Capitalizing Geographical Names Write the words that should be capitalized. Use correct capitalization.

1. The gaspé peninsula is part of quebec province.
2. Are the rocky mountains higher than the andes mountains?
3. The isthmus of panama was a likely place to build a canal.
4. From that spot, it's forty miles to the caribbean sea.
5. Lake geneva borders switzerland and france.
6. The state's official name is rhode island and providence plantations.
7. My parents were delighted to see the chicago skyline.
8. Farms in the midwest are not like farms in the east.
9. Visit vicksburg national park when you're in the south.
10. On that hot beach, my mouth felt like death valley.

C Capitalizing Organizations, History, and Time Write the following sentences, using correct capitalization.

1. The dark ages lasted from a.d. 500 to a.d. 1000.
2. Rosemont high school has winter break in january.

3. We memorized the gettysburg address for English class.
4. The international products company owns s & z vegetables.
5. The gregory art museum is closed on the fourth of july.
6. At the 1977 geneva convention, human rights were an issue.
7. I broke my arm at jones hardware, near the hospital.
8. During the depression, some people ate oatmeal at all meals.
9. On thanksgiving, Dad makes his special cornbread stuffing.
10. Last spring, I visited my uncle's farm every tuesday.

D Capitalizing Languages, Peoples, Courses, Transportation, and Abbreviations Write the words that should be capitalized.

1. Milo decided to take algebra I this year.
2. In the french revolution, Marie Antoinette was executed.
3. I plan to study german next semester.
4. The *queen mary* is docked in Long Beach, California.
5. In japanese, the letters are called characters.
6. My sister took psychology 101 in college.
7. Tim likes exploring sunken ships, like the *andrea doria*.
8. Ancient romans built the appian way in 312 b.c.
9. The original jamaicans came from ethiopia.
10. My sister is a french/english translator at the united nations.

E Capitalizing First Words Write the words that should be capitalized. Use correct capitalization.

1. "There will be a quiz today," said Mr. Sims. "it will cover *moby dick*."
2. Have you read Walt Whitman's poem "song of myself"?
3. We all enjoyed *the adventures of huckleberry finn*.
4. I.   making outlines
        A.   gathering materials
5. our school library subscribes to *newsweek* and *time*.
6. do not go gentle into that good night,
   rage, rage against the dying of the light.
7. The class representative said, "we've read and understood the school board's ruling."
8. The sculptures *moses* and *david* were made by Michelangelo.
9. Sasha's letter began, "dear ms. tracy"
10. She ended her letter, "yours regretfully."

Chapter Review

A Using Capital Letters Correctly Write the following sentences, using correct capitalization.

1. Caroline learned the portuguese language in brazil.
2. We read the bible and discussed the ten commandments.
3. captain klee directed the plane west, over the pacific ocean.
4. The exploration of the west was tied to the search for gold in california.
5. the girl scouts start their cookie sale in april.
6. My friend satit is a buddhist from thailand.
7. did king arthur live during the middle ages?
8. At middleview high school we are reading Plato's *the republic*.
9. Take the chicago and northwestern commuter train to evanston.
10. You'll enjoy a walk through the campus of northwestern university.

B Using Capital Letters Correctly Write the following sentences and other groups of words, using correct capitalization.

1. thomas jefferson wrote the declaration of independence in sixteen days during june of 1776.
2. patrick henry spoke against the stamp act.
3. napoleon bonaparte sold the louisiana territory to the united states.
4. easter is a christian holiday.
5. old king cole was a merry old soul, a merry old soul was he . . .
6. dear sir:
     yours truly,
7. "take my copy of *irish stories*," said dad, "and read it."
8. It was patrick henry who said, "give me liberty or give me death."
9. The name of Thomas jefferson's home in charlottesville, virginia, is monticello.
10. It was samuel adams who headed the boston tea party.

31
Punctuation

On-Off   Open-Close   Stop-Start

Nothing would get done in our push-button world without the signals that control machines. Writing, too, needs signals; punctuation marks provide those signals.

Punctuation marks add emphasis and show where sentences end. They indicate questions and exclamations. They show pauses and interruptions. They link and they clarify. In this chapter you will study the ways you can use punctuation to direct your writing.

1
End Marks

Use a *period*, a *question mark,* or an *exclamation mark* to end a sentence.

The tone of voice you use to communicate a message tells a great deal about what you are saying. Your tone may tell whether your message is a complete thought, a question, or something about which you are terribly excited. When you write, punctuation marks called **end marks** do the job your tone of voice does when you speak.

End marks show where sentences end. There are three kinds of end marks: the **period,** the **question mark,** and the **exclamation point** (or **exclamation mark**).

The Period

Use a period at the end of a declarative sentence.

A **declarative sentence** is a sentence that makes a statement. You use it to tell something, that is, to give information.

> My favorite team is the Dallas Cowboys.
> Some Chinese musical instruments are extremely old.

Use a period at the end of an imperative sentence.

An **imperative sentence** is a sentence that makes a request or tells someone to do something. It is followed by a period except when it expresses strong emotion. Then it is followed by an exclamation point.

> Please give your name.   Take care!

Use a period at the end of an indirect question.

An **indirect question** tells what someone asked, without using the person's exact words. If you use the person's exact words, however, that is a **direct question**. A direct question ends with a question mark. This question mark should always appear within the quotation marks that set off the person's exact words.

| Indirect Question | The speaker asked if anyone had read her book. |
| Direct Question | Jan Gray asked, "Has anyone read my book?" |

The Question Mark

Use a question mark at the end of an interrogative sentence.

An **interrogative sentence** is a sentence that asks a question.

What time will you arrive?   Did you see the plane land?

The Exclamation Point

Use an exclamation point at the end of an exclamatory sentence and following an interjection.

An **exclamatory sentence** is a sentence that expresses strong feeling. An **interjection** is a word or group of words that expresses strong feeling.

| Exclamatory Sentence | What speed that runner has! |
| Interjections | Wow!   Great!   Alas!   Oh no! |

You may also use the exclamation point at the end of an imperative sentence that expresses strong feeling.

Come here at once!

Exclamation points can be used to add more feeling or emphasis to declarative sentences.

The bridge fell into the water.
Oh no! The bridge fell into the water!

Exercise

Some of the end marks that follow the sentences and interjections below are used incorrectly. Write the end marks that would correctly complete these sentences and interjections. Write *Correct* for those that are punctuated correctly.

1. I asked, "Why were covered wagons called *prairie schooners*."
2. Maria wanted to know if they got this name because their huge white tops looked like the sails of a ship?

3. Families traveling across the plains to California usually banded together to form a wagon train!

4. Did you realize that wagon trains traveled only fifteen to twenty miles a day!

5. As long as the pioneers did not settle on the Native Americans' hunting grounds, were the Native Americans good to them.

6. Yes. They supplied the pioneers with meat and vegetables and helped them in dangerous river crossings.

7. Amazing. You would never learn that from old Hollywood movies about the West.

8. Pioneers followed one rule that saved many lives!

9. Keep moving! Stop only at noon and nightfall.

10. By following this rule, pioneers who began their journey in the spring could arrive just before the first snows fell!

Other Uses of the Period

Without periods not only would sentences run together, but titles and initials would run together with people's names. All abbreviations would look like words. The letters and numbers of outlines and lists would run into the items beside them. Without periods, your writing would be so confusing that no one could understand it.

Use a period after an initial and after most abbreviations.

Rev. J. L. Haeger, Jr.   2:00 P.M.

Some abbreviations do not require periods. When you are not sure whether you should use periods following the initials of an abbreviation, look up the abbreviation in a dictionary.

mph *(miles per hour)*   AM *(amplitude modulation)*

Use a period after each number or letter that shows a division of an outline or that precedes an item in a list.

Outline	List
I. Poets	1. art gum eraser
A. American	2. soft lead pencils
1. Robert Frost	3. sketch pad
2. Emily Dickinson	4. 2 sheets of good paper
B. British	5. 3 metal clips
1. Dylan Thomas	6. India ink
2. Christina Rossetti	7. brushes
II. Painters	

Use a period between numerals representing dollars and cents and before a decimal.

$18.98   4.853   33.3%

Exercise

Write on your paper the following sentences or phrases, adding periods where necessary.

1. Dwight D Eisenhower became President in 1953
2. Our car gets 296 mpg
3. The check for lunch was $1366
4. I Plays
       A Naturalistic
           1 Settings and time
           2 Plots
       B Experimental
     II Fiction
5. Ramon likes FM stations better than AM stations
6. The Rev James M Butler was guest speaker at the dinner
7. The UN was established in 1945
8. Shopping List
       1 milk
       2 orange juice
       3 brick cheese
       4 rye bread
9. The plane that left Atlanta at 6:00 PM is due here at noon
10. Mr. Loo's mail goes to his PO Box

2
Commas That Separate Ideas

When you speak, the tone of your voice and the pauses you take punctuate what you are saying. However, when you write, you use commas to indicate your pauses and to show which words belong together.

Commas in Compound Sentences

Use a comma before the conjunction that joins the clauses in a compound sentence.

Two or more simple sentences joined by a conjunction become a compound sentence made up of independent clauses.

> Dawn arrived at last, and we started the search.
> Pete joined us, but he was late.

A comma is not required in a very short compound sentence in which the parts are joined by *and*. However, always use a comma before the conjunctions *but* and *or*.

> They were hot *and* they were tired.
> They were hot, *but* they were not tired.

A comma is not required before the conjunction that joins a compound predicate unless it has more than two parts.

> Nita turned on the radio and listened to the news.
> Jeffrey caught the ball, threw it, and ran.

Exercises

A Write on your paper the following sentences, adding and deleting commas where necessary.

1. Maria finished practice, and raced home.
2. Do you like plays or do you prefer movies?

3. I read *Roots* but I preferred the television series.
4. The snow will begin falling in the afternoon, and will continue falling into the evening.
5. I read about space travel but I'm more interested in undersea exploration.
6. Kurt ran to the door opened it wide and let in the dog.
7. We drove to the lake, and camped there.
8. Jesse went ice skating and she really enjoyed it.
9. They will stay here and we will meet them tomorrow.
10. The tire keeps going flat but I can't find the cause.

B Write the following sentences, adding and deleting commas where necessary. If a sentence is already correct, write *Correct*.

Child laborer, cloth mill.

1. Farm women of the early 1700's spun their own thread, and wove their own cloth.
2. Then the *spinning jenny* and the *spinning mule* were invented and mills became the centers for cloth manufacturing.
3. The *spinning jenny* and the *spinning mule* could spin a number of threads at once but the *spinning mule* produced finer yarn.
4. Soon machines could produce cloth more cheaply than hand weavers, and many people stopped making cloth at home.
5. Many families gave up their farms, and went to live near the clothing mills.
6. The mills provided work for these families but mill work was filled with dangers and terrible hardships.
7. Young children worked hard put in long hours, and earned very little pay.
8. Dr. Elizabeth Shapleigh was aware of these hardships and concerned about them.
9. Few laws protected workers and those laws were disobeyed.
10. Stronger laws were eventually passed and enforced but that occurred only after many people had fought long and hard for them.

Commas in a Series

Use a comma after every item in a series except the last.

There are always three or more items of the same kind in a series. These items may be nouns, verbs, adjectives, adverbs, phrases, independent clauses, or other parts of a sentence.

Leslie, John, Meg, and Martina went skiing. (nouns)
Sam jumped, barked, and yelped with joy. (verbs)
The road winds up and down, over and back, and in and out. (groups of adverbs)
The commuter train stops at Colony Road, at City Center, and at Bay Street Terminal. (prepositional phrases)
The movie was over, the crowd had gone, and Jason began the long walk home. (simple sentences)

In the examples above, a comma followed by a conjunction precedes the last item in each series. That comma is always used.

When two or more adjectives precede a noun, use a comma after each adjective except the last one.

The *Swan* is a sleek, shiny, trim boat.
He was a proud, dignified person.

If two adjectives express closely related thoughts, they are not usually separated by a comma.

Our house is the *little green* cottage.
Look at the *big round* moon.

Read the above sentences aloud. Notice that you do not pause between the adjectives.

Use commas after the adverbs *first, second, third,* and so on, when these adverbs introduce items in a series.

We had three reasons: first, we were tired; second, we had no transportation; third, we had other things to do.

Exercises

A Write the following sentences, adding commas where necessary. If a sentence is already correct, write *Correct*.

1. A strong northerly wind swept snow against the door.
2. Open your books turn to page 40 and read that page.

3. Rena Lena Mina and Geraldine formed a singing quartet.
4. My sister can play the guitar the banjo and the mandolin.
5. A little red car is parked on the driveway.
6. George Washington was a soldier a statesman and a land surveyor.
7. I have three ideas: first we could picnic at the lake; second we could barbecue here; third we could each bring food.
8. I am very fond of that old blue sweatshirt.
9. They visited Quebec City Montreal and Toronto on the trip.
10. My home is a small green peaceful island.

B Write the following sentences, adding and deleting commas where necessary. If a sentence is already correct, write *Correct*.

1. There are three steps to being a better student: first study hard; second listen hard; third work hard.
2. We bought chicken corn baked beans and fruit.
3. The committee discussed analyzed and accepted the superintendent's report.
4. Handball racquetball and squash are similar sports.
5. The long sleek black limousine pulled into traffic.
6. The speaker addressed the assembly in a loud, clear voice.
7. The game is played as follows: first you form a circle; second the leader begins to tell a story; third someone else continues the story, and so on.
8. A shy, little, colt watched us from a distance.
9. Are you feverish shivery or achey?
10. The frail old structure could not withstand the storm.

c *Proofreading* Proofread the following paragraph, then rewrite it correctly. Be sure to watch for comma errors.

People have made pets of all sorts of wonderfuly, unusual animals. Farm, children often make pets of animals such as pigs chickens and, calfs. Some Circus performers have even made pets of elephants lions and, grizzly bears. However, these wilder animals are best kept as pets only when they are young. Adult, wild animals can be short-temperred, and dangerous.

3
Commas That Set Off Special Elements

Use a comma to set off introductory elements, interrupters, nouns of direct address, and appositives.

In speaking, you pause to indicate the presence of a special element. In writing, punctuation does the work of these pauses.

Special elements add specific information to a sentence, but they are not essential. Any sentence is complete without its special elements.

Commas After Introductory Elements

Use a comma to separate an introductory word, phrase, or clause from the rest of the sentence.

> Yes, I am coming.
> After circling twice, the plane landed.
> Arriving home late, I saw a light in Gretchen's window.

Read the above examples aloud. If you would pause only slightly after the introductory element you may omit the comma.

> At first I wasn't sure.
> Finally the rain stopped.

Commas with Interrupters

Use commas to set off interrupters.

Interrupters are words or phrases that break, or interrupt, the flow of thought in a sentence. The commas around the interrupters indicate a pause before and after the interruption.

> The report, moreover, is inaccurate.
> The name of the spy, I suppose, is a secret.
> Miko, nevertheless, wanted to tell his story.

Exercise

A Write the following sentences, adding and deleting commas where necessary.

1. Mrs. Cassini was quite pleased as a matter of fact with our panel discussion.
2. No there are no mail deliveries on Sundays and holidays.
3. Franklin D. Roosevelt's New Deal was in actual fact a group of economic and social reforms.
4. Although, the pool is nearby I don't go swimming much.
5. My grandmother however still runs two miles a day.
6. Since, it is a holiday there schools in New Orleans are closed during Mardi Gras.
7. After a week of snow the city reeled under an ice storm.
8. You don't know, I suppose who wrote that television drama.
9. Recently I received a letter but it is not I regret from Paris.
10. Due to the response the rock star will play an extra concert.

B *Write Now* You use introductory elements and interrupters often when you speak. Recall recent conversations you have had or overheard. Make a list of the introductory elements and interrupters you and the other speakers used. Add to this list any other introductory elements and interrupters that come to mind. Then, write a one-page dialogue, using as many different introductory elements and interrupters from your list as possible. Set up your dialogue in the same way as the following example.

> *Sheri* Excuse me, do you know the time?
> *Julie* It is, unfortunately, already 9:30 P.M.

Commas with Nouns of Direct Address

Use commas to set off nouns of direct address.

You often address by name the person to whom you are speaking. When you do this, you are using the **noun of direct address**. Nouns of direct address are the names of persons you address.

> On your way out, *Sanford*, check the bulletin board.
> Your team did a fine job today, *Coach Wong*.

Commas with Appositives

Use commas to set off most appositives.

An **appositive** is a word or group of words used directly after another word to explain it. Most appositives are nouns. Nouns used as appositives are called **nouns in apposition**. When an appositive is used with modifiers, the whole group of words is set off with commas. In the following sentences, *co-captains* and *gymnast* are nouns in apposition.

> Karen and Maria, *our co-captains,* accepted the trophy.
> Rosalinda, *the gymnast standing on her head,* is my cousin.

When the noun in apposition is a short name, it is not usually set off by commas.

> There is the actress *Rhonda Henking.*

Exercise

Write the following sentences, punctuating them correctly by adding and deleting commas where necessary. If a sentence is already correct, write *Correct.*

1. Karen did you know that our school is putting on a play about Helen Keller?
2. William Gibson an American playwright wrote this play and titled it *The Miracle Worker.*
3. *The Miracle Worker,* has two main characters, Helen Keller and Annie Sullivan.
4. The role of Helen, a child blind and deaf since age two, is difficult to perform.
5. The character Annie Sullivan, Helen's governess and teacher is also a demanding part.
6. Annie, while going blind herself, was a student and teacher at the Perkins Institute a school for blind children.
7. When Annie tries to teach Helen, the two have bitter fights.
8. The climax of the play takes place at a water pump, when Helen speaks her first word *water* and "writes" it.
9. Friends at last Helen and Annie, walk away hand-in-hand.
10. Roberta you should try out for the part of Annie.

Grammar in Action

When speaking, you can attract a person's attention by using his or her name. You also clarify for whom your statement is intended. The following draft of a pep talk to the debate team could be improved by adding nouns of direct address.

> Now, we've done our research, right team? We have spent hours in the library gathering facts. So let's show them what we know. Straighten your tie. Don't mumble. How you answer is as important as what you answer. Remember how well we did in our practice? We're bound to do well in the real debate.

Writing Activity Rewrite the pep talk above, adding nouns of direct address to make it more direct, clear, and attention-getting. Then, write a paragraph-length pep talk for a group or team of your choice. Use nouns of direct address.

The Runners, 1926. Robert Delaunay.

4
Other Uses of the Comma

Use a comma to set off quotations, dates, addresses, and parts of a letter.

Certain elements in your writing require commas to separate them from the rest of the sentence. In this section, you will learn when to use such commas.

Commas with Quotations

Use commas to set off the explanatory words of a direct quotation.

When you use the exact words of a speaker or writer, you are using a **direct quotation**.

When you make a direct quotation, you usually include explanatory words such as *Margaret asked, Lawrence said,* or *Jill replied*. If the explanatory words precede the direct quotation, you place a comma after the last explanatory word. When the explanatory words follow the quotation, place a comma after the last word in the quotation.

> Mark Twain said, "When in doubt, tell the truth."
> "The last show is about to start," the cashier said.

When the explanatory words interrupt the quotation, this is called a **divided quotation**. Place another comma after the last explanatory word in the quotation.

> "Try to get here early," said Carol, "while it's still light."

The quotations you have just looked at are all direct quotations. When you rephrase the words of a speaker or writer, you are giving an **indirect quotation**. You need not set these words off with commas. In most cases, however, you should credit the quotation to the original speaker or writer.

> Oscar Wilde said that *experience is the name that people give to their mistakes.*

Exercise

Write the following sentences, adding and deleting commas where necessary. If a sentence is already correct, write *Correct.*

1. Julius Caesar said "I came, I saw, I conquered."
2. Carlton said that his family was moving to Tennessee.
3. "Has my watch stopped" Ann asked "or is that the time?"
4. Terra explained that she had lost her favorite pet.
5. "Please don't bother me when I'm writing" I said.
6. "I didn't think it would bother you if I offered to do your proofreading" he said.
7. "I'll wash the car" I said "but I have no time to wax it."
8. Perry explained, that his trip to Kansas had been postponed.
9. Nicola said "Wally has a good suggestion for a festival."
10. Kate told us, that the party had been canceled.

Grammar in Action

The ability to write direct and indirect quotations will come in handy when you are writing essays and research papers. You can emphasize a point by using a direct quotation or summarize information with an indirect quotation. Study the way direct and indirect quotations are used in the paragraph below.

> Acid rain is one of the most serious environmental problems we face today. One ecologist, Dr. Pectin, says that we are already seeing widespread damage to many places and things we hold dear. "The Statue of Liberty," says Dr. Pectin, "was one of the most famous victims of acid rain." The doctor goes on to say that other national monuments, buildings, and even forests are suffering from rain that in some places is "as strong as lemon juice."

Writing Activity Research a topic of interest to you. Then, write a paragraph on this topic using direct and indirect quotations as in the paragraph above.

Commas in Dates, Addresses, and Letters

When you are writing dates, place a comma after the day of the month.

You should use a comma after a date when the date falls in the middle of the sentence. When only a month and year are given, no commas are necessary between them.

> February 14, 1990   July 4, 1776   August 1914

> The letter wasn't delivered until July 1975, although the postmark was March 1, 1945, from Chicago.

For geographical locations, place a comma between the name of the town or city and the name of the state, district, or country. For a postal address used in a sentence, place a comma after each part of the address.

> Miami, Florida   Munich, Germany
> Please forward our mail to 651 Sentinel Drive, Newark, New Jersey 07124, until the end of the year.

Note that there is no comma between the state and the ZIP code.

Use a comma after the greeting in a friendly letter and after the closing of a friendly or business letter.

> Dear Andria,   Yours truly,

Exercise

Write on your paper the following sentences, adding any necessary commas and deleting any unnecessary commas.

1. Dear Allison
     I've finally arrived in Washington D.C.
2. My train left Lexington Kentucky on July 15.
3. I'm staying at 35 Wisconsin Avenue Washington D.C. 10017.
4. I've learned so much about this city. Did you know that the famous dome on the Capitol building wasn't completed until December, 1863?
5. On May 30, 1922 the Lincoln Memorial was dedicated.

6. I visited 1600 Pennsylvania Avenue Washington D.C.
7. In November 1800 President Adams and his family became the first residents of the White House.
8. Did you know that on August 24 1814 the city burned down?
9. The new White House was completed in September 1817 to replace the building that had been destroyed in the fire.
10. Your friend
    Oona

Commas to Prevent Misreading

When speaking, you sometimes insert pauses in your statements to keep your listeners from misunderstanding what you mean to say. In writing, commas prevent similar misunderstandings from occurring. Even when a comma is not strictly required, you may insert one to prevent misreading. Notice the way the following sentences change in meaning when commas are added.

> Soon after the family packs sandwiches and heads for the beach.
> Soon after, the family packs sandwiches, and heads for the beach.
>
> On waking my aunt goes jogging.
> On waking, my aunt goes jogging.

Exercise

Write on your paper the following sentences, adding commas where necessary.

1. Before baking Al suggests that you gather your ingredients.
2. Frightened the children stopped listening to the story.
3. After we called the phone went dead.
4. While pitching the player strained her back.
5. After washing the children sat down to lunch.
6. Reacting quickly Juan caught the glass as it was falling.
7. When Holly walked in mud lay on the carpet.
8. As soon as she ate the sparrows came looking for crumbs.
9. Without warning the door let in a cold gust of wind.
10. Calling to Mel Sylvia leapt onto the trampoline, laughing.

5
The Semicolon and the Colon

Use a *semicolon* to separate parts of a compound sentence.

Use a *colon* to introduce lists of items, to follow the greeting of a business letter, and to separate hours from minutes in time expressions.

The Semicolon

Semicolons frequently punctuate compound sentences. A compound sentence is made up of two or more independent clauses.

Use a semicolon to separate the parts of a compound sentence when no conjunction is used.

> Directions are included, but they are not complete. Directions are included; they are not complete.

Note that the semicolon replaces the comma and the coordinating conjunction *but.* Conjunctions commonly replaced by semicolons are *and, but, or, for,* and *nor.*

Use a semicolon before a conjunctive adverb that joins the clauses of a compound sentence.

Conjunctive adverbs commonly used are *therefore, however, hence, so, then, moreover, besides, nevertheless, yet,* and *consequently.*

> The classes were filled; *however,* room was made for me.

Use semicolons to separate items in a series that are already separated by commas.

Like commas, semicolons are used in sentences to prevent misreading. If you list a group of cities and their states without semicolons, the list would confuse a reader.

> In the past year, I have visited Hartford, New Haven, and Norwich, Connecticut; Springfield and Worcester, Massachusetts; and Pine Bridge, New York.

The Colon

Use a colon to introduce a list of items.

In speaking and writing, people often use lists. Someone tells you what to pick up at the store. You tell a friend the list of characters in a movie you saw. You make lists to remind you to do certain things. You use them in your schoolwork as well. You should introduce these lists with a colon.

> The backpack contained the following items: a compass, a Swiss army knife, eating utensils, two packets of dried fruit, and a wallet containing five dollars.

Never place a colon immediately after a preposition or a verb.

Incorrect   Among the papers were: a passport, foreign currency, several letters, and an address book.

Correct   Among the papers were the following items: a passport, foreign currency, several letters, and an address book.

Always place a colon after the greeting of a business letter.

> Dear Mr. Trillingham:
> Thank you for replying to our letter so promptly.

Use a colon between the numerals that represent hours and minutes.

> 10:00 P.M.   2:30 A.M.

Exercises

A Write on your paper the following sentences, adding semicolons and colons where necessary. If a sentence is already correct, write *Correct*.

1. Jon prepared dinner Paula set the table.
2. The snow was blinding however, we found our way home.
3. My train should arrive at 930 P.M.
4. Dear Ms. Stein
    We have enclosed the catalog you requested.
5. In the magpie's nest were the following items a strand of colored yarn, a piece of shiny metal, a part of a gold chain, and a square of tinfoil.

6. We visited Jonesboro, Arkansas Topeka, Kansas and St. Louis, Missouri.
7. Bring a drawing pencil and a sketch pad to class tomorrow.
8. Matt's speech was interesting Pat's speech was boring.
9. The band will sell tickets the cheerleaders will usher.
10. The meeting begins at 1045 A.M. everyone should be seated by 1030.

B Write on your paper the following sentences, adding semicolons and colons where they are needed. If a sentence is already correct, write *Correct*.

1. The following items were reported missing two watches, a gold ring, a jade bracelet, and an onyx pendant.
2. San Francisco, Los Angeles, and Oakland, California Dallas and Houston, Texas and New York and Buffalo, New York, have professional teams.
3. We're arriving at 130, and we're meeting at 200 and 300 P.M.
4. For rehearsal, you need a skirt, make-up, and tap shoes.
5. Dear Mrs. Colombo
    We apologize for making an error on your bill.
6. Monica liked to travel besides, she could afford it.
7. The temperature was only 5° nevertheless, my car still started.
8. Dear Mr. Crossley
    Do you hire eighth grade students to deliver morning newspapers?
9. My dream cities include Nome, Alaska Louisville, Kentucky New Orleans, Louisiana and Honolulu, Hawaii.
10. This case bears investigation I'll put someone on it.

6
The Hyphen

> Use a *hyphen* to mark the division of a word at the end of a line.
>   Use a hyphen in compound numbers, nouns, and adjectives.

The **hyphen** has no equivalent in speech. Only in writing are you concerned, for example, with breaking words at the end of a line.

Use a hyphen to divide a word at the end of a line of writing.

Only words of two or more syllables may be divided at the end of a line. Words should only be divided between syllables.

> The Springville Township Library has several authorita-
>   tive books on solar energy.

Never divide a word of one syllable. Do not divide words to leave a single letter at the end or at the beginning of a line.

Incorrect   h-istorian   monke-y
Correct   histo-rian   mon-key

Use the hyphen in compound numbers from twenty-one through ninety-nine and in fractions.

> twenty-three cents   forty-seven members

The law passed by a two-thirds majority.

Use hyphens in such compound nouns as *great-aunt* and *commander-in-chief*, and between words that form a compound adjective preceding a noun.

> This is an up-to-date edition of the almanac.

When the above phrase is not used as a compound adjective, it is written *up to date*.

> I will try to keep you *up to date*.

Check the dictionary if you don't know how to punctuate a compound adjective correctly.

Exercises

A Write these sentences, adding hyphens where necessary.

1. The store has a new, up to the minute catalog.
2. Her self restraint in the record store was admirable.
3. Our much loved cat eats only tuna fish with onions.
4. In the largest showing in recent years, ninety three stu
   dents voted for a new student government.
5. A check for one hundred and seventy six dollars is due.
6. María has two great grandmothers, one age
   eighty nine and the other age ninety one.
7. The President is also Commander in Chief of the army.
8. The old fashioned dress I want is cotton and lace.
9. Tom is three quarters of the way through the book.
10. The witness gave a first hand report of the accident.

B Write the following sentences, adding and deleting hyphens where necessary. If a sentence is already correct, write *Correct*.

1. When the Erie-Canal was finally built, it was three hun
   dred and sixty four miles long.
2. The canal had eighty three locks and took about eight-and-
   one quarter years to build.
3. The canal linked Lake Erie and the Hudson River, two
   important waterways in the still expanding nation.
4. General George Washington, Commander in Chief of the
   American army, had seen the need to improve navigation.
5. In the early 1800's, rock-strewn trails of mud became impass-
   able in bad weather.
6. An east west canal, it was agreed, would allow for a speedier
   delivery of people and much needed supplies.
7. Principal workers on the Erie-Canal were the Irish-immi
   grants, who worked under back breaking conditions.
8. Wages for the workers varied from thirty seven-and-one half
   cents to one half dollar a day.
9. Machines invented for the hard digging included a gigan
   tic stump puller with sixteen inch wheels.
10. Fifty six farmers in one section offered their land free to the
    land hungry canal builders; others were equally-generous.

7
The Apostrophe

> Use an *apostrophe* to show possession; to form the plurals of letters, figures, and words used as words; and to show where letters are omitted in a contraction.

The apostrophe is another punctuation mark that is only useful in writing. Listeners are not confused by a missing or misplaced apostrophe, but readers are. Apostrophes show possession, represent omitted letters in contractions, and help form some plurals.

Forming Possessives and Plurals

To form the possessive of a singular noun, add an apostrophe and an *s*.

The boss's desk	Parker's bone
Gladys's report	Marilyn's apartment

The above rule applies, even when the singular noun ends in *s*.

To form the possessive of a plural noun that does not end in *s*, add an apostrophe and an *s*.

women's   children's

To form the possessive of a plural noun that ends in *s*, add only an apostrophe.

drivers'   pilots'

To form the possessive of indefinite pronouns, use an apostrophe and an *s*.

someone's   anyone's   anybody's

Never use an apostrophe with a possessive pronoun.

our   yours   hers   theirs

Use an apostrophe and an *s* to form the plurals of letters, figures, and words used as words.

two *m*'s   four *6*'s   no *if*'s, *and*'s, or *but*'s

In names of organizations and businesses, in hyphenated words, and in joint ownership, show possession in the last word only.

Georgina and Terry's trip
great-grandfather's gold watch
The Organization of American States' meeting

Forming Contractions

Use an apostrophe in a contraction.

In contractions, the apostrophe replaces omitted letters.

he's = he is	aren't = are not	I'm = I am
it's = it is	isn't = is not	I've = I have
won't = will not	don't = do not	we've = we have

If you remember the rule that an apostrophe replaces one or more omitted letters, you will be less likely to confuse *it's* with *its*. *It's* is the contraction of it is. *Its* is a possessive pronoun. Note that *won't* is the exception to the apostrophe rule.

Use an apostrophe to show that part of a date has been omitted.

The class of '80 (the class of 1980)
The Gold Rush of '49 (The Gold Rush of 1849)

Exercises

A Write the following sentences, adding and deleting apostrophes where necessary.

1. Someones car hit your's while you were gone.
2. Allen and Peggys computer "speaks" to ours.
3. Diana Rosss performance was outstanding.
4. We didnt go to the concert.
5. The teachers meetings are held in the schools library.
6. Charless room is always messier than her's.
7. Its a gift from the class of 56, donated in 86.
8. Im having trouble distinguishing your *m*s from your *n*s.
9. Weve kept our half of the bargain, and theyve kept theirs.
10. The womens volleyball team carefully watched all their opponents practices.

B Write the following sentences, adding and deleting apostrophes where necessary.

1. The *I*s and the *7*s in the 85 ledger are so faint that Albert Swanson and Associates have questioned them.
2. Whose scooter is parked in the Burtons driveway, between the babys buggy and Silass bike?
3. Although she was the Space Ages first woman in space, Valentina Tereshkovas name is not well known in the West.
4. The womens gymnastic meet is the week following the mens gymnastic events.
5. All of the players equipment lay on the ground after their championship games'.
6. Niagara-on-the-Lakes Shaw Festival attracts audiences who are devoted to George Bernard Shaw.
7. If you cant spend the weekend with us, wont you try to spend at least a day at the "Everyones Welcome Lodge"?
8. Its hungry babies' waited in the nest while the wren pecked at the hard ground.
9. Its anyones guess which of Les's businesses' will succeed, but I hope his are more successful than ours.
10. My great-grandfathers favorite subject is the war of 39 to 45; my great-grandmothers favorite is the peace of 45.

c *Write Now*   Imagine that you took the following science class notes in a hurry. Now you plan to lend them to a friend, but you have noticed that you did not make the singular and plural possessives clear. This makes the notes confusing. Clear up this confusion by rewriting the notes, adding apostrophes where they are needed. Use an encyclopedia to check the facts if necessary.

Notes on Mercury

Mercury—like most planets names, comes from
　　Roman mythology
density—second only to Earths density
daylight—(a) sun rises on Mercury once every 176 of
　　　　　Earths days
　　　　　(b) Mercurys day equals two of the planets
　　　　　revolutions around the sun

8
Quotation Marks

> Use *quotation marks* at the beginning and end of direct quotations and to set off titles of short works.

When you use another person's exact written or spoken words, you are giving a **direct quotation**. On the other hand, when you use the person's words but do not quote him or her exactly, you are giving an **indirect quotation**.

Use quotation marks to enclose a direct quotation. Indirect quotations need no quotation marks.

Direct My drama teacher said, "I can teach you the tech-
Quotation niques of acting, but you must find the feelings."

Indirect My drama teacher told me that she can teach me
Quotation acting techniques but that I have to do the rest.

Remember to place the quotation marks before the first word and after the last word of a direct quotation.

Always begin a direct quotation with a capital letter.

Ms. Greene said, "**W**e have been visited by unfriendly aliens."

When a direct quotation is divided by explanatory words, begin the second part of the quotation with a lowercase letter.
If the second part of the quotation is a complete sentence, the first word of this sentence is capitalized.

"If this is the situation," said Li, "**c**ount me out."
"I have to go," said Janet. "**T**ell Cass I'll call later."

Place commas and periods inside quotation marks. Place semicolons and colons outside the quotation marks.

"One of these days," said Tom, "I must mow the lawn."
Gil warned Al, "It's dangerous"; however, Gil was
  wrong.
Examine these elements as you read "The Tell-Tale
Heart": plot, characterization, and point of view.

Place question marks and exclamation points inside quotation marks if they belong to the quotation. Place them outside if they do not belong to the quotation.

> Burton asked, "Whose backpack is sitting on the steps?"
> Did Pilar answer, "I don't know"?
> "I repeat," Pilar answered, "I don't know"!
> "Don't shout!" yelled Bradley.

Use single quotation marks to enclose one quotation within another. If the quotation within the quotation ends the sentence, use both the single and double quotation marks after the last word of the quotations.

> "I heard you say, 'Tell Kate' as you left the office."
> "I heard you say, 'Tell Kate.'"

In a quotation of more than one paragraph, use quotation marks at the beginning of each paragraph and at the end of the final paragraph.

> "Walking is the thinking person's sport," said the speaker, "because the pace is so slow.
> "I find it much easier to think at such a slow pace. When I walk I usually think about the grass growing and the wind blowing."

Exercise

Write on your paper the sentences below, following the rules for correctly punctuating quotations. If a sentence is already correct, write *Correct*.

1. Theodore Roosevelt said, the only man who makes no mistakes is the man who never does anything.
2. Is it true that Jimmy Carter said, I can get up at nine and be rested, or I can get up at six and be President
3. "Always take the job, but never yourself, seriously," said Dwight D. Eisenhower.
4. We stand today, said the Democratic presidential candidate John F. Kennedy, On the edge of a new frontier.
5. President Herbert Hoover had promised Americans, A chicken in every pot; the Depression spoiled his promise.

6. "There is a homely adage that runs: Speak softly and carry a big stick; you will go far."
7. Let me assert my firm belief said Franklin D. Roosevelt, that the only thing we have to fear is fear itself.
8. Our first President let it be known that it was American policy to make no permanent foreign alliances.
9. "No President," said Teddy Roosevelt, Has ever enjoyed himself as much as I.
10. I should like to quote President Grant, said Helena, who said, Let us have peace, in his acceptance letter.

Punctuating Dialogue

There is one simple rule to remember when you write dialogue: begin a new paragraph each time you quote a different speaker.

"What did you say to him?" I asked.

He said," If your house seems too crowded, bring a goat home to live with you and your family."

I couldn't believe this. "Why would taking in a goat help?"

"Well, once you live with a goat for a few days, a house seems very spacious when you remove it."

Punctuating Titles

Use quotation marks to enclose the titles of poems, short stories, songs, reports, articles, and chapters of books.

Poem	"Annabel Lee"
Short Story	"The Headless Horseman"
Song	"Somewhere Over the Rainbow"

Underline titles of books, plays, magazines, newspapers, television series, works of art, musical compositions, and motion pictures. Titles that are underlined will be italicized in print.

Book	A Wind in the Door
Magazine	National Geographic
Television Series	The Bill Cosby Show
Motion Picture	The Wizard of Oz

Exercise

Write these sentences, adding and deleting punctuation where necessary. Use the proper form for dialogue.

1. Where is my book? she asked. I lost it. I'm sorry, I answered sheepishly.
2. That television station shows reruns of I Love Lucy.
3. Which article do you want, Shells of the Sea or Sea Shells?
4. We played music from 2001 before the big game.
5. What did you say? asked Jean. I said, "It's noisy!"
6. Shall we see a movie tonight? John asked. Yes, let's see Casablanca, Gail answered.
7. Rescue Party is a short story by Arthur C. Clarke.
8. The musical My Fair Lady is based on the play Pygmalion.
9. My favorite television series is Star Trek.
10. Why do you want to see the file? he asked. You know why, Kay answered. I need to see what it says.

Grammar in Action

Characters in stories seem most alive when they are speaking. Compare the following ways of telling the same thing.

> Tara and James discussed the design of the newsletter.
>
> or
>
> Tara said, "The headline is too large. It ruins the page."
> James replied, "I disagree. I like the big headline."

Writing Activity Imagine you have written the following passage:

> Anita and Jimmy wanted to know more about being a stunt person. They asked Roy questions about it, and Roy answered them patiently.

Now, rewrite the passage to include dialogue between the characters. Your revised passage should be much more vivid and informative. Use an encyclopedia to gather facts if necessary.

Linking Mechanics & Writing

A You have just met and talked with a famous person. You want to tell your friend about the conversation you had with this celebrity. In a paragraph, describe the conversation you had. Use indirect quotations rather than direct quotations. Then, because your friend wants to know exactly what was said, write the same conversation again, using direct quotations rather than indirect quotations.

B Imagine that you are the secretary of any club you choose. As secretary, you must take the minutes of the meetings. That means you must write everything that is said. Imagine that you are at one meeting in which all the club members are trying to talk at the same time. Write a page of minutes from this meeting. Use at least five different interrupters and five different introductory elements in the dialogue you write.

C Suppose that you are having a party to which you have invited ten people that do not know each other. Write ten sentences to introduce each of the ten strangers. Use nouns of direct address in five of the sentences and nouns in apposition in the remaining five sentences.

D Imagine that your family is planning to move. Make a list of twenty items that you want the movers to move particularly carefully. Choose items that belong to various members of your family. Use possessives to show to whom each item belongs. Some items may belong to two or more people. Others may belong to your entire family.

Additional Practice

Part 1 End Marks Write the following sentences and phrases, adding punctuation where necessary.

1. Does Canada have a larger land area than the United States
2. Oh no Father forgot to pay the electric bill
3. The film will be shown at 8:15 P M
4. Dr Marta Estevez is the oral surgeon who pulled my tooth
5. Shopping List
   1 hammer
   2 nails
   3 picture wire
   4 masking tape
6. King Akhenaton was the ruler of Egypt from 1367 to 1350 B C
7. What are your plans for summer vacation
8. Barbara C Jordan served in the United States House of Representatives during the 1970's
9. Great We can really see the field from these seats
10. Were you able to shake the governor's hand at the town meeting

Parts 2-4 Commas Write the following sentences, adding and deleting commas where necessary.

11. Mother assembled the bird house and I painted it.
12. The salad contained lettuce tomatoes grated carrots and shredded cheese.
13. Kim however does not like football and she never attends our school's games.
14. Gabriela Mistral a Chilean poet won the Nobel Prize, for literature in 1945.
15. Come outside Jeff and help me prune the trees.
16. Pardon me I didn't mean to bump you, with my grocery cart.
17. Shakespeare's Hamlet said "To be, or not to be—that is the question."

18. Elena told me, that she is designing and sewing a dress for the party.
19. Luther Burbank the famous horticulturist, was born on March 7 1849.
20. After striking out Fred dropped his bat in disgust.

Part 5 Semicolons and Colons Write the following sentences, adding semicolons and colons where necessary.

21. I played volleyball at the beach my little sister built a sand castle.
22. Thomas Edison improved the following inventions the electric generator, the telephone, and the motion picture.
23. Dear Mrs. Sendak
    Our university would like to award you an honorary degree.
24. Jim thinks most cartoon characters are silly however, he finds Porky Pig and Daffy Duck amusing.
25. On our European tour, we visited Brussels, Belgium Bonn, West Germany Bern, Switzerland and Lyon, France.

Parts 6 and 7 Hyphens and Apostrophes Write the following sentences, adding hyphens and apostrophes where needed.

26. This is a state of the art computer system.
27. What is the sum of two thirds and five sixths?
28. The mens clothing department is on the third floor.
29. Its a shame that you cant stay another few days.
30. The United States celebrated its bicentennial in 76.

Part 8 Quotation Marks and Other Punctuation Write the following sentences, adding punctuation where needed.

31. Thomas Jefferson said, Never trouble another for what you can do yourself.
32. Have you ever read the Robert Frost poem called Birches?
33. Call me later, said Diana, and give me your decision.
34. The radio announcer said, Don't forget to turn your clocks back one hour."
35. I have seen the movie E.T.: The Extra-Terrestrial twice.

Application and Review

Lesson Review

A Using End Marks Write on your paper the following sentences, adding periods and other end marks where necessary.

1. Address the memo to Capt T E Conklin, Jr
2. Jacinto Watch out That vase was created in 500 BC
3. Oh! I forgot to tell you that Eileen asked to use your bike.
4. Tell Ana to pay me the $350 she owes me for the album.
5. "Wow Are you really going to see the Indianapolis 500" Janice asked.
6. Don't forget the last two items on the list:
   5 plates
   6 silverware
7. We will discuss NATO at our next meeting
8. Be careful That box contains china and glassware
9. If Dr Cimino chaperones the dance, will you assist her
10. Here is my outline:
    I Architecture
      A Pre-modern
        1 Georgian
        2 Victorian
      B Modern
    II Design

B Using Commas That Separate Ideas Write the following sentences, adding commas where necessary. If a sentence is already correct, write *Correct.*

1. They could not decide whether to visit the old mansion or to go to the hotel and have lunch.
2. Meg saw that the sun was shining and she was thrilled.
3. The team practiced showered and went home to rest.
4. Jo agreed to join us for lunch but she wants to eat soon.
5. We arrived at seven worked until nine and took a break.

6. These are my chores: first fix the shed door; second mow the lawn; third trim the hedges.
7. The narrow, winding staircase is the subject of my painting.
8. James hasn't arrived but we expect him in the morning.
9. Should we help cook or should we arrive just in time for dinner?
10. Paul Tomi Ed and Sam signed their names in the book.

C Using Commas That Set Off Special Elements Write on your paper the following sentences, adding commas where necessary.

1. Yes I've read Agatha Christie; however I prefer P.D. James.
2. After mashing them Niki likes to reheat the potatoes.
3. This is my sister Jackie the photographer in our family.
4. You're not sure I suppose when the winner will be named.
5. Gary to tell the truth was quite satisfied; nevertheless I asked for another opinion.
6. Did you see someone pass by the window Ms. Ferguson?
7. Your decision moreover will affect our future plans.
8. You gave a great report Susan.
9. As you know, Bruce Jenner the Olympic decathlon champion spoke at the club luncheon.
10. An elderly woman a survivor of the *Titanic* disaster described in vivid detail her memories of that night.

D Using Commas in Other Ways Write the following sentences, adding commas where necessary. If a sentence is correct, write *Correct*.

1. As Liz said "I think it will rain" there was a cloudburst.
2. Send the package to Ms. Elena Wright 2439 North Granville Avenue Marion Ohio 43302.
3. "Entries postmarked after January 25 1986" Barry explained "are not eligible for the award."
4. Dear Laura
   Your birthday gift was just what I wanted. Thank you Laura.
      Yours sincerely
      Katie

5. Do you mean Kansas City Missouri or Kansas City Kansas?
6. Jim said that he wants to play ice hockey this winter.
7. Is your birthday May 9 1977 or May 9 1978?
8. We moved from 1289 Aspen Drive Langstown to 389 Des Plaines Avenue Merryville.
9. "Whatever you do, do it well" is an old saying.
10. "What I want" said Joan "is to win that contest."

E Using Semicolons and Colons Write the following sentences, adding semicolons and colons where necessary.

1. Jack passed the history exam I did also.
2. These are the guidebook shopping suggestions leather from Barcelona, Spain, or Florence, Italy wool from London, England, or Edinburgh, Scotland and crystal from Waterford, Ireland, or Stockholm, Sweden.
3. The play is sold out nevertheless, I can get tickets to it.
4. Dear Sir or Madam
   A refund check for nine dollars is enclosed.
5. Kay cleaned the porch Pop painted the stairs.
6. Brian was willing to pay his share however, Willis was not.
7. To make the dessert you need two apples, green or tart red ones two lemons; and a lime.
8. Bring these items to art class a charcoal pencil, a sketch pad, and fruit to make a still life.
9. The first train is at 600 A.M., the second at 730 A.M., and the last at 745 A.M.
10. The bus drives through traffic the train runs overhead.

F Using Hyphens Write on your paper the following sentences, adding hyphens where necessary.

1. Mr. Perez's daughter in law is an up and coming lawyer.
2. Although one hundred and thirty six teenagers applied for the camp, only ninety eight were accepted.
3. Julie's paintings received many awards, but her sculptures went unnoticed.
4. My great aunt and great uncle are both eighty three.
5. The vice president's recommendation won a three fifths approval.

G Using Apostrophes Write the following sentences, adding apostrophes where necessary.

1. The head coachs decision was applauded by our two teams representatives.
2. The actresss costume was covered in jewels, but they werent genuine, of course.
3. Dont you think that growing up in the 1950s would be more fun than growing up in the 1980s?
4. Sandy and Pams duet improves with each rehearsal.
5. In printing, dashes are measured in *m*s and *n*s.
6. Because I forgot mine, I need to borrow someones pencil.
7. Taste Pedros and Lilas rice dishes, and tell me whether you prefer his or hers.
8. The Canadians symbol is a maple leaf.
9. The athletic departments new sweatshirts resemble ours.
10. My jacket is the one with "Class of 87" on the back.

H Using Quotation Marks Write the following sentences, adding punctuation where necessary. If a sentence is already correct, write *Correct.*

1. I asked, Did Tolstoy write, If you want to be happy, be?
2. Wendy asked, Is anyone entering work in the fair?
3. Step Back into the Future: the Abacus in the Modern World, was the title of Rachel's essay.
4. We need these items, the announcement began, food, clothing, blankets, dishes, and housewares.
5. I like animals; I'm going to be a veterinarian, Callie explained. That's why I work in the animal shelter.
6. Eve Merriam's poems have a special meaning for me, stated Monique.
7. I didn't believe Steven when he said, I won the race, Emmet told us, but then he showed me his trophy.
8. Why does the notice on the bulletin board read, Volunteers, give us one hour out of your week ?
9. Read the chapter called Memory from The Mind's Eye.
10. Doug told us that his family albums contain pictures of ancestors who lived during the Civil War.

Chapter Review

A Using Punctuation Write the following selection, adding punctuation marks where necessary. Some punctuation marks have already been provided. Use the correct form for dialogue.

Places everyone called the director. Are we all ready to rehearse the scene Yolanda, is something bothering you Yes replied Yolanda I cant find my script Oh no exclaimed Maya How can we expect to rehearse? Thats when Ellie entered and saved the day. Look she said Here's the sought after script, and she handed the script to the much relieved Yolanda. Now said the director. let's go to work!

B Revising Punctuation Rewrite the following selection, adding and deleting punctuation where necessary.

September, 12 1988

Community Zoo
1000 Lincoln Avenue
Laingsburg Michigan, 48848

To Whom It May Concern;

After reading the article Helping Zoos Care for Their Babies in this months "Zoo Magazine," I decided to offer you my help. I love animals helping them is important to me. I have in fact a collection of stray pets that includes the following a baby raccoon four kittens two puppies and an old dog. In addition I sometimes care for a friends rabbit. Also I feed the ducklings in the springtime. I can work for you every Thursday afternoon from 400 PM to 500 PM
If you would like my help please let me know as soon as possible. I am eager to hear from you.

Sincerely
Gwen Goodheart

Cumulative Review

A **Using Capitalization** Write the words that contain capitalization errors in the sentences below. Correct the errors.

1. my aunt lynette and uncle george met the senator from their state, senator barbara s. granley.
2. a famous american president was known as j.f.k.
3. christopher columbus had spanish approval for his voyage.
4. please tell mom that aunt lillian can use my room.
5. my aunt read out loud from the book of genesis.
6. mother said that i have to go to the doctor tomorrow.
7. ask mr. karantinos to explain again what happened the day the president was assassinated.
8. the travelers planned to visit religious shrines in europe and asia.
9. it is much faster to sail through the panama canal than to sail all around south america.
10. travel east on the kennedy expressway until you come to an exit for fullerton avenue.
11. the buffalo in the west almost became extinct.
12. we want to drive through yosemite national park.
13. the mississippi river empties into the gulf of mexico.
14. houses that face north are often cold.
15. is it as hot and dry in nevada as it is in the sahara desert?
16. the family went to church together this sunday.
17. we sometimes call july 4 independence day.
18. the smithsonian institute has many fascinating exhibits.
19. sheila attended smith college after high school.
20. everyone in my school takes courses in french and latir
21. the corvair was an american car with a rear engine.
22. as early as 753 b.c., rome was inhabited.
23. the poem begins, "once upon a midnight dreary .
24. "where," she asked, "is my other shoe?"
25. have you read the book *a tale of two cities?*

B Using Punctuation Write the following sentences on your paper, adding correct punctuation where necessary.

1. Look out Those rocks are falling
2. Bill asked Whose picture is this
3. The first section of the outline was I American authors unite
4. Gov J B Engle was not elected again
5. Remarkable How did you do that
6. I went to the front door quickly but the caller had left
7. The tall elegant fragile cream pitcher fell to the floor
8. Yolanda ran to the window and opened it
9. Grover Cleveland Herbert Clark Hoover and Calvin Coolidge were each elected President of our country
10. Roger Hill my favorite neighbor is moving to Boston Massachusetts how I will miss him
11. Wait called Albert What time should I be there
12. We went to see the famous painting called the Mona Lisa
13. I brought the plates Terry brought the silverware
14. She has only twenty five cents to her name
15. Dads plan is to reach the city by nightfall
16. Where is your great grandmothers house asked Sal
17. The doors open at 530 dont be late
18. Ive visited Houston Texas Stowe Vermont and Toledo Ohio
19. He made a spur of the moment decision
20. It must have been difficult to survive in the 1700s

C Combined Review Write the following sentences on your paper, using correct capitalization and punctuation.

1. welcome said the president to the white house
2. the group of moslems faced east and prayed to allah
3. the school on warren ave is closed on saturday
4. the titanic sank in the atlantic many people drowned
5. jan owns an antique edsel
6. didnt robert louis stevenson write the book treasure island
7. giorgio a new student at park high smiled then he stood
8. the package goes to po box 450 rawlings virginia
9. On dec twenty fifth we open presents then we sing carols
10. wow this is fun exclaimed phylliss aunt

Writer's Handbook

Ideas for Writing

You can find ideas for writing anywhere, if you keep your mind open to the many possibilities around you. The following lists of ideas can help you explore various topics. For other writing ideas, see Starting Points on pages 41-53. Then use the thinking skills and prewriting strategies you learned in Chapters 2 and 3 to develop your writing topic.

Ideas for Writing

Descriptive
a time capsule
a boat in water
the inside of a restaurant
a city street in the rain
a dancer in motion
a movie theater
someone wearing a hat
the face of a stranger
an animal in its natural environment
two people on a park bench

Narrative
a midnight phone call
a day everything went wrong
a difficult, but rewarding job
a misadventure
a team effort
learning from a mistake
a time someone helped you

Expository
(Process)
how automobiles are manufactured
how a telephone works
how to save money
how to make basic bicycle repairs
how bridges are built across water
how electricity is generated
how a furnace works

(Cause/Effect)
how the sun and moon affect tides
What causes dental decay?
Martin Luther King, Jr.'s, effect on America's Civil Rights Movement
What causes blindness?
the effect of radiation on the human body
What causes a headache?

(Compare/Contrast)
hard/soft contact lenses
beneficial/harmful insects
traditional Japanese home/American home
electronic keyboard/piano
helicopter/airplane
judo/karate
rock music/classical music

Persuasive
Should teaching machines replace teachers?
Should America's space program continue?
Why become a foster parent?
Is nuclear energy safe?
Should teen-agers be allowed to vote?
Should teen-agers buy clothes in off-price stores?

Ideas for Writing in Subject Areas

Art
Islamic mosques
African art
public sculpture
Gothic cathedrals
illustrating
  children's books
Chinese watercolor
  paintings
the architecture of
  Mies Van Der Rohe
making paper
  sculptures
how to paint a
  mural

Consumerism
What causes
  inflation?
the high cost of
  credit cards
how interest is
  calculated
Should you buy
  counterfeit perfumes?
how to extend the
  life of photographs
Should you open a
  certificate of deposit?

Health
Why are premature
  babies placed in
  incubators?
Can influenza be
  prevented?
why the human
  body needs iodine
how tuberculosis is
  diagnosed and treated
how to control
  blood pressure
why people blink

Math
the origins of
  flowcharts
mathematical tricks
  with numbers
geometry in
  surveying land
the mathematics of
  the electoral vote
probability and
  games
calculating the
  momentum of
  moving objects
determining the
  speed of light

Music
the swing era in
  jazz
stringed musical
  instruments of
  India
how to play the
  bagpipes
the origin of the
  electric guitar
percussion
  instruments
chamber music
composing
  soundtracks for
  motion pictures
how radio stations
  program music
musical comedies
mariachi players

Science
how the smallpox
  vaccine was
  discovered
How are icebergs
  formed?
how blood clots
modern inventions
Why protect bats?
carbon-14 dating
left-brain and
  right-brain people
treatment of coro-
  nary artery disease
how hydrofoils work
medieval medicine
What is a silicon chip?
why people forget
how oil is
  discovered

Social Studies
What is the Wailing
  Wall in Jerusalem?
illiteracy in
  America
Who are today's
  immigrants?
What effect did
  Mohandas Gandhi
  have in India's
  struggle for
  independence?
Mother Theresa's
  effect on the lives
  of the poor in
  Calcutta, India
hairstyles throughout
  the ages
educating migrant
  school children
compare/contrast

Outlines and Other Graphic Organizers

Graphic aids can help you plan your writing and organize information in a logical way. You might use them to write a report or to record important facts from a class discussion.

Correct Outline Form

A **formal outline** organizes the main points and supporting details of a topic. These main points are arranged to show the relationships between ideas.

Formal outlines can be either sentence outlines or topic outlines. A **sentence outline** uses complete sentences to explain the main points and subpoints. In a **topic outline,** the main points and subpoints are written in words or phrases. Here is part of a topic outline.

Zoos

I. Purpose of zoos   (Main point)
   A. Entertainment/education   (First subpoint)
      1. Service to general public ⎫
      2. Group tours and lectures ⎬ (Details for A)
      3. Children's zoos ⎭
   B. Scientific research (Second subpoint)
      1. Study of animal bodies ⎫
      2. Study of animal behavior ⎬ (Details for B)
   C. Wildlife conservation (Third subpoint)
      1. Animals bred in captivity
      2. Some animals returned to the wild after breeding
         a. European bison ⎫
         b. Hawaiian goose ⎬ (Subdetails for 2)

II. Care of zoo animals
   A. Display
      1. Protection and comfort of animals and visitors
      2. Special means of displays
         a. Moats to isolate large animals
         b. Night-lighting for nocturnal animals
         c. Re-creation of natural habitats
   B. Feeding
   C. Veterinary care

Follow these steps when writing a sentence or topic outline.

1. Write the title at the top of the outline. The title, introduction, and conclusion are not considered parts of the outline.
2. Arrange main points and subpoints as shown on the previous page. Main points are indicated by Roman numerals.
3. Indent each division of the outline. Align letters or numbers as shown on the previous page.
4. Do not use a single subheading. A heading should not be broken down unless it can be divided into at least two points. For example, if there is a *1* under *A,* there must be at least a *2.*
5. In a topic outline, keep items of the same rank in the same form. For example, if *A* is a noun, then *B* and *C* should also be nouns. Subtopics need not be in the same form as main topics.
6. Begin each item with a capital letter. Do not use end punctuation in a topic outline.

Writing an Informal Outline

An **informal outline** organizes information quickly and concisely. Main ideas are written in separate headings, with supporting details placed beneath each heading. Because informal outlines are generally for personal use, the format varies. Any form that helps you to organize information is acceptable.

An informal outline can help you organize class notes, prepare a speech, or review test material. Here is an example.

I. Ways to see Grand Canyon
—drive along park roads and stop at scenic points
—walk along rim of canyon
—hike along park trails
—ride mules into canyon
—boat or raft into canyon on Colorado River
II. What to see in park
—spectacular canyons carved out of rock
—300 species of birds
—rare animals found only in Grand Canyon
—fossilized footprints of prehistoric animals

Other Graphic Organizers

Other graphic organizers can help you organize information that you have gathered for a speech or report.

Sequence Chain A **sequence chain** can be used to plan or analyze the plot of a narrative, to analyze a process, or to trace historical or social events. Like a time line (see page 20), a sequence chain shows chronological relationships. However, in a sequence chain there is a direct relationship from one event to the next.

To make a sequence chain, draw a rectangular box in the upper left-hand corner of a page, then write in the first event of your sequence. Continue to draw rectangular boxes from left to right and from top to bottom until you have reached the end of your sequence.

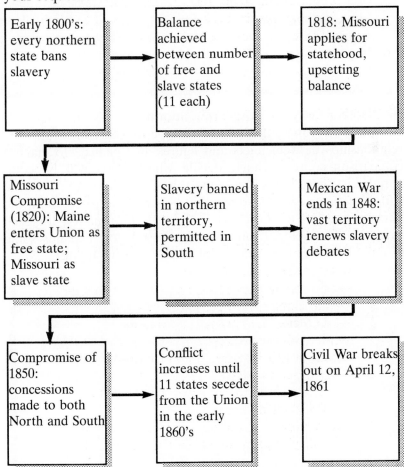

Charts A **cause-and-effect chart** illustrates how one thing happens because of something else. The cause-and-effect chart on the next page shows what causes a rabbit population to increase and decrease.

Rabbit Population

Cause	Effect
Favorable temperatures and amount of rainfall	—increased food supply for rabbits —large, healthy rabbit litters —rabbit population increases
Increased population among rabbits	—not enough food and shelter for rabbits —weaker members starve or migrate —rabbits become easy targets for predators such as hawks
Increased population among hawks	—more rabbits hunted by hawks —number of rabbits continues to shrink until rabbit population can survive with existing food and shelter

Another way to organize information is to make a **comparison–contrast chart.** This type of chart illustrates the relationships between facts and figures at a glance. To make a comparison–contrast chart, decide which items will be compared. List these items across the top of the chart. Then list the various categories or headings that you will use to compare the items at the left of the chart. Fill in the information for each category. The comparison–contrast chart below explains some of the differences between the planets Mars and Jupiter.

Mars and Jupiter

	Mars	Jupiter
size	about half the diameter of earth	diameter about eleven times that of earth
water	no large or visible bodies of water	probably has no water
atmosphere	thin atmosphere allowing dangerous radiation to reach ground	mostly gases that would suffocate living things on earth
noteworthy feature	giant dust storms periodically sweep entire planet	Great Red Spot—a hurricane-force storm that has been raging for centuries

Common Usage Problems

This section explains common writing problems. Review the items from time to time or use them as a guide for proofreading.

Abbreviations

In most instances, abbreviations should be avoided in formal writing. Exceptions are permitted for titles (Mr., Mrs., Ms., Dr.), dates, and times (A.M., P.M., B.C., A.D.).

See also pages 607-608.

Clichés

A **cliché** is an overused expression, such as *slow as molasses in January* or *putting your nose to the grindstone.* Use fresh words to express your ideas instead of clichés.

Double Negatives

Negatives are words such as *no, not, never, nothing,* and *none.* Contractions that end in *n't* are also negatives. A **double negative** occurs when two negatives are used where only one is needed. Double negatives should always be avoided.

Incorrect Our club does*n't* have *no* money left.
Correct Our club does*n't* have *any* money left.

See also page 524.

Infinitives, Split

An **infinitive** is a verb form that usually begins with the word *to.* A **split infinitive** occurs when a modifier comes between *to* and the verb. Avoiding splitting an infinitive.

Awkward Mark planned *to* promptly *serve* dinner at 6:00 P.M.
Better Mark planned *to serve* dinner promptly at 6:00 P.M.

See also pages 584-585.

Jargon

Jargon is the specialized language of people within the same profession. For example, lawyers talk of *allegations, appeals,* and *litigation.* While these words are understood by those within the same field, others may find jargon confusing. When you write, use vocabulary your audience will understand.

Modifiers

Adjective-Adverb Confusion In some cases, you may not know whether to use an adjective or an adverb. First, determine which word is being modified. Remember, adjectives modify nouns or pronouns. Adverbs modify verbs, adjectives, or other adverbs.

See also pages 512-513.

Good-Well The words *good* and *well* are often confused. *Good* is always an adjective. It modifies nouns or pronouns.

> Dana felt *good* when she finished painting her room. (predicate adjective—"felt good" means *happy* or *satisfied*)

Well is usually an adverb modifying an action verb. *Well* is an adjective when it modifies a noun or a pronoun and means "healthy."

> Angela ran *well* in yesterday's race. (adverb)
> I felt *well* when I awoke. (predicate adjective—"felt well" means *healthy*)

See also page 514.

Bad-Badly *Bad* is an adjective, modifying a noun or a pronoun. *Badly* is an adverb that modifies action verbs.

> The losing team felt *bad*. (predicate adjective)
> The guitarist performed *badly* last night. (adverb)

Comparative and Superlative Forms Use the **comparative form** to compare two items. Use the **superlative form** to compare three or more. Do not use *-er* and *more* or *-est* and *most* together.

> That ski slope is *steeper* than this one.
> It is the *steepest* slope on the mountain.

> Your photograph is *more interesting* than mine.
> It is the *most interesting* photograph in the contest.

See also pages 516-519.

Pronouns

Agreement A pronoun must agree with its antecedent in number. Singular pronouns are used with singular antecedents. Plural pronouns are used with plural antecedents.

Incorrect	Any *passenger* must pay *their* fare before boarding.
Correct	*Passengers* must pay *their* fares before boarding.

When two singular antecedents are jointed by *or* or *nor,* use a singular pronoun.

Either Jane or Sarah will read *her* composition next.

Indefinite Pronouns An **indefinite pronoun** does not refer to any specific person or thing. The indefinite pronouns listed below are always singular and take a singular verb. Remember that the phrase following an indefinite pronoun does not affect agreement.

another	anything	everybody	neither	one
anybody	each	everyone	nobody	somebody
anyone	either	everything	no one	someone

Incorrect *One* of the boys *jump* rope for exercise.
Correct *One* of the boys *jumps* rope for exercise.

Use the possessive pronouns *his, her,* and *its* with singular indefinite pronouns.

Somebody must have lost *her* ring.
Has *anyone* finished *his* or *her* art project yet?

The following indefinite pronouns are always plural: *both, few, many,* and *several.* Use them with the plural possessive pronouns *our* and *their* and with plural verbs.

Few of the group stayed in *their* seats. (pronoun agreement)
Many of us *favor* that idea. (subject-verb agreement)

Some indefinite pronouns may be either singular or plural depending on their meaning in a sentence: *all, any, most, none, some,* and *much.*

Most of the building had *its* original woodwork. (singular)
Most of the passengers fastened *their* seat belts. (plural)

Lack of Antecedents Do not use a pronoun without an antecedent.

Unclear When you are troubled, talk to someone about *it.* (*It* needs to be specified.)

Clear When you are troubled, talk to someone about your problem.

Possessive Pronouns Do not confuse possessive pronouns, such as *its, your,* and *their,* with the contractions they resemble. Possessive pronouns show ownership. A contraction combines two words and is always written with an apostrophe: *it's, you're,* and *they're.*

Subject and Object Pronouns The subject pronouns are *I, you, he, she, it, we,* and *they.* Use these pronouns as subjects of sentences and as predicate pronouns after linking verbs.

I have been studying ballet for three years. (subject)
The doctor on call is *he*. (predicate pronoun)

The object pronouns—*me, you, him, her, it, us,* and *them*—are used as direct objects, indirect objects, and objects of prepositions.

The horse threw *me* from my saddle. (direct object)
Mr. Stevens gave *him* another form. (indirect object)
Everyone is going except *them*. (object of preposition)

To use compound subject and object pronouns correctly, use the same pronoun that you would use if the pronoun stood alone.

Compound Subject	*She* and *I* tried out for the school play. (*She* tried out, *I* tried out)
Compound Object	Bring *me* and *her* some ice cream. (bring *me*, bring *her*)

Unclear Reference The reference of a pronoun is unclear if the pronoun may refer to more than one word in a sentence.

Unclear	If there are onions on the hamburgers, Uncle Bob won't eat *them*.
Clear	If there are onions on the hamburgers, Uncle Bob won't eat the onions.

Sentence Errors
Fragments Unlike a sentence, a **fragment** does not express a complete thought. It may be missing a subject, a predicate, or both.

Fragment	Pulled the rug up the stairs. (missing subject)
Sentence	*Ted* pulled the rug up the stairs.

Run-on Sentences A **run-on sentence** occurs when two or more sentences are written incorrectly as one.

Run-on	Strong winds knocked down power lines, our electricity was off for several hours.
Correct	Strong winds knocked down power lines. Our electricity was off for several hours.

Slang
Colorful words and phrases spoken by a particular group of people or during a specific time period are called **slang**. Slang is acceptable only in very casual settings. It should always be avoided in formal speaking and writing. The following words and phrases are examples of slang.

nerd   a person who is out of fashion, dull, troublesome, annoying

clueless   lacking knowledge or insight; confused or distracted

Verb

Active and Passive Verbs A verb is **active** when the subject of the sentence performs the action. A verb is **passive** when the subject receives the action. Change passive verbs to active verbs whenever possible to make your writing more direct.

Passive   The geraniums in the garden were trampled by my dog.
Active   My dog trampled the geraniums in the garden.

Agreement with Subject A subject and its verb must agree in number, even when the subject comes after the verb.

> Into the harbor *sail* the fishing *boats.*
> Here *are* the brass *candlesticks* for the dinner party.

Use a plural verb to join two or more parts of a compound subject joined by *and.* When the subjects are joined by *or* or *nor,* the verb agrees with the nearer subject.

> *Prokofiev* and *Tchaikovsky were* both Russian composers.
> Either the *physician* or the *paramedics are* on the scene.
> The *stamps* or the *envelope is* in the desk drawer.

If a prepositional phrase comes between the subject and the verb, the verb must still agree with its subject.

Singular   The *sunlight* in these rooms *is* quite bright.
Plural   The *seams* in the white carpet *are* very noticeable.

Tenses Verbs have different forms called **tenses** to indicate when an action or event takes place. When you write, do not change tenses in the middle of a sentence.

Incorrect   Paulette *loses* her footing on the mountain and *fell* twenty feet.
Correct   Paulette *lost* her footing on the mountain and *fell* twenty feet.

Who and *Whom*

Who is the subject form of the pronoun; *whom* is the object form.

> *Who* left the back door open again? (*Who* is the subject of the verb *left.*)
> *Whom* did you meet at the bus stop? (*Whom* is the direct object of the verb *did meet.*)

Quick Guide to Capitalization

Proper Nouns and Proper Adjectives

1. Capitalize the names of persons and also the initials or abbreviations that stand for those names.
2. Capitalize titles used with names of persons and capitalize the initials and/or abbreviations standing for those titles. Capitalize the titles *Mr., Mrs., Ms.,* and *Miss.*
3. Capitalize titles of people in unique positions whose rank is very important, even when the titles are used without proper names: *The President will meet with his staff.* Do not capitalize titles that are used as common nouns.
4. Capitalize such words as *mother, father, aunt,* and *uncle* when these words are used as names.
5. Capitalize the pronoun *I.*
6. Capitalize all words referring to the Deity, to holy books, and to religious scriptures.
7. Capitalize personal pronouns referring to the Deity.

Geographical Names

1. Capitalize names of sections of the country but not directions of the compass.
2. Capitalize proper adjectives derived from names of sections of the country or the world. Do not capitalize adjectives derived from words indicating directions.

Organizations, History, and Time

1. Capitalize all the important words in the names of organizations and institutions, including their abbreviations.
2. Capitalize the names of historical events, documents, and periods of time.
3. Capitalize the names of months, days, and holidays, but not the names of seasons.

Languages, Peoples, Transportation, and Abbreviations

1. Capitalize the names of languages, races, nationalities, and religions, and also the adjectives derived from them.

2. Do not capitalize the names of school subjects unless they are languages or unless a course name is followed by a number.
3. Capitalize the names of ships, trains, and aircraft. Capitalize brand names of automobiles.
4. Capitalize the abbreviations *B.C., A.D., A.M.,* and *P.M.*

First Words
1. Capitalize the first word of every sentence.
2. Capitalize the first word in most lines of poetry.
3. Capitalize the first word of a direct quotation.
4. Capitalize all the important words in the greeting of a letter. In the closing, capitalize only the first word.
5. Capitalize the first word in each entry of an outline.
6. Capitalize the first word, the last word, and all important words in the titles of books, poems, short stories, articles, newspapers, magazines, plays, motion pictures, works of art, television programs, and musical compositions.

Quick Guide to Punctuation

The Period
1. Use a period at the end of a declarative sentence.
2. Use a period at the end of an imperative sentence.
3. Use a period at the end of an indirect question, that is, a question that reports what someone said without using the speaker's exact words.
4. Use a period after most abbreviations and after initials.
5. Use a period after the letters or numbers in an outline or list.
6. Use a period between numerals representing dollars and cents and before a decimal.

The Question Mark and the Exclamation Point
1. Use a question mark at the end of an interrogative sentence.
2. Use an exclamation point at the end of an exclamatory sentence and following an interjection.

The Comma

1. Use a comma before the conjunction that joins the two parts of a compound sentence. In a very short compound sentence, it is not necessary to put a comma before *and,* but one must be used before *but* or *or.*
2. Use a comma after each item in a series except the last.
3. When two or more adjectives precede a noun but do not express a closely related thought, use a comma after each adjective except the last one.
4. Use commas after the adverbs *first, second, third,* and so on, when these adverbs introduce items in a series.
5. Use a comma to separate an introductory word or phrase from the rest of the sentence.
6. Use commas before and after interrupters.
7. Use commas to set off all nouns used in direct address.
8. Use commas to set off most appositives.
9. When writing dates, place a comma after the day of the month.
10. For geographical locations, place a comma between the name of the town or city and the names of the state, district, or country.
11. Use a comma after the greeting in a friendly letter and after the closing of a friendly or business letter.
12. Use a comma to set off the explanatory words of a direct quotation, such as *Margaret asked, Lawrence said,* or *Jill replied.*
13. Use a comma to separate any sentence parts that might be improperly joined or misunderstood without the comma.

The Semicolon and the Colon

1. Use a semicolon to separate the parts of a compound sentence when you do not connect them with a coordinating conjunction.
2. Use a semicolon between the parts of a compound sentence when these clauses are long, complicated, or punctuated.
3. Use a colon to introduce a list of items.
4. Use a colon after the greeting of a business letter.
5. Use a colon between numbers that represent hours and minutes in expressions of time.

The Hyphen and the Apostrophe

1. Use a hyphen to separate the parts of a word at the end of a line.

2. Use a hyphen in compound adjectives when they precede the word they modify.
3. Add 's to form the possessive of singular nouns.
4. Add only an apostrophe to form the possessive of a plural noun that ends in *s*.
5. Add 's to form the possessive of a plural noun that does not end in *s*.

Quotation Marks

1. Use quotation marks to enclose direct quotations.
2. When a direct quotation is divided by explanatory words, begin the second part of the quotation with a lower-case letter, unless it is the beginning of a new sentence.
3. Place commas and periods inside quotation marks. Place semicolons and colons outside the quotation marks.
4. Place question marks and exclamation points inside quotation marks if they belong to the quotation. Place them outside if they do not belong to the quotation.
5. Use single quotation marks to enclose quotations within one another. If the quotation within the quotation ends the sentence, use both the single and double quotation marks after the last words of the quotations.
6. In a quotation of more than one paragraph, use quotation marks at the beginning of each paragraph and at the end of the final paragraph.
7. Use quotation marks to enclose the titles of poems, short stories, songs, reports, articles, and chapters of books.
8. Underline titles of books, plays, magazines, newspapers, television series, works of art, musical compositions, and motion pictures. Also underline the names of ships, airplanes (but not the type of plane), spacecraft, and trains.

Thesaurus

A thesaurus is a resource that writers use to help them choose more precise words. A thesaurus lists synonyms—words with similar meanings—in groups. A thesaurus can help you find the best word to express an idea, and it can also help you broaden the range of words you use in speaking and writing.

Using This Thesaurus

To locate synonyms for a word, first look up the word in the index on pages 682–683. The index lists, in alphabetical order, every synonym that is defined in the thesaurus. Notice the format of the following portion of the index.

> **ENTHUSIASTIC**
> **erroneous** *see* WRONG
> **essential** *see* IMPORTANT
> **evil** *see* BAD
> **exhausted** *see* TIRED
> **EXPLAIN**

Words printed in capital letters in the index are called **entry words**. These entry words have general meanings. They are the headlines under which more specific synonyms are grouped. *Enthusiastic* and *explain* are entry words.

Words printed in lower case, or small letters, in the index are synonyms for entry words. Thus, *evil* is a synonym for BAD.

If you wanted to find a synonym for the word *essential*, you would find *essential* in the index. The index would tell you to look at the entry for IMPORTANT.

The entry begins with the entry word, IMPORTANT. This general word is defined and used in an example sentence. Following the definition and example sentence are synonyms for IMPORTANT. These synonyms include *essential, momentous, urgent,* and *vital*. Each synonym is defined and used in an example sentence. Read all the synonyms before deciding which one best expresses your idea.

At the end of most entries, you will find a list of other synonyms that are not defined and not used in example sentences. Some entries may also include antonyms—words with opposite meanings. Be careful about using these words. If you choose one, look it up in a dictionary before you use it.

ACTIVE *Active* and its synonyms share the meanings "full of action" or "inclined to action." • People who lead active lives need extra calories.

agile *Agile* suggests quickness and good coordination. • Only an exceptionally agile skater can complete a triple jump.

energetic *Energetic* indicates that a person has a high level of energy and does not easily tire. • Linda is the most energetic volunteer at the hospital.

frisky *Frisky* emphasizes a playful attitude. • You can see how frisky the puppies are today.

spirited *Spirited* suggests a special liveliness, independence, and strong will. • When you are a better rider, you can try a more spirited horse.

Other Synonyms: athletic, busy, lively, spry, vital, vivacious

Antonyms: inactive, lazy, sluggish

AFRAID The words in this group mean "feeling fear." *Afraid* suggests a continuing fear. • Theresa is afraid to fly on an airplane.

anxious An anxious person feels anxiety, a fretful worry. • Sandy paced the floor anxiously, waiting for news that Dan was safe. Many people use *anxious* to mean "eager," but when it is used in that way it should have a suggestion of worry. • Beth is anxious to succeed in her new job.

fearful A fearful person is concerned about a potential danger. • I was fearful that the boat would run aground in the storm.

terrified A terrified person is overwhelmed by fear. • When the father saw his child almost hit by a car, he was terrified.

worried A worried person is mildly frightened by the expectation that something troubling might happen. • I was worried that the bus would leave without us.

Other Synonyms: alarmed, frightened, nervous, panicky, scared, wary

Antonyms: calm, unafraid; *see also* BRAVE

ALONE *Alone* and the other words in this group share the meanings "by oneself" or "by itself." • If my sister can't go with me, I'll have to go alone.

lonely Use *lonely* to suggest unhappiness, even gloom. • In the corner one lonely child stood weeping.

lonesome Use *lonesome* to suggest a longing for companionship. • This will be a lonesome town after you move to New York.

solitary Use *solitary* to emphasize the idea that something is the only one. • After an hour's discussion we had only a solitary idea.

solo Use *solo* to emphasize the idea that something is done single-handedly. • Tomorrow's concert will be my first solo performance.

Other Synonyms: isolated, unique

ANGRY *Angry* and the other words in this group share the general meaning "upset by something that hurts or opposes me." • His opponent's name-calling made Senator Hobbs angry.

furious Use *furious* to show extreme rage to the point of being out of control. • I was so furious that I didn't know what I was doing.

irate Use *irate* to suggest righteous anger or anger that comes from the feeling that one has been wronged. • Seeing that driver throw trash out the window made me irate.

irritated Use *irritated* when someone is mildly annoyed, especially by something that continues. • I became irritated by her constant bragging.

Other Synonyms: annoyed, enraged, indignant, mad, resentful, upset
Antonyms: glad, happy, pleased

ANSWER These synonyms share the general meaning "to react to a question or request." To answer is to say, write, or do something, as a situation requires. • The mayor agreed to answer the charges at her press conference.

acknowledge To acknowledge is merely to show that a message has been received and understood. • They sent a card to acknowledge my order, but I haven't received the tapes.

react To react is to respond to a stimulus in some way. • When he heard the news, he reacted with a shrug.

retort To retort is to answer in an angry or clever way. • "I can't understand your ideas because they don't make sense," he retorted.

Other Synonyms: rebut, reply, respond
Antonyms: see ASK

ASK The words in this group mean "to request something that is wanted." *Ask* may indicate a request for an answer, for information, or for help. • "What is the capital of Poland?" she asked.

beg Use *beg* to suggest asking for something in an especially humble or earnest way. • I beg you to do something before it is too late.

demand *Demand* indicates that a person believes he or she has a right to what is requested. • He demanded that he be allowed to call his attorney.

plead *Plead* suggests that the request has been made often without success. • The class pleaded with Ms. Hill, but she refused to delay the exam.

request *Request* indicates asking in a polite and formal way. • We request a short recess, your honor.

Other Synonyms: beseech, entreat, implore, inquire, question, quiz, seek
Antonyms: see ANSWER

BAD *Bad* has two groups of synonyms. One group shares the meaning "not satisfactory." • A few of the apples were bad. The other group shares the meaning "evil." • If you want to stay out of trouble, stay away from bad people. **Caution:** Describing what is wrong is usually better than using *bad* or a synonym.

dreadful Use *dreadful* for something so bad that it makes a person feel dread or terror. Compare *horrible*. • The jagged edge of the can gave Sam a dreadful cut.

evil *Evil* suggests deliberate wrongdoing. • The evil dictator punished hundreds of innocent people.

horrible *Horrible* suggests something so bad that it makes a person feel horror. • A horrible cry came from the darkness on the moor.

malicious *Malicious* suggests something done out of hatred or spite. • Jealousy is behind these malicious rumors.

Other Synonyms: careless, incorrect, repulsive, revolting, vicious, vile, wicked; *see also* MEAN, WRONG
Antonyms: fine, good

BEAUTIFUL These synonyms mean "pleasing one or more of the senses." Use *beautiful* to suggest that a thing approaches the ideal for its type. • The countryside around Santa Fe is the most beautiful in the Southwest.

attractive Use *attractive* for beauty that draws a person's attention. • That certainly is an attractive haircut.

dazzling Use *dazzling* for beauty that is brilliant and splendid. • The museum has a dazzling collection of gold artifacts from Peru.

elegant Use *elegant* to suggest refined beauty, good taste, grace, and excellence. • The architect designed an elegant marble lobby for the new theater.

gorgeous Use *gorgeous* to indicate beauty that is bright and colorful. • We took a drive to see the gorgeous autumn foliage.

Other Synonyms: fair, handsome, lovely, pretty, stunning
Antonyms: hideous, homely, ugly

BEST *Best* and its synonyms mean "as good as can be" or "better than any other of its type." Use *best* to emphasize the idea that something is above all others of its type. • Cory's Restaurant makes the best steak in town.

finest *Finest* emphasizes the idea that a thing's qualities are nearly perfect. • This necklace is made of the finest platinum.

foremost *Foremost* emphasizes that something is first in a ranking of things. • Allow me to introduce the foremost actor of our time.

inimitable *Inimitable* indicates that something is so good or unusual that any imitation would fall far short. • Billie Holiday's inimitable singing style won her many fans.

superior *Superior* indicates that something is better than most, even if it is not the very best. • Though she is a superior swimmer, she did not qualify for the Olympic team.

Other Synonyms: supreme, unparalleled
Antonyms: inferior, least, worst

BRAVE The words in this group mean "fearless in meeting danger or difficulty." • You were brave to speak your mind.

adventurous Use *adventurous* to suggest an eagerness to face danger or difficulty. • He has an adventurous plan to climb Mount McKinley.

daring *Daring* suggests a certain pleasure in taking risks and facing danger. • Sheila made a daring dive to rescue the boy from the icy water.

fearless *Fearless* suggests that a person acts without even thinking about personal safety. • Fearless doctors battled the highly contagious disease.

heroic *Heroic* is the strongest word in this group; save it for extreme bravery and exceptional daring. • Only a heroic effort can save the miners.

Other Synonyms: courageous, hardy, indomitable, plucky, valiant
Antonyms: see AFRAID

BREAK These synonyms mean "to cause to come apart." *Break* expresses the general idea of dividing something into pieces by force. • If you twist the handle, you'll break it.

crack *Crack* means "split something without making the pieces come completely apart." • The plaster cracked in a jagged pattern.

crumble *Crumble* means "break something into small bits." Something that crumbles is often easy to break. • This delicate cake crumbles at the touch of a fork.

demolish *Demolish* means "destroy something completely," often deliberately. • His negative answer demolished our hopes.

raze *Raze* means "to tear down, to level completely." It is usually used for the destruction of buildings. • The old firehouse will be razed to build a parking garage.

Other Synonyms: dismantle, shatter, smash, snap, split, wreck

BRIGHT The words in this group mean "reflecting light well" or "shining with its own light." *Bright* suggests that the light is strong. • Bright sunlight makes me squint.

glowing *Glowing* suggests warm, even light coming from something, especially something heated until it gives off light. Compare *radiant*. • The mirror in the living room reflected the glowing light of the fire.

luminous *Luminous* suggests an object full of light, especially white, phosphorescent light. • Between the clouds we could see the luminous moon.

radiant Use *radiant* to suggest a brighter light than *glowing* suggests; it is also used metaphorically to suggest warmth. • Her radiant smile makes me feel welcome.

sparkling Use *sparkling* to suggest many tiny points of light that last a brief time, like sparks. • The night was lit with sparkling fireflies.

Other Synonyms: blazing, brilliant, gleaming, glistening, shiny

Antonyms: dark, dim

ENERGY *Energy* and its synonyms mean "the quality that is necessary to do work or to be active." • The energy of the sun can be put directly to work.

force *Force* is energy that works against something. • The force of the blast rattled windows in the town.

power *Power* is great energy, especially energy that is put to use. • Restaurant appliances have more power than home models.

strength *Strength* is energy compared to a standard. • It is a small dog, but it has the strength of a husky.

vitality *Vitality* is the energy needed to continue living or to endure. • Every election proves the vitality of democracy.

Other Synonyms: might, stamina, verve, vigor, vim

ENTHUSIASTIC *Enthusiastic* and its synonyms share the meaning "having or showing interest." They vary in the degree and type of interest and the way it is shown. *Enthusiastic* itself suggests strong favorable feelings and eagerness. • They are enthusiastic about our plans for the trip.

eager *Eager* emphasizes the impatience a person feels when waiting for something desired. • I'm eager to see Ralph.

earnest *Earnest* suggests enthusiasm that comes after careful thought. • We want a candidate who will make an earnest effort to win.

fervent *Fervent* suggests burning enthusiasm; it comes from a root meaning "burn." • Derek has a fervent desire to become a musician.

sincere *Sincere* emphasizes honesty and lack of pretense; a sincere person may not advertise his or her enthusiasm. • Evans gave a quiet, sincere speech in support of the project.

Other Synonyms: avid, fanatical, passionate, zealous

Antonyms: bored, reluctant, unenthusiastic, uninterested

EXPLAIN The words in this group share the meaning "to make more understandable." To *explain* is to make plain or clear. • Please explain the causes of inflation.

clarify *Clarify* means "to make

clear." It suggests that something was confusing before it was explained.

• We called the company to have someone clarify the misleading instructions.

criticize *Criticize* means "to examine something carefully, explain it, and show where it is good and bad." • Ursula criticizes new record releases for the school paper. A second meaning of *criticize* is "finding fault" (possibly because many critics find more to blame than to praise). • Don't be too quick to criticize what you don't understand.

define To define is to give the meaning of a word or to explain something showing what its limits are.

• Chapter 2 defines the power of the Supreme Court.

demonstrate To *demonstrate* means "to explain by showing." A demonstration may show how something works or why something is so.

• Next I will demonstrate the separation of oxygen and hydrogen.

Other Synonyms: clear up, comment, describe, detail, develop, interpret

FUNNY *Funny* and its synonyms mean "inspiring smiles or laughter."

• The book was so funny that I laughed out loud.

laughable Use *laughable* for something that is funny unintentionally. • Our football team is so bad that it's laughable.

whimsical Use *whimsical* for humor that is odd and unpredictable.

• In one whimsical scene, a group of hippos in tutus dances a ballet.

witty Use *witty* for something funny because it is clever. Wit usually relies on the humorous use of words.

• My parents are always making witty comments about the news.

Other Synonyms: amusing, comical, hilarious, humorous, playful, silly

Antonyms: grave, serious

GET The words in this group share the general meaning of *get*, "to come to have" or "to become the owner of." • If this watch can't be fixed, I'll have to get a new one.

acquire *Acquire* suggests that getting a thing took considerable time. • Tanya is acquiring a reputation as an excellent artist.

amass *Amass* comes from a Latin root meaning "to pile up." It is often used for collecting or accumulating things. • The Ryans have amassed a valuable collection of gold coins.

obtain *Obtain* suggests working to get something strongly desired. • Mr. Darrow obtained special permission to visit the laboratory.

procure Use *procure* to suggest that something was obtained only after considerable effort. • The underwater explorers procured samples from the ocean floor.

Other Synonyms: buy, collect, earn, gain, purchase, receive, take, win

Antonym: give

GROUP These synonyms mean "a number of people, animals, or things considered together." • We will be traveling in a group.

association Use *association* for a formal group of people with similar interests. • We plan to form a dog owners' association.

company A *company* is a group organized for a purpose. • This construction company has built many office buildings. *Company* originally meant "people sharing bread." That meaning survives in our use of *compa-*

ny to mean "guests." • Vacuum the rug before our company arrives.

crowd Use *crowd* to suggest a large, disorderly group squeezed into a small space. • A crowd waited in the lobby for tickets to go on sale.

throng Use *throng* for a crowd that moves toward a destination or that moves aimlessly. • A throng of shoppers arrived for the sale.

Other Synonyms: band, clique, crew, faction, gang, horde, mob, set

HARD *Hard* has several meanings. The one that is the focus of this group of synonyms is "demanding great effort or labor." • Last night's assignment was really hard.

arduous *Arduous* suggests that a long struggle is required. • Removing and resetting those stones will be arduous work.

demanding *Demanding* suggests a task that requires more and more effort. • Alice's job is so demanding that she has no time for fun.

difficult *Difficult* is appropriate for a job that requires mental rather than physical work. • It is a difficult problem, but I think we can solve it.

Other Synonyms: formidable, laborious, onerous, tough

Antonym: easy

HELP The words in this group share the general meaning of *help* "to make things easier or better." • I'd be happy to help you wash the windows.

assist Use *assist* when the help given is much less important than the rest of the work. • Steve earns spending money by assisting the librarian.

bolster Use *bolster* for helping by supporting an effort. *Bolster* sug-

gests that the support is not absolutely necessary. • Tina played records to bolster the cleanup crew's spirits.

foster To foster is to encourage. • His optimism fostered hope among the rest of us.

Other Synonyms: abet, aid, foment, rescue, serve, succor, support, sustain

Antonyms: hinder, interfere

IMPORTANT The words in this group share the meaning of *important*, "having great meaning or great influence." • I have an important message for you.

essential Use *essential* for something so important that it is absolutely necessary. • Vitamins are essential to good health.

momentous Something momentous is so important that it captures everyone's attention. • A momentous announcement came over the radio.

urgent Use *urgent* for something so important that it should get immediate attention. • The needs of the flood victims are urgent.

vital *Vital* indicates that something is absolutely necessary. Its original meaning is "necessary to life." • It is vital that you change these bandages twice a day.

Other Synonyms: critical, notable, prominent, serious, weighty

Antonyms: insignificant, trivial, unimportant

LIKE *Like* and its synonyms mean "to be pleased with, to enjoy." • I like New York in June.

appreciate To appreciate is to like something as a result of understanding its value. • I appreciate the piano technique of McCoy Tyner.

cherish Use *cherish* to suggest tender affection for something. • You will cherish the memory of these times.

love Use *love* to indicate a strong, deep, and tender affection. • I love to visit my uncle's farm. In formal writing, don't waste *love* by using it to exaggerate feelings.

prefer *Prefer* indicates a liking for one thing over another. • Frank prefers broiled fish.

Other Synonyms: admire, enjoy, fancy, favor, idolize, prize, relish, revere

Antonyms: despise, disdain, dislike

MAKE The words in this group share the meaning of make, "bring into being." • We always make Yorkshire pudding to go with the roast beef.

assemble *Assemble* means "to complete something by putting its parts together." • The bicycle comes partially assembled.

build *Build* means "to make something, especially a building, by putting materials or parts together." • Work is underway to build a tunnel linking England and France.

create *Create* means "to bring into being something that did not exist before." • The discovery of gold created a stampede to California.

produce *Produce* is often used for manufacturing. • This plant produces light trucks.

Other Synonyms: construct, establish, fabricate, manufacture

Antonyms: break, destroy, dismantle

MANY *Many* and its synonyms mean "a great number of." **Caution:** It is usually better to tell how many than to use *many* or one of its synonyms. The second of the following sentences is preferable. • Many cars had defective

tires. Eighteen percent of the cars had defective tires.

a lot The phrase *a lot* is used colloquially to mean "very many" or "very much." However, you should avoid it in most writing and speaking.

myriad *Myriad* comes from a Greek word meaning "ten thousand." It is often used to mean "too many to count," but it is best used to mean "thousands." • Myriad beads were embroidered into the star's costume.

various *Various* emphasizes the idea of many different things. • Various solutions were suggested.

Other Synonyms: countless, numerous, several, sundry

Antonym: few

MEAN Two of the meanings of the word *mean* are "bad-tempered or unkind" and "stingy or miserly." • Nora was hurt by Curt's mean treatment.

petty Use *petty* to indicate meanness about even the smallest things. • Her petty attitude blinds her to Rick's good qualities.

selfish *Selfish* suggests that a person cares too much for his or her own interests and not enough for others. • It was selfish of you not to give Ted equal time to speak.

spiteful Use *spiteful* for meanness that comes from a desire to get even. • Letting the air out of my tires was a spiteful act.

unkind *Unkind* indicates harsh or cruel treatment, often the result of thoughtlessness. • Leaving those dishes for me to wash was unkind.

Other Synonyms: nasty, vicious

Antonyms: considerate, generous

NEW The words in this group share the general meaning of *new*, "appearing for the first time." • Have you seen this year's new cars?

fresh *Fresh* suggests something very new or surprisingly different from what has come before. • We need some fresh ideas for the fall dance.

innovative *Innovative* suggests that something introduces new ideas or a new standard. • The company announced an innovative computer.

original *Original* emphasizes that something is the first of its kind. • Jack's group has a fresh, original sound.

Other Synonyms: modern, novel, recent, untried

Antonyms: antique, old, out-of-date

OFFEND *Offend* and its synonyms share the general meanings "to hurt the feelings of, to make angry." • The play offended people.

affront *Affront* suggests a deliberate insult or offense. • Her remarks were an affront to the entire community.

annoy *Annoy* means "to cause a mild temporary disturbance." • It's annoying to sit near someone who talks during a movie.

displease To displease is to offend slightly. • Sloppiness displeases me.

insult To insult is to commit an offense so strong that it causes deep pain or anger. • Ken insulted me with his false accusations.

Other Synonyms: disgust, hurt, provoke, upset, vex

Antonym: please

QUIET *Quiet* and its synonyms share the general meaning "without sound." *Quiet* also suggests calm and orderliness. • We sat at a quiet table.

calm Use *calm* to suggest still-ness and serenity. • The classroom is calm now, but wait until the bell rings!

noiseless Use *noiseless* to stress the complete absence of noise. It also suggests movement without sound. • Noiselessly, the cat stalked a mole in the yard.

serene Use *serene* to suggest a dignified, peaceful silence. • The empty church was serene.

still *Still* indicates that there is no sound or movement. • When Will finished speaking, the hall was still.

Other Synonyms: hushed, peaceful, restrained, silent, tranquil

Antonyms: loud, noisy

RIGHT The words in this group share two general meanings of *right*, "correct" and "proper." • Are we on the right road?

accurate *Accurate* emphasizes meeting a standard very precisely. • This compass is amazingly accurate.

fit *Fit* and *fitting* mean "just what a situation or purpose requires." • "Who cares?" is not a fitting answer to my question.

proper *Proper* designates a thing that good judgment says is appropriate or suitable. • These are the proper skates for hockey.

suitable *Suitable* means useful for a certain purpose. • This lamp is suitable for reading.

Other Synonyms: correct, exact, just, precise, reasonable, true

Antonym: see WRONG

RUN The words in this group share one of the general meanings of *run*, "to go by moving the legs faster than in walking." • Can you run fast?

scamper *Scamper* suggests small, quick movements, like those of a small animal. • Children scampered across the playground.

scurry *Scurry* is similar to *scamper*, with the added suggestion of hurrying. • We scurried around, trying to get the house in order.

sprint *Sprint* suggests very rapid running over a short distance. • I sprinted to the bus stop.

Other Synonyms: dash, gallop, jog

SAY The words in this group share the general meaning of *say*, "to utter words; to speak." • He said that the posters were ready.

assert *Assert* means "to say something in a positive, forceful way." • She asserted that her position was the only right one.

blurt *Blurt* means "to say without thinking." • "But you're not the real Sherlock Holmes," he blurted.

comment *Comment* means "to make a remark that explains, criticizes, or gives an opinion." • "This is fine, careful work," he commented.

declare *Declare* means "to say something emphatically." • She declared that she intended to vote for him.

state *State* means "to say in a definite, precise way, to specify." • He stated that no one would be admitted before two o'clock.

Other Synonyms: announce, boast, cry, exclaim, growl, grumble, remark, roar, shout, whisper

SEE *See* and its synonyms mean "to get information through the eyes." • Did you actually see what happened?

behold Use *behold* for seeing with awe or wonder. • Then we beheld a whale leaping from the sea.

inspect Use *inspect* for looking at something carefully, examining it.

• These machines inspect each computer chip for flaws.

observe Use *observe* for looking at something with special attention or a special purpose. • A team of reporters observed the missile test.

perceive Use *perceive* for seeing that involves awareness of fine differences or features. • We could barely perceive the oncoming cars in the fog.

sight Use *sight* for seeing something for which one has been looking. • Helicopter crews have sighted the life raft!

watch Use *watch* for observing something closely for a purpose. • Nurses watch for a change in heart rate. However, *watch* also means "to look at something *without* paying close attention." • We lay on our backs, watching the clouds drift by.

Other Synonyms: ascertain, discern, glimpse, spot, view

SIGN *Sign* and its synonyms denote something that stands for something else. • Yawning is a sign of fatigue.

mark A mark is a trace or impression on a surface. • That line of seaweed is the mark of the high tide.

signal A signal is a sign made deliberately. • Flash your lights as a signal that you want to pass.

symbol A symbol is an object that stands for an abstract idea. • A handshake is a symbol of welcome.

Other Synonyms: emblem, indication, omen, symptom, token, trace

SMART *Smart* and its synonyms share the general meanings "intelligent, alert, clever." *Smart* is an informal word. • Marty is smart, but his work is careless.

astute *Astute* suggests cleverness combined with wisdom. • Nan had some astute suggestions for improving my paper.

intelligent *Intelligent* emphasizes the ability to learn or to adapt to new situations. • A flexible plan is an intelligent plan.

shrewd *Shrewd* suggests a quick mind, great insight or sharpness, and a practical approach. • Senator Olson is a shrewd negotiator.

Other Synonyms: bright, clever, gifted, perceptive

STRANGE *Strange* and its synonyms share the general meanings, "out of the ordinary, peculiar, or odd." • A strange voice called to us from the dark.

bizarre Use *bizarre* to suggest something extremely strange and unexpected. • He gave us a bizarre excuse involving a gorilla and a truck.

eccentric Use *eccentric* to suggest deliberately being unusual or flouting convention. • The old woman's eccentric manner of dress includes flowered hats and long, flowing capes.

mysterious Use *mysterious* to suggest the unknown, unexplained, or secret. • Every night we hear a mysterious whirring in the basement.

peculiar Use *peculiar* to suggest something puzzling or difficult to explain. • I feel a peculiar shudder in the steering wheel.

Other Synonyms: curious, odd, quaint, unusual, weird

Antonyms: familiar, ordinary, usual

TERRIFIC The words in this group are often used in casual speech to mean "unusually fine or enjoyable." However, this is not the best use for them, since each word has a specific meaning of its own. *Terrific*, for example, means "terrifying, horrifying." • Terrific winds buffeted the tower.

amazing Something that is amazing is so surprising or astonishing that it leaves a person confused for a minute. • We stared in awe at the amazing stunt performed by the tightrope walker.

astounding Something that is astounding is so shocking that it stuns a person. • Karen told us the astounding news that she was leaving town.

marvelous Something marvelous makes a person stop and marvel, or stare. • On the peak of the roof was a marvelous golden grasshopper.

wonderful Something wonderful causes wonder or amazement. • This wonderful cake was twelve feet (nearly four meters) high.

Other Synonyms: astonishing, fabulous, miraculous, remarkable, sensational

THINK *Think* and its synonyms share the general meaning "to use the mind in one way or another." To think is to use the mind reasonably, to form ideas or reach conclusions. • What do you think of the President's announcement?

believe *Believe* means "to accept something as true, even when it cannot be completely supported by evidence." • The officer believed that the nephew had stolen the jewel.

consider *Consider* means "to accept something in order to reach a decision." • Consider my offer and give me your answer tomorrow.

feel *Feel* means "to believe something based on emotion, not on thinking." Avoid using *feel* when *think* is the appropriate word. • I feel that she is sincere in her beliefs, but I think her policies would not work.

wonder *Wonder* means "to be curious about, to want to know about." • I wonder whether the universe will continue to expand.

Other Synonyms: contemplate, deliberate, ponder, reflect, speculate

TIRED The words in this group share the meaning "low on energy, rundown." *Tired* indicates a loss of energy from hard work or long hours. • We were tired after walking all day.

exhausted *Exhausted* indicates complete loss of energy. • The exhausted rescue workers had gone forty-eight hours without sleep.

fatigued *Fatigued* indicates tiredness great enough to require immediate rest. • Anderson was fatigued after the long tennis match.

weary *Weary* indicates such extreme tiredness that a person can't keep working. • By nightfall, I was too weary to take another step.

Other Synonyms: drowsy, sleepy

TRAVEL The words in this group share the general meaning of *travel*, "to go from one place to another." • Jon traveled to Europe last fall.

emigrate *Emigrate* means "to go from one country to stay permanently in another." • Our former neighbors emigrated to France.

immigrate *Immigrate* means "to come into one country from another country to stay permanently." • Our neighbors immigrated from Haiti.

migrate *Migrate* means "to move to another place to live, but not permanently." • Monarch butterflies migrate to Mexico.

tour *Tour* means "to travel for the purpose of sightseeing." • In the winter we will tour Norway. It can also mean to travel for the purpose of performing. • After its New York run, the play will tour the U.S. for a year.

Other Synonyms: journey, roam, traverse, wander

WALK The words in this group share the general meaning of *walk*, "to go on foot at a normal pace, not running." • You can walk to the harbor from here.

amble *Amble* indicates walking in a relaxed manner. • I enjoy ambling along, looking in the shop windows.

stride *Stride* indicates walking with long steps in a vigorous or bold way. • The candidates strode to the podiums and began the debate.

tramp *Tramp* indicates walking with heavy steps. • The troops tramped through the streets.

trudge *Trudge* indicates a tired or weary way of walking. • Sue trudged home after the exam.

Other Synonyms: hike, march, pace, parade, step, stroll, strut, tread

WRONG *Wrong* and its synonyms share the meaning "not what is true, correct, or wanted." • That clock must be wrong by about half an hour.

erroneous *Erroneous* indicates that something is based on an error. • She had the erroneous impression that I had given her secret away.

false *False* suggests that the lack of truth is deliberate. • The information he gave the police was false.

faulty *Faulty* indicates that there are small errors in something basically correct. • One faulty switch delayed the launch.

Other Synonyms: fallacious, illogical, inaccurate, incorrect, mistaken, untrue; *see also* BAD

Antonyms: see RIGHT

mark *see* SIGN
marvelous *see* TERRIFIC
MEAN
migrate *see* TRAVEL
momentous *see* IMPOR-
TANT
myriad *see* MANY
mysterious *see*
STRANGE

N
NEW
noiseless *see* QUIET

O
observe *see* SEE
obtain *see* GET
OFFEND
original *see* NEW

P
peculiar *see* STRANGE
perceive *see* SEE
petty *see* MEAN
plead *see* ASK
power *see* ENERGY
prefer *see* LIKE
procure *see* GET
produce *see* MAKE
proper *see* RIGHT

Q
QUIET

R
radiant *see* BRIGHT
raze *see* BREAK
react *see* ANSWER
request *see* ASK
retort *see* ANSWER
RIGHT
RUN

S
SAY
scamper *see* RUN

scurry *see* RUN
SEE
selfish *see* MEAN
serene *see* QUIET
shrewd *see* SMART
sight *see* SEE
SIGN
signal *see* SIGN
sincere *see* ENTHUSIAS-
TIC
SMART
solitary *see* ALONE
solo *see* ALONE
sparkling *see* BRIGHT
spirited *see* ACTIVE
spiteful *see* MEAN
sprint *see* RUN
state *see* SAY
still *see* QUIET
STRANGE
strength *see* ENERGY
stride *see* WALK
suitable *see* RIGHT
superior *see* BEST
symbol *see* SIGN

T
TERRIFIC
terrified *see* AFRAID
THINK
throng *see* GROUP
TIRED
tour *see* TRAVEL
tramp *see* WALK
TRAVEL
trudge *see* WALK

U
unkind *see* MEAN
urgent *see* IMPORTANT

V
various *see* MANY
vital *see* IMPORTANT
vitality *see* ENERGY

W
WALK

watch *see* SEE
weary *see* TIRED
whimsical *see* FUNNY
witty *see* FUNNY
wonder *see* THINK
wonderful *see* TERRIFIC
worried *see* AFRAID
WRONG

Index

A

Abbreviations
  capitalization of, 605, 607
  in dictionaries, 332
  problems with, 661
  punctuating, 620
Acronyms, 279
Action verbs, 468, 514
Active verbs, 491, 665
Addresses
  in letters, 379, 381, 382
  commas in, 632
  on envelopes, 383
Adjective clauses, 557–59
  diagraming, 558–59
  relative pronouns in, 557–58
Adjective phrases, 536, 557
Adjectives, 505–508, 512–19
  adverbs modifying, 509–10
  articles, 508
  commas between, 624
  comparative form, 224, 516–18
  compound, 637
  confused with adverbs, 512–13, 662
  defined, 505
  in descriptive writing, 170
  infinitives as, 585
  irregular, 518
  in narrative writing, 194
  participles as, 587
  predicate, 409, 505, 513–14
  pronouns used as, 506
  proper, 505, 600–601
  superlative form, 516–18
Adverb clauses, 559–60
  diagraming, 560
Adverb phrases, 536, 559–60
Adverbs, 509–15, 520–22
  with adjectives or other adverbs, 509–10
  comparative form, 520–22
  confused with adjectives, 512–13, 662
  confused with direct objects, 406
  confused with prepositions, 534
  conjunctive, 634
  defined, 509
  diagraming, 401
  forming, 510
  infinitives as, 585

  in narrative writing, 194
  superlative form, 520–22
  as transitional words, 123
Agreement
  pronoun-antecedent, 456–57, 663–64
  subject-verb, 568, 570–77, 666
Almanacs, in reference sections, 323
Analogy questions, 368–69
Analyzing, 26–27, 58, 63
  audience, 60
  descriptive writing, 154–55
  expository writing, 204–205
  narrative writing, 178–79
  paragraphs, 94–95
  persuasive writing, 230–31
  in reports, 252–53
and
  sentences combined with, 132, 133, 550, 551
  in stringy sentences, 144
  words added to sentences with, 143
Anecdotes 102, 265
Antecedents
  agreement of pronouns with, 456–57, 663–64
  defined, 456
Antonyms, 284
Apostrophes, 452, 639–40
Appositives, commas with, 628
Art
  capitalization of titles of works of, 610
  underlining for titles of works of, 644
Articles (*a, an, the*), 508
  definite, 508
  indefinite, 508
  in titles, 315, 320
Articles (written)
  capitalization of titles of, 610
  quotation marks with titles of, 644
Atlases, 323
Audience, 119
  analyzing, 59, 60–61
  and expository writing, 211
  and persuasive writing, 231, 235–36
  and purpose, 59
  and reports, 253
Author cards, in card catalog, 319–20
Authors
  on card catalog cards, 318, 320, 321

English and Social Studies, 246, 308
Cumulative Reviews, 464–65, 546–47, 596–97, 652–53
Cutter numbers, 318, 320, 321

D

Dates
  in letters, 378, 379, 382
  punctuation in, 632, 640
Declarative sentences, 99, 618
Definite article, 508
Definitions
  as context clue, 286
  to develop paragraphs, 102
  in dictionaries, 331–33
  for report introductions, 265
Demonstrative pronouns, 444
Dependent clauses. *See* Subordinate clauses
Descriptive writing, 152–75
  analyzing, 154–55
  drafting, 167–70
  figurative language in, 168–69
  ideas for, 655
  in Literature, 156–59
  modifiers in, 507, 511, 522
  mood in, 160–61
  in narrative writing, 187
  organization of, 163–66
  in paragraphs, 94
  prewriting, 160–62
  revising/editing, 171–72
  sensory details in, 161–62, 167
  specific words in, 167–68
Dewey Decimal System, 315–16, 318
Diacritical marks, 330–31
Diagraming
  adjective clauses, 558–59
  adverb clauses, 560
  adverbs, 401
  compound objects of verbs, 413
  compound predicate words, 413
  compound sentences, 551–52
  compound subjects, 412
  compound verbs, 412
  direct objects, 407
  indirect objects, 407
  introductory words, 401
  noun clauses, 562
  predicate words, 410
  predicates, 397
  prepositional phrases, 537
  subjects, 397

Dialogue
  in narrative writing, 193, 197
  punctuating, 644
Dictionaries, 330–37
  definitions in, 331–33
  parts of speech in, 332
  pronunciation in, 330–31
  synonyms in, 334–35
  word division in, 330
  word origins in, 335–36
Dieties, capitalization of names of, 601
Direct address, commas after nouns of, 627, 629
Directions
  for filling out forms, 384
  following, 350–51
  reading, on tests, 372
Direct objects, 405–406, 413
  compound, 413
  diagraming, 407
Direct quotations, 258, 611
  capitalization of, 609
  punctuating, 630, 642
Discussions. *See* Group discussions
Divided quotations, punctuating, 630
do, forms of, and subject-verb agreement, 576
Documents, capitalization of, 605
Double negatives, 524, 661
Drafting, 56, 70–79
  bridge building, 75–76
  descriptive writing, 167–70
  expository writing, 210–12, 217, 222–23
  highly structured, 75
  loosely structured, 74
  narrative writing, 191–94
  persuasive writing, 242–43
  quick draft, 76
  reflecting after, 77
  reports, 264–69
  slow draft, 76
Drawing conclusions, 32–33
  from graphic aids, 359

E

-e, silent, spelling problems with, 339
Echoic words, 279
-ed
  past tense formed with, 486
  words ending with, 134, 137
Editing. *See* Peer editing; Proofreading; Revising/Editing
ei and *ie,* spelling problems with, 341
Empty sentences, 142–43

O

Object of the preposition, 532
  noun clauses as, 561
Objective writing, 240
Objects
  compound, 413
  gerunds as, 589
  infinitives as, 585
  noun clauses as, 561
  pronouns as, 447
  see also Direct objects; Indirect objects
Observing, 23, 161
Opinions
  in persuasive writing, 235
  and reports, 253
  see also Fact and opinion
or, sentences combined with, 132, 133, 550, 551
Order of familiarity, 67, 217
Order of importance, 67, 107, 108, 216
  transitions that show, 121
Order of impression, 165–66
Organization
  of cause and effect explanations, 216–17
  of comparison and contrasts, 222
  of descriptive writing, 163–66
  of expository writing, 210, 216–17
  of group discussions, 299, 300
  of narrative writing, 187–89
  of paragraphs, 106–109
  of persuasive writing, 236–37, 242
  of reports, 260–63
  see also Outlines
Organizations, capitalization of, 605
Organizing ideas, 66–67
  charting, 20–21
  graphic organizers, 659–60
Outlines, 657–58
  capitalization in, 610
  for notetaking, 355
  punctuation with, 621
  for reports, 261–63
  types of, 657–58
Overgeneralization, 241

P

Padded sentences, 147–49
Paragraphs, 92–111
  analyzing, 94–95
  coherence in, 106–109
  defined, 94
  descriptive, 94
  developing, 101–103

expository, 94
  main idea of, 96
  narrative, 94
  organization in, 106–109
  persuasive, 94
  topic sentences, 96–98
  unity in, 104–105
Participial phrases, 587
Participles, 587
  confused with gerunds, 589–90
Parts of speech
  in dictionaries, 332
  see also Adjectives; Adverbs; Conjunctions; Interjections; Nouns; Prepositions; Pronouns; Verbs
Passive verbs, 491, 665
Past participles, 472, 587
Past perfect tense, 487
Past tense, 486
Peer editors, 82
  checklists for, 83, 171, 196, 212, 218, 224, 244
Perfect tenses, 487
Periodicals, 313
  see also Magazines
Periods
  with abbreviations, 620
  with lists, 621
  with numbers, 621
  with outlines, 621
  with quotation marks, 642
  with sentences, 618–19
Person, of pronouns, 438
Personal pronouns, 438
  compound, 440
  defined, 438
Persuasive writing, 228–47
  analyzing, 230–31
  audience and, 231, 235–36
  connotations of words and, 240
  drafting, 242–43
  generalization and, 241
  ideas for, 655
  judgment words and, 238–39
  in Literature, 232–33
  opinions in, 235
  organizing, 236–37
  in paragraphs, 94
  presenting, 244–45
  prewriting, 234–37
  revising/editing, 244–45
Phrases
  adjective, 536, 557
  adverb, 536, 559–60

exclamation points, 619
hyphens, 637
periods, 618–19, 620–21
question marks, 619
quotation marks, 642–45
semicolons, 550–51, 634
Purpose
and descriptive writing, 160
determining, in prewriting, 59–60, 62
listening for, 301
and reports, 252–53

Q

Qualifying generalizations, 241
Question marks
at ends of sentences, 618, 619
with quotation marks, 643
Questions, 99, 618, 619
punctuating, 618, 619
in SQ3R, 353
"what if," 185
see also Test questions
Quotation marks
with dialogue, 197, 644
with direct quotations, 642
with other punctuation marks, 642, 643
with quotations of more than one paragraph, 643
single, 643
with titles, 644
Quotations
capitalization in, 609
commas with, 630, 631
direct, 258, 611
indirect, 630
punctuating, 630, 642–43

R

Readers' Guide to Periodical Literature, 256, 313, 323, 324–25
Reading, 30–31, 58
a draft, 77
in-depth, 357
scanning, 357
skimming, 357
in SQ3R, 353
taking notes when, 355
Reference sections, in libraries, 313, 323–25
Reflecting, 64, 77, 184, 234, 235
Reflexive pronouns, 440
Regular verbs, 472
Relationships, 24–25, 66–67
Relative pronouns, 557–58

Repetition, in empty sentences, 142
Reports, 248–73
audience and, 253
bibliographies for, 269
body paragraphs, 266–68
conclusions, 268–69
drafting, 264–69
fact and opinions and, 253
introductions to, 264–65
organization of, 260–63
outlines for, 261–63
presenting, 270
prewriting, 250–51, 252–55, 260–63
purpose and, 252–53
revising, 270
sources for, 258
taking notes, 256–59
Research, 252–59
evaluating sources, 356
notetaking, 256–69
preparing for, 252–55
using the library, 310–27
Research papers. *See* Reports
Restatement, as context clue, 286
Return addresses, 383
Reviewing, test answers, 372
Revising/Editing, 56, 80, 82–83
compositions, 125–26
descriptive writing, 171–72
expository writing, 212, 218, 224
methods of, 82
narrative writing, 195–96
persuasive writing, 244–45
proofreading, 84–85
reports, 270
see also Peer editors
Run-on sentences, 415, 553, 665

S

Salutations, in letters, 378, 379, 381, 382
Scanning, 357
School subjects, capitalization of, 607
Second person, 438
Self-editing, 82
Semicolons
in compound sentences, 550, 551
with quotation marks, 642
Senses, using, 6–7
observing and, 23
Sensory details
in descriptive writing, 161–62
in narrative writing, 192
Sensory images, 167
Sentence outlines, 657

Subject cards, in card catalog, 321
Subjective writing, 240
Subject-verb agreement, 568, 570–77, 666
    compound subjects, 572
    forms of *do* and, 576
    indefinite pronouns and, 574
    in number, 570
    in sentences beginning with *here, there, where,* 576
Subjects, 394, 396–97, 403, 412
    agreement of, with verb, 568, 570–77
    complete, 397
    compound, 412, 572
    defined, 394
    diagraming, 397
    gerunds as, 589
    infinitives as, 585
    noun clauses as, 561
    order of, in sentence, 403
    pronouns as, 446
    simple, 396
Subordinate clauses, 554–55, 557–63
    adjective clauses, 557, 557–59
    adverb clauses, 559–60
    diagraming, 558–59, 560, 562
    noun clauses, 561–62
Subordinating conjunctions, 554–55
Suffixes, 280, 281–82
    spelling problems and, 339, 340–41
Superlative forms
    adjectives, 516–18
    adverbs, 520–22
Syllables, 330, 637
Synonyms, 284, 334
Synonymy, 334, 335

T

Taste words, 7
Television
    capitalization of titles of programs, 610
    underlining for titles of series on, 644
Tenses, of verbs, 486–87, 666
Term papers. *See* Reports
Test questions, 366–71
    analogy, 368–69
    essay, 371
    fill-in-the-blanks, 368
    matching, 368
    multiple-choice, 367
    short-answer, 370
    true-false, 366
Tests, 362–87
    answer sheets, 372–73

course, 364
    planning for, 364–65
    standardized, 365
    textbook, 364
    see also Test questions
that
    avoiding vague use of, 213
    combining sentences with, 139–41
    words added to sentences with, 139–40
Thesauruses, 284, 671–83
Thinking skills
    analyzing, 26–27, 58, 63
    brainstorming, 18, 21, 58, 184
    charting, 20–21, 26
    classifying, 27
    clustering, 19, 21, 58, 184
    comparing and contrasting, 27–28
    creative, 36–37, 58
    drawing conclusions, 32–33, 212, 217, 223, 242, 268–69
    free writing, 18, 21, 58, 184, 185
    gleaning, 58, 64–65, 184, 234, 235
    imaging, 19–20, 21, 162
    inference, 32
    inquiring, 24, 63
    interviewing, 30
    observing, 23, 161
    reading, 30–31, 58
    reflecting, 64, 77, 184, 234, 235
    relationships, 24–25, 66–67
    writing and, 16–40
Third person, 438
Time
    colons in numerical notation of, 635
    organization by, 107
    relationships of, 24, 66
    transitions that show, 121
Time lines, 20
Title cards, in card catalog, 320
Titles, personal, capitalization of, 600–601
Titles, of written works
    capitalization of, 610
    on card catalog cards, 318, 320, 321
    of books, on note cards, 256
    of encyclopedia articles, on note cards, 257
    of magazines, on note cards, 257
    quotation marks with, 644
    in *Readers' Guide,* 324
    underlining with, 644
to, sign of the infinitive, 584
Topic sentences, 96–98
    position of, 96–97

Editorial Credits

Director of Program Planning and Development: Bonnie L. Dobkin
Senior Editor: Julie A. Schumacher
Associate Editor: Christine Iversen
Assistant Editor: Peter P. Kaye
Project Assistance: Ligature, Inc.

Acknowledgments

Sources of Quoted Materials

The authors and editors have made every effort to trace the ownership of all copyrighted selections found in this book and to make full acknowledgment for their use. Grateful acknowledgment is made to the following sources for permission to reprint copyrighted materials.

9: *Chicago Tribune.* For "O'Hare cougar lets a probe of transport out of the bag" by Jack Houston, *Chicago Tribune,* 1/8/87; **12-13:** Harvard University Press: For an excerpt from *One Writer's Beginnings* by Eudora Welty, Harvard University Press; copyright © 1983, 1984 by Eudora Welty, reprinted by permission of the publisher. **92:** James Reeves Estate: For two lines from "Beech Leaves" by James Reeves; copyright © James Reeves Estate. **112:** Mary Britton Miller: For four lines from "Houses" by Mary Britton Miller, from *Poems Children Will Sit Still For,* edited by Beatrice Schenk de Regniers, et al. **154:** Harcourt Brace Jovanovich, Inc. and Faber & Farber, Ltd.: For "Prelude I," from *Collected Poems 1909-1962* by T.S. Eliot; copyright 1936 by Harcourt Brace Jovanovich, Inc., copyright © 1963, 1964 by T.S. Eliot, reprinted by permission of the publisher; **156-159:** Curtis Brown, Ltd.: For excerpts from *A Bevy of Beasts* by Gerald Durrell; copyright © 1973 by Gerald Durrell. **176:** Houghton Mifflin Company: For the first four lines from "A Song of Greatness," from *The Children Sing in the Far West* by Mary Austin; © 1928 by Mary Austin, copyright renewed 1956 by Kenneth M. Chapman and Mary Wheelwright; **180-183:** Delacorte Press: For an excerpt from *Whale Watch* by Ada and Frank Graham, Jr.: copyright © 1978 by Ada and Frank Graham, Jr.; **188:** The Writer, Inc.: For an excerpt from Chapter 26, "Springboard to Suspense Fiction" by Phyllis A. Whitney, from *Writing Mystery and Crime Fiction,* edited by Sylvia K. Burack; copyright © 1976, 1985 by The Writer, Inc., Publishers, Boston, MA. **206-207:** Cobblestone Publications, Inc.: For "The Bloomer Outfit" by Jean McLeod, from *Cobblestone,* October 1985 issue *American Clothing;* copyright © 1985, Cobblestone Publications, Inc.; **220:** Harper & Row, Publishers, Inc.: For an excerpt from *One Man's Meat* by E. B. White; copyright © 1983 Harper & Row. **231:** Classroom Computer Learning: For an excerpt from "Is It Time to Boot Out Cursive Writing?" by Jack McGarvey, from *Classroom Computer Learning,* March 1986, Vol. 6, No. 6, reprinted by permission of the publisher, Peter Li, Inc., 2451 E. River Road., Dayton, OH 45439; **232-233:** Prometheus Books: For excerpts from *Opus 300* by Isaac Asimov; reprinted from *The Roving Mind;* © 1983 by Isaac Asimov. **258:** World Book, Inc.: For entry "Ganges River," from *The World Book Encyclopedia,* 1986 edition; copyright © 1987, World Book, Inc. **324:** H. W. Wilson Company: For entries from *The Readers' Guide to Periodical Literature:* copyright © 1985 by H. W. Wilson Company. **331, 332, 333, 334:** For entries from *Webster's New World Dictionary,* Students Edition, copyright © 1976, 1981.

Unit Art

Unit 1: Marcia Teusink. *Red Barn in Winter.* New Jersey State Teen Arts Program (Joseph Schembri) **Unit 2:** Peter J. Grabowsky. *An Autumn View.* New Jersey State Teen Arts Program (Joseph Schembri) **Unit 3:** Courtesy of the International Collection of Children's Art, University Museums, Illinois State University

Photographs

Assignment photography: Vito Palmisano: **5, 17, 29,** *r* **41,** *b* **43,** *b* **45, 46-47,** *r* **47,** *l* **48,** *tl* **52,** *c* **53, 57, 71, 220, 249** *t* **291, 302, 311, 363, 374, 390, 505, 569, 583** Ralph Brunke: *tr* **53, 65, 78, 97, 108, 118, 135, 142-143, 149, 174,** *t* **279, 287,** *r* **291, 292, 305, 328, 344, 360, 362, 377, 407, 487-488, 494, 515, 523, 541, 559, 571, 582, 610, 4:** © John Bova, Photo Researchers **7:** © Brett Froomer, The Image Bank **9:** *Chicago Sun-Times* **14:** Three Lions **16:** © Peter C. Poulides, PhotoUnique **22:** National Gallery, London **31:** SCALA/Art Resource **34:** T.D.F. Kendall* **39:** *l* © Dan McCoy, Rainbow, *r* © M.R. Schneps, The Image Bank **41:** *l* Culver Pictures, *br* National Museum of American History, Smithsonian Institution **42:** *t* Culver Pictures, *c* © George Von Kantor, PhotoUnique, *b* National Museum of American History, Smithsonian Institution **43:** *tl* The Bettmann Archive **44:** *t* © Mel DiGiacomo, The Image Bank, *b* © Thomas Hart Benton **45:** *t* © Claudia Parks, The Stock Market, *l* Culver Pictures, *r* © R. Hamilton Smith, **46:** *t* © Jim Whitmer, Nawrocki Stock Photo, *r* © Susan Jones, Animals Animals **47:** *t Peanuts* by Charles Schulz.

Permission of United Features Syndicate, Inc., *l* © Gabe Palmer, The Stock Market, *r* © Jim Brandenburg, Frozen Images, *b* © Luis Castaneda, The Image Bank **48-49:** © Chip Clark **49:** *l* © Tom & Nancy Falley, Aperture, *r* © Wayne Eastep, PhotoUnique **50:** *l* © Galen Rowell, After-Image *r* © Judith McClung, FPG, *b* © John Dominis, Wheeler Pictures **51:** *t* Musée d 'Orsay, Paris, SPADEM/ARS (Art Resource) *r* © Ashod Francis, Animals, Animals, *b* © Keith Gunnar, West Stock **52:** *tr* Three Lions, *c* © Michael Philip Manheim, Gartman Agency, *b* © Cezus, Click/Chicago **53:** *l* © Nancy Pierce **54-55:** © Michael Philip Manheim, Gartman Agency **60:** T.D.F. Kendall* **63:** *Chasing the Bowhead Whale* (Tom Sadowski, Alaska Photo) **68:** © Jim Pickerell, Click/Chicago **70:** Photri/Gartman Agency **73:** New Jersey State Teen Arts Program (Nancy Roberts-Lawler) **80:** © Cathy Melloan, Click/Chicago **81:** © Henley & Savage, PhotoUnique **85:** © Rich Browne/Stock, Boston **86:** T.D.F. Kendall* **88:** © Richard Kolar, Animals Animals **89:** © A.R. Miller, FPG, **92:** © Frank Oberle, After-Image **93:** © Willard Clay, Click/Chicago **100:** © Vito Palmisano **110:** © Billy Barnes, Jeroboam **112:** © Robert Frerck, Click/Chicago **113:** © Dale R. Thompson, After-Image **122:** © Donald Smetzer, Click/Chicago **127:** Culver Pictures **130:** © Jim Goodwin, Photo Researchers **131:** © Michael Mauney, Click/Chicago **136:** The Bettmann Archive **138:** © Lee Boltin, **150:** © 1939 Loew's Inc. Ren. 1966 by Metro-Goldwyn-Mayer, Inc. **152:** © Charles Seaborn, Odessy Productions **153:** © G&J Images, The Image Bank **161:** Museum of Modern Art, Paris ARS/ADAGP (Art Resource) **164:** Tommy Miyasaki **167:** © Gene Marshall, Tom Stack & Assoc. **176:** © Bob Shaw, The Stock Market, **177:** © Willard Clay, Click/Chicago **180:** © Michael Bertan, Click/Chicago **182:** © Vince Streano, Click/Chicago **185:** Amon Carter Museum, Fort Worth (SCALA/Art Resource) **188:** © Shannon O'Cork **190:** © Brian Seed, Click/Chicago **194:** © Steve Dunwell, The Image Bank **199:** © Bill Pierce, Rainbow **202:** © George Shelley, Earth Images **203:** © G.D. Plage, Bruce Coleman, Inc. **209:** © Stephan Dalton, Animals Animals **214:** The Bettmann Archive **217:** © Billy Barnes, Click/Chicago **219:** © Michael Bertan, Click/Chicago **229:** © Mark William Talbot **233:** Collection of Mr. & Mrs. Graham Gund (Art Resource) **237:** © Vic Bider, The Stock Market **238:** © Barbara Thomas **246:** © Diana Rasche **248:** © Vito Palmisano **253:** © Michael O'Brien, Archive Pictures **259:** © Seth Joel, Wheeler Pictures **265:** © Berenholtz, PhotoUnique **270:** *Wild Meat for Wild Men,* Amon Carter Museum, Fort Worth. **271:** *l* © Miguel, The Image Bank, *r* © Patti McConville, The Image Bank **272:** *l* © Stephan Dunn, Focus West, *r* © Todd Friedman, Focus West **276:** © Francois Robert, **277:** © Stan Osolinski, The Stock Market **279:** *c* © Charles Krebs, The Stock Market **283:** © Tom Dietrich, Click/Chicago **294:** © Ellis Herwig, Gartman Agency **295:** © Jim Whitmer **299:** © Ellis Herwig, Gartman Agency **310:** © Steve Elmore, West Stock **314:** © Jon Riley, The Stock Shop **317:** Chicago Public Library **329:** © Tim Bieber, The Image Bank **336:** Historical Pictures Service **341:** © Joseph K. Lange, Stock Imagery, **346:** New Jersey Teen Arts Program (Joseph Schembri) **348:** © Gloubus Brothers, The Stock Market **349:** © Vloo, Stock Imagery **357, 364:** The FAR SIDE © 1982. Reprinted by permission of Chronicle Features. **365:** Three Lions **376:** © Robert Frerck, Odessy Productions **385:** Three Lions **391:** © Ray Morsch, The Stock Market **392:** The FAR SIDE © 1980. Reprinted by permission of Chronicle Features. **395:** © Robert Frerck, Odessy Productions **400:** © Vladimir Lange, The Image Bank **404:** © Joe McDonald, Tom Stack & Assoc. **416:** © Peter Turner, The Image Bank **422:** © Donald Smetzer, Click/Chicago **423:** © Stephen Brown, The Stock Market **429:** © Vito Palmisano **432:** Historical Pictures Service **436:** © Cezus, Click/Chicago **437:** © J. Sapinsky, The Stock Market **441:** The Bettmann Archive **445:** © E. R. Degginer, After-Image **466:** © Jim Richardson, Click/Chicago **467:** © William Meyer, Click/Chicago **490:** © Jay Ward Productions **496:** © Berlitz, Click/Chicago **502:** © Stock Imagery **503:** © Gabe Palmer, The Stock Market **507:** The Museum of Modern Art, New York, The Lillie P. Bliss Bequest **522:** © Christopher Kean **526:** © Walter Chandoha, **530:** © Vito Palmisano **531:** © John Coletti, The Picture Cube **535:** © Brian Seed, Click/Chicago **542:** © J. Blackman, The Stock Market **548:** © Robert Amft, Nawrocki Stock Photo **549:** T.D.F. Kendall* **563:** © Charles Harbutt, Archive Pictures **568:** © Pankaj Shah, The Stock Market **575:** © Leverett Bradley, After-Image, **578:** National Palace, Mexico City (Jose M. Pavon, Shostal Associates) **591:** The Bettmann Archive **592:** © L.L.T. Rhodes, Click/Chicago **598-599:** © Robert Frerck, Odessy Productions **602:** © Ira Kirschenbaum/Stock, Boston **606:** © Charles Harbutt, Archive Pictures **612:** © Lenore Weber, Taurus Photos **616-617:** © Bill Floyd **619:** © Wayne Eastep, PhotoUnique **620, 623:** The Bettmann Archive **629:** Museum of Modern Art, Paris. ARS/ADAGP (Giraudon/Art Resource) **643:** © William S. Nawrocki, Nawrocki Stock Photo.

*Indicates exlusive property of McDougal, Littell & Company.

Illustrations

13, 173, 308, 316, 319, 326; Jeff Mellander **25, 198, 285, 367, 458, 646:** Dianne Bennett **76, 312, 393, 471, 511, 538:** Judy Reed **90, 171:** Dirk Hagner **95, 145, 223, 264, 268:** Pam Rossi **103, 380, 424, 564, 636:** Cathy Pavia **107, 124, 170, 211, 371, 411, 556:** Doug Schneider **155, 179, 519:** Ken Raney **157:** Manuel Garcia **192, 586:** Ross Adcock **213:** Debra Stine **226:** Lynne Fischer **255, 553, 609:** Avalyn Lundgren-Ellis **Handwriting:** Michael Kecsez, Pen Graphics Studio, Inc.